The
Mobilization
of Intellect

The Mobilization of Intellect

French Scholars and Writers during the Great War

MARTHA HANNA

HARVARD UNIVERSITY PRESS
Cambridge, Massachusetts
London, England
1996

Library of Congress Cataloging-in-Publication Data

Hanna, Martha.
    The mobilization of intellect : French scholars and writers during
the Great War / Martha Hanna.
        p.   cm.
    Includes bibliographical references (p.) and index.
    ISBN 0-674-57755-8
    1. World War, 1914–1918—France.   2. France—Intellectual
life—20th century.   3. Intellectuals—France—Biography.
I. Title.
940.53′44—dc20   95-42544
                                                                CIP

In Memory of
Edward Gerrard Clarke
and
Reginald Duncan Hinch

Acknowledgments

On 2 October 1916 a shell, fired into the Canadian front lines northeast of Amiens, exploded and killed my great-grandfather. It was a 1914 recruitment film that had prompted him to enlist, so Private Edward Gerrard Clarke was well aware of noncombatants' efforts to sustain the war effort. But unlike many of the men whose names appear in the pages of this book, he was not a scholar-in-arms. A skilled craftsman who knew little (if any) French and nothing of German philosophy, he served in France for eighteen months, all the while remaining unfamiliar with and unaffected by the efforts of French intellectuals. Thus this book, which examines how and to what effect noncombatant French scholars contributed their energies to the war effort, devotes itself to an analysis of aspects of the war unknown to my great-grandfather. No doubt he would have been astonished to learn that while he was fighting on the Somme, French scholars and writers were debating—with impassioned intensity—whether Immanuel Kant could be held responsible for the First World War.

If the war that my great-grandfather experienced and the war French scholars constructed were worlds apart, this book nonetheless owes something to his experience. Edward Clarke was survived by a wife and seven children, the youngest a toddler not yet two years old, the oldest boy only thirteen. With six siblings to help support, the young teenager left school to apprentice to a plumber. He always regretted his own incomplete education and resolved that his children, of whom my mother is the oldest, would receive the schooling circumstances had denied him. Thus for my mother a respect for education became one of the most lasting legacies of her grandfather's death in the First World War. It was this regard for scholarship, which my father always firmly reinforced, that sustained me through graduate school and beyond. Without their conviction that scholarship was a worthy enterprise, I would never have written this book.

My research, writing, and revisions have benefited from the advice and encouragement of many colleagues, friends, and experts in the field. I owe a great deal first to Sandra Horvath-Peterson for her conscientious, kind, and rigorous dissertation supervision. In the past five years this project has been transformed from a dissertation concerned with the intellectual culture of the Action Française to a monograph analyzing the intellectual enterprise of republicans and antirepublicans alike. During this metamorphosis, many scholars have shared with me their professional expertise. I am grateful to my colleagues at the University of Colorado who agreed—always graciously—to comment on individual chapters: to Fred and Virginia Anderson, Barbara Engel, Steven Epstein, David Gross, Robert Pois, and Edward Ruestow, thank you. And I am especially indebted to several fellow French historians. Both Stuart Campbell and Natalie Zemon Davis offered their advice and encouragement; William Keylor, Paul Mazgaj, and Robert J. Young read and recommended revisions to the initial draft of the manuscript; and the recommendations of the two readers for Harvard University Press guided my final revisions. Anita Safran has been a conscientious and careful editor.

Much of the material upon which this book is based appeared originally in pamphlets and periodical articles. To begin research into this literature, I spent months during the summers of 1990 and 1991 in the stacks at Sterling Memorial Library. I am grateful to Yale University for granting me access to this collection. I also wish to acknowledge the help of Alan Solomon and Mary Dean, who shared with me their professional expertise and their hospitality while I undertook my research in New Haven. Most of the sources essential to my project could be obtained only with the assistance of the Inter-Library Loan staff at the University of Colorado. They always greeted my requests for obscure articles and long-forgotten essays with good grace, and processed them with exemplary efficiency. Sources that could not be obtained through Inter-Library Loan were located in Paris, where the staff at the Archives Nationales and the Bibliothèque Nationale offered me their assistance. I could not have undertaken research in France without the financial support of the Graduate Committee for Arts and Humanities at the University of Colorado.

While I studied in Paris, my husband and my daughter awaited my return home. This book owes more to their patience, good humor, and unflagging encouragement than I can calculate. Bob has been steadily supportive and a source of professional expertise from the very beginning; his lucid explanations of Kant were particularly valuable. And my interest in the First World War has been nurtured by his own familial affection for another soldier of the Great War. His grandfather, Reginald Duncan Hinch, who served with dedication and distinction, inspired in his grandsons profound respect and abiding regard. Although our daughter, Beth, never knew her great-grandfather, she is nonetheless very much a descendant of the generation of 1914. While she has made me promise that my next book will be for her and her father, we all agreed that this one rightly belongs to the memory of Edward Clarke and Reginald Hinch.

Contents

Introduction

In the early months of the First World War, Raymond Poincaré, President of France, called upon the members of the Académie Française to contribute to the war effort with "their pens and their words."[1] The mobilization of intellect was, he insisted, as essential to the defense of France as the mobilization of arms. Many of France's most prominent scholars and writers, whose age or physical infirmity disqualified them from active military service, responded enthusiastically to Poincaré's exhortation. Indeed, by September 1915, one commentator observed approvingly that the "war was being waged with blood and with *matériel*, but it was also being waged with ideas." That men of intellect would come together to serve *la patrie* was, the author argued, an honorable development: "all forces ought to be brought together and placed at the service of the nation."[2] Borrowing the title of this brief article, my book examines how the "mobilization of intellect" came about, and why many of the most established and distinguished intellectuals of early twentieth-century France (including Henri Bergson, Pierre Duhem, Emile Durkheim, and Ernest Lavisse) chose to contribute to this enterprise. Along the way, it scrutinizes the major intellectual debates that dominated the war years. And it concludes that the mobilization of intellect positively influenced the morale of civilians and combatants alike and contributed directly to a reorientation of culture evident during and after the war.

So many individuals of all political persuasions participated in this intellectual defense of the French war effort, that a new spirit of cooperation and reconciliation appeared to replace the acrimony and animosity of prewar intellectual life. Alfred Croiset, Dean of Letters at the University of Paris, spoke of how the "internal quarrels" (which Germany had mistaken for "irremediable disunity") had, with the declaration of war, "disappeared, as if by magic."[3] Pierre Imbart de la Tour, a conservative Catholic historian, agreed: although prewar France had been a "country divided" and debilitated by "factional quarrels," the aftermath of August 1914 brought out "the most noble virtues—endurance, sacrifice, . . . [and] the union of all thought."[4] Speaking in the same vein, Victor Giraud, literary editor of the *Revue des deux mondes,* also lamented the internal divisions that had made France appear decadent and indecisive before the outbreak of war, and celebrated their disappearance. While Croiset considered the emergence of this intellectual *union sacrée* a magical occurrence, Giraud, more inclined to religious explanations, spoke of the "miracle" thus effected in French intellectual life.[5]

For those who had observed or participated in the culture wars of the early Third Republic, the reconciliation of scholars and writers that took place in August 1914 must indeed have seemed both magical and miraculous. Those who offered their pens and their words to the national war effort and rejoiced in the apparent emergence of an intellectual *union sacrée* had previously been, as Chapter 1 will show, sworn enemies. In one camp, the leading scholars of the French academic establishment had defended a vision of French intellectual culture that was secular, scientistic, and cosmopolitan: the scholar's task, in this view, was to investigate the natural world, apply with rigor and integrity the methods of scientific inquiry, and pursue knowledge in cooperation with all men of intellectual goodwill. In the opposing camp, men of letters alienated from the university culture that came into being at the end of the nineteenth century, ill-disposed to the political ideals of the Third Republic, and nostalgic for an age of order, hierarchy, and faith, defended a traditionalist and Catholic intellectual order radically at odds with the progressive spirit and anticlerical practices of the Republic. After 1900, this "counterintelligentsia" (to borrow a phrase from William Keylor) found its most vigorous spokesmen among the neoroyalists of the Action Française.

Divided over questions of loyalty to the Third Republic, and also split in their defense or denunciation of Alfred Dreyfus, the nation's two "spiritual families" disputed for decades the political, cultural, and educational principles according to which France ought to be governed. Not only did they carry into the twentieth century political divisions that had originated with the Revolution of 1789, but they revived in their own terms the great literary and pedagogical debate of the late seventeenth century: the "Quarrel of the Ancients and the Moderns."[6] In their considerations of literary aesthetics, the latter-day Moderns were secular individualists who rejected as oppressive the restrictive character of classicist aesthetics and embraced instead the individualist, self-expressive, and radically autonomous ethos of Romanticism. The Ancients—Catholic and conservative traditionalists, who believed the world was rendered orderly by the preservation of political, social, and intellectual hierarchy—acclaimed the intellectual discipline and political order of seventeenth-century classicism. And eager to revive the values that Revolutionary politics, rampant individualism, and reform-minded educators had undermined, they demanded that France return to an educational system that would defend the classical tradition from modernist onslaught.

Conservatives and modernists tended to articulate their differences—and make manifest the fundamental cultural discord that beset their nation—in ongoing debates over French education. Modernists believed that to become internationally competitive, industrially advanced, and militarily secure, the Republic should learn the essential lesson of Sedan: that the nation with the most comprehensive and sophisticated system of public schooling wins. Drawing impetus from the French defeat of 1870 and deriving inspiration from German examples, they demanded that France adopt an educational system committed at the elementary level to compulsory, universal, and secular instruction, and at more advanced levels to the study of the natural sciences and modern languages. Eschewing the traditional classical curriculum, with its heavy emphasis on learning ancient languages, as suitable only for a nation of dilettantes, they insisted upon—and, in 1902, brought into being—a radical reform of secondary education. Traditionalists, inspired by their vision of France as inherently classical and essentially Catholic, denounced the modernist spirit of this new curriculum. More attentive to physics than to ancient philosophy, more committed to understanding the natural world than to speculating about the supernatural, it represented all that they found reprehensible in the intellectual culture of modern-day republicanism. Two radically incommensurable visions of France thus translated into protracted and divisive debate over the proper character and appropriate content of French education.

Anticipating a short war, scholars and writers on both sides of this cultural divide agreed in August 1914 to set their intellectual, literary, and pedagogical differences aside while they de-

voted themselves to the defense of France. Armed with a patriotic conviction in the justice of their cause, noncombatant intellectuals worked
indefatigably to raise funds, provide moral and material support for the
casualties of war, and strengthen the nation's morale. Much maligned
after 1918 for their patriotic enthusiasm and their putative indifference
to the war's relentless slaughter, these civilians, scholars, and writers did
not lend their unconditional support to the French war effort because
they were ignorant of or unmoved by the fate of their younger colleagues.
Chapter 2, based in large part on the archival records of the University
of Paris and the Ecole Normale Supérieure, suggests just the opposite:
noncombatant scholars, often regular correspondents with troops at the
front, knew well enough what conditions of combat were like, and their
knowledge often caused them considerable anguish. In 1916 Ernest Lavisse, Director of the Ecole Normale Supérieure, tormented by his own
inability to share the sufferings of his former students, determined to
bring their experience of the war into the public domain. Denouncing as
insulting the "banal optimism" of the French daily press, with its notoriously unrealistic representations of combat, he insisted that those who
could not fight should at least honor those who did by accepting nothing
less than the truth. To this end he commended to the people of France
Maurice Genevoix's novel, *Sous Verdun.* Lavisse believed that the stark
realism Genevoix brought to the war was a fitting tribute to his *normalien* education: the pursuit of truth prevailed in his "sincere testimony" to the war.[7]

Archival records also show that noncombatant scholars and writers
worked diligently to assist, comfort, and console their friends, colleagues,
students, and sons at the front. They mourned their deaths; feared that
these losses would place in jeopardy the future of intellectual life in
France; and did what they could to sustain their morale, give moral and
material assistance to their families, and minimize their risk of death. To
keep the spirit of intellectual life alive even in the trenches, scholars sent
books to students at the front and to those held as prisoners of war. To
assist families impoverished by the war, they created and donated generously to national charities. And to protect their students from the ravages of the front—but not to exempt them from the responsibility of
military service—they intervened frequently with the Ministry of War.
Lavisse worked diligently to effect transfers for students out of the infantry and into the somewhat safer artillery branch or the much more
secure confines of the General Staff. Anxious to pursue their war-related

research with the help of qualified research assistants, scientists, too, sought the transfer of their most promising prewar students.

There is, however, no evidence in the archival record that noncombatant scholars tried to secure absolute exemptions from military service for their students; nor is there any evidence that their students sought such exemptions. Whether at the front or behind the lines, the intellectual community, like the nation at large, remained resolute in its support of the war because they perceived it as a worthy struggle. The front-line troops, even those of most humble origins, were animated by an intense love of country and remained convinced for most of the war that the French cause was just, and that the Army had to liberate the nation from the invader's grasp.[8] Veterans continued to believe in the justice of the French cause long after the war was over; although opposed to future wars, they believed firmly that France had defended the cause of justice and liberty. Antoine Prost considers the "pacifist patriotism" of French veterans a consequence of their schooling. The national educational system established in the 1880s had successfully inculcated in almost all fighting men a conviction that France represented the progressive values of liberty, equality, and fraternity.[9]

The proposition that patriotism was cultivated in the classroom opens the door to understanding the patriotism of noncombatant intellectuals. That the integral nationalists of the radical right, venomous in their dislike of Germany, should have supported the war effort with their literary labor is not surprising. But to understand why scholars and writers on the left, who had hoped to create a cosmopolitan community of scholars by improving relations with Germany, who had defied the status quo, the government, and the Army with their insistence that Dreyfus receive a fair trial, and who after the Dreyfus Affair had thought of the Army as the enemy of justice, supported the French war effort, one must remember that they, too, were formed by, and in many cases were the formative forces within, the nation's educational system.

Neither scholars nor students ever doubted that combatants and noncombatants alike should do their utmost to defend France. They were after all unequivocal patriots who had thrived in and helped constitute a culture that cultivated an intense love of country and honored civic duty. This was true of all intellectuals, even those most vehemently opposed to republican academic culture. Joseph Moody has argued that the educational system was so effective in teaching civics that, "unless he was unusually resistant," every French student "was likely to depart [the

schoolroom] with a love for the common fatherland."[10] Intellectual patriotism combined with a passionate commitment to the Third Republic
was most evident, however, among the leaders of the reformed university
system created in the 1890s. After 1880, scholars eager to establish the
autonomy and professionalization of academic life entered into a relationship of mutual support with leaders of the Republic whose endorsement, enthusiasm, and funding were essential to the success of the academics' project. In *Academy and Community* William Keylor argues that
the professional historians of the University of Paris, as committed as
their colleagues in other disciplines to bring rigor, discipline, and respectability to French academic life, were also determined to effect a national
revival comparable to that which had occurred in Prussia after 1807. To
instill a patriotic enthusiasm in the minds of young citizens, they put
their historical scholarship at the service of the Republic. Keylor concludes that professional historians became of their own volition "func-
tionaries of the republican state and messengers bearing the republican
catechism"; and George Weisz concurs: the reformed university became
"the ideological arm of the state."[11]

The scholars of the reformed university were patriots ardent in their
love of France and republicans intent upon the preservation of the Third
Republic. Seasoned Dreyfusards, they were also committed to the cause
of intellectual engagement. Respectful of the rule of law, convinced that
all citizens were entitled to a fair and open trial, and animated by their
suspicion of the Army as a bastion of clerical and royalist sentiment,
many of the scholars who devoted themselves to the cause of intellectual
action during the Great War had rallied to the defense of Alfred Dreyfus,
the Army captain who had been so grievously wronged by forces apparently indifferent to justice and antipathetic to the Republic.[12] Dreyfusard
scholars were persuaded that *as intellectuals* they had a responsibility to
take a public stand in defense of truth; and with the formation of the
Radical Republic that ultimately exonerated Dreyfus, they did not hesitate to use their scholarship to its advantage. In this manner, historians
"placed their scholarly and pedagogical talents at the disposal of the
harried regime with the intention of repairing the republican consensus
that had been disrupted by the political turmoil of the fin de siècle."[13]

For scholars who had encouraged the culti-
vation of patriotic sentiments, rallied to the Republic, and entered the
public domain in defense of universal principles, the mobilization of intellectuals that occurred between 1914 and 1918 was not (as their critics

would subsequently contend) a repudiation of their Dreyfusard idealism but a continuation of it. The same moral imperative to defend justice, together with a political imperative to support the embattled Republic that had moved Dreyfusard intellectuals to act in 1898, informed their actions in 1914. The war, however, presented them with radically different circumstances. In 1898 Dreyfusards challenged the authority of the Army and assumed an oppositional stance. This opposition came most easily to scholars who found themselves on the margins of established academic respectability and had no vested interest in the preservation of the status quo—those who integrated the new or radically reformed disciplines—than to those in the established fields of literature and the law.[14] In 1898, therefore, dissent was a privilege of the dispossessed. With the triumph of the Radical Republic, however, the outsiders of the late nineteenth century became, in Weisz's words, "the academic oligarchy" of the early twentieth century. By 1914 the reformers were dominating, rather than being dominated by, the academic establishment. With everything to lose if the nation were defeated or the Republic overturned, they were far from challenging the status quo. Instead, they embraced the national cause as their own, supported the Army they had once so bitterly disparaged, and legitimated its actions with their approbation.

Although united by their love of France and firm in their determination to contribute to its defense, noncombatant intellectuals, so bitterly divided before the war, neither buried nor transcended all their profound intellectual disagreements during the war. For all but a few moments, the cultural consensus so eagerly acclaimed in August 1914 was more fictive than real. Scholars and writers did agree on certain points: that France should fight for the defense of civilization, the liberation of occupied territory, and the unconditional surrender of the enemy. As Chapter 3 makes clear, most believed that German *Kultur,* which scholars across the Rhine defended as the very essence of German identity, was directly responsible for the aggressive actions of the modern German state. And all agreed (without any hint of self-referential irony) that German intellectuals betrayed their professional vocation by sacrificing scholarly objectivity on the altar of national loyalty. In October 1914, ninety-three of Germany's most distinguished men of letters and science produced one of the most controversial cultural documents of the war. Intended for distribution to neutral audiences, "An Appeal to the Civilized World" defended German military action as essential to the defense of German *Kultur*. This document, also known as the Manifesto of 93, established the tone of nearly all subsequent German intellectual action and at the same time significantly influenced the character of French intellectual enterprise for the duration of the war.

French scholars denounced what they took to be the intellectual servility, lack of objectivity, and craven spirit of the manifesto's signatories. They hoped to underline the difference between themselves and their counterparts across the Rhine by their scrupulous attention to scholarly method, and to demonstrate thereby that it was possible to display independent judgment and be a loyal citizen. They did not always succeed in this endeavor. Keylor charges that many of the most distinguished professional historians of the Third Republic "rapidly abandoned their prewar commitment to higher truths in the summer of 1914 and surrendered to the basest form of jingoist hysteria during the next five years."[15] This is a harsh evaluation indeed, and, as Chapter 3 reveals, not entirely unjustified. Lavisse and Charles Andler, for example, published at least one pamphlet that was more sensationalistic than scholarly; others hid patriotic invective behind a transparent veil of pseudo-objectivity. But French intellectuals continued to pay considerable attention to the question of scholarly objectivity in order to reassure themselves, and the world, that the first principles of intellectual life, under siege in Germany, remained alive and honored in France.

Although French scholars and writers agreed on what France was fighting against, when they tried to establish what France was fighting for, consensus was much harder to come by. They divided along well-established lines over three questions: (1) Was there anything within the German cultural tradition that remained worthy of respect? (2) What did it mean for the cultural and educational institutions of France to insist that French culture was the modern heir of ancient Greece and Rome? and (3) Was science a product of German *Kultur* (and hence unworthy), or an intellectual enterprise rooted in the philosophical traditions of France and Britain (and hence worthy of respect)? Because these questions were central to the very definition of intellectual culture in France, each of these debates brought to the fore the most fundamental political and sectarian divisions—between monarchists and republicans, conservatives and progressives, nationalists and internationalists, Catholics and anticlericals—that had riven the French intellectual community since at least the turn of the century.

Nowhere was the fragility of the intellectual *union sacrée* more evident than in the controversy over the philosophy of Immanuel Kant that raged in France throughout the First World War. Chapter 4 argues that radical conservative and Catholic scholars denounced Kant in part because they perceived in his ethics and epistemology the foundations of unrestrained individualism, subjectivism, and atheism; and in part because they hoped to discredit the republican school system, predicated as it was on Kantian notions of rights and duties. By contrast, scholars who situated themselves on the left recognized in Kant an ideal candidate for republican admiration and defended him as vigorously as their domestic opponents denounced him. Kant had spoken favorably of the French Revolution and had developed a theory of moral obligation that was well suited to the political culture of the Third Republic, committed as it was to both individual autonomy and patriotic obligation. In the decades before the war, French republicans had made Kant's concept of individual responsibility founded in human reason the cornerstone of republican civics, and Kantian rationalism the centerpiece of university philosophy.[16] During the war they continued to find sustenance in his concept of individual responsibility and found in his essay on *Perpetual Peace* the principles of collective security and the promise of peaceful coexistence through a league of nations.

In their defense of Kant, republican scholars invoked the well-established thesis of "two Germanies." This theory—in which Kant was a pivotal figure—was a powerful force in the formation of French intellectual culture between 1870 and 1914. Although French scholars had long suspected that Germany was plagued by a particularly virulent strain of cultural schizophrenia, it was only in the wake of the Franco-Prussian War that this seemed incontrovertible. In December 1870, E. Caro, writing in the *Revue des deux mondes,* juxtaposed the evidence of Prussian troops encircling Paris with an acknowledgment of German accomplishments in the arts and the humanities, and concluded that "it could indeed be said that there are two Germanies." One Germany was mystical and metaphysical, the other materialistic and militaristic. The former had reached its apotheosis in the transcendental idealism of Kant; the latter—having turned its back on Kant, embraced the politics of national ambition, supplanted transcendental metaphysics with a philosophy of materialism, and subordinated the interests and rights of the individual to the interests and ambitions of the state—had triumphed at Sedan. For Caro and subsequent French proponents of the two-Germanies thesis, the second tradition originated with Hegel.[17]

Scholars intent on restoring French prestige after 1870 recognized that the thesis of two Germanies would allow educational reformers in good conscience to take from Germany that which they found compatible with republican ideals, and to discard that which they found objectionable. In a process of selective imitation, they embraced the epistemological rationalism, ethical deontology, and political cosmopolitanism of Kant, while rejecting the hubristic nationalism of Hegel. Before 1914 many Dreyfusard scholars had embraced the cause of intellectual cosmopolitanism. Working diligently to improve relations and hence to preserve peace between France and Germany, they had cultivated in their students respect for and knowledge of German culture, and had encouraged exchanges between French and German scholars.[18] It was in keeping with this spirit of international cooperation and intellectual fraternity that Emile Boutroux, an indefatigable internationalist whose contacts extended throughout Europe and North America, traveled to Berlin in the spring of 1914 to address an assembly of scholars on the subject of "French and German Thought: The Mutual Advantages Each Can Offer the Other." The lecture was a great success, and both German and French participants hoped that Boutroux's visit would be but the first instance in an ongoing, cordial, and fruitful exchange of scholars.[19]

The war doomed this project, but did not destroy entirely the French scholars' cosmopolitan outlook. Committed by loyalty to their country and by intellectual conviction to the universality of reason, many French scholars were anxious to prove that one could be both a patriot and an honest advocate of intellectual internationalism. With their endorsement of Kantian ethics and their definition of universal classicism (discussed in Chapters 4 and 5, respectively), republican scholars hoped to reconcile these competing political and professional loyalties. Defending Kant, they showed themselves to be respectful of that which was most universal within German culture, and in this way they distinguished themselves from narrow-minded nationalists on both sides of the border who refused to recognize any virtue in the other's culture. Defining classicism as inherently cosmopolitan, they hoped to keep alive the borderless commerce of intellectual life.

During the war years, when discipline, obedience, and self-abnegation became civic virtues essential to the nation's survival, France grew ever more appreciative of the strictly regulated moral and aesthetic order of classicism. Chapter 5 argues that a classicist revival—evident in art, theater, and public oratory—came to characterize much of the intellectual culture of wartime France. Modernist intellectuals, eager to make classicism compatible with the most progressive ideals of the Third Republic, posited what might be called an essentially republican definition of classicism. The cultural and political principles of Greece and Rome—rationalism, the rule of law, and the autonomy of the individual—were, in this view, the classical precursors of liberty, progress, and international peace. Greece had bequeathed to France a legacy of individual liberty predicated on the essential rationality of all individuals; Rome had taught reverence for the rule of law and republicanism; and Christianity, the final element in the French classical equation, preached universal brotherhood. When combined, the Graeco-Roman and Christian traditions gave rise to the famous fundamental principles of French republicanism, Liberty, Equality, and Fraternity.

Republican scholars were not, however, the principal beneficiaries of this neoclassicist revival. That torch passed to the neoroyalist nationalists of the Action Française, who had long demanded that France abandon its infatuation with modern ideas, cosmopolitan culture, and Germanic institutions. Mark Antliff has argued that the classicist spirit espoused by some avant-garde artistic communities before the war was distinct in spirit and origin from the Graeco-Roman classicism acclaimed by the Action Française, and he thus challenges those who insist that the Action Française exerted a powerful influence in the domain of modern art *before* 1914.[20] Carrying the story into the war years, however, Kenneth Silver proposed that after August 1914 the neoroyalists directly influenced public perceptions of modern art as alien. When the great modernist innovators of the early century—led by Picasso and Matisse—abandoned Cubism in response to this public outrage and sought a more authentically French form of artistic expression, they embraced a classicism unlike that of the prewar avant-garde and definitely Latin in spirit. This recognizably traditional idiom continued to shape their work through the early 1920s.[21]

Proponents of classicism wished not only to purge French art of modernist impulses but to liberate French education from what they contended were the errors and excesses of its modern curriculum. Their greatest ambition was to overturn the reform program of 1902 that permitted secondary school students to specialize in the sciences and modern languages and thus qualify for admission to university without any knowledge of Latin or Greek. In their desire to preserve France's classical heritage, classicists insisted that all secondary school students have a firm grounding in the classics and called for the reintroduction of mandatory Latin and Greek to the secondary school curriculum. Because this demand proved ever more popular in the conservative national atmosphere of the Great War, it intensified the anxieties of French scientists, who feared that the classics could be restored to all sections of the secondary school curriculum only at the expense of instruction in the sciences.

French scientists found themselves in an awkward position at the beginning of the war. Like many of their colleagues in the humanities, they had developed many contacts with their German counterparts, had encouraged academic exchange programs with German students, and had praised Germany as an international leader in scientific research, development, and application. In the process they had contributed to a belief, widely held in France as elsewhere, that science was—if not uniquely, then at least especially—a German enterprise. As Chapter 6 reveals, this perception made science increasingly suspect in France. Associating science with the enemy (an association reinforced in April 1915, when the German Army was the first belligerent power to use poison gas in the field of combat), French citizens perceived science as brutal and alien. Those who identified science with *Kultur* came to believe that scientific acumen was the regrettable product of a materialist ethos, indifferent to everything but brute domination. Scientists and educational reformers, fearing that this popular suspicion of science would undermine the legitimacy of scientific enterprise in France and alarmed that the classicist revival would endanger hard-won educational reforms, launched a counteroffensive. Revisiting the history of science, they discovered that science was not unique to Germany but indigenous to England and France, and only subsequently developed in Germany. Acknowledging German contributions, French scientists insisted nonetheless that the most important and original initiatives had always been French or English. Indeed, German science was essentially derivative, for German scientists, devoid of the gift of creative insight Pascal had called the *esprit de finesse,* had been adept only at developing applications of others' discoveries.

The scientists who contributed to the mobilization of intellect were, with very few exceptions, leading members of the Paris-based Académie des Sciences and the Faculty of Sciences at the University of Paris. (Even Pierre Duhem, who taught at the University of Bordeaux, held a seat on the Académie des Sciences—a distinction no other provincial scientist enjoyed.) And in their efforts to rehabilitate science in France, they reflected and articulated one of the most deep-seated prejudices of the Parisian scientific elite: that applied science was inferior to pure research.

For several decades, applied science had been anathema to the scientists affiliated with the University of Paris and the Ecole Normale, because they feared "that basic research and basic scientific teaching was being sacrificed to a short-sighted vocationalism."[22] Given that the prestige of French education derived traditionally from its disinterested, distinctly nonutilitarian character, anything that smacked of vocationalism was abhorrent to those who considered themselves the caretakers of France's intellectual culture.

Even though many Parisian scientists devoted themselves to war-related research and worked diligently to apply principles of physics and chemistry to problems of modern warfare, the war only intensified their antipathy to applied science.[23] Many of France's most promising young research scientists died in uniform; and of those who survived the war, many pragmatically assessed the economic realities of the early 1920s and opted for the remunerative employment of industry rather than the disinterested satisfactions of teaching and research. Thus there occurred during and after the war a crisis in recruitment into the pure sciences that chronic underfunding and inflation exacerbated. Fearing the irremediable damage these problems would bring to scientific development, the French scientific elite vigorously resisted all initiatives to expand the domain of applied science any further. On this front as on the classicist front, scientists came up against the persistent opposition of the cultural and political right. A curious and not entirely consistent pattern emerged from the cultural debates of the war years: on the one hand, cultural conservatives challenged what they took to be the hegemonic authority of science in French intellectual culture by calling for a return to classicism and the classical curriculum; and yet, as nationalists fearful for future French security, they also demanded that France develop its expertise in applied science, despite its unfortunate identification with the enemy. Both developments worried the nation's scientific elite, which wished to preserve the modern curriculum with its heavy emphasis on the sciences yet inhibit the expansion of applied science at the expense of pure research.

Patrick Fridenson has recently observed that "most [of the] conflicts dividing French society continued during the war."[24] This conclusion applies with equal force to the cultural history of wartime France, when the French intellectual community remained radically divided. But to note that the quarrel of the Ancients and the Moderns went on unabated during the war years is not to say that the war and the debates it generated had no significant effect on the cultural character of France during the war and after the Armistice. Quite the contrary, in fact. The Great War effected a transformation in the cultural orientation of France comparable to the "deep transformations" in the nation's social and economic development. As the social and economic conflicts of French society unfolded in the context of the war, they brought about decisive alterations that made it "impossible for France [after the Armistice] to go back to normalcy." The world of prewar France was lost forever, and a new world—more politically conservative and more tolerant of government intervention in the economy; dependent upon foreign labor, technocratic in spirit, and corporatist in organization—emerged in its wake. So fundamental were the changes wrought by the war that many of the attributes of this new society remain familiar even to citizens of modern-day France; and certainly many were familiar to citizens of Vichy.[25] This is as true of the cultural history of France as of its social and economic history.

The First World War made the French nation more introspective, more suspicious of foreign influences, and more susceptible to calls for a "return to French culture" (to borrow the title of one of the most discussed and most influential essays of the war years). Cultural modernists, whose self-identification with the cause of cosmopolitanism made them increasingly suspect, did not disappear entirely—had they done so there would have been no cultural conflict during and after the war— but their ideas, once predominant, no longer prevailed absolutely. They were challenged with increasing efficacy by an emerging cultural conservatism that was comparable to and compatible with the political conservatism of the Bloc National government elected in 1919.[26] This shift to the right was evident in the careers of some prominent scholars: Gustave Lanson, an ardent Dreyfusard, impassioned supporter of educational reform, and cofounder with Jean Jaurès of L'Humanité in 1904, moved so far to the right during the war that he supported the Bloc National after 1919. Hubert Bourgin's political sympathies moved along a similar trajectory.[27] More generally, this cultural reorientation towards the right could be observed after 1919 in the emergence of "intellectual nationalism," a stridently nationalistic, xenophobic, and anti-Semitic cultural program that infiltrated student culture, did battle with the academic cosmopolitanism of the postwar Sorbonne, and helped transform the Action Française from a group of marginal monarchist cranks into a movement of major cultural critics. As cultural conservatism became increasingly influential, it also contributed to a restructuring of French education in the early 1920s. In 1923, against the vociferous opposition of academic modernists, Léon Bérard reformed boys' secondary education by reintroducing compulsory Latin and Greek to the secondary school curriculum. In the emergence of intellectual nationalism and a concomitant educational reformism, it is possible to perceive, foreshadowed but not yet full-blown, the cultural agenda of Vichy.

This, then, is a history of France during the First World War that is more concerned with the debates of scholars than with the details of battles. As analysis of the intellectual culture of France between 1914 and 1918, it is situated at the intersection of two historiographical fields: the history of noncombatant France, and the cultural history of the Great War. In recent years, scholars influenced by the methodologies and principles of social and cultural history have argued that in order to appreciate the full impact of the First World War on European society, one must examine it from the vantage point of the home front as well as the military front. Those who have turned their attention to the French home front have arrived at three overarching conclusions. (1) France endured and survived four years of unprecedented bloodletting because its citizens, united in their conviction that the French cause was just, applied their muscular energy and lent their moral authority to the relentless prosecution of the war. (2) Much of what happened to France during the First World War prefigured the social, political, and economic development of France during the Second World War. (3) The French experience of the First World War was, if not unique, then at least sufficiently unlike that of the other major belligerents to merit examination on its own terms. On each of these points, this book reinforces and contributes to the existing historiography of France during the First World War.

With the publication in 1983 of *Les Français dans la grande guerre*, Jean-Jacques Becker adopted as his own the *poilus'* famous supposition that "if the civilians [held] out," the nation would not fall.[28] Through a careful analysis of the morale and material well-being of French civilians between 1914 and 1918, he established that the success of the French war effort depended not only upon the endurance of the French Army and the combined resources of its allies, but also upon the collective efforts and determined consensus of the nation's noncombatants. Working in the fields and laboring in factories, women, children, and the elderly moved with alacrity and quiet determination to fill positions once occupied by men called to the front. In the process, they guaranteed that the nation's economy would adapt successfully to the demands of wartime production. Middle-class professionals applied themselves just as energetically to the war effort. With more than half of the nation's elementary school teachers away at the front, elderly teachers returned from retirement to join forces with young women in the nation's much disrupted classrooms. There they taught their pupils about the perfidy of Germany and the justice of France, the importance of national resolve, the necessity of unconditional victory, and the virtue of civic duty. When the school day was finished, these same teachers addressed patriotic lectures to their pupils' parents, urging generous contributions to war charities and prompt subscriptions to war bonds.

Even though citizens proved themselves willing to work at whatever their task to reinforce the nation's ability to fight, civilian morale held firm in part because the French government left so little to chance. With close censorship of the press, it controlled the content of printed information and thus made certain that bad news would not deflate civilian confidence. The government also intervened in the economy to maintain tolerable standards of living. From the very outset, it issued allowances to families with men at the front and guaranteed supplies of essential commodities; for the first three years of the war, it successfully maintained wages and thus was able—until 1917—to prevent outbreaks of industrial action injurious to the war effort. Although Becker argues that censorship and material well-being were important to bolster civilian morale, he does not ultimately suggest that civilians continued to support the war only because they remained well fed, well paid, and well clear of the front. The French people remained resolute in their support of the war because, inspired by the arguments of teachers, writers, and clergymen, they were convinced that France was fighting on the side of justice. In the final analysis, "the real explanation of French steadfastness . . . lay in the intellectual, spiritual, and political leadership of the people."[29] When bound together by this triple cord, the will of France was not easily broken.

If the secret to French endurance resided in the formation of a resilient *mentalité* rather than only in the preservation of material conditions, it follows that the intellectual and spiritual leaders of the nation were indispensable to the national war effort. Indeed, among the teachers, writers, and clergymen a "near consensus . . . existed when it came to the need to defend their country."[30] United by a rare ecumenical enthusiasm, priests, pastors, and rabbis preached on the justice of the French war effort while other religious leaders formed publishing committees dedicated to the patriotic education of domestic and foreign readers. They distributed pamphlets in French, Spanish, and English, and sent representatives abroad to exercise their moral influence upon coreligionists in neutral countries. Restricting their efforts to more local enterprises, teachers and principals cultivated in their students sentiments of national resolve and coordinated the considerable charitable efforts of pupils and parents alike. Recent studies by Jacques Fontana, with his analysis of how French Catholics responded and contributed to the war, and Jo Burr Margadant, who has examined how the teachers and principals of girls' *lycées* dedicated themselves during the war to tasks of philanthropy and public education, have reaffirmed Becker's contention that the efforts of teachers and clergymen were essential to the survival of the nation at war.[31]

When historians have turned their attention to the role of noncombatant intellectuals in the French war effort, they have tended to pay more attention to the prodigious efforts of literary writers than to the initiatives of scholars. Writers resolved to bolster national morale with innumerable tales of moral heroism. They hoped thereby to give a moral dimension and an element of dignity to the war, but all too often their descriptions of combat were so devoid of realism and their portrayals of trench warfare so anaesthetized that front-line troops were more insulted than honored by the relentlessly romanticized *bourrage de crâne* of noncombatant writers. Of all the patriotic literary men who applied their imaginative energies to this task none was more indefatigable (and subsequently more defamed) than Maurice Barrès: his collected essays of patriotic effusion filled fourteen published volumes. Indeed, Barrès was so energetic, so prolific, and so undaunting in his apparent enthusiasm for the war that subsequent critics of intellectual mobilization singled him out for their particular opprobrium.

The tendency to examine the impact of noncombatant writers at the expense of noncombatant scholars has been evident on both sides of the Channel. Geneviève Colin, who contributed the chapter "Writers and the War" to *The Great War and the French People*, considers at some length the many ways in which writers contributed to the French war effort, but says almost nothing of scholars and academics; and in *British and French Writers of the First World War* Frank Field is even more dismissive. In his determination to examine the "intellectual and spiritual history, the *Geistesgeschichte*, of the war years and the years that surround them," he, too, looks closely at Barrès, on the one hand, and at Romain Rolland, on the other, even though Rolland enjoyed almost no support within France during the war years.[32] By restricting his focus to writers, however, Field grasps only part of the "intellectual and spiritual history" of wartime France. The importance of writers—whether as critics or celebrants of the war—cannot be gainsaid. But those who hope to understand the scope of noncombatant mobilization and the character of intellectual culture of France before, during, and after the Great War must necessarily examine with equal care the critical role of academics.

Prominent scholars were perhaps less prolific than Barrès, but they were nonetheless eager to make themselves useful. They believed (with an almost Socratic conviction) that as citizens they owed a moral debt to the nation that had nurtured them. To redeem that debt they devoted themselves tirelessly to works of public welfare: they coordinated sewing workshops, organized medical dispensaries, administered military hospitals, and donated generously to war-related charities that provided financial support to the wounded, the widows, and the orphans of France. In their commitment to philanthropic enterprise, the nation's most distinguished scholars and writers closely resembled the small-town schoolteachers of provincial France, who also gave unstintingly of their time and their salaries. The female teachers who volunteered their good will and offered their good works to the war effort transferred the ethos of self-abnegation expected of all middle-class women from the domestic to the public domain.[33] By contrast, the nation's most prominent men of intellect devoted themselves to works of good will because they believed that philanthropy was a moral obligation for citizens committed to the preservation of a secular and civic-minded republic. During the Second Empire philanthropy occupied an important place in the voluntary associations of republican educational reformers. By committing themselves to acts of public charity, the republicans of the 1860s hoped to establish a secular society independent of the charity of the Catholic Church and committed to the cultivation of civic responsibility.[34] The republican scholars of the Great War were the direct heirs of this reform-minded "radical bourgeoisie," which had been instrumental in demanding and initiating the far-ranging educational reforms of the Third Republic; and in devoting themselves to acts of public assistance, the intelligentsia of 1914 carried the traditions of their spiritual ancestors into the twentieth century.

Recognizing that ordinary citizens looked to the intellectual elite for enlightenment as well as moral example, the French intelligentsia of the Great War believed, however, that they could not fulfill their patriotic obligation through philanthropy alone. As the nation's intellectual leaders, occupying prominent and prestigious positions within the University of Paris, the Collège de France, and the Institut de France, theirs was a unique responsibility. They were expected to offer and were uniquely qualified to articulate an intellectual rationale for why the nation was at war. This they did with innumerable pamphlets, articles, and public lectures. With an energy that was unusual for men of their age, they defined what was at stake in the war, defended the French war effort, and proselytized abroad in search of new allies.

These patriotic intellectuals, ardent in their defense of the war, seem uncomfortable ancestors of an intellectual elite subsequently defined as "critical dissenters." Whether as brave souls who risked death in the Resistance, radical (and perhaps morally myopic) critics of the bourgeois status quo, or determined opponents of the Algerian War, the twentieth-century French intelligentsia has become identified with the politics of opposition.[35] And within this typology there has been neither room nor sympathy for the obedient patriots of the First World War. The noncombatant scholars of the Great War have become, therefore, not only the forgotten elements of that war, but also the unstudied intellectuals of twentieth-century France. This oblivion is perhaps one of the most enduring and ironic consequences of their wartime mobilization. In the interwar years, left-wing scholars held their elders responsible for the horrendous slaughter of the war and banished them henceforth from the genealogy of respectable, engaged intellectuals.[36]

Stigmatized as pariahs, the "patriotic intellectuals" of the Great War have until recently remained outside the community and beyond the purview of academic scholarship. Only in the last few years have historians begun to rescue these scholars from the ignominy of oblivion. Both Jean-François Sirinelli and Jacques Fontana acknowledge the important role noncombatant intellectuals assumed during the war, but neither one discusses the scholarly discourse of the war years in extensive detail or examines the context of cultural contestation in which the scholarly debates were embedded. Fontana, to be sure, identifies and analyzes the anti-Kantianism of French Catholics and shows that Catholic clerics and lay scholars perceived in Kant the intellectual descendant of Luther.[37] But his analysis does not suggest that the Catholic attack on Kant was directed as much at intellectual opponents in France as at theological heterodoxy in Germany. It is only upon delving into the details of this and other wartime debates that one discovers the depth of wartime intellectual division.

Social historians who have examined in close detail the character of civilian society during the war have determined that although French citizens remained faithful to the cause of national defense, the *union sacrée* to which they subscribed neither precluded nor prevented genuine, far-reaching civil disagreement: "the *union sacrée* was nothing but a temporary and exceptional alliance for the *practical* purposes of national defense."[38] In politics it effected a much trumpeted, albeit temporary, truce between the nationalist right and the socialist left, but it did not (and could not) oblige either side to agree on anything but their determination to defend *la patrie*. Nor could adherence to the *union sacrée* compel either employers and employees or Catholics and anticlericals to shelve indefinitely their ongoing struggles. Indeed, as the war dragged on and the nation accommodated itself accordingly, long-festering animosities, only temporarily set aside, resurfaced to disturb the civil peace. Hence industrial relations between employees and employers, acrimonious and discordant before 1914, did not entirely lose their edge after August 1914: "as the war progressed it appeared that exhortations to rally together masked persisting antagonisms less and less, especially between employers and workers."[39] Fontana makes a comparable point in his detailed study of relations between Catholics and anticlericals during the First World War.[40]

Just as there was no separate peace in the religious and labor wars of the Third Republic, neither was it all quiet on the nation's cultural front. If anything, the war deepened the old cultural divide. On this point, this book parts company with the historians who have argued that as scholars and men of letters united in their defense of the war effort, the rift that had divided the French intelligentsia before 1914 closed for the duration of the war years.[41] The intelligentsia did unite in its defense of the war, but the rift that had long separated Dreyfusards from anti-Dreyfusards, and modernists from traditionalists, remained. Whether denouncing Kant or demanding a return to the classical curriculum, intellectual nationalists intensified their assault upon the academic establishment and progressively eroded its authority. Insisting that the cultural conflict of the prewar era continued unabated through the war years, this study thus seeks to qualify Ory and Sirinelli's conclusion that it was only in the early 1920s that French intellectual culture returned to the bitter bipolarity of the post-Dreyfus Republic, with ardent neoroyalists once again, and ever more forcefully, challenging the republican establishment.[42] This they did, but a close reading of the intellectual debates of the war years suggests that neither the bitterness nor the bipolarity disappeared between 1914 and 1918.

The mobilization of intellect was, all scholars of the Great War agree, an international phenomenon. And in many of their responses to the war French academics and writers resembled their intellectual contemporaries in Germany and Britain. German scholars were, as the Manifesto of 93 made clear, as convinced of the righteousness of their cause as British and French scholars were of their own. Fritz Ringer argues that the German professoriate, especially those in the humanities and social sciences, "greeted the war with a sense of relief," in large part because they saw in the conflict an opportunity to reverse, or at least to slow down, the process of industrialization that was rendering scholars ever more irrelevant, their prestige ever more precarious. When war broke out and the German people rallied to the cause with an unexpected enthusiasm, the German mandarins believed that it would usher in a new age for the nation, an age that, free of politics and internal division, would be capable of producing genuine social cohesion. For this reason, most members of the German academic community (those whom Ringer designates as "the orthodox") remained unrepentant pan-German expansionists throughout the war. Only a minority eschewed as exaggerated and unrealistic the pan-Germanists' demands for territorial expansion.[43]

Ringer contends that the German intellectuals directed their animosity more to England than to France: England, they believed, represented the true threat to German hegemony and the true source of the materialistic, industrial, entrepreneurial culture the German professors despised and feared. More recently, Eberhard Demm has offered a useful qualification to this conclusion. While German intellectual action was directed primarily against Britain and German scholars occasionally treated France with condescending dismissal, they did not ignore France entirely. Eager to defend the conservative political system of the Wilhelmine Empire that kept the threat of popular sovereignty at bay, they disparaged the principles of the French Revolution as outmoded and insisted that Germany would replace the petty individualism of personal rights with an organic, collectivist spirit of liberty. With his "Confessions of a Non-Political

Man," Thomas Mann became the most famous German intellectual to denounce French democracy and the principles of 1789 as decadent and passé; but he was by no means the only one.[44]

Recent scholarship in the cultural history of Britain during the Great War makes it clear that British scholars, writers, and artists were as antipathetic to Germany as German scholars were to Britain, and as ardent in their enthusiasm for the war effort as were the French. Like the French, they "perceived the war against Germany as a war . . . in defence of civilization, against a barbarous, many-headed enemy."[45] With so much at stake, everything became important and every individual indispensable. Cultural controversies raged even over concert programs, for the most ardent patriots feared that one could not be true to Britain while listening to Brahms. And the mobilization of intellect was as much a feature of academic life in Britain as in France. British scholars, outraged by evidence of German intellectual subservience to the state, nonetheless voluntarily "enlisted" for a government-organized propaganda campaign that found its headquarters at Wellington House in London. Like their counterparts across the Channel, these patriotic scholars took it upon themselves to educate the nation through public lectures and written pamphlets. Paul Fussell observed almost two decades ago that the Great War was the first literary war: troops, schooled and literate, crossed the Channel with Thomas Hardy in their pockets, and rendered the war immortal in their poetry.[46] Widespread literacy affected the character of the noncombatants' war, too. In a nation transformed by mandatory public education and dependent—until 1916—upon voluntary enlistment, noncombatant scholars sought to woo the national electorate through writing.[47] Above all, they hoped that their lectures and their essays would stimulate enlistment by arousing the patriotic indignation of working-class men.

Committed as they were to their country, English academics nevertheless confronted several crises of intellectual conscience. They too had long admired German scholarship and held German scholars in high regard. Thus with the outbreak of war they had to learn to dislike the men they had so recently admired and to disdain the academic system they had sought to emulate. Yet esteem for things German quickly withered, and scholars who had once praised German academic institutions and placed German science in a class by itself soon recanted. The war effectively "demoted German universities from their former position as models for university reformers" and confined German scientific accomplishment to the shadows.[48] In Britain as in France scientists soon became conspicuously proud of their own nation's scientific accomplishments and less impressed with those of Germany. Philosophers, however, found it much more intellectually problematic to rid themselves of their prewar regard for German philosophy. Hegelianism had indelibly marked British Idealism, the most influential school of philosophical thought in Britain before 1914, and British philosophers consequently sought refuge in the thesis of "two Germanies." While French republican scholars hoped to immunize Kant from public calumny, the British Idealists wished to protect Hegel (toward whom French philosophers of the early twentieth century were notably indifferent), and as a consequence insisted that "Hegelianism had been superseded by other less noble ideals in Germany."[49] Perhaps it is somewhat exaggerated to call "the rescue of Hegel . . . a matter of life and death for some philosophers," but the general point—that the war created crises of intellectual conscience in which the preservation of established academic principles was a serious issue—is as valid for France as for Britain.[50]

Although scholars as prominent as Bertrand Russell and G. E. Moore publicly opposed the war, they represented the minority. For the duration of the war, nearly all British academics rallied enthusiastically to their nation's cause: as in France, they addressed themselves to domestic and foreign audiences alike, and worked with especial vigor to win over academic opinion in the United States.[51] But while the mobilization of British intellect resembled that of France in many ways, the mobilization of French intellectuals was of much greater import and more far-reaching effect. The mobilization of British intellectuals did not significantly affect the cultural character of postwar Britain. Indeed, ultimately the "professors' war" waged in Great Britain between 1914 and 1918 was of little consequence: "bitterly fought while it went on . . . in the end it simply ceased to matter."[52] It was much different in France, where the arguments of noncombatant intellectuals helped bring about a reorientation of intellectual culture after the war and positively influenced the attitudes of French combatants and civilians during the war.

Many years after the war, Marc Bloch recalled that front-line troops usually found the propaganda of the patriotic press so distasteful that many came to regard the written word with bitter mistrust.[53] Upon reading the wartime correspondence of France's most educated front-line troops, however, it becomes apparent that these troops retained some regard for the written word. Although they found the notorious *bourrage de crâne* of the daily press offensive and intolerable, they were often much more tolerant of the more sophisticated and more nuanced essays of the noncombatant intelligentsia published in the nation's scholarly journals. Not only did front-line scholars and former students have relatively easy access to these journals, but, unlike their British counterparts, whose alienation from the home front has become legendary, they often found themselves in agreement with the arguments they read in the pages of the *Revue des deux mondes* or the *Revue de Paris*. Rather than divorcing themselves absolutely from the patriotism of the home front, rather than fighting only to maintain solidarity with their comrades-in-arms, these men shared the idealism and many of the antipathies of their former mentors and senior colleagues. They too conceived of the war as a moral—and mortal—combat against barbarism and unrestrained materialism; and they were willing to die to defend the eternal, immutable values of France: liberty, the rule of law, and the classical tradition. The meaning they bestowed upon the Great War, the "myth" that nurtured them at the front was, in many ways, the myth of the war noncombatant intellectuals manufactured behind the lines.

A recent analysis of French newspapers produced for and by front-line troops concludes that "there was no real rift between the soldiers and the rest of the national community."[54] Yet reasons for demoralization were greater in the French ranks than elsewhere along the Western Front—inefficiency of operations made the French trenches even more inhospitable than those of the British and the German front lines, and French mortality rates were higher, too. But French troops held out because, like the civilians with whom they communicated on a regular basis, they remained confident that their cause was just and the liberation of their country essential.[55] Whatever their grumblings and legitimate complaints, the *poilus* remained determined defenders of the French war effort because they believed that France should not declare an end to the war until its soil was liberated, its civilization secure, and its victory decisive.

Even if the "professors' war" mattered little to the history of English culture after 1918, it proved of singular importance to the development of intellectual culture in interwar France, where the major questions informing wartime debates continued for several years to shape the nation's cultural discourse. In a nation more fundamentally divided than Britain, the cessation of hostilities in 1918 did not strip these debates of either their importance or their power to command intellectual attention. Indeed, scholars on both sides of the ideological divide were convinced that the victory so dearly purchased on the fields of northern France could be secured, and the nation's future guaranteed, only if ultimate answers to essential questions about the cultural identity of France were determined. Thus the debates, now colored by the anxieties and expectations of a badly battered but nonetheless victorious nation continued, albeit in an unfamiliar new key. Because the right-wing intelligentsia made significant gains within the nation at large, the cultural hegemony of the *universitaires* eroded noticeably after 1914. Régis Debray has argued that the cultural history of France since 1870 may be divided into three distinct stages: the age of the scholar, from 1870 through the interwar years; the age of the writer, from 1920 to approximately 1960, and most recently the age of the celebrity.[56] It was during the Great War that the scholars, the cultural brokers of the first half of the Third Republic, saw their dominance begin to decline, and the writers of the right-wing intelligentsia gained their foothold.

CHAPTER ONE

The Discord
of the Elders

The intellectual discord of the Great War was as old as the Third Republic itself. From 1870 onwards, intellectuals split into two hostile camps that differed fundamentally over questions of politics, philosophy, and educational reform. Academic modernists affiliated themselves for ideological and pragmatic reasons with the republicans who secured power definitively in 1879, and—like their political allies—were determined to complete the unfinished agenda of 1789. They hoped to inaugurate at last an age of genuine liberty, equality, and fraternity. But to do so they would first have to make the Republic secure, by weaning the French citizenry of its disturbing political appetite for authoritarianism, and by breaking the cultural authority of the Catholic Church. For centuries the church had controlled all of the nation's elementary schools and many of its most prestigious secondary schools, and in the past century it had categorically opposed the politics of republicanism and—with varying degrees of enthusiasm—had supported instead Bourbon and Bonapartist experiments in illiberal government. Convinced that no accommodation was possible with an institution so resolutely antithetical to their ideals, reform-minded scholars and republican politicians were anticlericists in their politics and secular philosophical empiricists in their world-view. Inspired by the progressive spirit of the Revolution, Darwinian science, and Comtean positivism, they believed that the world was moving ever closer to perfection, whether through the mysterious process of natural selection, the agency of man, or the power of science. Like many educated men of the nineteenth century, they were particularly enamored of science, since they were convinced it could both explain and improve the world. So powerful indeed was their faith in science that they believed all that was worth knowing could be gleaned from scientific investigation.

This quintessentially nineteenth-century world-view appalled political and philosophical traditionalists, who saw their control of French cultural institutions erode as their republican opponents gained authority. Monarchists and Catholics contemplated the political triumph of anticlerical republicanism and academic modernism with horror. Not only did they repudiate as inherently disorderly the revolutionary ethos of individualism and egalitarianism, they rejected the evolutionism of Comte and Darwin as unbridled materialism entirely indifferent—if not absolutely hostile—to the consideration of spiritual matters. And they denied that either man or his world could achieve perfection independently of divine intervention. Dismissing as specious the dream of progress, they wanted France to return to its pre-1789 past, not to embrace its republican future.

Confronting one another across a chasm of mistrust and incomprehension, modernists and traditionalists were wont to articulate their differences in acrimonious, impassioned debates over the character of French education. Both sides knew that control of education was of the essence, for—as George Mosse would observe a century later—"the solidity of [a] human society depends in large measure upon the effective transformation of its ideals into educational institutions."[1] Reformers hoped to infuse every level of French education with their values. Thus they set for themselves the daunting task of systematic educational reform. From 1880 onwards, they introduced legislation to make elementary schooling secular, compulsory, and civic-minded; to attune the secondary school curriculum to the demands of an emerging industrial society; and to bring rigorous scientific method to higher education.[2] Unconcerned that the two schools of thought were philosophically incompatible, the reformers created an intellectual culture predicated jointly upon Comtean positivism and Kantian ethics. Their conservative antagonists, opposed as they were to any comprehensive reform of French education that would reduce the influence of the Catholic Church or advance republican ideals, denounced both the scientism and the neo-Kantianism of republican intellectual culture. They insisted that French culture remain true to its own traditions and French education preserve its resolutely classical (and clerical) character.

Republican Intellectual Culture

The educational reforms of the Third Republic traced their origins to the Second Empire. Reform-minded scholars and politicians, uncomfortable with the clerical character of early education, uneasy with what they took to be the archaic classical curriculum of secondary education, and embarrassed by the academic laxity of higher education, emerged in the 1860s to demand free, secular education at the primary level, a curriculum suited to the demands of the modern age at the secondary level, and rigorous intellectual inquiry for higher education.[3] Leaving the thorny issue of elementary reform to another day, Victor Duruy, Napoleon III's innovative Minister of Education, took some significant steps to overcome the most grievous inadequacies of secondary and postsecondary education. As every subsequent advocate and opponent of modern pedagogy would remember, it was Duruy who introduced the option of a modern curriculum to secondary education. Reviving an unsuccessful eighteenth-century experiment that would have made French (rather than Latin) the principal language of instruction and would have offered courses in geography, the sciences, and modern languages, Duruy's *enseignement spécial* ran aground in the 1860s on the shoals of clerical opposition and bourgeois snobbery. Duruy's second major innovation in modern education proved, however, more immediately successful. With the founding of the Ecole Pratique des Hautes Etudes in 1868, Duruy offered French scholars the opportunity to become familiar with the techniques of the research seminar, an innovation that would forever change the character of higher education in France. From Duruy's two initiatives would emerge the Third Republic's reform program for secondary and higher education.[4]

Upon the fall of the Second Empire in 1870, Duruy's experiments in educational modernization came to an end. But his vision remained, and in the wake of military defeat would-be reformers grew ever more committed to his cause. The Franco-Prussian War persuaded scholars as prominent as Ernest Renan and Louis Pasteur that Prussia's advantage on the battlefield had originated in the classrooms, laboratories, and seminars of its schools, *gymnasia,* and universities. At the elementary levels, Prussian classrooms promoted discipline and literacy among the nation's conscripts; at more advanced levels, laboratories and seminars instructed students in the methods of science. Pasteur charged that German dedication to science had proved decisive in 1870: for more than fifty years, while the French had absorbed themselves in searches for the perfect political system, the Prussians had invested heavily in scientific education and had encouraged the coordination of scientific efforts with emerging industry.[5] By 1870 the manifold advantages of a rigorous national education based on the scientific method were evident to all observers. Not only had the conquest of science allowed Prussia to conquer both Austria and France, nations that had remained indifferent to science; it had made German education the envy of the world. Students from France, Britain, and the United States had flocked to Prussian universities in search of an incontestably superior education. And German professors, armed with an indomitable confidence in the scientific method, had proved such prodigious scholars that they had earned an international reputation for scholarship their counterparts in France could only envy. With such evidence before them, French educational reformers, persuaded of the professional and national advantages to be accrued from serious science-based education, determined to overcome previous inadequacies in French higher education by means of the sincerest form of flattery: extensive imitation of German educational practices.[6]

Unlike university education in Prussia, which was admired around the world, higher education in France was an embarrassment. Although the *grandes écoles* offered highly specialized training to a handful of talented students destined for careers in the military, in industry, and in teaching, there were no multi-faculty universities in France before 1896. There were, instead, independent faculties (of letters, science, law, medicine, and—until 1888—theology) that offered public audiences lectures notable more for the rhetorical power of the lecturer than the rigor of his interpretation; these faculties also examined candidates for state-granted degrees. Physical facilities were run-down, ill-equipped, and underfunded: Pasteur had made monumental advances in the study of bacteriology in spite of and not thanks to the facilities in which he labored. Although French professors were not noticeably overworked, they were in truth notoriously ill paid. Anxious to redeem the honor of their profession, ambitious scholars joined with republican politicians—who knew that France could never hope to compete economically with Germany and feared that she could not defend herself militarily against future aggression if French education remained so deplorably backward— to demand a far-reaching structural reform of higher education.

The Société d'Enseignement Supérieur (which published the *Revue internationale de l'enseignement*) was "a pressure group on behalf of reform," and the vision of reformers who congregated in the Société fundamentally shaped the character of higher education from 1880 to 1914.[7] Many of the scholars who would participate in the wartime mobilization of intellect were longtime members of this organization: François Picavet served as editor of its journal for twenty years, and members included Paul Appell, Alphonse Aulard, Emile Boutroux, Alfred Croiset, and Ernest Lavisse. They hoped to bring to French scholarship the status it deserved by establishing institutional autonomy for universities, increasing faculty salaries, and improving the academic standards of all degree programs. Only then would higher education in France be comparable in quality and structure to that offered in Germany, and only thus could scholars rightly expect the respect German scholars already enjoyed. Reforms introduced after 1880 went a long way to accommodate the demands of the Société, by granting faculty members administrative control over their institutions and by restructuring the institutions and teaching methods of higher education.

Louis Liard, who had worked closely with Duruy in the 1860s and who proved a powerful voice for the Société within the Ministry of Public Instruction, coordinated the reform of higher education in France. His most notable accomplishment was the creation in 1896 of a system of academically rigorous, multi-faculty universities dedicated to the pursuit of original research based on scientific models.[8] Insisting upon the construction of modern facilities at the University of Paris, Liard helped create the *nouvelle* Sorbonne, where scholars gladly abandoned the large lecture-halls that had served as auditoriums for public lectures directed at dabblers in scholarly life, and concentrated their energies instead on newly created seminar courses open only to degree students. It was in these seminar rooms that professors worked to form future generations of scholars by instructing them in the methods of academic criticism and analysis.

The Scientism of the *Nouvelle* Sorbonne

One of the most notable features of the reformed university was its respect for the scientific method which, Weisz concluded, "became the official ideology of the university establishment."[9] Science became the secular faith of the Third Republic for many reasons: it was compatible with the positivist, progressive social vision of the early Republic; its strenuous empiricism defied the superstitious supernaturalism of organized religion and was thus an essential ally of anticlericalism; and (as Pasteur had noted) it promised the nation military security. Thus the Republic worked assiduously to improve the quality of scientific education; to develop fruitful working relationships between science and industry; and to bring the rigor of scientific analysis to fields of academic inquiry as yet untouched by the scientific method. Although the Republic made significant (and often underrated) advances in scientific education and industrial development, efforts to infuse the study of literature, history, and philosophy with the scientific spirit provoked by the 1890s a storm of controversy within and outside the halls of higher education.

Ever mindful of Pasteur's indictment that in 1870 France had paid the price for its ignorance and indifference to science, French educational reformers and influential politicians took systematic steps to improve the quality and expand the domain of scientific instruction. New faculty positions in the sciences opened up, and enrollment in faculties of science increased almost exponentially, from a meager 300 in 1876 to more than 6,000 in 1911. Simultaneously, republican reformers set aside their fears that the decentralization of education would play into the hands of monarchists, and "found in the German example of competing regional universities a model for creating provincial educational and scientific centers as rivals to Paris." New universities—in Bordeaux, Nantes, Marseille and elsewhere—took science into the countryside.[10]

Those responsible for the expansion of science into the provinces were determined to develop the economic potential of applied science. The dramatic industrial development of Germany that occurred in the last decades of the nineteenth century and that depended heavily on advances in chemistry, made all observers aware of the economic advantages to be gained from a close alliance between science and industry. Fearful of being swamped by German industrial and technological might, French politicians and businessmen hoped to bring about a comparable alliance in France. By and large, they succeeded more than anyone ever admitted. In the provincial universities, faculties that concentrated on applied science—notably those of Grenoble, Toulouse, and Nancy—recruited large numbers of students and made significant contributions to regional economic development.[11] As Weisz concludes, "the belief that French academic scientists in the 19th century were resistant to change and uninterested in practical economic needs thus does not stand up to close scrutiny. Professors of science in France seem on the contrary to have been far more willing to serve industrial interests than their opposite numbers in German universities."[12]

French science was not as backward, unproductive, or dominated by Paris as contemporary observers believed and historians of science have subsequently argued. The preponderant belief that French science was inferior to that of Germany before 1914 (or to the United States thereafter) is overstated. Pasteur was not an "isolated achievement," for "a great deal of important medical research was carried on" in late-nineteenth-century France. Nor was it the case that the most significant advances in French science occurred in Paris: Pasteur's achievements in Lille and Pierre Duhem's in Bordeaux suggest that much of great merit was accomplished in the provinces. Nonetheless the perception remained at the time (and persisted well into the twentieth century) that Germany was the dominant scientific power of the late century and outstripped France in the domain of applied science, in large part because Germany's industrial economy so far exceeded that of France. When reviewing the relative accomplishments of France and Germany, Harry Paul concludes that one must keep in mind that "there is . . . a difference between the decline of French science, which remains to be shown, and the rise of German science, which is not at issue, and its putative surpassing of French science, which was not by any means stagnant."[13]

Had the scientific method been confined to the laboratories of provincial and Parisian faculties of sciences, few would have complained. Even the leaders of the Action Française, who would become vociferous opponents of the "scientism" of republican higher education, conceded that empirical observation, induction, and deduction were appropriate enough in the laboratories of Louis Pasteur and Pierre Curie. They objected strenuously, however, when these principles of scientific investigation were applied to the study of history, literature, and philosophy. Yet the Republic's regard for the positivism of science was so pervasive that it did indeed penetrate faculties of letters, where professors become ardent practitioners of "scientific" scholarship. Frustrated that French academic life had traditionally undervalued serious scholarship, scholars believed that if their research and their teaching bore the mark of "science" and were based on the careful accumulation and dispassionate interpretation of data, then their enterprise would earn the esteem it so richly deserved.[14] Thus in the reformed universities of late-nineteenth-century France the scrupulously thorough collection and analysis of data became the dominant method of academic research. Historians encouraged their students to mine untapped archives, to catalog and collate evidence, and to produce richly detailed but interpretively timid monographs on the most arcane subjects. According to their detractors, literary critics enamored of the scientific method eschewed the analysis of the most profound themes of literature because this required scholars to exercise their subjective judgment; they preferred to lose themselves in the much more objective study of the rhetorical patterns and syntactical practices of great writers. And philosophers dominated by the positivism of Auguste Comte, Ernest Renan, and Hippolyte Taine were—in the main—content to restrict their attention to the study of that which could be known about the natural world with comparative certainty.[15]

Neo-Kantianism and Republican Civics

Republican intellectual culture of the 1870s and 1880s combined—in a not entirely internally consistent synthesis—a reverent regard for scientism and an appropriation of Kantian ethics. Even though the progressive, positivist, and materialist presuppositions of scientism offered republicans a theory of knowledge that was at once radically at odds with the epistemological foundations of Catholicism and compatible with the secular and anticlerical spirit of the new republic, scientism—or, to use a more current term, "naturalism"—proved an incomplete philosophical system for the reformers of the Third Republic. Concerned only with the way things are, and not with how they ought to be, naturalism offered the nation little in the way of moral guidance. For the Republic to provide a moral justification for its political principles and a viable alternative to the moral precepts of the Catholic Church, its ideologists had to discover and promulgate a secular ethic. Republicans found such an ethic in Kant's moral philosophy, which offered a philosophical system compatible with the defense of individual rights, the establishment of universal education, and the cultivation of civic responsibility.[16]

Although the expansion of neo-Kantianism became most evident during the decades after the debacle of Sedan, it would be inappropriate to conclude (as neoroyalists would subsequently do) that Kantian ethics came to France in the knapsacks of the Prussian conquerors. Charles Renouvier, for example, developed in the 1860s a neo-Kantian philosophy of individual liberty predicated upon human rationality. An unequivocal republican frustrated by the authoritarian politics and clerical educational system of the Second Empire, Renouvier found in Kantian ethics an alternative philosophical foundation that was both compatible with the principles of 1789 and indispensable to those intent upon the systematic reform of French education. Deriving his inspiration directly from Kant, he believed that all human beings are, by virtue of their rationality, both free and inherently equal; and he insisted that rational beings could exercise their freedom only if given the opportunity to cultivate their reason. Hence for Renouvier (as for Kant), comprehensive, secular public education was essential to the formation and preservation of a free society.[17]

Kant's ethics did more, however, than offer secular republicans a rationale for sweeping educational reform. His moral philosophy, predicated upon the belief that freedom entails duty, also insisted that as free and rational beings, citizens of a free society have civic obligations that cannot be ignored. Unlike animals bereft of reason, rational beings are free because they have the ability (although not always the inclination) to act in accordance with the dictates of universal reason. But if rationality endows rational beings with freedom, it also compels them to honor and not impinge upon the autonomy of other rational beings. A free man does not do whatever he pleases; his reason dictates that he act towards others in such a way that his actions could become the basis of universal law. Thus one's obligation to others is a necessary consequence of one's freedom.

For republican politicians and scholars who hoped to create a republic that was at once free and orderly, Kant's emphasis on the moral obligation and—by extension—civic responsibility of citizens proved most compelling. It informed (albeit in a much watered-down form) the civics curriculum taught in elementary schools across the nation.[18] And it inspired the self-abnegating, secular ethos of girls' secondary education.[19] Even more noticeably, Kantian ideas infiltrated the philosophy curriculum of boys' secondary education, where republican professors gave *lycée* students an enthusiastic introduction to deontological ethics. Certainly the most famous of the neo-Kantian *lycée* instructors was Auguste Burdeau, who taught philosophy at the Lycée Louis-le-Grand in Paris until he entered politics as an Opportunist deputy for Lyon in 1885. Although many students remembered his classes with great fondness, not every one appreciated Burdeau's enthusiasm for Kant. Integral nationalists were indignant that he should have embraced with such enthusiasm a philosophical system originating in Germany, and when Maurice Barrès set out in *Les Déracinés* to denounce the alien—and alienating—character of republican education, he created in Professor Bouteiller an easily recognized caricature of Burdeau.[20] Léon Daudet, who attended Louis-le-Grand in the mid-1880s, nursed for decades his bitter memories of Burdeau's philosophy class. He claimed many years after the fact that Burdeau used to open the *Critique of Pure Reason* and interpret significant passages to his bedazzled students. Having rendered the text in French, Burdeau would often then read the original text aloud in German. Daudet, disgusted by what he took to be this reverence for the language of the enemy, believed that Burdeau was thus insinuating that German was "the language of pure thought."[21]

It is probable that Daudet's memory deceived him. Burdeau was best known for his interpretations of Kantian ethics, and it is more likely that he read to his students sections of the *Critique of Practical Reason* than passages from the *Critique of Pure Reason*. Unlike Kantian ethics, Kantian epistemology infiltrated French thought and education only very slowly. Until the late 1880s the philosophical naturalism of Ernest Renan and Hippolyte Taine dominated the philosophy taught at the University of Paris, and Kant's antinaturalist transcendental epistemology (which rejected as inadequate the reductionist spirit of Humean empiricism) found few enthusiasts there. It was only after 1890 that French philosophers, increasingly dissatisfied with the scientism of their age and seeking a more philosophically satisfying system of explanation, turned in large numbers to Kant.

French neo-Kantianism established its first foothold at the Ecole Normale Supérieure, where a few prominently placed scholars and teachers laid the foundations for the philosophical rejection of naturalism that marked the 1890s. No scholar was more influential in this regard than Jules Lachelier, who during his tenure at the ENS from 1864 until 1875 encouraged his students to investigate the limits of empirically derived knowledge. Lachelier was not a prolific scholar, although his thesis, *On the Foundations of Induction,* published originally in 1871, became a text of singular importance for generations of *normaliens.*[22] He was, however, a dynamic and inspiring teacher whose unpublished lecture-notes circulated in manuscript form among students enthused by his explication of Kant and eager to familiarize themselves with a more satisfying systematic philosophy than that offered by Renan or Taine.[23] By introducing his students to Kant, Lachelier profoundly influenced the philosophical formation of the nation's *lycée* teachers and forever changed the philosophical orientation of French academic life.

Of all the students Lachelier taught at the Ecole Normale, none was more important to the development and dissemination of neo-Kantianism in France than Emile Boutroux. A philosopher of science who developed a meta-scientific critique of scientific method, Boutroux made his mark upon French philosophy with the publication in 1874 of his doctoral thesis, *On the Contingency of Laws of Nature.* Insisting upon the epistemological limitations of scientific inquiry and on the need to subject the laws of science to the scrutiny of rational critique, his dissertation challenged the first principles of French positivism.[24] An internationally esteemed philosopher and much admired teacher, Boutroux inherited Lachelier's mantle when in 1877, two years after the retirement of his mentor, he secured a teaching position at the Ecole Normale. One of the most important philosophers of his day, Boutroux directly influenced the intellectual formation of Henri Bergson (who entered the ENS in the *promotion* of 1881), Victor Delbos (of the *promotion* of 1882), and Charles Andler (of the *promotion* of 1884). Whether at the ENS or subsequently at the University of Paris, where he remained until his death in 1921, Boutroux drew successive generations of students to neo-Kantianism.

By the early 1890s it was evident that French philosophers had abandoned naturalism in favor of neo-Kantianism. New translations of major Kantian texts appeared throughout the years of the *belle époque,* and many of the scholars who would defend Kant with an uncommon academic ardor during the Great War established their philosophical reputations in the two decades before the war. Unlike Renouvier, who had never been able to read Kant in the original German, Victor Delbos and his contemporaries—Victor Basch, Emile Picavet, and Charles Andler— were not only original scholars but proficient linguists whose interpretations and translations of major Kantian texts transformed the character of French philosophy after 1890. Picavet issued a new translation of Kant's *Critique of Practical Reason* in 1888; Andler, working in collaboration with Edouard Chavannes, produced the first French translation of *The Metaphysical Foundations of Natural Science* in 1891; and in 1902 Delbos received his *doctorat d'état* for a thesis on Kant's ethics. Appointed *maître de conférences* at the Sorbonne, five years later he published his definitive translation of the *Foundations of the Metaphysics of Morals.*

The intense and rigorous interest in Kantian philosophy that characterized French philosophy at the turn of the century was indicative of two larger movements in French academic life: a systematic rejection of naturalism and the development of an interdisciplinary interest in German culture. Allan Mitchell has noted that in the aftermath of the Franco-Prussian War French *germanistes,* once known only for their detailed analysis of German literature, were no longer content to study the masterworks of literature in cultural isolation. Eager to understand the nation that had so effectively humiliated France in 1870, they hoped to develop a comprehensive understanding of German culture in its many manifestations. And thus scholars like Delbos and Andler, who came of age in the 1890s, studied German philosophy, art, and society with unprecedented enthusiasm.[25] Building upon the "two Germanies" thesis that Caro had articulated twenty years earlier, their studies of the German tradition emphasized that which they found most admirable, most worthy of emulation, and most consistent with the ideals of French republicanism.

The neo-Kantianism of the 1890s was also indicative of an antipositivist revolt that occurred simultaneously, but with fundamentally different intentions and effects, both inside and outside the academic community.[26] Within the reformed university, philosophers were not alone in questioning the merits of naturalism. Even though sociologists sought to establish a science of human society, they found the narrow focus of "scientistic" scholarship unsatisfying and like some historians of the same generation they joined with their colleagues in philosophy to express their serious reservations. Two of the most vehement critics of the scientism of the new Sorbonne were Emile Durkheim and Henri Berr. Berr contended that compiling a catalog of facts, unearthed from necessarily incomplete archival sources, did not constitute historical explanation, and he called for a more broadly "synthetic" study of history. Durkheim also charged that with their obsessive emphasis on the idiosyncratic and *événementiel* character of the past, historians of the new school did nothing to advance understanding of the essential character of human society.[27]

When historians, philosophers, and sociologists launched an internal challenge against the scientism of the reformed university, they did not intend thereby to undermine the philosophical foundations or discredit the political ideals of French republicanism. Not only was the neo-Kantianism of the 1890s entirely consistent with the principles of republicanism, but the scholars within the university most closely identified with the attack on philosophical naturalism were dedicated democrats devoted to the preservation and moral improvement of the Third Republic. This became evident at the end of the decade, when many of them rallied to the cause of Alfred Dreyfus. Support for Dreyfus was most widespread within the academic disciplines most directly affected by and amenable to curricular reform and academic modernization: history, philosophy, and the social sciences.[28] Indeed, the Dreyfus Affair effected an ideological (if not an intellectual) reconciliation between naturalists and antinaturalists within the Faculty of Letters at the University of Paris. Fearing that if the forces of traditionalism were to prevail, the Republic would be overthrown and the reforms introduced to higher education reversed, they transcended their academic differences in defense of the Republic.

The Revolt of the Right-Wing Intelligentsia

Opponents of scientism outside the republican university and hostile to the progressive principles of the Third Republic also participated in the antipositivist revolt of the 1890s. But whether as Catholics or as nationalists, they did so in order to discredit the Republic, to challenge its secular, individualist, and cosmopolitan ideology, and to oppose its initiatives at educational reform. Constituting an antirepublican oppositional intelligentsia, they decried all evidence of Germanic (and Protestant) influence in French life and denounced the university's excessive respect for scientific method as materialistic and injurious to faith. They articulated their opposition to the spirit of the reformed university in the literary journals that existed independently of academic life—the *Revue des deux mondes, Mercure de France,* and the Catholic *Le Correspondant*—and after 1890 they found many powerful allies—including Ferdinand Brunetière and Maurice Barrès—in the conservative wing of the Académie Française.

In 1895 Ferdinand Brunetière, writing in the pages of the *Revue des deux mondes,* issued the decade's most famous challenge to the scientism of the republican university: "Après une visite au Vatican." Asserting the "bankruptcy of science" and challenging the scientistic belief that "everything true could be discovered by reason and catalogued by science,"[29] Brunetière (like the neo-Kantians) argued that empiricism alone was not an adequate epistemological foundation for understanding humanity. Vehemently attacked by the distinguished physiologist Charles Richet, he nonetheless found many allies among Catholic intellectuals who were indifferent to the appeal of neo-Kantianism and who believed that the materialism and scientism propagated for so long within the academic institutions of the Third Republic were inimical to true faith. Antipathy to philosophical naturalism led Boutroux and Delbos to neo-Kantianism, which seemed to hold out some promise of spiritualism; but it inclined other Catholic philosophers, especially those suspicious of Kant's Pietist, Protestant origins and uncomfortable with the individualism of his ethics and the subjectivism of his epistemology, away from modern rationalism and towards neoscholasticism. After the publication of Leo XIII's encyclical "Aeterni Patris" in 1879, a neo-Thomist revival dominated Catholic thought. This may have constituted a conscious effort on the part of Catholic intellectuals to reconcile the teachings of the Church with the teachings of science. Aspiring to the Thomistic synthesis of faith and reason, they came to accept evolutionary theory as consistent with their faith.[30] They did not, however, rally to the cause of the Republic.

No single biography traces the conversion from scientism to neo-Thomism more dramatically than that of Jacques Maritain. Born in 1882 of liberal, republican, and Protestant parents, Maritain as a youth embraced the humanistic socialism of Jean Jaurès, scorned religious commitment, and decided to pursue a career in science. In 1900, however, while enrolled in the Faculty of Sciences at the University of Paris, his ideals changed irrevocably: he and a fellow student soon discovered that the study of the physical sciences offered them only inadequate answers to the ontological questions that haunted them both. During the summer of 1901, profoundly disillusioned with the scientific empiricism still prevalent within the Faculty of Sciences, Jacques Maritain and Raïssa Oumansoff concluded a suicide pact. If they could not find a more satisfactory philosophical system within a year, they would abandon life as a futile enterprise.[31] Charles Péguy saved them from suicide when he took them to hear Henri Bergson lecture at the Collège de France, and for a while Maritain became an enthusiastic Bergsonian. He felt uncomfortable, however, with the anti-intellectual bias of Bergson's intuitionism and continued to search for a system more responsive to his yearning for "the absolute." Having converted to Catholicism in 1906, he found such a system in neo-Thomism.

Many Catholic scholars and writers found themselves increasingly at odds with the intellectual values of the Third Republic for a more practical reason: they suffered the consequences of anticlerical discrimination. In the eras of most intense anticlerical activity—the 1880s and the first decade of the twentieth century—the Third Republic clearly discriminated against Catholic scholars, many of whom were removed from or denied access to positions of academic responsibility and prestige. Catholic scientists fared somewhat better than Catholic humanists: because the Republic "made a fetish of rewarding individuals for their contributions to science," it rarely dismissed Catholic scientists.[32] Nonetheless academic promotion often eluded them. In 1903 Paul Tannery, a Catholic historian of science, received forty of forty-seven votes for election to the chair of history of science at the Collège de France, only to have the anticlerical government of Emile Combes overturn his nomination and appoint an ardent positivist to the position instead.[33] Pierre Duhem was an even more celebrated victim of anticlerical discrimination. A practicing Catholic, a prominent physicist, and a historian of science, Duhem was consistently refused promotion to the University of Paris—even though none of his peers contested his preeminence in physics—and was obliged to spend his academic career at the University of Bordeaux. Only in the years immediately preceding the war, when anticlericalism abated, did this academic persecution decline, and Raymond Thamin (who would become an active supporter of Bérard's reforms) took active steps to recognize and reward Duhem's genuine contributions to the world of science.[34]

Although Duhem demonstrated with his dedication to physics that not all Catholics were irremediably hostile to science, most Catholic intellectuals of the prewar era remained extremely hostile to the post-Cartesian rationalism upon which modern science was predicated. In an important essay published in 1910 entitled "Reason and Modern Science," Maritain denounced the pretensions of modern science to universal applicability and lamented the intellectual sovereignty of science in the modern world. The essay examined the relationship that obtained between "reason," as understood in the post-Cartesian philosophical tradition, and the intellectual dominance of modern science; and contended that modern "reason" was in fact an inversion of true reason. Maritain defined reason in terms of divinely given Intelligence: it was "the methodical exercise of Intelligence [a gift of the Holy Spirit] and the means by which it [Intelligence] arrives at an understanding of reality." The modern world, however, denied divinity and supplanted intelligence with a self-sufficient reason. This modern reason, which Maritain characterized as "pseudo-reason," insisted that nothing was real except that which could be explained mathematically; it denied the reality of anything which could not be made into a formula. As rationalism could make no sense of the supernatural and the divine, it denied their existence. Only the observable, calculable, physical world was deemed to be real. Insofar as Cartesian rationalism favored *a priori* knowledge of the natural—as opposed to the supernatural—world, it promoted the age of science.[35]

Just as the reason of modern philosophy was in Maritain's eyes "pseudo-reason" because it failed to take into account, or account for, the nature of divinity and the supernatural, modern science was only "pseudo-science." It was, nonetheless, an intellectual error of immense power. Modern science, having usurped true faith, became "an idol worshipped in primary schools, a fortress of the world spirit, a shop stocked with confusions and false ideas where error constantly supplies itself with ammunition." Maritain thus railed against the aggressive materialism and secularism of modern science and set himself against the established intellectual orthodoxies of his day.[36]

Catholics were not the only critics of the academic culture of the Third Republic. From the mid-1890s through 1914 right-wing nationalists, with Maurice Barrès and Charles Maurras in the vanguard, attacked the intellectual foundations of the reformed university and denounced the political allegiances of the nation's most prominent scholars. They specifically denigrated the scientism and the neo-Kantianism of the new Sorbonne as Teutonic and alien. In fact, neither was a direct import from Germany: with its materialist faith in progress, the scientism of the 1880s derived more directly from Comtean positivism and Darwinian evolutionism than from Hegelian dialectic; and the success of French neo-Kantianism owed more to the efforts of Charles Renouvier than to Prussian conquest. Nonetheless, critics of the Republic contended that in introducing to French higher education pedagogical practices perfected in Germany and philosophical systems that originated on the other side of the Rhine, the reformers had slavishly imitated the enemy.

Frustrated by General Georges Boulanger's failure to lead a nationalist, revanchist coup in 1889, French nationalists became even more vehemently antipathetic to all things German. Unlike the *germanistes* of the Sorbonne, who acquired a familiarity and sympathy for German culture in the 1890s, many of the men who would emerge as leaders of the Action Française in the first decade of the twentieth century forged their anti-German nationalism in the same decade. Jacques Bainville, Léon Daudet, and Maurice Pujo all traveled to Germany as students in the 1890s and returned home as confirmed French nationalists hostile to all German influence.[37] Like Barrès, who identified Bouteiller as the archetypal republican academic who corrupted modern French youth with his passion for Kantian philosophy, they repudiated the Republic's apparent preference for alien traditions, its unfounded faith in pure reason, and its advocacy of intellectual cosmopolitanism.[38] These integral nationalists resented the alacrity with which republican reformers looked for inspiration to German examples, and maintained that cultural imitation was antithetical to cultural authenticity.

This oppositional intelligentsia, comprising Catholics and integral nationalists, remained an inchoate force until the formation of the Action Française in the wake of the Dreyfus Affair. Dedicated to the politics of monarchical restoration and hostile to the ideology of the reformed university, the Action française categorically opposed both the political and intellectual culture of the Third Republic and from 1905 through 1914 made its opposition clear through an extensive campaign against the *nouvelle* Sorbonne. Neither the scientistic spirit, the neo-Kantianism, nor the political sympathies of the reformed university escaped the neoroyalists' opprobrium. The dominance of scientism at the Sorbonne was, they contended, symptomatic of the intellectual subservience of French scholarship to the victors of Sedan. Disparaging the historical monographs of Ernest Lavisse, Gabriel Monod, and Charles Seignobos as exercises in statistical accounting rather than analyses of the past glories of France, the Action Française lamented that this new historiography rejected the time-honored, elegant, narrative style traditional to France and imitated instead the Ranke-inspired historiography of modern Germany.[39]

The Action Française objected not only to the sort of scholarship produced by applying principles of scientific analysis to the study of non-scientific subjects, but also to the presuppositions which made science the epistemological analogue of democracy, and democracy the political analogue of science. Although Durkheim was no slavish imitator of German methodology, the neoroyalists took exception to his scholarship too, because they could not tolerate his politics. By insisting that "a democracy would be unfaithful to its principle if it did not have a faith in science," Durkheim implied a necessary connection between the intellectual premises upon which modern science rested and the political premises undergirding democracy.[40] Both systems postulated the autonomy of the rational individual and both denied the epistemic need for external authority: scientific truth was evident to the rational mind and thus did not need the intercession of specially qualified or ordained interpreters. Of one mind, science and democracy asserted an equality of status for all individuals based on universal rationality.

The Action Française denounced the *nouvelle* Sorbonne as much for its defense of Dreyfus as for its modern methodologies. The University of Paris was by no means unanimous in its defense of Dreyfus, but because many academic Dreyfusards (including Charles Andler, Victor Basch, Gustave Lanson, and Charles Seignobos) enjoyed prominent positions within the reformed university, it was not difficult to tar the entire university with the brush of Dreyfusism. In the decade before the First World War, when the intellectual civil war of prewar France reached its greatest intensity, the Action Française systematically subjected these scholars and their academic allies to verbal assault. Thus in May 1908, they criticized the initiative of Charles Andler to improve Franco-German understanding. They were outraged that Andler, who held the chair in German studies at the Sorbonne, had arranged, with the support of the university administration, for a group of students to visit Germany in the spring of 1908. Such overtures of intellectual reconciliation were, in the eyes of the neoroyalists, unconscionable. A true patriot would not teach his students to learn to like Germans but to look constantly for opportunities to avenge the loss of Alsace and Lorraine. Representing Andler's initiative as a "pilgrimage to Berlin," the Action Française, fired by the fighting enthusiasm of the newly formed Camelots du Roi, took to the streets of the Latin Quarter in protest.[41]

The events of May 1908 were but a dress rehearsal for the neoroyalists' major production of that winter, the Thalamas Affair. In the most noteworthy and notorious episode in their campaign against the *nouvelle* Sorbonne, the Action Française took to the streets in violent protest and stormed the classroom of Alfred Croiset, Dean of Letters. Even though Croiset was more moderate in his politics than many of his colleagues— he had, for example, tried to effect a reconciliation of scholars divided by the Dreyfus Affair—as Dean of the new Sorbonne he was so closely associated with the cause of academic reform and the repudiation of classicism that he became an especial target of attack.[42] Castigated as the "Dean of the Jews and of Thalamas," Croiset had to attend his classes during the winter of 1908–09 with a police escort.

In the months and years that followed the Thalamas Affair, Pierre Lasserre, an embittered academic *manqué* and the neoroyalists' self-appointed critic of republican higher education, devoted himself single-mindedly to attacking the "official doctrine of the University" and the scholars who had thwarted his ambition. Insisting that the Sorbonne worked "conscientiously to weaken and corrode the spirit of French patriotism," he was particularly critical of the scientistic tone of Gustave Lanson's literary criticism.[43] As the foremost scholar of French literature at the Sorbonne, Lanson had done more than anyone else to bring the methods of science to the study of literature and had in the process destroyed the didactic and morally elevating character of literary inquiry that France had cultivated over centuries. Lasserre argued that in his search for scientific certainty Lanson had dismissed as entirely inappropriate all subjective judgments: "the originality of the new Sorbonne was to have discovered and defined that which could be considered objective in the study of literature, and to have restricted it to that alone." Thus Lanson, whose project was to determine through a statistical analysis of Bossuet and Fénelon the characteristics of good prose, denied subjective judgment any place in literary analysis: "as for myself," he protested, "I have no literary preferences." This aspiration to scientific objectivity was anathema to the Action Française, which insisted that the study of literature had first and foremost to concern itself with aesthetic and moral judgment.[44]

The Quarrel of the Ancients
and the Moderns Revived

When conservative Catholics challenged the intellectual premises of modern science, post-Cartesian rationalism, and (by extension) neo-Kantianism, and when integral nationalists took to the streets to denounce the intellectual spirit and political affiliation of the new Sorbonne, they revealed the depth of the divide that separated them from the academic establishment. Having nothing but contempt for the curricular innovations and "alien" ideologies of republican education, they worked persistently to discredit both. Thus in the culture wars of Third Republic—which Phyllis Stock-Morton has so justly described as a "new Quarrel of Ancients and Moderns"—the counterintelligentsia firmly and proudly situated itself in the camp of the Ancients.[45] This conservative, traditional impulse was evident not only in their assault on higher education, but also in their vocal opposition to the Republic's modernist reform of secondary education.

At the end of the nineteenth century, with reform of higher education complete, reformers turned their attention to what they took to be the inadequacies of secondary education. Like Duruy before them, they hoped to modernize secondary education by modifying (but not entirely eliminating) the traditional classical curriculum, with its heavy emphasis on rhetoric and classical languages. Reformers feared that for the modern world of the late nineteenth century the classical curriculum was dangerously anachronistic. A *lycée* education that emphasized Latin and Greek at the expense of science, mathematics, and modern languages gave students an inadequate preparation for the demands of the modern world. And reforms undertaken between 1880 and 1890 to introduce a modern curriculum had been undermined by one fundamental flaw: unlike students who graduated with a classical *baccalauréat* and enjoyed unrestricted access to higher education, those who opted for the shorter modern curriculum were, by and large, shut out. To rectify this inequality, a parliamentary commission under the direction of Alexandre Ribot recommended that the classical and modern curricula be granted equality of status.

The recommendations of the Ribot commission became the blueprint for the *lycée* reforms of 1902, which abolished the unsatisfactory division between classical and modern degrees and created instead one secondary school diploma, attainable through one of four streams: "A", "B", "C", and "D." Students who opted for "A" would continue with the established classical curriculum, but students with a bent for the sciences or a distaste for Greek could pursue a *baccalauréat* of equal weight in one of three other ways. "B" offered the option of studying Latin *and* a modern language; "C" balanced modern and classical curricula by combining study of Latin with extensive preparation in the sciences; and "D"—the most controversial innovation of all—allowed students to study modern languages and sciences and required no Latin. Students who earned their *baccalauréat* in science and modern languages were ineligible for admission to the nation's faculties of letters, which continued to require Latin of all students until after the First World War, but they remained eligible for admission to faculties of medicine, law, and sciences.

Proponents of the 1902 reforms believed that the four options allowed students to pursue the course of studies best-suited to their intellectual inclinations. If a student demonstrated an aptitude for scientific inquiry, it was appropriate to provide him with the background necessary to pursue further study. By the same token, students who struggled with classical languages or whose anticipated career path made knowledge of Latin and Greek unnecessary should not be required to undertake such studies, and they certainly should not be denied access to higher education for want of them. But a modern curriculum also responded to the economic, social, and military needs of the nation. Louis Liard, who now served as Vice Rector of the Academy of Paris and Rector of the University of Paris, was so convinced that this was true that he insisted that "a system of national education that was not resolutely modern, in both substance and spirit, would be not just an offensive anachronism, but a national danger."[46]

Liard's conservative critics—the neoroyalists of the Action Française, leaders of French commerce and industry, and spokesmen for the Ligue pour la Culture Française—retorted that the reforms themselves were a danger to the nation. Critics argued repeatedly that the 1902 curriculum burdened students with excessive work; imposed upon young minds the pressure of premature academic specialization; bestowed upon practical education—in modern languages and the sciences—the same authority traditionally granted the disinterested classical curriculum; and contributed directly to a crisis of national literacy. The 1902 curriculum was, they contended, so laden with new courses and unnecessary content that it left little time for adequate instruction in French composition, spelling, and grammar. As any teacher obliged to evaluate the written answers of *baccalauréat* examinations could attest, French secondary schools graduated students who could not write lucidly in French, could not analyze arguments critically, and could not spell. Opponents of 1902 charged, moreover, that the modern curriculum would be the nation's ruin. Students who knew no Latin and less Greek lacked a sense of the French cultural legacy and the intellectual tools required for critical, reasoned analysis. If France were to preserve its cultural heritage, it had to restore the classical curriculum—with compulsory Latin and Greek as its cornerstone—to its central place in secondary education.

Until 1910, the modern curriculum seemed impregnable. In the aftermath of the Dreyfus Affair, the modernists—Liard, Lanson, Andler, Seignobos, and Lavisse—dominated the political and administrative institutions responsible for education, and their opinions prevailed. Those who had originally criticized the reformed curriculum either converted to the cause of modern education—as was the case with Alfred Croiset, who had defended the classical curriculum in 1899 but lined up with the modernists by 1911—or lamented their inability to garner public support for their cause. Their fortunes improved significantly, however, with the celebrated publication in the summer of 1910 of a series of articles by the pseudonymous "Agathon" (co-authored in fact by Alfred de Tarde and Henri Massis).[47] Charging that scholars at the new Sorbonne, more competent in German than in French, were unable to give students the education they deserved, Agathon concluded that modern education had created a crisis of French literacy. Modernists seemed hardpressed to defend themselves. When Croiset addressed the students and faculty of the University of Paris in November 1910, he retorted that if students were illiterate it was not the fault of the Sorbonne but of the *lycées* which prepared them for university.[48] This, of course, was just the admission critics of the 1902 reforms had been waiting to hear.

Agathon's charge that modern education had to be held accountable for *la crise du français* hit a nerve. Public concern that the nation was lapsing into illiteracy prompted the Chamber of Deputies to initiate a national inquiry in 1913 into the consequences of the 1902 reforms. The committee hearings hoped to answer two fundamental questions. Was it true that French high-school graduates of 1913 were less literate than their predecessors of previous decades? And if so, was the 1902 curriculum to blame? Testifying against the reform, the Ligue pour la Culture Française, formed in May 1911 to "defend the study of the classics compromised by the most recent reforms in secondary education," expressed its conviction that a compulsory classical education provided the best foundation for future scholarship in *all* disciplines. The society feared that the lamentable illiteracy of *lycée* graduates was "the most clear consequence" of the 1902 reforms and called upon parliament to reinstate a unified, single curriculum that would require instruction in Latin and Greek through the first six years of *lycée* education. Only upon completion of the first part of the *baccalauréat,* at the end of what was called the *première* class, could students appropriately begin their specialization and choose to study either a "modern" curriculum with a strong emphasis in the sciences, or a "classical" curriculum with continued study in Greek, Latin, and French. The Ligue was convinced that this curriculum would in no way compromise French expertise in the sciences, for experience demonstrated that science had never suffered under a classical curriculum. Was it not true that Henri Poincaré, France's most distinguished mathematician of the early twentieth century, had benefited from a classical education and publicly acclaimed its advantages?[49]

The Association of Philosophy teachers at French *collèges* agreed that only graduates of the "A" option were adequately prepared for higher education. Of the three other options, "B" and "D" were particularly troubling. The former failed to achieve an honorable balance between the humanities and the sciences because, offering but a smattering of these disciplines, it seemed to draw students who preferred to avoid both the rigors of Greek and the demands of sciences. And the much maligned "D" option was even worse. Depriving students of any knowledge of the classics, it was too utilitarian to merit inclusion in the secondary curriculum.[50]

When the philosophy teachers dismissed the modern curriculum as suitable, perhaps, for the formation of efficient businessmen and engineers, their condescension must have enraged France's corporate elite, for few constituencies were as firm in their defense of classical education as the nation's chambers of commerce. The reforms of 1902 had been undertaken to provide an education "more suited to the modern world"; but if the opinions and laments of France's commercial and industrial elite were anything to go by, the modern curriculum had failed miserably in this endeavor. Complaints were legion about the inadequate preparation of students aspiring to positions in business and industry; graduates of the "B" and "D" options lacked the skills necessary to communicate effectively, to reason convincingly, or to address problems creatively. Thus in 1913, when the Paris Chamber of Commerce submitted its opinion to the parliamentary committee, it reiterated its support—expressed a decade earlier to the Ribot Commission—for classical education: "a strong classical education was the best preparation for life, even for life in industry or business."[51]

Those who defended the reforms of 1902 feared that compulsory Latin and more French could be accommodated within the secondary school curriculum only at the expense of science and modern languages. Thus in their depositions to the parliamentary committee, and in subsequent debates about secondary school reform that ran through 1923, they fiercely defended the time given to the sciences and to modern languages in the French secondary school curriculum. Charles Lallemand, President of the Association for the Advancement of Science, entered the fray on behalf of scientific education in 1911. In his presidential address to the fortieth congress of the society, he disputed the contention that the 1902 reforms had precipitated a *crise du français* and suggested that modern-day scientists needed modern languages more than they needed Latin. He reminded his audience that the 1902 reforms had been introduced to bring French education into line with advances in science and to provide students with the means to communicate with their international neighbors. In a world that was becoming increasingly scientific and international, *lycée* graduates needed to know science and modern languages; they did not need to know Latin.

Lallemand acknowledged the importance of literacy to the pursuit of science; to be effective, science had to be communicated in clear, precise language: "une langue précise et correcte—je ne dis pas élégante—est donc l'instrument nécessaire à toute bonne culture scientifique." He denied, however, that one needed Latin to attain clarity and precision in French. Charging that students were no less adept in French in 1911 than they had been a generation before, he conceded only that this generation of students could not spell. This, however, was of little consequence. In an age of advanced technology—he was thinking of the advent of the typewriter—spelling would become less the responsibility of scholars than of secretaries. Lallemand's testimony thus revealed the fundamental concern of the scientific community that any reform of the 1902 curriculum would only jeopardize the advances recently made in scientific education. The Ancients could win only at the Moderns' expense.[52]

This was Hubert Gillot's fear, too. In early 1914 Gillot, a scholar of French literature at the University of Strasbourg, a friend of Gustave Lanson, and an unabashed advocate of educational innovation, published *La Querelle des anciens et des modernes*. Although Gillot appeared on first reading to concern himself only with the literary quarrels of the *ancien régime,* his book was by no means unaware of the cultural division that characterized France before 1914. No mere chronicler of the seventeenth-century quarrel, Gillot was an enthusiastic celebrant of its outcome. Dismissing the Ancients as unimaginative, authoritarian, and dogmatic, he disparaged their reverence for the classics as intellectually stultifying, as was any curriculum that reflected that regard. By contrast he acclaimed the Moderns as progressive champions of free inquiry and cosmopolitanism, eager to introduce an educational system consonant with their ideals and responsive to the demands of the contemporary world. Gillot stressed that the regard of the Moderns for modern languages made possible the emergence in the eighteenth century of an international community of scholars committed to the open exchange of ideas.[53]

It was not difficult to perceive in Gillot's resolutely republican scholarship—which judged the "triumph of the Moderns" that occurred at the end of Louis XIV's reign a cultural victory for progress—an apologia for the modern curriculum of 1902. Like Lallemand, Gillot contended that the attention paid to foreign languages and physical sciences in the modern curriculum made it the educational program best suited to a democratic, progressive, cosmopolitan Republic. By contrast, classical instruction, with its reverential regard for ancient languages and its disdainful dismissal of innovation, advanced the cause of authoritarianism. It was surely not surprising that it continued to find favor among those predisposed to despise republican principles. Between these two political visions, and the educational systems that sustained them, there was, he contended, no room for compromise or accommodation.

CHAPTER TWO

The Impiety of War

In 1940, as he reflected on France's "strange defeat," Marc Bloch recalled Herodotus's dictum that "the great impiety of war is that it forces fathers to consign their children to the tomb."[1] Time, Bloch knew, had not diminished the pertinence of this ancient observation, which could serve especially well as a classical epitaph for the Great War. His own father, a medieval historian at the Sorbonne, had been spared that anguish personally, but many of Gustave Bloch's academic colleagues had experienced directly the "impiety of war." Emile Durkheim, Gustave Lanson, and Emile Picard each lost a son in 1915; and by the time Camille Jordan assumed the presidency of the Académie des Sciences in 1917, three of his sons had been killed. Even those with no sons to sacrifice were not immune to grief, for the deaths of their students moved them profoundly. French noncombatant scholars were by no means the complacent "old men" despised by British war poets for watching with indifference as the younger generation went to its death. Indeed, the very opposite was true. The knowledge that colleagues, students, and sons were at the front affected fundamentally the way noncombatant intellectuals responded to and mobilized on behalf of the war. As Pascal Ory and Jean-François Sirinelli have written, "at the very moment when their students or their readers, often also their sons, fell by entire ranks, certain intellectuals felt that they had a patriotic duty to fulfil."[2]

On occasion, this sense of patriotic duty prompted aging academics and writers to join their sons in active military service. Thus Charles Bayet (1849–1918) enlisted in 1914 at the age of sixty-five. A volunteer in the Franco-Prussian War, he had served thereafter as Dean of Letters and Rector of the University of Paris and Director of Higher Education within the Ministry of Public Instruction. In 1914, he left the comfort and safety of educational administration to serve once again in the French Army. He went to the front in August 1914, where he resumed his rank of sublieutenant. Not surprisingly, the rigors of the 1914 campaign took their toll, and fatigue forced him out of the trenches and into a staff position in early 1915. Physically enervated and spiritually overwhelmed by the death of his younger son, Bayet fell ill in 1917 and died two months before the Armistice, on September 17, 1918.[3]

More often than not, however, physical incapacity or competing responsibilities made active military service impractical. Most academics and writers of Bayet's generation realized that they would have to contribute to the war effort in other ways. Many volunteered their energies and lent their considerable prestige to national and local philanthropic enterprises: they raised money for war orphans, ran hospitals for wounded troops, and intervened frequently to help the families of mobilized students and colleagues. Yet for many scholars and writers the "practical action" of philanthropy remained essentially insufficient. Convinced that intellectuals should exert themselves in the public arena by exercising their unique talents and exploiting their special stature, they believed that to spend the war changing bandages or visiting the wounded was to waste their energies and abandon their proper function. As Etienne Lamy reminded them, they alone could use the opportunities created by the war to define the nature of French science and culture, to educate the nation, and inform the world of what was at stake in the war. A task of national and international education awaited them, and it was to this project of "intellectual action" that they also directed their energies.

The Anguish of Inaction

In the early weeks of the war noncombatant intellectuals agonized over their own inability to serve. Raymond Thamin, who watched his son leave for the front, later recalled the "pain of feeling useless in the days of August 1914."[4] Pierre Duhem, physics professor at the University of Bordeaux and noted philosopher of science, confessed that he felt a "profound anguish" and an immense "sorrow, brought about by a sense of uselessness," as his students departed for active service.[5] Emile Hovelaque, an Inspector of Schools, recognized that he was "incapable of serving the sacred cause in any other way, but . . . wanted at least to give the impression of not remaining, at such a time, completely inactive."[6]

Victor Giraud, a principal contributor to the *Revue des deux mondes,* wrote of similar regret: "*immobilisé* like so many others, I wanted at least to try and *serve,* in my own way."[7] And Alfred Baudrillart, Rector of the Institut Catholique in Paris, recalled how in August 1914 his colleague Alfred Rébelliau came to his house, despondent at his own inaction, as "desolate as I was myself, at not being able to offer to the country that service that only the young [were] capable of giving."[8]

This pervasive sense of uselessness was particularly intense among those whose philosophical principles or personal circumstances made action a moral imperative. Maurice Blondel, who had made his reputation as a Catholic philosopher twenty years earlier with the publication of *L'Action,* found his military incapacity particularly irksome. For Blondel, action was an essential condition of human existence and an implicit recognition of the interdependence of all creation.[9] When war came, he longed to act. He wrote to a student in uniform that "those who truly acted . . . seemed to be the only ones in their proper places."[10] This desire to fill one's "proper place" was particularly acute for many (but not all) who were young enough to serve but were medically disqualified.[11] Jacques Maritain (1882–1973), exempt from military service on medical grounds, resolved to "make himself useful in civilian life" by doing "double duty as a professor" at the Institut Catholique in Paris, the Collège Stanislas, and the Petit Seminaire de Versailles.[12] Teaching also absorbed the energies of students at the Ecole Normale who could not join up; they often volunteered to teach in *lycées,* chronically understaffed because of general mobilization.[13] One *normalien,* whose delicate health obliged him to spend the war in the mountains of Switzerland, hoped to make himself useful by preparing adolescent Alsatian refugees for the rigors of the *baccalauréat,* and by lecturing to the social elite of Basel on the merits of the French war effort.[14]

Patriotic Duty and Practical Action

The anguish (and embarrassment) of inactivity quickly gave way to practical action. With the nation in danger, everyone was anxious to contribute to its defense. Some decided to suspend intellectual life: Elie Halévy spent the best part of the war as a volunteer at two military hospitals. François Mauriac (1885–1970), tormented by the "horror of feeling useless," volunteered in 1915 to serve as an ambulance driver.[15] Posted to Salonika in December 1916, he fell ill with malaria and returned to France to convalesce in 1917. Others hoped to reconcile duty and artistic inclination: Marcel Proust, practically bedridden throughout the war, endeavored nonetheless to visit convalescent soldiers and collected items for distribution among the military hospitals in Paris. At the same time, he devoted himself to revising *A la recherche du temps perdu*. Gonzague Truc, a literary critic who wrote frequently during and after the war about the social responsibility of intellectuals, would have applauded Proust's priorities, for Truc insisted that "the most intelligent" members of the noncombatant intellectual community had decided to "devote themselves to hospital work or to genuine scholarship, continuing their real work while ever mindful of the struggle going on around them."[16]

In the early months of the war, however, many prominent scholars and writers sacrificed the "real work" of scholarship to the pressing demands of public service. Members of the Institut de France, France's most prestigious intellectual establishment, led the way. At the very outset of the war the Institut, anticipating a short war, funded the establishment of a military hospital in the *hôtel* Thiers; and Emile Picard, a member of the Académie des Sciences and president of the central administrative committee of the Institut, supervised the financial administration of the hospital. Initially, the Institut committed itself to provide funds sufficient to maintain a fifty-bed hospital. Expecting that the hospital would stay open for no more than three months, Picard allocated an operating budget of three francs per patient per day. Because "necessity" required the Institut to renew its commitment beyond three months, the hospital remained open for the duration of the war, under the joint administration of the Association des Dames Françaises (which ran military hospitals throughout France) and the Institut.[17] Frédéric Masson of the Académie des Sciences Morales et Politiques supervised the daily operations of the hospital, and, when necessary, attended the funerals of those who died.[18]

Whether acting as official appointees of the Institut de France or as private individuals, members of the five academies of the Institute, convinced that their distinguished stature conferred upon them a unique authority and responsibility to lead the nation by example, directed their energies towards several projects of public utility. Not only did Frédéric Masson administer the Thiers hospital, but he and several of his colleagues within the Académie des Sciences Morales et Politiques established a mutual assistance society for war widows, which distributed 40,000 francs in its first six months. Requests for assistance were so numerous that the Académie had to provide Masson's society with regular financial support. Other members of the Institut coordinated efforts to assist orphans and blind veterans.[19]

Emile Boutroux, a member of both the Académie des Sciences Morales et Politiques and the Académie Française, exploited a family connection in an effort to improve the quality of medical care available to French troops. During a visit to the hospital wards of the *hôtel* Thiers in April 1916, he learned that Dr. Alexis Carrel had devised an effective technique that allowed for the safe transport of wounded troops from the front to hospitals in the rear. Dr. Carrel, who had received the Nobel prize for medicine in 1912, was a French surgeon who had spent the previous decade in North America. Returning to France in 1914 to serve in the French medical corps, Carrel worked with a British surgeon to develop the Dakin-Carrel procedure for cleaning wounds: combining an innovative use of antiseptic and bandaging, they were able to keep wounds clean and less susceptible to secondary infection; when put into practice the procedure brought about a "considerable reduction" in the number of amputations needed. The doctor who described this technique to Boutroux considered the new procedure "marvelous." Boutroux was obviously convinced, because he immediately wrote to Raymond Poincaré, his cousin-in-law, urging him to look into the merits of the procedure.[20] An intellectual's inclination to practical action, combined with a most convenient family connection, may have saved numerous French lives.

Another initiative of the Institut de France was the establishment of a sewing workshop—an "ouvroir"—installed in the offices of the Secretariat of the Académie Française. Adamant that the project "remain under the patronage of the administrative committee of the Académie and a certain number of wives and daughters of members of the Institut," Picard recommended that direction of the workshop be assigned to Mme Vallery-Radot, wife of René Vallery-Radot of the Académie des Sciences Morales et Politiques and daughter of Louis Pasteur. Under her supervision, the administrative offices of the Académie Française became the site of a highbrow sweatshop. The wives of members of the Institut sought out "worthy" women from the neighborhood who had been impoverished by the onset of war. By the end of August 1914, 150 appropriately deserving women were on the payroll of the Académie Française; half worked at home, half at the Institut. At first all items produced in the workshop went directly to the Red Cross, but because all clothing produced in the workshop was donated, the initial budget of 12,000 francs soon proved inadequate.[21] By the end of September 1914, Picard, wishing to expand the scope of the workshop, urged Lamy, as Permanent Secretary of the Académie Française, to approve additional funding so that the women now employed as seamstresses in his offices could produce enough personal linens to outfit completely each soldier leaving the hospital.[22] At the end of October, the Institut renewed its funding for the *ouvroir,* with a small increase of 500 francs and the proviso that the Red Cross and the Thiers hospital share the output equally. This helped the hospital but did nothing to increase funds available for wages. Donations from individual members of the Institut supplemented the official grant by more than 4,000 francs; nonetheless, by the beginning of January 1915, the *ouvroir* had less than 500 francs in its account. Temporary layoffs followed; from a full complement of 150 workers, the payroll dropped to 118. And in an effort to raise funds and return to full employment, the Institut authorized the production of some items for sale.[23]

Wages at the workshop were low, but working conditions were, without a doubt, unusual, at least by established standards of the day.[24] Even taking for granted that coal was in short supply, the offices of the Académie Française constituted no ordinary sweatshop. To keep the moral tone appropriately elevated, Mme Vallery-Radot's daughter suggested that all would benefit if the wives and daughters of members of the Institut volunteered to read aloud while the seamstresses worked. Mme Boutroux and Mme Masson were among the wives who regularly provided "patriotic readings" on suitable subjects from the past as well as reflections on the nature of the current crisis. Mme Vallery-Radot believed that the seamstresses, when thus informed of their national heritage, worked all the more diligently at their machines.[25] Whether hearing stories of Joan of Arc's exploits read by President Poincaré's cousin and Pasteur's granddaughter really motivated the employees to work ever more productively is, of course, unknown; but it is clear that those who organized the *ouvroir* of the Institut de France hoped that their efforts would provide both moral and material sustenance to the women they employed and the soldiers they indirectly served.

Noncombatant intellectuals were generous in their contributions to worthy causes. Not only did members of the Institut subsidize many of its philanthropic enterprises; they also contributed to collections organized by the University of Paris and the Patronage National des Blessés. Ernest Lavisse, historian, Director of the Ecole Normale, and member of the Académie Française, presided over this latter organization and Paul Appell, Henri Bergson, and Emile Boutroux were among the members of the intellectual community who contributed their time, money, and national prestige to its projects. It set itself a basic goal: to provide medical stations at the front with sufficient supplies of iodine, essential medical equipment (even thermometers were in short supply), and X-ray machines. Marie Curie coordinated the radiology services.[26] From the very beginning of the war she had applied her expertise (and exerted her considerable influence in social circles) to this end. Persuaded that the Army medical corps needed mobile radiology units, at first she informally requisitioned vehicles owned by Parisian society women and transformed them into vans outfitted with X-ray equipment. By early 1915 the efforts of the Patronage National des Blessés replaced these informal arrangements, and for the duration of the war the gray vans, known to all along the front as "petites Curies," provided essential X-ray facilities to wounded troops.[27] The scholars who coordinated and helped finance these critical services believed, justifiably enough, that they had thereby made themselves useful.[28]

A powerful sense of civic obligation informed the initiatives of the Institut de France and the philanthropic efforts of prominent intellectuals. But the initiatives financed and organized by the Secours Universitaire of the University of Paris suggest that an equally powerful personal imperative—to sustain the morale and support the efforts of former students and colleagues—also compelled noncombatant intellectuals to contribute to the war effort. In October 1914 Louis Liard, then Rector of the University of Paris, proposed to the Conseil de l'Université (the administrative committee that represented all faculties and schools within the university) that faculty members voluntarily contribute the equivalent of one day's salary per month to two separate charitable organizations: the Secours National, a national charity devoted to helping families bereaved and economically distressed by the war, and a comparable Secours Universitaire that would provide material assistance to the families of students, staff, and faculty at the front. Paul Appell, speaking not so much as the dean of the Faculty of Sciences but as president of the Secours National, suggested that the university should imitate the example of other public service employees and donate all contributions exclusively to the Secours National. Liard disagreed. Acknowledging the importance of that organization, he nonetheless contended that the university community had a special obligation to care for its own members. The university council voted to support Liard's proposal.[29]

Through their contributions to the Secours Universitaire, noncombatant faculty members provided material aid to families of staff and faculty at the front, to returning, demobilized students, and to prisoners of war. One project financed in part by the Secours Universitaire bought and shipped books to French students and scholars held prisoner in Germany. Etienne Gilson (later one of France's most distinguished medieval scholars), probably benefited directly from this initiative. Having graduated from the Sorbonne with an *agrégation* in philosophy in 1907, and a *doctorat d'état* in 1913, he had been mobilized in the massive call-up of August 2 and entered the army as a sergeant. Captured during the initial German assault on Verdun, he spent the remainder of the war as a prisoner of war, teaching himself Russian and his fellow prisoners philosophy.[30] Gilson's protéges were by no means the only beneficiaries of the books-to-prisoners program. When the university committee charged with coordinating this endeavor addressed the Conseil de l'Université in January 1918, it reported that Allied prisoners of war had received more than 18,000 books since the Swiss scientist, Professor Louis Maillard of the University of Lausanne, had initiated the project; and 50,000 francs had been spent.[31]

Demands placed upon the generosity of the Secours Universitaire were numerous, for the Great War had a devastating impact on the nation's academic elite. The military service law of 1889, passed in the wake of the Boulanger Affair, had abolished the exemption from military service previously granted to clerics, students, teachers, and professors. As a result, when war came in 1914, thousands of young scholars were called to the colors; and they died in such numbers as to seem to place in jeopardy the very future of higher education in France. Wartime casualties created critical gaps throughout the ranks of national education, but the immediate and longterm effects of the war on French higher education were nothing short of staggering.[32] Because aspiring scholars ordinarily passed their years of academic apprenticeship teaching in provincial *lycées,* the academic future of France depended upon the existence of an established university faculty to train future scholars and the survival of an intellectually ambitious secondary-school professoriate and a graduate student population that could ultimately expect to assume the positions left vacant by retiring university professors. The war decimated each essential constituency. By 1919, when the *Revue universitaire* published its grim tally, 460 high-school teachers and 260 university professors had died in combat. Given that France in 1914 had approximately 1,000 university professors, one quarter of all French faculty members had died in uniform.[33]

These alarming but anonymous statistics referred to some of the most promising young intellectuals of the Third Republic. And the archival record demonstrates that neither teachers nor colleagues were indifferent to the dangers these scholars-in-arms confronted or unmoved by their deaths. Eager to keep alive the spirit of intellectual community they had cultivated in peacetime, noncombatant scholars frequently corresponded with former colleagues and students at the front, sending them books, articles, and journals. Victor Delbos, a professor at the Sorbonne, mailed philosophy books to the trenches for Gilson; Pierre Duhem forwarded offprints of articles to his former students.[34] Curious care-packages indeed; but genuinely welcome reading for men committed to scholarly careers.

Nowhere was the intellectual community's conviction that it constituted an extended family bound by affection and moral obligation to men at the front more evident than in the ongoing correspondence between noncombatant scholars and Maurice Masson. Masson (1879–1916) was, by his own estimation, almost a grizzled old man when he left for the front at the age of thirty-five. A graduate of the ENS, he had spent the decade before the war teaching French literature at the University of Fribourg in Switzerland from where he quickly made his mark in French literary studies. A prodigious scholar, he published works on Fénelon, Mme de Tencin, and Lamartine (both *Mme de Tencin (1682–1749)* and *Lamartine* won recognition from the Académie Française), and prepared his *thèse d'état* under the direction of Gustave Lanson at the Sorbonne. Mobilized as soon as war broke out, Masson spent his spare minutes in the trenches writing exquisitely crafted letters to his wife, mother, and family friends; engaging academic colleagues in scholarly debate; and revising his dissertation manuscript. In early 1916 he applied for and—after several infuriating delays—was granted permission to return to Paris to defend his dissertation, a three-volume study entitled *La Religion de J. J. Rousseau*. The defense, scheduled for March 4, 1916 at 4 P.M., never took place. Confronted by the German offensive at Verdun, the French high command cancelled all leaves, and Masson remained at the front where he died in action on April 16, 1916.

When the Faculty of Letters at the University of Paris met shortly after Masson's death to consider, among other items of business, the merits of his dissertation, Lanson spoke not only of the quality of the manuscript but also of the qualities of the man who wrote it. He told his colleagues that Masson was a man of profound compassion, generosity, and honor.[35] Lanson knew of what he spoke. When Michel Lanson had died in the Champagne offensive six months earlier, Masson had written to his mentor a most poignant letter of condolence.[36] But he had also written and revised over the past ten years the six-hundred-page dissertation which Lanson judged "one of the most remarkable ever submitted for our evaluation." Even scholars unsympathetic to the unapologetically

Catholic interpretation that informed Masson's analysis were impressed by the "impartial, sincere, and intelligent" character of his scholarship. Alphonse Aulard, who had read the chapters pertaining to the French Revolution, acclaimed his originality and his "admirable critical spirit." Upon hearing such high praise, the faculty recommended that the University bestow upon Maurice Masson the posthumous distinction of a *doctorat d'état*. The recommendation was accepted.[37]

To read Lanson's written assessment of Masson's dissertation is to glimpse the grief of a noncombatant scholar coming to terms with the death of one of his finest students. To read Emile Durkheim's obituary for his son, prepared for publication in the yearbook of the ENS, is to eavesdrop on anguish of a higher order. Writing of his son's brief life, Durkheim portrayed him as a young man of high moral character, outraged by social injustice, and of extraordinary intellectual promise. André Durkheim was by all accounts a brilliant student. Taught at home by his father until the age of ten, he attended the Lycée Montaigne thereafter, where he was consistently the best student in his class. Durkheim *fils* won admission to the ENS before he turned eighteen, and then fulfilled his year of compulsory military service before starting classes in the fall of 1911. In the next three years he completed his *licence,* his *diplôme d'études supérieures,* and, eager to develop further his interest in the philosophy of language, he began to prepare for his *agrégation.* Like any father supervising the apprenticeship of a beloved son in the family business, Emile Durkheim delighted in the prospect of André, whom he considered his closest intellectual companion, pursuing advanced philosophical study. He wrote that "the intellectual intimacy that existed between us was as complete as it could possibly be."[38] Then the war came. Mobilized immediately, André Durkheim saw action in Belgium in early August 1914; wounded on the western front in June 1915, he recovered sufficiently to accompany his regiment when it set sail for the Balkans that fall. His parents watched his departure with intense trepidation: "of course, from the very beginning of hostilities, we lived with the thought of the almost inevitable sacrifice [that awaited us]; but we had never had, to the same degree, the sense that he was threatened and that we had to prepare ourselves" for his death. In mid-December of 1915, following days of intense fighting in the Salonika campaign, André Durkheim died of wounds in the distant village of Davidova, Macedonia. He was twenty-three years old. The founder of modern sociology never fully recovered from the irreparable loss caused by his son's death.

Letters and other unpublished documents testify that even men who had neither a son nor a brother in uniform felt what amounted to a familial obligation to care for the material and moral concerns of colleagues and former students at the front. Victor Giraud, who had helped Maurice Masson secure his teaching position at Fribourg, felt especially close to that bereaved family. In 1917, he prepared the preface to Masson's war letters, and when Raymond Poincaré wished to convey his respects to Masson's widow, mother, and sister, he turned to Giraud for the appropriate information.[39] The familial feeling that one senses in Giraud's relationship with Masson was characteristic of *normaliens,* for the Ecole Normale worked diligently to create within its walls a spirit of intellectual intimacy.

Because tradition dictated that the Ecole Normale encourage close ties between students and masters, Ernest Lavisse and Paul Dupuy were determined to keep them strong even in the "exceptional circumstances" of the war. As Lavisse explained to a skeptical staff officer unfamiliar with the school's ethos, those who remained at the school felt "a duty to maintain and to tighten" this essential "intimacy."[40] Corresponding with men at the front thus became as essential to the administrators and alumni of the ENS as it was to any wartime family. Although the archival record here is incomplete, it is clear that both Lavisse and Dupuy maintained regular correspondence with former students. The project they initiated to publish an anthology of letters received from former students, a project that Lavisse described to the alumni of the Ecole at its annual meeting in 1917, never materialized, but the school's wartime files show an ongoing correspondence among Lavisse, Dupuy, and their former students.[41] At least one of these correspondences became part of the French literary tradition: Maurice Genevoix corresponded regularly with Dupuy from the front, and when he came to write of his combat experience, he integrated this correspondence into the text of *Ceux de 14.*[42] It is also clear from the school's records that early in the war Lavisse wrote to recent students, many of whom were forced to remain behind the lines awaiting commissions, impressing upon them the virtues of patience and submission to discipline.[43] (At the same time he was badgering the General Staff with impatient requests for immediate action on his students' behalf.) Believing that it was as important for classmates as for family members to communicate with one another, Dupuy set up what amounted to a postal clearing-station at the school. Letters from the front could be sent to the school and then redirected to the intended recipient.[44]

Dupuy and Lavisse, prompted in part by requests expressed in students' letters, spent many hours acting on behalf of *normaliens* and their families.[45] Lavisse did not hesitate to use his many connections within the government to help advance the careers of former students or protect the interests of their families. Like a parent convinced that his children were especially clever, talented, and worthy, he wrote directly to the Minister of War to complain in November 1914 that the Army unjustly overlooked *normaliens* eligible for promotion.[46] By the terms of the 1913 three-year service law, students who entered St-Cyr (the French military college) or the Ecole Polytéchnique in 1913 automatically assumed the rank of sublieutenant upon mobilization in August 1914; *normaliens* of the *promotion* of 1913 were eligible for a commission only when the Army determined that "their practical military education was deemed sufficient."[47] Lavisse and his students believed that the distinction thus made between *normaliens* and *polytechniciens* cast doubt upon the quality of military training given at the school and undermined the morale of its students. But his protests were to no avail; the law governing the terms under which *normaliens* qualified for commissions changed only in October 1916.[48]

Lavisse also acted as an intermediary with the ministry for his students' families. Early in the war he wrote the Ministry of War requesting that two mothers whose sons had died in action be allowed to travel to the front to visit their sons' graves; this moving but highly impractical request was denied.[49] On a subsequent occasion he pleaded on behalf of a widow whose *normalien* husband had died at the front. The Army had allocated her a pension of 104 francs, but Lavisse believed that if the soldier's military service undertaken at the ENS were included in the Army's calculations, Mme Pannetier should receive 240 francs.[50] The Army disagreed, and Mme Pannetier's pension remained unchanged. Judging from this and many other curt, usually unaccommodating responses from General Headquarters, the Army certainly did not appreciate Lavisse's frequent interventions on behalf of former students; but one suspects that families of mobilized *normaliens* were profoundly grateful for his many efforts on their behalf.

He probably fared better with requests submitted to the Ministry of Public Instruction, where ties of friendship abounded and sensitive issues of national security were less likely to intervene. On one occasion he wrote Liard, then Vice-Rector of the Academy of Paris and a close friend, on behalf of a Mlle Andrée Morillon. The sister of a *normalien* who had been missing in action since August 1914 and presumed dead, Mlle Morillon alone remained to care for her working-class parents, and thus hoped to obtain a transfer from the private school in which she taught to a public school in the *département* of Cher. Lavisse hoped that Liard would approve this request, even though the young woman, who had been teaching since the age of fifteen, lacked the formal qualifications required for teaching in the public school system. A year later he asked the Minister of Public Instruction to approve the transfer of a young woman to a teaching position in Paris. Her three brothers, including one former student of the school, had all been killed, and she wished to return to Paris to care for her mother.[51]

Ongoing correspondence with former students prompted Lavisse's démarches in various ways. He willingly interceded on many occasions with the War Ministry, hoping to secure promotions or transfers for his former students, although the Army rejected nearly all such requests, and even *normaliens* fluent in foreign languages often failed to secure positions as translators or liaison officers. In October 1914 Lavisse recommended thirty-nine *normaliens* for service as military translators: twenty-four were fluent in English and could serve as liaison officers with the British Army; the thirteen who were fluent in German could act as translators and interpreters.[52] It is unclear what became of these recommendations, but a staff officer informed Lavisse on January 3, 1915, that only one of the three *normaliens* he had recommended for service as military interpreters would be admitted to the training program. The urgent need for officers at the front had to be given first priority.[53]

The Army's policy of keeping all available infantry officers in the front line was understandable given the military conditions of 1915, but it proved disastrous for *normaliens,* who were required by law to serve in the infantry. By the spring of 1915, Lavisse and Dupuy, who kept vigilant records detailing the military service of *normaliens,* recognized the danger compulsory service in the infantry represented to their students. An interim tally of casualty rates among students and graduates of the Ecole Normale, completed after six months of combat, showed that of the 255 *normaliens* mobilized since August 1914, only 95 were as yet unscathed: 55 were dead; 16 were missing in action; 64 were wounded; and 25 were prisoners of war.[54] From the *promotions* of 1908 through 1914, 41 were dead and 12 missing.[55] *Normaliens* at the front heard so often of classmates and former colleagues being killed in action that one young sub-lieutenant, from the *promotion* (or entering class) of 1911, expressed amazement in November 1915 that even one other *normalien* remained "intact."[56] By the end of the war more than 800 *normaliens* had seen military service, nearly all in the infantry; 239 had died in action. The *promotions* of 1908 through 1913, the nucleus of French scholarship for the future, were devastated: from the *promotions* of 1908 through 1910, of the seventy-nine *normaliens* who served, thirty-nine, or 49 percent, died; for the classes of 1911 through 1913, 161 enlisted, eighty-one, or 50.3 percent, died, and sixty-four were wounded.[57] To place these statistics in comparative perspective, of all Oxford students who matriculated between the years 1905 and 1909 and saw military service in France, 23 percent died; the rate for those who matriculated in the years between 1910 and 1914 was 29.3 percent.[58] Only when compared to losses within their French intellectual cohort could such mortality rates seem modest.

Military regulations that required *normaliens* to serve in the infantry, and thus contributed to these horrifying casualty rates, prompted Lavisse to lobby vigilantly for a fundamental change in the military service law. For much of the war he directed his energies to an initiative that, if successful, would allow *normaliens* to qualify for service in the artillery. Several factors seem to have influenced him in this regard. Certainly he knew of the effect of compulsory service in the infantry and feared that the wholesale destruction of young *normaliens* would jeopardize the future of higher education in France; but it is also clear from his correspondence that he knew of, and was tormented by, the horrifying nature of service in the infantry as individual students experienced it. His private papers show that, starting in January 1916, his correspondents effectively disabused him of whatever illusions about trench warfare he might still have had, and prompted in him feelings of profound dismay. An unidentified correspondent suggested that those who enjoyed the comfort and security of civilian life could never imagine the savage, barbarous, and primitive conditions of life at the front.[59] He did not argue that they *should* know immediately the horrors of trench warfare, but he did believe that all, combatants and noncombatants alike, should share in the suffering of the front. "A Prayer for Those at the Front (to be said by those who are in the rear)," dated January 1916, suggests that Lavisse did indeed share this burden. Invoking the tone, while inverting the spirit, of the Beatitudes, the prayer begged God for:

> Pity for all those who each day touch the very depths of human misery, who live each day exposed to the most hideous of deaths, who hold fast without respite, who eat without sating their hunger and drink without satisfying their thirst; who no longer know true rest; who are gnawed at by vermin, tormented by rats, frozen by the cold and the damp; and for those who, above all else, live, separated from all who love them, with broken hearts . . . But most of all, my God, have pity

on me; I did not wish to share their suffering and, like Pilate, washed my hands of them.[60]

Whether Lavisse composed or merely copied this heart-rending lament is unclear; it appears without attribution among a series of handwritten notes (some dated, others not) in his private papers. These documents suggest, however, that by 1916 Lavisse was tormented by what he knew of the conditions of trench warfare, and by the moral burden such knowledge entailed for those who did not (or could not) fight. It was not true, however, that Lavisse had "washed his hands" of his students' suffering. He empathized profoundly with their agony, even though he could not experience it directly, and he took to heart their call for effective action. His unidentified correspondent called upon friends behind the lines to devote themselves to "action, more action, and still more action."[61] Lavisse did just that by lobbying successfully for a change in the law that required *normaliens* to serve in the infantry.

On August 5, 1916, the French government modified the law of 1889 to allow students admitted to the *promotion* of 1916 to serve alongside students from the Ecole Polytéchnique in the artillery. At first the law made no distinction between humanists and scientists; all secured automatic admission to the artillery training college at Fontainebleau. Subsequently, the government amended the law to require that students who had gained admission to the ENS in Letters pass an entrance examination to Fontainebleau. Lavisse found this unacceptable; even if students in letters lacked the background in mathematics that their colleagues in sciences enjoyed, they should be judged equally admissible on the grounds of their "good will, their intelligence, and their *culture générale*."[62] In a letter dated 15 June 1917, Lavisse urged the Minister of War to reinstate the law's original terms and admit all students from the *promotion* of 1917 to the artillery training course. He believed that if such a provision had been in effect in August 1914, the school would not have suffered the "appalling losses" it had sustained since then.[63] It was too late to save the 117 *normaliens* who had already died. But it was not too late to protect those about to be called up.

The change in the law seems to have made a difference. All students mobilized from the *promotions* of 1910 through 1913 served in the infantry; by May 1917, almost half of them were dead. By contrast, sixteen of the forty-four students from the *promotion* of 1914 were assigned or transferred to the artillery. By the spring of 1917, of the twenty-eight serving in infantry regiments, eight were dead and sixteen wounded; of those assigned to the artillery, only one was dead and one was wounded.[64] The *promotions* of 1916 and 1917 were small because most students eligible for admission to the school went directly into the army before taking the Ecole's entrance examination; but casualty rates for the few who entered the school before reaching military age and were subsequently conscripted as *normaliens* were comparatively low. Twenty-seven students from the *promotions* of 1916 and 1917 saw military service; four (14.8 percent) died. No doubt some credit for these lower casualty rates belongs to changes in military strategy brought about by the failure of the Nivelle offensive in the spring of 1917 and the ensuing mutinies; but if one extrapolates from the experience of the *promotion* of 1914, one must conclude that efforts to place *normaliens* in the artillery rather than in the infantry helped save some of these students.

Intellectual Action

A pseudonymous observer writing in *La Grande Revue* in early 1915 assessed the practical initiatives of noncombatant scholars with a somewhat skeptical eye. He understood why during the early weeks of a war that everyone believed would be quickly won, intellectuals had plunged into "practical action," but he feared it was not quite French to abandon the life of the mind entirely. Ultimately, it would become necessary to think about the fundamental issues at stake in the war. Reassuring himself that the "intellectual silence" that had recently descended upon France would not last, "Brutus" argued that only by reinforcing the efforts of the army with the reflections of reason could the French intelligentsia remain true to itself and to an honorable French tradition, dating from the Revolution, of "thinking under fire."[65]

Judging by their actions, most French intellectuals of the First World War agreed. Not content to raise funds, supervise sewing workshops, and campaign on behalf of men at the front, they also wrote essays, addressed domestic and international audiences, and engaged one another in impassioned debates about the essential character of French culture and the necessary attributes of French education. They did so because profound disruptions in academic and literary life changed for the duration of the war the character of intellectual discourse and the audience for public education. But they were also moved to embrace the cause of "intellectual action" in response to calls from prominent political and intellectual leaders. The President of the Republic, the Permanent Secretary of the Académie Française, and the Dean of Letters at the University of Paris each called publicly upon noncombatant scholars and writers to remember that as intellectuals they had specific duties to the nation and the war effort that could be honored only through writing, thinking, and teaching. Theirs was a unique responsibility to educate the nation about the war and the fundamental issues at stake; to help thereby to sustain the nation's morale; and to persuade potential allies in neutral powers of the merits of the French cause.

When President Poincaré reminded the members of the Académie Française of the importance of intellectual action in late 1914, his was by no means a lone voice. Several months earlier Albert Sarraut, the Minister of Public Instruction, had emphasized the important function schools and universities had to fulfill. Teachers at all levels had a sacred duty "to keep the flame of French thought alive, bright and clear," and to inspire in their young students the qualities of will and intellect that the nation would need in the future.[66] While troops at the front confronted death, those who could not fight were obliged to protect, preserve, and propagate something that would never die: the "eternal idea" of France.[67] This, too, was the message Alfred Croiset delivered to the scholars of the Sorbonne when classes resumed in November 1914. He acknowledged that it was difficult to focus one's thoughts on the classroom when "all thoughts were with [one's] colleagues" at the front, but he urged students and faculty alike to devote themselves to the academic enterprise.[68] "The life of the nation goes on," he told them, and "each one must work according to his own abilities to prepare" for the peace. This did not mean that academics should be oblivious to the war and the problems posed by it; far from it. But they should recognize that they had a specific responsibility to discharge in the life of a nation at war. They had "to work to defend French civilization."[69]

Etienne Lamy, who devoted himself equally to practical and intellectual action, also believed that the French intelligentsia had to exercise its gifts of public persuasion. Echoing Poincaré, he too urged his colleagues within the Académie Française to educate the nation. Intellectuals, he emphasized, and especially those of the stature of academicians, had a unique ability "to make truth accessible to all"; thus individual members of the French intellectual elite were obligated to teach the nation (through public lectures and extensive publication) "what it had to know." If they honored this commitment to "become persuasive educators of their contemporaries," then "men of thought would become men of action."[70]

In September 1915 the Minister of Public Instruction reiterated this moral charge. Preparing the nation for the opening of another wartime school year, Sarraut argued that French universities shared with primary and secondary education a moral responsibility to demonstrate to the nation at large—to soldiers at the front and civilians behind the lines—why France was at war: "The role of the *Université*, in effect, is to make known to the entire country why it is fighting, for what past and for what future, for what facts and what ideas; by illuminating national feeling with its specific knowledge, [the *Université*] will sustain and fortify the nation with an unshakeable confidence and a will for total victory."[71] If the educational establishment fulfilled this task of national enlightenment and invigoration, schools at every level would become "the moral center of the nation."

This sweeping invocation to the *Université* as a corporate entity did not seem to distinguish the obligations of higher education from those of primary or secondary schooling. But Sarraut recognized that those who taught in the nation's universities had unique responsibilities, and he insisted, as Croiset had done a year earlier, that "whatever the difficulties," the academic enterprise in its entirety had to continue "for the sake of the country itself; for the sake of foreigners; and for the future of France."[72] He identified four essential tasks that French higher education had to perform: it had to assure wounded, demobilized soldiers that they could resume their studies; to allow young women, eager to prepare themselves for the task of postwar national revival, to pursue the requisite degree programs; and to present to foreign students (who represented a sizeable proportion of all degree students attending French universities during the war) a clear vision of the character of French culture. Even courses not directly related to the war were important in this endeavor because they could "rally to our cause all minds enamoured of beauty and justice [*éprises de beauté et de justice*]."[73] And finally, the universities had to remain open because they alone could provide the intellectual leadership—particularly in the sciences—the nation would need in the postwar world. Throughout the war, the academic community endeavored to honor each of these responsibilities through public lectures, extensive publication, and ongoing research.

To keep universities open and intellectual conversation alive was by no means a simple task. Mobilization profoundly disrupted intellectual life throughout France. Classrooms lost teachers and students; journals and publishers lost writers and technical staff; and many who remained out of the fighting lost—at least initially—the will to write. This was evident at the *Revue critique des idées et des livres,* a culturally conservative literary review founded in 1908 and dedicated to a revival of classicism. In August of 1914 most of the young writers associated with the

Revue critique went to the front; of the regular contributors to the review, seventeen died in front-line action, three more were missing and presumed dead, and three others died while on military service.[74] Too old for active service, Pierre Lasserre was deeply moved by the mobilization of his many colleagues at the *Revue critique;* as he watched them leave for the front, he remained behind, tormented by his inability to take up arms and reluctant to write.[75]

The *Revue critique* was but one of many academic and literary journals that had contributed in the decade before the war to the rich—and often acrimonious—literary and scholarly life of the nation; in 1919 Fernand Baldensperger of the Sorbonne mentioned more than two dozen journals that had shaped prewar intellectual culture.[76] Individual circumstances dictated how these journals responded to the war. Some closed for the duration, as their editorial staffs donned army uniforms. This was particularly true of the literary journals founded in the decade before the war. Thus both the *Revue critique* and the *Nouvelle Revue française* suspended publication in August 1914. Journals with older editorial staffs remained active throughout the war, although disruptions in the publication schedule were common in the first months of the war. With compositors at the front, supply routes disrupted, and other difficulties to overcome, the *Revue historique* published its first wartime issue several weeks behind schedule; the November 1914 issue of the *Revue de métaphysique et de morale* appeared, after even more considerable delay, in the fall of 1915.

Even if material circumstances had allowed for uninterrupted publication, moral compunction often precluded it. In the first weeks of the war theaters closed, writers abandoned their prewar projects, and silence prevailed. Writing seemed neither an adequate nor an appropriate response to the war. As François LeGrix, writing in the *Revue hebdomadaire,* explained: "Many of our best minds went to war, and those of us who remained behind were hardly in a mood to read or to write . . . We live[d] without books and theatres, and we live[d] better."[77] The editorial committee of the *Mercure de France* contributed to this collective silence by suspending publication at the beginning of the war. In April 1915, when publication resumed, Alfred Vallette explained the journal's initial decision. At first the war had seemed to compel men of letters to silence: "Our endeavors became the games of mandarins, to which it had become indecent to devote oneself." There was "nothing to do but remain silent."[78] André Gide made a similar argument. He found that with the onset of war he could not write; and, like many other noncombatant scholars and writers, he turned his energies to volunteer work which he found both "interesting" and "useful."[79]

For many academics and writers, however, prolonged silence was untenable. The need to talk about the war, whether directly or indirectly, became imperative. Thus when Parisian theaters reopened, they played heroic dramas of the seventeenth century that attested to the glories of French military leadership and the genius of French writers; these became the staple product of the French stage.[80] Victor Giraud, who welcomed this return to the classical tradition, also felt compelled to address the issues of the day. No longer able to absorb himself in disinterested scholarship, he believed he had to apply himself to something he judged "necessary." Thus he "abandoned studies that [he] had started on the history of literature and ethics, and made it a point of honor to write only on that which was 'uniquely necessary'."[81] Maurice Blondel, concerned that speculative philosophy was, for the moment at least, "unreal" and "alien," determined to use his classroom to talk about the war. He was convinced that those who remained behind, "mobilisé sur le front de l'enseignement," had to "translate into acts and ideas the deaths of soldiers who had fallen for a cause that surpassed both them" and those who were soldiering at their studies.[82]

Concentration on prewar projects was even more difficult and attention to the issues of the day even more pressing for those whose sons were in uniform. In late October 1914, Durkheim wrote that neither teachers nor students "showed much interest in university life."[83] But he and many others with sons at the front were scholars of international reputation; for them, the abrupt abandonment of scholarship would have been unthinkable. And so they chose to redirect their intellectual energies to the war effort. Durkheim wrote essays that denounced German aggression; Picard defended the independence and superiority of French science compared to that of Germany; and Lanson felt compelled to forsake the internationalist *esprit de corps* that had characterized Sorbonne life before the war. Until France was free of German troops, he would commit himself to denouncing publicly the offenses committed by the invaders.[84]

At the same time, they resumed their responsibilities as teachers. In October 1914, Louis Liard circulated a notice to all university administrators within the Academy of Paris, urging them to prepare as best they could for the scheduled resumption of classes. The Ministry of Public Instruction recognized that the University of Lille, deep within the territory occupied by the German Army, had no choice but to close; all other public universities, however, were to remain open "as if the war did not exist."[85] Scholars applied themselves to the task, and a month before classes were scheduled to resume, Paul Appell and Alfred Croiset informed the Conseil de l'Université that the faculties of sciences and of letters would offer courses in most areas of undergraduate specialization and would give priority to courses required of candidates pursuing teaching certificates.[86] With its teaching staff reduced by mobilization, the University of Paris was hard-pressed, however, to offer a full complement of graduate courses. Recognizing that most graduate students were at the front, Appell and Croiset proposed reductions in graduate course offerings and the Ministry of Public Instruction suspended, at least for 1914–15, the competition for the advanced *agrégation* degree.[87] By preserving intact the undergraduate curriculum that prepared students for teaching positions in *lycées* and *collèges,* the faculties endeavored to protect secondary education from the worst ravages of mass mobilization. Protecting the university itself from the effects of mobilization proved much more difficult.

Ministerial directives notwithstanding, it proved well nigh impossible to resume academic life "as if they war did not exist." The war brought with it material inconveniences—enforced budgetary austerity, insufficient fuel supplies, and the possibility of aerial bombardment—as well as critical reductions in faculty numbers and student enrollments.[88] It also created new academic priorities. Noncombatant scholars, believing that the academic elite of the future was (for the most part) away at war, and encouraged by government officials and fellow scholars to educate the public about why France was at war, adjusted their course offerings to accommodate both the circumstances of the day and changes in the university population. Public courses, open to students and interested outsiders alike, became instruments of academic propaganda by which scholars taught the nation what was at stake in the war.

The most obvious effect of the war was on student enrollments. Jean-François Sirinelli has calculated that, on average, enrollment in higher education declined by 60 percent during the war years.[89] For some schools the decline was even more dramatic. The University of Paris enrollment plummeted from more than 14,000 students on the eve of the war to 3,300 a year later; at the Ecole Libre des Sciences Politiques, a prewar enrollment of 800 students dropped to seventy-two, of whom one third were foreigners; and the experience of the Ecole Normale was comparable. From a prewar student population of more than 150, enrollment dropped to a mere twenty students in March 1915.[90] Indeed, academic life at the Ecole Normale barely resembled that of the prewar years. In accordance with a law passed in 1888 and put into effect on August 1, 1914, the dormitories and most physical facilities of the Ecole were converted into a military hospital under the direction of the Union des Femmes Françaises. Draped with the flag of the Red Cross, the school remained open in name more than in spirit. The handful of students who continued to register had access only to the library, a few study halls, and the geology laboratory; all other facilities were requisitioned by the hospital or by scientists conducting secret research for the war. Forced to live out and take all their classes at the Sorbonne, temporarily barred from earning graduate degrees, the few students who continued to enroll enjoyed none of the customary camaraderie of *normalien* life. As Lavisse described the mournful atmosphere of the wartime Ecole in 1915, former students, now serving as military doctors, wandered the hushed halls and thought sadly of their colleagues at the front and of lost days of college exuberance.[91]

Even schools and universities not subjected to these additional burdens of war were profoundly affected by declining enrollments and the changing demographic character of higher education. The radical reduction in university enrollment brought with it a serious fiscal crisis. In peacetime, university budgets counted on a fixed allocation from the state and income derived from student tuition. Although the government contribution initially remained unchanged, tuition income, which ordinarily represented half of a university's operating budget, dropped dramatically. This forced the University of Paris, for example, to reduce faculty budgets for 1915 by 25 percent.[92] Costs, however, did not decline proportionately. As was customary for all government employees, mobilized staff and faculty continued to receive financial support from their peacetime employer; this allowed their families to supplement the meager wages allocated for military service. In 1914 the University of Paris faculty voted to extend this practice to fellowship students. For the duration of the war, students in the Faculty of Sciences who held the rank of soldier received half of their scholarship income; those who served as commissioned officers received one quarter of their fellowship stipend.[93] All other university operating costs thus became subject to severe scrutiny.

In October 1914 Liard informed Lavisse that "the exigencies of national defense" made frugality in the operation of the Ecole Normale imperative. Henceforth, "all acquisitions for laboratories, libraries, and other collections were to be put on hold."[94] Lavisse and his peers, who remembered the Franco-Prussian War and the "irreparable" damage it had caused to university collections, were anxious to preserve library budgets, especially for the ongoing purchase of periodicals.[95] They thus began to look for other places to cut expenditures and also sought alternate sources of university income. During the war faculty members saw their salaries decline; and although donations to the Secours National and the Secours Universitaire suggest that reductions in salaries, however unwelcome, were not overly burdensome in the first years of the war, with the onset of inflation in 1916 faculty salaries were probably sadly inadequate.[96]

As early as 1915, the university also began to investigate seriously the possibility of increasing foreign student enrollment to offset temporary (and anticipated long-term) enrollment declines that resulted from mobilization and massive casualties. Addressing the Conseil de l'Université in April 1915, Liard admitted to a grave concern for the future of the university: given the obvious fact that there could only be a decrease (relative to prewar standards) in enrollment after the war, it was essential that the faculty consider ways to attract foreign students to Paris.[97] To this end, a scholarly committee with Durkheim as its chairman examined in careful detail the academic and social needs of foreign students and recommended appropriate curricular changes; other scholars, including Lanson, traveled abroad to convince scholars in neutral countries of the advantages French higher education could offer their students.

Foreign students represented a potential source of new, much needed income; so did female students. Full-time female enrollment at the University of Paris doubled between 1914 and 1915 and continued to grow thereafter. For the 1915–16 academic year, the University of Paris enrolled 50 women in the Faculty of Law, 186 in Medicine, 18 in Pharmacy, 179 in Sciences, and 196 in Arts; of those in Arts and Sciences, the majority prepared for the *licence* degree, the teaching certificate to allow them to teach in the *lycées;* anticipating a serious shortfall in qualified male candidates, the women took it upon themselves to fill their ranks in the *lycées* and *collèges* of France.[98] Liard, who knew how short-staffed secondary schools were and were likely to remain, did nevertheless express doubts about women's ability to compete successfully with men in the degree programs of higher education. He feared that their academic preparation was inadequate: as *baccalauréat* students they had flocked to the Latin Modern languages curriculum because it was deemed the easiest program of study, and they had succeeded in this program in large part on the strength of "female intuition." He worried that once they arrived at the Sorbonne, their second-rate secondary education would prove a serious liability. Liard's anxieties notwithstanding, women persevered and female enrollment at the University of Paris almost tripled between 1914 and 1921 (from 1,209 to 3,192).[99]

Female attendance at lectures caused professors and contemporary observers considerable concern. One writer, observing the changing demographics of the Sorbonne, suggested that the young women and elderly men who frequented the public courses at the Sorbonne in 1914–15 were academic dilettantes.[100] Liard's judgment was less hostile: he knew that young women attended the Sorbonne with serious purpose. Yet his concerns about their academic preparation carried with them the implication that as the population of the university changed, the character of its curriculum must change accordingly. Discussion of curricular reforms dominated faculty council meetings for much of the war and ultimately gave rise to several significant innovations. The most immediate change in the curricular character of the university concerned the importance assigned to public lectures. Before 1914, public lecture courses, an established tradition within French higher education, were an academic responsibility that many scholars resented. In the heady days of academic reform, university scholars had objected to the requirement that they offer courses accessible to the general public; as scholars, their duty was to form a scholarly elite for the future, not to entertain the bored and frivolous.[101] The war changed all this. Courses restricted to degree candidates remained in place—Maurice Blondel, in spite of his reservations about the relevance of speculative philosophy, continued to offer classes on ontology and the history of philosophy at the University of Aix-Marseille—but public lectures became essential expressions of "intellectual action."

Convinced that public lectures would contribute to the cause of national education, academics around the country directed their energies to the war effort by lecturing extensively on the war. From his lectern at the Institut Catholique, Jacques Maritain tried to persuade his audience that German philosophy was responsible for German militarism. Maurice Blondel offered a public course in 1914–15 on German philosophy and the lessons of the war; in the following year, he spoke on the task of philosophy and the responsibility of intellectuals during wartime.[102] At the Sorbonne, the faculty offered courses on modern German history, European diplomatic history, military architecture, and the history of the Balkans. The Société des Amis de l'Université coordinated a lecture series, held at the Sorbonne from January through March 1915, to address issues the war had raised. Lavisse opened the series with a lecture on the history of Prussia; Charles Andler spoke on the military culture of nineteenth-century Germany; and Aulard lectured on the French Revolution and the war.[103] The committee organized comparable lecture series each spring for the duration of the war.

This contemporary curriculum met with uneven success. Charles Seignobos drew only two dozen students to his course on the historical origins of German unity. But Fortunat Strowski, who presented lectures on Verlaine and Mallarmé, attracted huge crowds. One observer commented that in the early months of the war at least, Parisians went to the Sorbonne to be distracted from the crises of the day; they tended to flock to the same public courses that had proved popular before the war.[104] Yet audiences did reveal a renewed interest in analyses of French literary and philosophical culture. Although Lanson's prewar critics had often berated him for his arid style and passionless analyses, in 1914, when he spoke on the development of the French concept of culture, he addressed himself to large and appreciative audiences. Philosophers, many of whom had been students of German Idealism, turned their attention to the French philosophical tradition. Lucien Lévy-Bruhl lectured to large audiences on eighteenth-century French philosophy, and Victor Delbos, whose lectures on Kant and post-Kantianism are still in print, turned his attention to an analysis of "la philosophie française" instead.

Public lectures were important but inadequate on their own. Whether presented at home or abroad, they could reach only a few hundred people at most. By contrast, the written word, more expansive in its scope and, when translated, more accessible to foreign readers, could reach thousands. Recognizing this, academics and writers combined forces with French publishers and editors to make writing an integral component of intellectual action. The efforts of French publishing houses were very important in this regard. From the beginning of the war major publishers collaborated with scholars and scholarly committees to produce essays and articles that addressed intellectual and cultural issues raised by the war. They also initiated projects that they considered of public utility. In 1915 Hachette undertook a French Authors series for which it sought the cooperation and endorsement of Sorbonne scholars. The publishers intended to prepare for distribution at home and abroad inexpensive but accurate scholarly editions of French classic works from the Middle Ages onwards. Many of the titles to appear under the Hachette imprint were already available to foreign readers—but only from German publishers! The Hachette project would rectify this anomalous situation by giving students around the world access to definitive French editions of essential texts. To give the project academic authority, Hachette sought and won the official endorsement of the University of Paris.[105]

With the active cooperation of French publishers, scholars and writers from across the political spectrum responded to Poincaré's invitation to wage war with their pens and their words. Charles Maurras was no friend of the Republic Poincaré represented, but he was eager nonetheless to contribute to the war effort by "defend[ing] French civilization." Unable to fight, he resolved on the first of August 1914 "to make [his] pen ever more useful."[106] This resolution took various forms. First, his writing turned to practical action when he used the columns of the *Action française* to demand higher wages for the nation's troops, and when he donated the proceeds from the publication of *L'Etang de Berre*, a collection of poems and essays, to the wounded. At the same time, however, he and his colleagues used their publishing house, the Nouvelle Librairie Française, as an instrument of intellectual action to denigrate German *Kultur*, denounce Kant, and defend classicism as the essential cultural voice of France. His colleagues Léon Daudet and Louis Dimier, who like Maurras watched with pride mingled with anxiety as the ardent young Camelots du roi of the Action Française left for the front, pledged to support their military efforts with intellectual enterprise. Dimier hoped that his writing would bolster the morale of those who fought; Daudet intended that his essays of intellectual criticism would complement the efforts of men in arms.[107]

Republican academics proved no less eager to lend their pens to the war effort. Lavisse, Boutroux, and Bergson, all members of the Institut de France, joined forces with Durkheim, Lanson, Andler, and Seignobos to create a Committee for Studies and Documents on the War. The committee resolved to publish scholarly, putatively objective analyses of the war, its prosecution, origins, and fundamental character. The Paris Chamber of Commerce subsidized its efforts, and pamphlets appeared in French for domestic distribution and were translated into seven foreign languages for circulation to citizens of neutral powers. Yves-Henri Nouailhat calculates that of all the English-language brochures printed, just under a quarter made their way to the United States, where pamphlets written by Joseph Bédier on German atrocities and by Emile Durkheim on German responsibility for the war were particularly well received.[108]

International distribution was essential to the success of French intellectual action, for neutrals had to be convinced of the righteousness of the Allied cause and reminded of the superior character of French culture.

Before the war, the moderately conservative weekly periodical *Revue hebdomadaire* had established a public lecture series devoted to cultural debate that continued to function during the war—the two lecture series slated for 1914–15 were "L'Espérance française" and "Les Villes martyres"—and became an instrument of international propaganda. For the duration of the war the Société des Conférences published and translated each lecture series into eleven foreign languages.[109] Catholic, Protestant, and Jewish groups organized similar publishing ventures to defend the French cause to coreligionists in neutral countries. Baudrillart and Rébelliou determined to serve France "par une action morale" directed to foreigners. Together with Lévy-Bruhl they initiated the *Bulletin de la guerre de l'Alliance française;* by 1916 the journal appeared in ten languages and enjoyed a circulation of 200,000. The Comité Catholique de Propagande Française à l'Étranger collaborated with the publishing house of Bloud and Gay to issue pamphlets (some of which were written by non-Catholics) in a series called *Pages actuelles;* by 1916 the committee had distributed more than one-and-one-half million copies of these pamphlets.[110]

Henry Bloud, who had relinquished direct control of the publishing house when he assumed a position on the bench of the Paris Court of Appeals, did not consider these efforts, extensive though they were, sufficient. In 1916 he approached Etienne Lamy with yet another proposal to extend French cultural and intellectual influence abroad. Alarmed by the extent of German propaganda overseas, Bloud believed that publishers and scholars had a responsibility to work together to combat the enemy on this intellectual front. He recommended that writers and publishers establish a national committee to coordinate the composition, publication, and distribution of French propaganda abroad.[111] In fact such a committee already existed. The Comité du Livre, which counted among its directorial committee Emile Picard, Maurice Croiset (brother of Alfred and administrator of the Collège de France), Louis Liard, and Etienne Lamy, worked assiduously in 1916 to extend France's cultural influence abroad. Although the committee did not adopt Bloud's proposals in their entirety, it did endeavor to produce, with the active cooperation of French publishers, inexpensive editions of current French scholarship for distribution overseas. It was hoped that such a project would effectively counterbalance comparable German efforts and convince the world of the vitality of contemporary French culture.[112]

Unlike many writers who wrote at length about the war, André Gide kept his counsel. His suspicion that those who wrote "on the war" did so "as an excuse for not being at the front" prompted him to continued silence.[113] Gide's judgment was harsh. There were certainly many writers and scholars who "wrote on the war" because they were not at the front. But intellectual action was not so much an "excuse" for not being at the front as an attempt to do something significant for the war in spite of their inability to fight. In waging war with their pens, noncombatant writers did not deceive themselves that their efforts alone were adequate: when Victor Giraud published a patriotic essay in 1917, he acknowledged that "all of this was very little, as I know; and if you were to tell me that all these ink-stained pages ("les pages noircies") were not worth a few good shots fired in the trenches—ah! how right you would be!"[114] Yet "les pages noircies" appeared throughout the war because noncombatant intellectuals believed that intellectual action was necessary to public education and crucial to the successful prosecution of the war. Although it was a sense of ethical obligation to the nation and to colleagues within the intellectual community that predisposed the noncombatant intelligentsia to act, it was moral outrage, provoked by the publication of the German manifesto "An Appeal to the Civilized World," that determined the specific character and content of their action.

CHAPTER THREE

The *Kultur* War

On October 13, 1914, the Paris daily *Le Temps* published a document that elicited an immediate, intense, and unanimously indignant response from the ranks of the French intelligentsia. The offending article, entitled "An Appeal to the Civilized World," was none other than the Manifesto of 93. Endorsed by scholars and writers as distinguished as Ernst Haeckel, Gerhart Hauptmann, Engelbert Humperdinck, Karl Lamprecht, Friedrich Naumann, Max Planck, and Wilhelm Wundt, the manifesto represented all branches of knowledge, from physics and chemistry through art and architecture, and seemed to express the collective opinion of the German intellectual elite. The Appeal article had appeared initially nine days earlier in the *Berliner Tageblatt,* had been quickly reprinted in Germany's many regional and local newspapers, and had already been distributed to readers in neutral countries; by the time it appeared in the French press, therefore, rumors of its existence had circulated for at least a week. Once the precise contents of the manifesto became known in France, indignation knew no bounds. The French intelligentsia took issue with each of the manifesto's claims, denounced as patently disingenuous its many denials of German culpability, and expressed outrage at the supine character of Germany's intellectual elite.

So numerous were French reactions to the manifesto that one commentator suggested that it alone galvanized the French intellectual community to mobilize for intellectual action: "in this regard, too, it was the Germans' mobilization which determined that of the French. The declarations, protestations and explanations of their intellectuals provoked ours to emerge from their self-imposed silence."[1] Such a judgment, appropriate enough for the cultural and academic institutions of wartime

France, is not entirely accurate for individual intellectuals, some of whom had already determined "to make their pens ever more useful" from the early days of August. For these intellectual activists, many considerations—from a sense of anguish at their own inaction to a determination to be useful—proved to be the moving factors. What is true, however, is that by presenting to the French intellectual community a catalogue of controversial claims that demanded responses, the manifesto gave a structure to subsequent French intellectual action. Hitherto undirected intentions came to focus on questions raised in or about the Manifesto. Thus its publication did open a critical chapter in the mobilization of French intellect.

French scholars could not simply denounce and then dismiss this text, because for reasons independent of the signatories' intentions the issues it covered were of fundamental importance to French intellectual culture. The Manifesto of 93 provoked in France controversial and divisive debates about the character of German *Kultur* and the essential qualities of French *civilisation;* about the place of science in modern society; and about the culpability of German philosophy—especially the philosophical tradition that started with Kant—for contemporary German crimes. The manifesto also called into question the very appropriateness of intellectual action. Because the document provided the world with uncomfortable evidence of "intellectual action" gone awry, would-be respondents had to consider why the most prominent men of German learning, men they had respected and in some cases revered, had abandoned established methods of intellectual inquiry and scruples of academic honesty to defend the unworthy behavior of their nation. What could possibly explain such aberrant behavior? Would-be French respondents had, therefore, to consider the implications of any comparable French action. If they, too, resorted to intellectual action, how could such a course of action be defended? How, in effect, could the French distinguish—and defend—their own intellectual action from the kind they, and so many others, denounced in the enemy?

The Manifesto of 93

The "Appeal to the Civilized World" was a simple, structurally symmetrical text with three distinct parts.[2] A two-paragraph preface and a two-paragraph conclusion enveloped six paragraphs of substantive arguments in which the signatories challenged the legitimacy of charges leveled against the German Army. In the preface the signatories established their credentials. They identified themselves as "representatives of German Science and Art" and "heralds of truth" called to defend Germany before the "civilized world" against the wicked calumnies and misrepresentations of the Entente powers. In the conclusion they situated themselves within an intellectual tradition of unimpeachable credibility. They appealed to neutral readers to "have faith" in their integrity: as the intellectual heirs of Goethe, Beethoven, and Kant, they and their nation would not act in any way that would dishonor or repudiate the values these great men of Germany had come to represent.

The substantive claims of the manifesto appeared as a litany of denials. "It is not true," the signatories repeated emphatically, that Germany had caused or even wanted the war: the Germans were a peace-loving people led by an Emperor committed to maintaining "universal peace." War came not because Germany had willed it, but because "a numerical superiority, which had been lying in wait on the frontiers, assailed" her people. Nor had Germany violated Belgian neutrality, committed atrocities against innocent civilians, scorned international law, and willfully ignored established conventions of appropriate conduct. Whatever the Entente powers suggested to the contrary, German warfare was responsible for "no undisciplined cruelty." Each of these assertions provoked indignant reactions from French scholars determined to prove that Germany had indeed both caused and wanted the war; had violated the rights of innocent nations and innocent civilians; and had scorned international law.

French Reactions to the Manifesto of 93

Quickly eclipsing Bethmann-Hollweg's infamous repudiation of international law—"necessity knows no law"—the Manifesto of 93 soon became the most vilified document to come out of Germany in the early war. In France, anticlerical republicans and ardent Catholics would come to disagree vehemently over details of interpretation, but in the immediate aftermath of publication they were unanimous in their condemnation of the document.[3] The collected faculties of the nation's public universities, responding to an initiative from the University of Paris, issued their own manifesto in rebuttal, as did the faculty of the Institut Catholique. Each of the five classes of the Institut de France repudiated the document, and by mid-1915 had moved to disbar from the ranks of honorary membership any German scholar who had signed the manifesto. Denounced by each of the Entente powers, the manifesto fared little better with audiences in neutral territory: responses castigating the signatories appeared promptly in the United States, Spain, Portugal, and Ireland. At the University of Dublin faculty members were dumbfounded by the document, and found themselves hard-pressed to explain how scholars "whom we formerly knew and respected could have signed their names to this completely untruthful declaration."[4] French academics carefully catalogued this response (and any other evidence of neutral indignation), for every expression of international disapprobation strengthened their own efforts to discredit the arguments German intellectuals articulated in their most infamous text.

In the week following the publication in France of the "Appeal to the Civilized World," the five classes of the Institut de France considered how best to respond to the document and its assertions. The Académie des Inscriptions et Belles-Lettres led the way with a draft response which expressed outrage at German atrocities; decried German attacks on Reims and Louvain, where the destruction of the university's library proved a particularly sore point for French intellectuals; and moved to terminate the honorary membership of any signatory previously granted associate status within the Academy. The Academy's reaction was significant for two reasons: the preliminary, unpublished text, when circulated to the other academies for their approval, generated a fundamental disagreement within the Institut de France itself; and once published, the Académie's response established publicly the importance of the Manifesto in galvanizing French intellectual action.

The document issued by the Académie des Inscriptions et Belles-Lettres admitted that the manifesto prompted them to act when earlier German acts, however despicable, had not. Until late October 1914, the Academy had made no public statement on war atrocities, not because it did not believe the reports filtering back to Paris from the occupied zones, but because it considered that sufficient public outrage had been expressed already on these counts. With the publication of the Manifesto of 93, however, the Academy decided it should no longer contain its indignation: "today the appeal which is addressed to international opinion by a certain number of German scholars no longer allows us to remain silent."[5] The intellectuals who had signed the manifesto had, in the eyes of these academicians, violated their duty as men of reason; they had lent the authority of their names and their reputations to the cause of violence, and had compromised their intellectual integrity by denying what was demonstrably true.

In mid-October Etienne Lamy circulated this draft to the presidents of the other four academies, asking that their members endorse it. Lamy hoped that if all five academies would agree to accept the draft response, the Institut de France could present the document at its scheduled public meeting on October 26 as a unanimous expression of the Institute's collective opinion. Three of the remaining four academies proved amenable to this plan, and endorsed the published response of the Académie des Inscriptions et Belles-Lettres: the Académie des Beaux-Arts on October 24, the Académie Française on October 29, and the Académie des Sciences Morales et Politiques two days later. Only the Académie des Sciences withheld its compliance.

On October 19, 1914, several days before the Académie des Inscriptions published its condemnation of the manifesto, Paul Appell wrote Etienne Lamy to explain the position of the Académie des Sciences. The Academy had held a closed meeting that day to discuss whether it should approve the text Lamy had circulated and to consider whether it should also strike from its list of honorary members any scientist whose name appeared on the manifesto. At that meeting, the Academy decided unanimously that it would neither disbar its German colleagues nor endorse the proposed French response. The membership contended that the manifesto expressed the opinions of individuals, not institutions, and concluded that collective action against individual signatories was inappropriate. Had the German Academy of Science issued or endorsed the manifesto, it might have been appropriate for the French body to reply in kind. But for institutions to respond to individuals was, in the circumstances, ill-advised.[6] Appell held out the possibility of some future response to the manifesto once the Académie des Sciences had consulted with its sister institutions in the other Allied countries, and the Academy did issue its own response to the Manifesto of 93 in early November 1914.[7] But Appell informed Lamy that, as of October 19, 1914, it would be impossible to represent the text prepared by the Académie des Inscriptions et Belles-Lettres as the expression of the Institut de France.

The division between humanists and scientists that split the Institut de France also appeared within the deliberations of the University of Paris, when it, too, considered how the intellectual community should respond to the Manifesto of 93. On October 26, 1914, the faculty council of the University of Paris debated the advantages and disadvantages of a public response. Liard, as Rector of the University and President of the committee, argued that if, as seemed to be the case, the Germans had distributed the manifesto to neutral countries, then the French scholarly community in its entirety had an obligation to respond publicly and forcefully to the document. And in order to assert the nation's unanimity and unity of purpose, the response should come not just from the faculty of the University of Paris but from all public universities in France. When recommending collective action, Liard appealed not to principle but to practical considerations. "A sector of national opinion," he said, expected and awaited a response. Durkheim agreed. Reminding his colleagues that scholars in Britain and Russia had already issued their responses, he insisted that the French could not remain silent. The public, whether rightly or wrongly, expected a formal response from the French academic community.[8] Yet neither Durkheim nor Liard was convinced that a formal French response would be efficacious. Liard recognized that it was not the citizens of France or other Entente powers that had to be disabused of the German arguments; it was the citizenry of neutral powers who had to be addressed, and a manifesto that merely contradicted the German claims would not suffice in this regard. A much more substantial campaign of public persuasion was required. Nonetheless, given that the French public, or at least an important section of it, awaited a response from the university community, some response was imperative.

Asked to vote on Liard's resolution that the University of Paris compose an appropriate reply to the Manifesto of 93 and then submit it for the approval of the other French universities, the faculty divided along disciplinary lines. The deans of Science and Medicine (Appell and Roger) and the Director of the School of Pharmacy (Borel) opposed the motion, arguing that it was not appropriate to present an institutional response to the manifesto; individuals could, if they desired, collect signatures and respond *as individuals* but as the Manifesto of 93 was the expression of individuals rather than institutions, it would be inappropriate to issue an institutional response. Borel thus moved that the French response should bear the names of individual members of university councils, not the names of the universities themselves. This motion, which Appell and Roger supported, failed to win sufficient support to pass. The scientific community, whether within the Institut de France or the University of Paris, was clearly at odds with humanists, who favored an immediate, unequivocal institutional response to the initiative of their German counterparts.[9]

Ultimately the university council agreed to form a committee, to which any member of the faculty could belong, authorized to compose a response on the part of the entire French university community to the Manifesto of 93. The committee met on October 28, 1914, prepared the text, and then submitted it that afternoon to the university council. The council accepted the text as presented, and forwarded it by telegram to the councils of the provincial universities. The minutes of the council meeting for October 28 do not record who attended the meeting, or whether the text was accepted unanimously. How the scientists reacted to this move is therefore unknown. But on November 3, 1914, the Manifesto of French Universities appeared in repudiation of the Manifesto of 93, endorsed by the faculty councils of all French public universities (excluding Lille, which was in the occupied zone), and with no public dissenters.

The republican academic establishment was not alone in its vehement rejection of the German manifesto. In mid-November the faculty of the Institut Catholique and the neoroyalists of the Action Française issued their own responses to the German intellectuals. Two considerations appear to have dominated the Catholic scholars' deliberations: they wanted to establish their own commitment to standards of scholarly inquiry and to distance themselves from the actions of the German Catholics. They needed to convince their own compatriots that Catholic scholarship was as rigorously "scientific" and as committed to truth as secular scholarship, and that French Catholics, whatever the calumnies directed against them, were as patriotic and loyal to France as any other citizen. As adherents to the *union sacrée,* the neoroyalists were equally eager to prove their patriotism by condemning the German signatories. The Action Française publishing house, the Nouvelle Librairie Nationale, published Louis Dimier's annotated and much acclaimed edition of the manifesto, *L'Appel des intellectuels allemands.*[10] In his introductory essay Dimier described the manifesto as an "official document of intellectual Germany . . . [that] bears witness to the support the Empire can count on from its collective of scholars."[11] At the end of the war, the neoroyalists congratulated themselves for having "published the first work of intellectual action to appear during the war, and the first work of general literature to appear since mobilization which dealt directly with the war."[12]

Interest in the Manifesto of 93, intense in the last months of 1914, did not abate. References to it continued to proliferate in essays, addresses, and pamphlets published throughout the war years; and formal reactions to the document appeared through the spring of 1915. In March, one hundred French artists, scientists, and men of letters joined forces to denounce the German manifesto and, not incidentally, to challenge the right of the Académie Française to represent itself as the unique voice of French culture.[13] Speaking as the defenders of eternal truths, intellectual honor, and independence, the French signatories condemned the "ninety-three" as a "maleficent band of Excellencies" for having "created, and codified in mystical language . . . a national catechism, adorned with the semblance of morality." If the Manifesto of 93 purported to represent all branches of German science and arts, the French Manifesto of 100 was consciously even more catholic in its scope. The literary and fine arts were more strongly represented in the French manifesto than in the German, and whereas the German manifesto included no female signatories, the French respondents garnered the support of six women writers.[14] Of all the signatures appended to the Manifesto of 100—which included those of Maurice Barrès, Emile Boutroux, Paul Claudel, Georges Clemenceau, Claude Debussy, Anatole France, André Gide, Henri Matisse, Claude Monet, and Camille Saint-Saëns—perhaps the most noteworthy was that of Paul Appell. Having opposed as inappropriate any institutional response to the Manifesto of 93, he did not hesitate to express his private indignation in this manner.

Rebutting the Manifesto

Some scholars and writers did little more than denounce publicly the German signatories; others, intent on fulfilling the promise of the Manifesto of French Universities, were determined to go much further: they would not rest easy until every German argument and assertion had been discredited. For every denial expressed in the Manifesto of 93, the Manifesto of French Universities posed these telling questions: Which nation had wanted war? Which nation had obstructed diplomatic initiatives designed to avoid war? Which nation had violated the neutrality of Belgium, destroyed the University of Louvain, and bombarded Reims cathedral? And for each unsubstantiated denial categorically asserted by the German intelligentsia, the French faculty members promised to provide irrefutable proof of German culpability. By compiling evidence from diplomatic sources, neutral inquiries into allegations of war atrocities, and German evidence from the field; by providing proof of the destruction of cultural monuments in France and Belgium; and by establishing that Germany did indeed desire war in order to advance its pan-Germanic ambitions, French academics would demonstrate that the German statements were "lies and misrepresentations."[15]

In the minds of French scholars and writers, one of the most outrageous lies perpetrated by the Manifesto of 93 was that German troops had committed no atrocities. As every French citizen knew by early October 1914, the German Army had burned the library at the University of Louvain and shelled Reims cathedral. Such incontrovertible evidence suggested that it was capable of any outrage. Led by "barbarians" whose indifference to culture was indisputable, German troops could just as easily have murdered civilians, burned villages, raped women, and brutalized children, as atrocity tales circulating in France alleged. Scholars affiliated with the Committee for Documents and Studies on the War resolved to make this case. In 1915 Ernest Lavisse and Charles Andler published *The German Theory and Practice of War* to document—sometimes with an almost unseemly relish—instances of German atrocities. These two distinguished scholars of German history and culture based their resumé of German atrocities on evidence gathered by French and Belgian commissions of inquiry. To skeptics who might question the impartiality of such investigations, Lavisse and Andler offered a rather lame explanation: the evidence could be trusted because of "the honor of [the] enquirers, the scrupulous care which they . . . employed in their task," and the "meticulous fairness" of each investigating team.

Perhaps aware that the evidence upon which Lavisse and Andler relied was not sufficiently convincing, the war committee subsequently published Joseph Bédier's pamphlet, "German Atrocities, from German Evidence."[16] John Horne and Alan Kramer have identified this pamphlet as one of the most important texts in the atrocities debate that absorbed German and French scholarly attention in 1915. Basing his investigation on the diaries of German soldiers captured or killed in September 1914, Bédier, a philologist trained in Germany and a scholar of medieval French literature at the Collège de France, concluded that in their advance through Belgium and northern and eastern France in August 1914, German troops had indeed razed villages, massacred civilians, killed prisoners of war, and brutalized women and children. In the face of such evidence from German eyewitnesses, Bédier insinuated that it was absurd for German scholars to assert—as they had done in the manifesto and would continue to do in repudiation of his pamphlet—that German troops had committed no atrocities. Indeed, in their determination to represent and thereby justify these documented acts of brutality against civilians and prisoners of war as legitimate acts of self-defense (which is what German scholars attempted to do), Bédier's opponents revealed their own moral bankruptcy.[17] Misled by a patriotism that perverted common sense, they forfeited their scholarly objectivity and their ethical integrity.

Documentation of atrocities might have discredited the German manifesto's claim that German warfare knew "no undisciplined cruelty," but such evidence did not prove that Germany had either wanted or actively planned for war. The French intellectual community, convinced as most French citizens were that their country was the innocent victim of German aggression, determined to make this point, too. Lacking direct documentary proof that Germany had issued Austria a "blank check" in its confrontation with Serbia, authors of articles, essays, and popular pamphlets appealed instead to evidence of pan-German ambition. In 1915 Andler argued in *Pan-Germanism: Its Plan for German Expansion in the World,* that with the accession of Wilhelm II in 1888 and the implementation thereafter of the "new course" in German diplomacy, the political, economic, and military agenda of territorial expansion and continental domination advocated most emphatically by the Pan-German League became the dominant ideology of the German Empire.[18] He cited the efforts of the German government to convert the Triple Alliance (which bound Germany, Austria-Hungary, and Italy in a strictly defensive diplomatic alliance) into a German-controlled Central European Customs Union that would include territory to the east and west of the Empire as evidence of German expansionism. Andler subsequently edited a multivolume work (to which he contributed a historical survey and a philosophical essay) that examined in greater depth the character and origins of pan-Germanism.

Andler's initial essay said nothing to suggest that pan-Germanism had roots in a long-established intellectual tradition. A year later, however, when discussing the "Philosophical Origins of Pan-Germanism," Andler (like many other French scholars who analyzed the character of that movement) argued that pan-Germanism found its roots in the philosophical ideas of Johann Gottlieb Fichte.[19] A student of Kant and a noted German Idealist of the early nineteenth century, Fichte was remembered by 1914 primarily as the author of *Addresses to the German Nation.* Composed in 1807–08, while Prussia suffered under the ignominy of French conquest and occupation, and presented as public lectures at the University of Berlin, Fichte's addresses had called upon the German people to transcend the tragedy of military defeat by forging a unified, self-sufficient nation integrating all German-speaking peoples.

When Andler identified Fichte as the spiritual father of German nationalism, he entered a philosophical debate intensified by (but not original to) the publication of the Manifesto of 93. At issue was the much-disputed relationship between German militarism and German culture *(Kultur).* Was militarism the product of *Kultur* (as Allied scholars would come to claim) or merely its protector (as the ninety-three signatories insisted)? And were the Allied armies fighting to destroy militarism or to eradicate *Kultur?* Germany's enemies had insisted from the outset of the war that they had taken up arms only against German militarism which, they charged, threatened the peace and stability of the Continent. They denied that in their determination to destroy German militarism they were also trying to destroy German *Kultur.* The signatories of the Manifesto of 93 rejected this disavowal as entirely specious: to declare war on German militarism, they retorted, was necessarily to declare war on *Kultur,* because *Kultur* could not survive without the protection of the German military. The manifesto made the point clearly enough: "Were it not for German militarism, German civilization would long since have been extirpated. For its protection it arose in a land which for centuries had been plagued by bands of robbers, as no other land has been." Insisting that "combat against our so-called militarism" was therefore also "combat against our civilization," the signatories proclaimed that the Entente powers were indeed engaged in a war against German *Kultur.*

Although French intellectuals were loath to agree with any part of the Manifesto of 93, on this point they could not genuinely disagree. The force of syllogistic logic compelled them to conclude that *Kultur* was the real cause of German militarism. If pan-Germanism was responsible for German aggression in 1914, and if Fichte and Hegel could be identified as the intellectual architects of the movement, then they could also be held responsible (at least indirectly) for the aggression. This syllogism permeated French essays of the war years. In "Trois idées allemandes," the principal parts of which were subsequently integrated into *The German Theory and Practice of War,* Lavisse insisted that pan-Germanism could not hide behind, or find exclusive justification in, arguments of material necessity. It was true that Germans believed that their nation needed to expand territorially in order to accommodate an ever-growing population, but they also believed that war was willed by both God and nature, and that Germany, because of its fundamentally superior cultural tradition, had a mission to govern the world for the greater good of humanity.[20] Although he cited Luther's defense of the inevitability of war, Lavisse blamed Fichte for the most insidious argument of all: that Germany was innately superior to all other nations. When propagated by "historians, philosophers, philologists, anthropologists, and poets," and popularized by German public education, this Fichtean conviction took firm root in nineteenth-century Germany and—Lavisse contended—ultimately became a rationalization for aggression. Thus German expansionism, although most evident in recent German political initiatives, was a product of an intellectual tradition that preceded the accession of Wilhelm II by almost a century. *Kultur* was responsible for the aggressive spirit of modern Germany, and *Kultur,* at least for Lavisse, originated with Fichte.

Of all the French scholars who addressed themselves to the intellectual origins of pan-Germanism, only Victor Basch, who taught German at the University of Paris, chose to defend Fichte from Lavisse's charge. Fichte, he insisted, was a "mystical Jacobin," a defender of individual liberties, and a worthy heir of an honorable philosophical tradition. His ideas had nothing in common with the aggressive nationalism and brutal expansionism of Wilhelmine Germany. Indeed, Basch asserted—somewhat implausibly—that there was not a trace of pan-Germanist mentality in Fichte's thought.[21] Few of Basch's colleagues agreed. Emile Boutroux, in a much-cited essay published in October 1914, wrote that Fichte was responsible for his nation's cultural conviction that Germany was distinct from and superior to the nations of the West; that German superiority was both a sign of divine grace and a justification for German aggression; and, consequently, that God had ordained the subjugation of Western Europe by Germany to bring about the moral improvement of the world.[22] In the spring of 1915, Victor Delbos, a colleague of Boutroux and Basch and a highly respected Kant scholar at the Sorbonne, expanded upon these themes. Not only had the early-nineteenth-century German Idealists abandoned the essential balance and moderation of their eighteenth-century predecessors—Delbos regretted their tendency to push every concept to its extreme—but they had also established the philosophical foundations of pan-German aggression. According to Delbos, when Fichte insisted in the *Addresses to the German Nation* that the Germans constituted a chosen people, he deviated significantly from established German philosophical tradition and set German philosophy on a new course. Thereafter German philosophy concentrated on immanent and particular ideas of nation and race, and abandoned philosophical inquiry into "the pure idea of truth." From Fichte's notion that Germany represented "the privileged depositary of culture and philosophy" Hegel went on to identify Prussia as the Idea made immanent in history. As such, Prussia was not bound by recognized moral restraints; it became instead "absolute power . . . God on earth."[23]

Lavisse, Delbos, and Boutroux were only the most prominent of many French scholars who identified Fichte as the progenitor, and nineteenth-century Idealism as the inspiration, of pan-Germanism. When Professor Edmond Goblot delivered a lecture to the Faculty of Letters at the University of Lyon in February 1915, he called the *Addresses to the German*

Nation "the philosophical origin of German madness." Goblot regretted that Fichte's famous text, translated into French only in 1895, had heretofore been little read in France, because he believed that the French could understand their adversary only if they understood properly the character and intellectual origins of German nationalism. Although Goblot was convinced that Fichte's work had been the "origin of pan-Germanism," he recognized that the philosopher's arguments in defense of German national identity were not identical in every detail to the arguments of later pan-Germanists.[24] Fichte, for example, had never argued that German superiority gave the German people the right to impose their will outside of Germany's natural boundaries. Indeed, Goblot considered the *Addresses* an "act of courage" because they were intended to inspire the German people to liberate themselves from the indignity of foreign domination.[25] Yet the *Addresses* had incubated the germ of German aggression, for Fichte had insisted that the German people represented a pure race, which, unsullied by cross-cultural contact, was superior to all others.

The dangerous but perhaps inchoate implications of the *Addresses to the German Nation* became frighteningly evident when Hegel, also a witness to Prussian defeat in 1807, expanded upon Fichte's notions of the national identity and innate superiority of the German people. This was clear to both Delbos and Edmond Barthélemy. Writing in the *Mercure de France* in June 1915, Barthélemy argued that German politics and German philosophy in the modern age, although direct products of Kantian and Fichtean transcendental idealism, found their true voice in Hegel, "the most representative of all Germans."[26] For the historian Pierre Imbart de la Tour, who believed—as did Lavisse—that German historians as well as German philosophers had contributed directly to the development of pan-Germanism, Hegel's philosophy of history constituted a critical juncture in German thought. Imbart de la Tour insisted that German expansionism was a direct consequence of a philosophy of history "which proclaims as a fact, a right, and a law the disappearance of small nations, the hegemony of German power throughout the world, and the triumph of Germanism." German historians of the early nineteenth century had argued that Germany constituted a distinct racial community that aspired constantly to internal autonomy and external hegemony. Spurning contact with its neighbors and resisting any foreign influences, Germany nonetheless yearned to dominate and impose its will on those people and nations who surrounded her. The philosophical justification for this political agenda was to be found in Hegel's philosophy of history. If the Idea that animates human history is instantiated in a nation or a state, and if its progression is inevitable and irresistible, then the nation that represents the advance of the Idea in history is endowed with an almost divine power to dominate others. "The Idea marches towards its final end with an irresistible élan, and this élan affects the entire world. Those that resist its force are vanquished, condemned to defeat and to historical oblivion."[27]

When Imbart de la Tour condemned the Hegelian notion of inevitable historical progression, he brought to his critique of nineteenth-century German Idealism an explicitly Bergsonian rejection of mechanistic determinism. For Imbart de la Tour, Hegel's philosophy of history, with its emphasis on the Idea as an indomitable force of development and progress, was both monocausal and mechanistic. It posited a progression through history that deprived individuals of free will: with their actions determined by forces beyond themselves, they became not agents but instruments of historical change. Such a philosophy of history failed to allow for the agency of individuals, and especially of individual genius, in history; it failed to contemplate the possibility of the unpredictable; and it stripped all history and all human action of moral freedom. If what happened in history was preordained, it was necessarily endowed with a moral authority that surpassed human understanding. The actual and the moral thus merged under the aegis of historical determinism, and might, which brought about change in history, became right. This criticism of Germany as "mechanistic"—functioning according to direct laws of material cause and effect—figured prominently in the critiques of *Kultur* articulated by both Paul Appell and Henri Bergson.

In his presidential address to the Institut de France delivered on October 26, 1914, Appell argued that the war had brought into play "two opposing conceptions" of human civilization. Although the two military forces that confronted one another across the trenches of northern France were of comparable material strength, their moral characters were "entirely different." Appell argued, and Bergson agreed, that Germany could boast "impeccable organization, lengthy, systematic detailed preparation . . . and the practical application of the most recent scientific discoveries." But behind the admirable material organization of the German Army was a most disturbing moral precept: Germany had come to believe that "Force, when organized and disciplined to perfection, creates Right, and is superior to all else: to the Truth, to treaties, to oral commitments, to the idea of fraternal freedom, and to respect for humanity and its works."[28] Borrowing a phrase that Jean-François de la Harpe had coined in the eighteenth century, Bergson captured the imagination of the nation's intellectual elite when he described this combination of organization, technical skill, and materialist indifference to moral law as "scientific barbarism."[29]

Upon assuming the presidency of the Académie des Sciences Morales et Politiques in December 1914, Bergson reminded his colleagues that through the eighteenth century two traditions had coexisted in Germany: one of metaphysical reverie, another of material realism. This latter tradition, which Bergson identified expressly with Prussia, was, he contended, the product of an "artificial" culture and a "mechanistic" worldview. Insofar as Prussia represented nothing more than the political will of the Hohenzollerns, it was not a "natural" political entity; yet since its emergence on the European stage, it had demonstrated the efficacy "of bending science to the satisfaction of material needs." This reliance on material power had become most evident in the nineteenth century, when Prussia, sustained by the century's faith in science, had applied its indisputable talents for organization, discipline, and tenacity to the domination of the material world. The nation flourished economically and militarily in the process, and came to believe in the divine character of material force: "if force had accomplished this miracle [of prosperity and power], if force had bestowed [on Prussia] glory and wealth, it could only be because force harbored within itself a mysterious, and divine, virtue."[30] By 1870, Prussian successes suggested to other German observers that material force was indeed endowed with divine authority. Having brought about the unification of Germany, Prussian might had achieved an indisputable moral stature. German culture thus succumbed to "scientific barbarism" because, following the lead of Prussia, it had come to honor material power as an expression of moral authority.

Bergson's exposé of "scientific barbarism," Imbart de la Tour's condemnation of Hegelian determinism, and Appell's castigation of German mechanism were all important elements of an extensive French critique of *Kultur*. When read together, these and comparable arguments suggested that German aggression was neither an accident nor a defensive reaction to a perceived danger of encirclement. Rather, aggression was the inevitable product of a nation's conviction that it constituted a superior, divinely ordained force in history. That conviction was, in turn, the logical consequence of an intellectual tradition—fostered by philosophers and historians alike—that bestowed moral authority on material force. *Kultur* was indeed inextricably linked to German militarism not because, as the German signatories claimed, it depended upon military might for its survival, but because *Kultur* begat militarism: "this brutal and inhuman militarism is indistinguishable from *Kultur*, it is its ultimate expression, its essential form."[31] The aggressive spirit of expansionism in Wilhelmine Germany grew out of an intellectual tradition that identified the German people as a chosen race, that endowed historical progression with a priori moral legitimacy, and that perceived in the state the voice of divine authority.

With its sustained assault on pan-Germanism, characterized most particularly by a persistent exposé of the intellectual origins of pan-German ambition, the French intelligentsia did more than assert German responsibility for the war; they also sought to explain— to themselves as much as to their audience—why German scholars had abandoned intellectual objectivity in their enthusiastic endorsement of the Manifesto of 93. Behind the protests and manifestos, the addresses and lengthy essays explaining German actions, there was evident within the discourse of the French intelligentsia a sense of dismay and disbelief. The Manifesto of 93, which Alfred Croiset lamented as one of several "scandalous manifestos recently signed by the most authentic representatives of [German] culture," suggested to indignant French scholars a serious lack of intellectual integrity and objectivity within the highest echelons of the German academy.[32] Willing to approve the violation of treaties and determined to deny German atrocities, in spite of evidence that made denials ludicrous, the German intelligentsia had, it seemed, lost its capacity for independent judgment and had become "anti-scientific."[33] Across the ideological spectrum, French scholars lamented this loss of scholarly objectivity. The scholars of the Institut Catholique perceived in the Manifesto of 93 no evidence of dispassionate reason. It was shot through with "passion and prejudice" that precluded honest analysis. Abandoning reason, evidence, and established standards of scholarly inquiry, the "ninety-three" had betrayed their vocation. Lucien Maury made this same point in the first issue of the *Revue bleue* to appear after the outbreak of war: by endorsing the Manifesto of 93, German intellectuals had "abdicated their intellectual independence and in the process [had] renounced their authority."[34]

Historians and scientists, whose respect for incontrovertible evidence defined their methodologies, were particularly alarmed by the evidence of scholarly servility suggested by the Manifesto of 93. The editors of the *Revue historique*, determined to maintain the academic character of their journal in spite of the exceptional circumstances, were appalled by the alacrity with which their German colleagues had abandoned scholarly methods. Charles Bémont and Christian Pfister lamented the signatories' loss of objectivity: instead of evaluating the available evidence, they had merely asserted the righteousness of the German cause; they had not demonstrated why the German war effort required the destruction of cultural monuments, but only asserted the necessity of such actions.[35] French scientists likewise regretted their German colleagues' apparent willingness to forfeit truth to patriotism. Like Bémont and Pfister, Albert Dastre, Director of the Ecole des Hautes Etudes and President of the Société de Biologie, criticized the signatories of the manifesto for having abandoned the scientific spirit.[36] Appell, who refused on principle to invoke the institutional authority of the Institut de France against the signatories, avoided direct mention of the German scholars in his presidential address. But he obliquely suggested disapproval of their actions: Germany, he told his colleagues, was so convinced that force was "superior to all else" that it had sacrificed truth—"la Verité"—on the altar of national interest. Those whose vocation compelled them to protect the truth, and whose actions could have defended the truth from its attackers, must ultimately be held accountable for this ignoble offering.[37] More than a year later, Charles Nordmann, writing in the *Revue des deux mondes,* made the same point more explicitly, when he argued that Wilhelm Ostwald, one of Germany's most celebrated chemists, had forfeited truth to the cause of national interest when he attached his signature to the Manifesto of 93.[38]

How could so many of the men with whom French scholars had communicated, corresponded, and cultivated friendships, have erred so gravely in judgment? What explained their willingness to abandon principle and intellectual integrity? Where, in effect, had the German intelligentsia gone wrong? The French found an answer to these disturbing questions in the cultural background that had formed the intellectuals. In their indictment of *Kultur* as the progenitor of pan-Germanism, French scholars asserted that German ideology, from at least Fichte onwards, was directly responsible for the aggressive, materialistic mind-set of modern Germany. As participants within and perpetrators of a cultural tradition that cultivated obedience rather than intellectual independence, that placed the interests of the state above the demands of intellectual inquiry, and that justified even illegal, immoral, and ignominious deeds, by appeals to raisons d'état, the signatories of the Manifesto of 93 had become, in the final analysis, incapable of independent judgment.

Although Imbart de la Tour did not mention the signatories of the German manifesto by name, his analysis of German historiography informed by Hegelian principles did propose—albeit obliquely—an explanation for their action. Hegel's philosophy of history endowed the State, as the instrument of the Idea in history, with an authority that made obedience to its will inescapable; Hegel thus granted the State and all its endeavors a moral authority that justified all its actions. This made individual moral actions necessarily subordinate to the will of the State: "It is only insofar as the individual participates in the State that he is capable of truth, morality, and freedom; because only the State possesses true freedom, which is to say the absence of all limits." Such a philosophy of history, according to which the state represents the genuine interests of all individuals, eliminates all discord between the interests of individuals and the interests of the state; obedience to the state thus becomes "a duty."[39] German scholars, Imbart de la Tour argued, were by no means immune to the logic of this argument. Convinced by a succession of German historians and philosophers of history that the German people constituted a distinct race and the German state a divinely ordained political authority to which obedience was due, they had voluntarily relinquished their independence of judgment and offered their obedience to the state.

German scholars and men of letters were more susceptible than most of their fellow citizens to the dangerous allure of the German cultural tradition because of their involvement with the nation's educational system. Several French commentators held German education and pedagogy ultimately responsible for the manifesto and the spirit of intellectual servility evident therein. Lavisse and Andler insisted that it was the nation's "universities, colleges, schools, the clergy and the press" which disseminated most effectively and most broadly the pan-German gospel.[40] Emile Hovelaque, who as Inspector of Schools held one of the most elevated positions within the French educational establishment, made the same point in almost identical words.[41] And Professor Goblot, careful to distinguish between Fichtean ideals and subsequent abuses of those ideals, also spoke of the moral burden German education carried with it. Fichte had recognized that political autonomy could be achieved only through a process of national education. But his vision of national schooling, derived equally from the pedagogical arguments of Rousseau and the Italian educational reformer Pestalozzi, and the moral precepts of Immanuel Kant, was progressive and liberal. Fichte believed that national education would create a "republic of free and reasoning people in which each individual is at once a legislator and a subject and in which all recognize one another as an *end in itself*." Over time, however, Fichte's principles, liberating in themselves, were "altered, deformed, and vulgarized." From Fichte's vision of a republic of free, autonomous citizens, the Prussian state constructed a system of public education that created "blind and docile subjects."[42]

According to M. Fridel-Cortelet, who contributed an article to *La Grande Revue* in October 1915, none was more docile in its acceptance nor more blind in the embrace of the Prussian state than the German professoriate. Fridel-Cortelet, who clearly appreciated the power of an arresting phrase, borrowed from a prewar essay the captivating title: "Der Professor ist die deutsche Nationalkrankheit" (The Professor is the German National Disease). He did not pretend to be original in this regard; in fact, his intention was to bring to his readers' attention an overlooked essay of the same title written by a M. Raphaël in 1908. Even his title had been consciously imitative; it derived originally from a phrase in Julius Langbehn's *Rembrandt as Educator*. However it was used, the point was unambiguous: when perceived as a form of cultural illness, German education was not something to emulate but something to abhor.

Raphaël had observed, and Fridel-Cortelet concurred, that the principal failing of German education, most evident in secondary and higher education, was that it destroyed independence of thought. A curriculum that required students to spend at least twenty-five hours in the classroom each week was neither liberating nor educational; rather, it "wore out the body, harassed the mind, and killed all personal initiative in intelligent students." The culture of the classroom, which compelled students to submit to the rigors of a barracks-like existence and the implacable demands of absolute obedience, cultivated an unquestioning acceptance of absolutist authority. The schools, having destroyed the intellectual curiosity and vitality of their students, succeeded masterfully in creating "a people docile and robust, firmly attached to national institutions." For all their pedagogical faults, such schools were without doubt a "marvelous instrument of government," for they gave moral strength to the "fortress of absolutism."[43]

However much students suffered under this yoke of excessive work, inadequate inspiration, and oppressive authority, they were not alone. Teachers, too, had to submit to the rigorous discipline of the national school system, and had to suppress any inclination to independence of thought. "All originality, all initiative became suspect. It was essential that one conform to innumerable orders, regulations, circulars, impose silence on one's spirit of independence and accept passivity as a duty and routine as a rule."[44] The schools had the cumulative effect of creating a national culture suspicious of foreigners, submissive to authority, and indoctrinated with love of country. "Professors, scholars, scientists, industrialists, and workers . . . all accept Prussian militarism as necessary to national life, and all are imbued with the cult of force and the habit of discipline. Inside everyone, from the first to the last, from the most distinguished to the most humble, resided the spirit of a Prussian corporal."[45] The "cult of force" and the "habit of discipline" inculcated in the German professoriate explained the supine submissiveness of those who signed the Manifesto of 93.

The Debate over Intellectual Action

So disturbing was the evidence of German intellectual servility that some French writers and scholars came to question the appropriateness of intellectual action itself. A handful of writers wondered aloud whether it was fitting for French intellectuals in their responses to the Manifesto of 93 to resort to German techniques and tactics. By issuing manifestos of their own, did not French intellectuals imitate and thus honor the much-reviled methods of their enemy? Gonzague Truc, writing in *La Grande Revue,* believed that French intellectuals should not have responded in kind to the "sordid levée of pens from across the Rhine"; they should have gone about their business as usual or found something "useful" to do: "it [was] not glorious to leave one's ranks except to receive fire."[46] In 1915 Dr. Grasset, a highly respected contributor to French medicine, refused, very politely, to provide an essay comparing the contributions of German and French scientists to medicine, because he feared that to do so would be to repeat the error of the German signatories. They had abandoned their true forum and had stepped beyond the bounds of their expertise when they discussed details of international law and denied accounts of German atrocities. Since no scientific knowledge informed their opinions, they spoke not as scientists but as citizens; yet they presented their opinions under the guise of their intellectual authority, and that was fundamentally dishonest. Grasset would not compound the error of German scientists by responding in kind.[47]

Francis de Miomandre believed that French literary and cultural leaders who had signed the Manifesto of 100 were similarly misguided in their actions, if not in their intentions. Imitation only honored the tactics of the enemy. He contended that manifestos, *enquêtes,* and petitions were fundamentally Germanic in spirit; their validity was asserted by an appeal to numbers rather than an appeal to reason. De Miomandre reminded his readers that the nation of Descartes established truth through irrefutable arguments, and he insisted that the time had come for France to liberate itself from imported, and essentially erroneous, intellectual habits; the French needed to remember that "a good argument and an apt citation" would always suffice. Intellectual action might be appropriate, but only if it shunned the methods and epistemological assumptions of German science.[48]

The most famous denunciation of intellectual action in thrall to national interests was, of course, Romain Rolland's essay, "Au-dessus de la mêlée" (Above the Fray). Originally published in September 1914, the essay railed against intellectuals on both sides of the Rhine who had abandoned their intellectual objectivity to become handmaidens of the state and apologists for all-out war. Rolland feared that in their enthusiasm for their nation's war effort all had lost sight of the essential internationalism of the life of the mind. Reminding French and German scholars alike that they had been nurtured by an international culture, he urged them to remain committed to its preservation. Men of intellect, dedicated to the pursuit of universal principles, should distance themselves from the passions of the moment. Duty-bound to defend eternal truths from the insidious, corrosive effects of national passion, they should unite in common cause "above the fray" in pursuit of international brotherhood.[49]

During the war, "Au-dessus de la mêlée" won few supporters in France. While the nation was at war, and its territory subjected to foreign occupation, the neutrality Rolland preached found few converts, either in the nation at large or in the ranks of the French intelligentsia. In April 1915, Henri Massis responded directly to Rolland with a characteristically acerbic denunciation of the internationalism and humanitarianism that informed the essay. Conceiving of the war as a Manichean struggle between good and evil, Massis contended that every man "worthy of the name" had a duty to defend the cause of France by "pursu[ing] and combat[ing] error." Each one had to "take a position, be a man, and not refuse to serve."[50] To the man who had "deserted" his country and his countrymen in their hour of greatest need, Massis retorted that neutrality and nonparticipation were no longer appropriate.

Even more interesting, given his subsequent denunciation of intellectual engagement inspired by nationalist passion, was Julien Benda's repudiation of Rolland, published in 1916. Benda agreed that since the beginning of the war some French scholars had indeed dishonored themselves with their base, unrefined, and unreflective denigration of Germany and its people. But this was not true of those who spoke out against the enemy from positions of intellectual authority. Citing Bergson's denunciation of German barbarism, Benda argued that individuals who resolved to use scholarship and reason to discredit the claims of the German intelligentsia and to defend the cause of justice did not deserve Rolland's condemnation. "The greatest minds [in France] did not believe that they had been untrue to their vocation if in rendering harsh judgments they had believed them to be just."[51] Justice was more important than kindness. When Rolland called upon men of principle on both sides of the Rhine to love their enemy and to unite in a spirit of international brotherhood that transcended national loyalties, he mistook what was at stake in the war. For Benda, the true function of the intellectual was to speak the truth and defend the cause of justice, and if that entailed defending the victims of aggression and denouncing the aggressor, so be it.

Benda's response to Rolland expressed a sentiment common to many French writers and scholars: French intellectual action was legitimate because it was fundamentally different in spirit from that practiced in Germany. On this point Catholic and anticlerical scholars found themselves in agreement. In defense of his countrymen, Alfred Croiset recalled that the Romans had proved adept imitators of their enemies and had conquered their foes in part through timely acts of imitation.[52] The faculty of the Institut Catholique pledged that in their efforts to expose as patently false German affirmations of innocence, they would scrupulously respect established standards of scholarly inquiry. Like their republican counterparts on the Committee for Documents and Studies on the War, they promised to support each of their own points with references to "the published diplomatic documents of several powers, public inquiries executed with a scrupulous respect for accuracy, and personal experience." Such evidence would prove that Germany had planned and prepared for war; had willfully rejected any efforts to avoid conflict through diplomatic negotiation; and had prosecuted the war in such a way as to "push civilization back to the age of the barbarian invasions."[53]

Paul Flat, editor-in-chief of the highly regarded *Revue bleue*, also failed to see either danger or dishonor in imitation. Convinced that the Institut, and especially the Académie Française, had a moral obligation to participate actively in the war effort, he argued that it was both essential and honorable that the Institut engage in intellectual action. Indeed Flat publicly chastised the institute for not having rallied sooner to the cause of intellectual action, and was openly critical of the Académie des Sciences for its tardy response to the manifesto.[54] It was not fitting for intellectuals to take refuge in silence and apparent indifference to the problems of the everyday; and they certainly should not leave political life and political issues to the politicians, because "only if intellectuals actively involved themselves in political life would the incompetence of politicians be avoided or overcome." He applauded those intellectuals, who "have understood that they have to fight with the weapons unique to them: the pen and the word, alongside those who fight in the trenches."[55]

Like Benda, Paul Flat distinguished the intellectual action of his compatriots, which he defined as dedicated to the pursuit of truth, from that of German intellectuals, who had "militarized themselves in the name of destruction and shame." The French scholars who "mobilized themselves" acted "from the depths of their souls and in full awareness of their spiritual duty."[56] With more than a modicum of self-righteous congratulation, Flat's subjects concurred with his assessment. Lucien Maury went so far as to define French intellect as essentially "disinterested."[57] Committed only to the pursuit of truth and the articulation of fundamental principles, French intellectuals entered the fray because they were convinced—as scholars rather than as patriots—that a German victory would mean the end of honest and free intellectual inquiry. The Manifesto of 93 proved to the world that Germany disdained the truth, was indifferent to the dictates of honest inquiry, and disrespectful of the fundamental methods of scholarship. The French would demonstrate that even if truth, honesty, and rigorous inquiry were now scorned in Germany, they were still honored in France.

This was the essential message of Etienne Lamy's address to his colleagues within the Institut de France in 1915. Convinced that the international reputation of French scholarship—and hence the efficacy of intellectual action—depended upon the preservation of scholarly first principles, he was adamant in his insistence that intellectuals could retain their unique authority and prove effective in the public arena only if they conquered their passions and continued to speak the truth:

> Whoever, wishing to instruct others on the facts of the war, allows himself from the beginning to be dominated by intense nationalist fever, informs himself of current popular opinion in order to make his opinions consistent with it, and from the beginning has his mind made

up, might be an admirable patriot . . . but he is not a judge. A judge is one whose curiosity is dictated by his conscience and whose conscience resists popular opinion; thus he imposes silence on his sentiments and on his legitimate antipathies.

Lamy implored his fellow intellectuals to remember always that honesty and objectivity should never succumb to national fervor: if the facts do not warrant a certain conclusion, do not draw it; if the failings of one's adversaries can be explained by extenuating circumstances, then such circumstances should not be ignored. However passionately he desired victory for France, the French intellectual should not blind himself to the truth: to the German cry of "Deutschland über alles," the Frenchman should respond: "Above all else, truth."[58]

This was a compelling argument, indeed. Calling upon French men of intellect to distinguish themselves from their German counterparts by honoring the truth, Lamy insisted that they could prove their patriotism by remaining true to their scholarly principles. Such an argument spoke directly to French scientists, who were as adamant in their defense of intellectual honesty as they were outraged by their German counterparts' abandonment of it. Objective, honest assessment of all available evidence was so essential to the scientific enterprise that to abandon it to patriotic fervor was, they feared, to forsake science itself. Charles Richet, Nobel laureate for chemistry in 1913, wrote in the spring of 1915 that he "did not wish, as a result of his ardent patriotism, to abandon himself to iniquity and error"; however much he despised the German leadership for provoking the war, he would speak the truth about German accomplishments in the natural sciences.[59] So, too, would Georges Lemoine, of the Académie des Sciences, who argued that it would be "unjust" to deny the genuine achievements of truly talented German chemists. That was also the feeling of Pierre Duhem, a renowned theoretical physicist who was unimpressed by Einstein but genuinely appreciative of the seminal contributions to physics of Carl Frederick Gauss and Hermann von Helmholtz.[60] Unlike their counterparts across the Rhine, whom French scholars repeatedly criticized for refusing to recognize any merit in the intellectual accomplishments of the enemy, French scientists would show the world that in their ranks at least patriotism had not effaced intellectual honesty.[61]

Intellectual honesty required that French scholars in other fields also give due credit to German accomplishments. Historian Charles Langlois, who with Charles Seignobos had written a textbook of historiographical method, did not hesitate to give credit to German leadership in his field.[62]

Alfred Croiset confessed that he had no desire to deny the obvious achievements of German scholars. For Croiset, a frank assessment of the intellectual power of the enemy was a patriotic duty. France gained nothing by denying Germany its due, and stood to lose a great deal if it ignored or underestimated the power of its adversary: "one cannot defeat that which one does not know, and it is dangerous not to know" one's enemy.[63] For others, to give credit to the enemy was a question of personal credibility. Had Langlois denied the merits of German scholarship, he would have done as much to damage his own intellectual credibility as that of the enemy. Because he was well known for his prewar admiration of German scholarship, honesty and honor prevented him, as it prevented Croiset, from now denouncing it as unworthy.

When Victor Basch resolved to examine "with complete impartiality, and with the sole preoccupation of seeing clearly and speaking truly" the putative connections between German philosophy and German aggression, he lived up to Lamy's standards of scholarly inquiry.[64] Defending both Fichte and Hegel from the charge of pan-Germanism, he presented an interpretation that went too far for even his most distinguished colleagues to endorse, and in the process demonstrated how well his conscience could resist the powerful pull of popular opinion. Moreover, in publishing Basch's essay, the *Revue de métaphysique et de morale* allowed for the free expression of independent opinion.

Other scholars proved less successful, however, at "imposing silence on their sentiments" and mastering their "legitimate antipathies." Emile Hovelaque, who believed he had a "duty" to understand the enemy with "cold clarity," resolved to "master within himself all feelings of revulsion in order to look directly at this monstrous Germany." But when in one sentence he described the German people as beset by all the "faults of the parvenu: vulgarity, presumptuousness, and tyrannical aggressiveness"; lamented "German pedantry, Prussian brutality" and condemned the "innate grossness of spirit and the incurable puerility of a race that cannot be civilized," his feelings of revulsion—his "legitimate antipathies"—clearly got the better of him.[65] Even the most distinguished French scholars were hard-pressed to contain their hatred of the enemy. With their scholarly investigations of alleged atrocities, Lavisse, Andler, and Bédier hoped to demonstrate not only that German denials were untenable but that the French intellectual community remained committed to recognized, honored methods of academic inquiry. Unlike the signatories of the Manifesto of 93, who merely asserted German innocence, the French respondents would provide incontrovertible proof that Germany was guilty as charged. Yet the sensationalistic tone with which *The German Theory and Practice of War* opened was far from scholarly. Determined to prove that atrocity tales were not exaggerated, Lavisse and Andler discussed in the first twenty pages of their inquiry four kinds of atrocity: "Murders," "Pillaging and Burning," "Hostages," and "Outrages." Employing a staccato-like syntax that captured the horror of German aggression in graphic, but consciously incomplete, sentence fragments, they wrote of "filthy bestiality let loose," "nuns outraged," and young girls killed. So horrible were the scenes of murder, mayhem, and rape that Lavisse and Andler lost their customary eloquence; all they could say on one occasion was "the outrage effected; fifteen soldiers."[66] Lurid tales and consciously incomplete sentences that did more to excite the imagination than protect gentle sensibilities or prove the guilt of the "fifteen soldiers" pandered to readers' baser instincts and dispensed with cool, dispassionate reason.

Equally disingenuous were those who damned the enemy with fulsome praise. René Pichon, writing in the *Revue des deux mondes,* acknowledged German contributions to the study of classical history. Adopting the same tone of generous recognition evident in other works of wartime scholarship, he insisted that he had no intention of denying "that German erudition, highly respected as it was, had its merits and rendered service [to the intellectual community], that it was diligent, patient, often ingenious, sometimes original and fecund." Nor did he begrudge Theodor Mommsen, Germany's renowned classical scholar, his obvious abilities: he was "indefatigable" in his application, "almost infallible" in his documentation, and "original and penetrating" in his interpretations. Indeed, Pichon denied that he intended any "systematic denigration" of Mommsen or his scholarship. Yet the purpose of Pichon's essay was to demonstrate that Mommsen was directly, albeit not uniquely, responsible for the "mentality of modern Germany." To this end, he spent the subsequent thirty pages of his article calling into question the quality of Mommsen's masterwork. For Pichon, this highly acclaimed analysis of ancient Rome was essentially "mechanistic" in its methodology: Mommsen's documentation was like "a well-ordered army, well-equipped and fully supplied, impeccable and formidable" but essentially lacking in human spirit. The master historian could marshal material resources, but he could not conquer his subject because he—like other German scholars—lacked the subtlety of psychological insight. When called upon to appreciate the qualities of non-German peoples, Mommsen proved himself mean-spirited. When required to understand the past, he was handicapped by the pervasive present-mindedness of his scholarship: "Mommsen, while dealing with the subject-matter of the past, was thinking only of the present-day. He always had in front of him, and uppermost in his mind, his own society, with its problems and its struggles." Ultimately, Mommsen's "history was as much a work of propaganda as a work of scholarship."[67] But so was Pichon's essay.

Although such evidence suggests that the objectivity of French intellectual action was, on occasion at least, more imaginary than real, it is nonetheless significant that aspirations to intellectual objectivity should have figured prominently in French scholarly discourse throughout the war. By acclaiming objectivity and honesty, scholars could suggest that truth was on the side of France; there was no need for the lies and misrepresentations that were the intellectual currency of wartime Germany. There was, however, also a political message embedded in the many encomia to intellectual honesty. French scholars could speak honestly—even about the enemy—because their nation defended freedom in all its guises. This was certainly the message of both Paul Appell and Alfred Croiset at the outset of the war. Appell believed that Germany was burdened with its tragically misguided mechanistic conception of moral authority because it lacked liberty: "this mechanistic conception, from which both intelligence and respect for the feelings of others are completely excluded, rests on a rigidly established social hierarchy." Because hierarchy demanded obedience, it precluded independence of thought and destroyed intellect. By contrast, France, infused with the principles of 1789, fought to defend Liberty and Justice for all.[68] Croiset concurred. The spirit of the Revolution inspired the French Army to defend freedom, secure justice, and preserve truth.[69] The French determination to speak the truth was therefore an intellectual obligation sustained by a political inheritance. Republican scholars proclaimed, and attempted to uphold, freedom of expression and intellectual inquiry because they could thereby demonstrate that—censorship notwithstanding—freedom, crushed in Germany, still thrived in the Third Republic.

By early 1915 Gaston Deschamps could write in the *Revue hebdomadaire* without any exaggeration that "we have all read with a feeling of horror combined with disgust this 'manifesto'."[70] And it was the unanimity of French revulsion that prompted contemporary observers to speak of the emergence of an intellectual *union sacrée*. It is true that in their eagerness to denounce the manifesto, French intellectuals found much upon which they could agree: the infamous

ninety-three had forfeited their right to be considered true men of intellect; *Kultur* with its pervasive amoral mechanism had perverted their
judgment and had directed Germany along a path of aggression and
atrocities. Professional French scholars and writers were convinced that
ideas had led Germany astray. They, by contrast, determined to remain
true to the French cultural tradition of free inquiry and scholarly objectivity, thereby distinguishing their intellectual action from that of the
enemy, and defining France as the cultural antithesis of all that prevailed
in Germany. On these points, agreement did exist.

The Manifesto of 93 did *not*, however, create a genuine intellectual
consensus in France. It raised disturbing questions about the civic responsibilities of intellectuals that generated some disagreement within
the intellectual community. More critically, the debates that the manifesto engendered exposed fundamental divisions within the French intellectual community, divisions that had animated the intellectual discord
of the prewar years and that did not disappear after August 1914. When
scholars moved beyond their common faith that *Kultur* was responsible
for German militarism and debated the deep implications of their attack
on *Kultur*, they disagreed vehemently among themselves. Three issues in
particular proved disruptive of the intellectual peace: the nature of the
German philosophical tradition; the character of French classicism; and
the legitimacy of science. Insofar as these intellectual debates arose in
response to the assertions and implications of the Manifesto of 93, they
illuminated serious sectarian fault-lines within the French intelligentsia
that anodyne appeals to a *union sacrée* could not obscure.

CHAPTER FOUR

The Controversy
over Kant

The campaign against *Kultur* did not create scholarly unanimity in the ranks of the French intelligentsia, for although most French intellectuals could agree that *Kultur* was responsible for the outbreak of war, they could not agree on exactly what *Kultur* was. Specifically, they disagreed vehemently over one major figure: was Immanuel Kant part of, or to be exempted from, the tradition of *Kultur* defended by the German intellectuals? The signatories of the "Appeal to the Civilized World" had insisted that modern Germany remained loyal to the spirit of Goethe and Beethoven and to the principles of Kant. French scholars rejected these assertions; some claimed that Goethe was essentially French in spirit, while others identified Beethoven as Flemish. But the real debate within France occurred over Kant. Republicans sympathetic to Kant's ethical and political philosophy employed the "two Germanies" thesis to argue persuasively that the author of *The Metaphysics of Morals* and *Perpetual Peace* would have disavowed the aggressive spirit of contemporary Germany. But two camps were as hostile to Kant as republican scholars were hospitable. Catholics, outraged by the secularism of modern society which they attributed to German Protestantism and Kantian epistemology, and neoroyalists, for whom Kant's notion of autonomy was nothing but an invitation to anarchy, placed him squarely within the realm of *Kultur*.

For France in 1914, Kant was bound to be a controversial figure. A German, and hence automatically suspect, he was, however, a well-known admirer of the French Revolution, of Rousseau, and of individual autonomy. An enemy of all opponents of republicanism, Kant was a valuable ally of those who would defend the Third Republic from internal opposition. Advocates of republicanism found in Kantian texts the philosophical foundations that sustained their political faith. Thus to denounce Kant as a progenitor of pan-Germanism would be to undermine the very legitimacy of republicanism. Kantian principles, always important to the preservation of the Republic, acquired an even greater relevance during the war. In a nation committed to individual rights but dependent for its very survival on the willingness of its citizens to do their duty, Kant's doctrine of duty—articulated in the famous "categorical imperative" that one should "act only according to that maxim by which one can at the same time will that it should become a universal law"—seemed to offer a philosophical justification for national sacrifice. And with his prescription for "perpetual peace," predicated upon the creation of an international organization committed to collective security, Kant offered a blueprint for postwar security. For scholars antecedently committed to the preservation of peace through international cooperation—as were those affiliated with the League for the Rights of Man and the Citizen and the Association of Peace through Law—Kant's work was indispensable.

During the war years two Kantian texts proved of critical importance to the republicans' case: the first part of *The Metaphysics of Morals* (1797), in which Kant gave specific content to the moral principles set forth initially in the *Foundations of the Metaphysics of Morals* (1785), and *Perpetual Peace* (1796). Within these texts two principles central to Kant's political and moral philosophy proved particularly compelling: that individuals as rational beings are autonomous moral agents with certain rights and duties directly entailed by their pure practical reason; and that as free rational beings they are bound only by those laws to which they have given their a priori assent. By contrast, those who identified Kant as part of an unbroken cultural tradition that began with Luther and culminated with the Kaiser paid little attention to his political philosophy. Rather, they based their critique of Kant on his epistemology and his moral philosophy. Neo-Thomists, convinced that knowledge of real essences (or things-in-themselves, as Kant would have it) was possible, found Kant's epistemology fundamentally unacceptable and considered Kant's ethics a logical (but lamentable) extension of an epistemology indifferent to metaphysics and theology. Neoroyalists, less concerned with underlying epistemological assumptions, were, however, equally antipathetic to Kant's moral philosophy. By situating moral authority in the hands of the autonomous moral agent, Kant undermined hierarchy and endorsed principles of revolutionary governance.

Whether practiced by republicans or neoroyalists, selective textual analysis corresponded to distinct political objectives. Those who cited *Perpetual Peace* had a clear postwar agenda in view; but so, too, did those who castigated Kant's epistemological and moral "subjectivism." In neither camp, therefore, was the analysis of Kant entirely disinterested. This is not to say that genuine differences over philosophical principles played no part in the French debate. It is only to point out that philosophical debate in the context of wartime France was also, and perhaps inevitably, intensely political.

French Republicanism and the Defense of Kant

Even before the publication of the Manifesto of 93, Emile Boutroux insisted that Kant could in no way be held accountable for the coming of war. In a letter written in late September 1914 and published in the *Revue des deux mondes* in mid-November, he drew upon his detailed knowledge of German philosophy to argue that until 1870 there had been two distinct philosophical traditions evident in Germany. He did not deny that pan-German ideas had taken root in nineteenth-century Germany: as a visiting student at Heidelberg in 1869–70, he had been subjected to such sentiments. But he had also witnessed a cosmopolitanism in the actions and attitudes of some of his German hosts, an attitude completely at odds with the one inspired by Fichte's *Addresses to the German Nation*. Remembering this "other" Germany, Boutroux argued in 1914 that the cosmopolitanism he had observed in pre-Wilhelmine Germany derived from the universal and humanitarian tradition best exemplified by Leibniz and Kant.[1] German philosophy of the seventeenth and eighteenth centuries had aspired to the reconciliation of opposites, the attainment of freedom for the individual, and the recognition of the moral equality of individuals and nation-states. Thus if *Kultur* could, and should, be held accountable for the outbreak of war, Kant—at least in the eyes of Emile Boutroux—could not.

Boutroux was only the first of many French scholars to invoke the concept of two Germanies that had served academic reformers so well in the wake of the Franco-Prussian War. When Lavisse argued that pan-Germanism began with Fichte, he suggested that the philosophical tradition that preceded Fichte—and of which Kant was such a central part—was not responsible for the aggressive nationalism that characterized nineteenth-century German politics and thought. The manifesto of French universities also distinguished between a pernicious tradition originating with Fichte and a more admirable philosophical tradition of the eighteenth century. The French professors insisted that German intellectuals of an earlier age—the "great minds of Germany"—had accepted the premise that "civilization is the work not of one special people [un peuple unique], but of all peoples." Thus, like Boutroux, the collective voice of fifteen French universities insisted that two distinct intellectual traditions had coexisted in Germany until 1870; and it was only after 1870 that modern Germany had "broke[n] with the traditions of the Germany of Leibniz, Kant, and Goethe."[2]

Intellectual integrity demanded that scholars like Boutroux, who had identified themselves as neo-Kantians before the war, neither abandon nor repudiate Kantian principles with the outbreak of war. Following the publication of the Manifesto of 93, Victor Delbos and Victor Basch, both of the University of Paris, denounced as outrageous the efforts of the signatories to associate Kant with *Kultur*. For both men, Kant was the essential voice of the "other" Germany, audible throughout the eighteenth century but extinguished by the end of the nineteenth. Delbos, who was probably France's most renowned scholar of Kantian ethics, was therefore "confounded by the cynicism" of those who invoked Kant's name in defense of German militarism and brute force.[3]

In a public lecture delivered in March 1915, Delbos contended that since the late eighteenth century two incompatible intellectual impulses had vied for control of the German spirit. One inclination, appreciative of "clear and distinct ideas" and aspiring always to clarity of thought through the rigorous use of reason, was rationalist and classical. Kant, who hoped to establish "the act of thinking [as] the fundamental condition of all knowledge," epitomized this rationalist spirit; and although he disagreed with Descartes in critical ways, insofar as he assigned to reason a pre-eminent authority, he "derive[d] directly from Descartes." Hegel represented the Germany of "confusion and obscurity" that had supplanted Kantian rationalism. The fundamental differences that separated Kant from Hegel, and the thought of eighteenth-century Germany from that of the nineteenth century, were their radically different attitudes towards war. Delbos insisted that Kant's moral philosophy, which was fundamentally antimechanistic, could never be used to justify wars of aggression. As the translator and editor of the *Foundations of the Metaphysics of Morals,* he knew that neither Kantian duty nor Kantian rights could be reduced to or derived from laws of physical causation: the "ought" could never be derived from the "is." War, therefore, could never be justified by appeal to natural necessity. Delbos went so far as to say that Kant "condemned war" (which was not strictly the case, though he did condemn what he called "offensive wars") and "the barbaric, perfidious and inhuman methods" with which it was executed. Hegel, by contrast, considered war "the means by which a State realized . . . the fullness of its nature." On the Hegelian view, if the State represented the Idea on earth, its will, effected through command of material power, could neither be questioned nor contradicted: what it willed was what would be. The state was, by necessity, absolutely autonomous—in its political deliberations it consulted only its own interests and considered only its power to realize those interests—and war became in such a system nothing but a "necessary aspect" of this "absolute autonomy." Because the autonomy of the Hegelian state was founded in material power, and was thus mechanistic, it shared nothing in common with Kant's concept of moral autonomy founded on pure reason.[4]

A renowned Kantian, Delbos was also a devout Catholic, and in 1915 these two loyalties pulled him in opposite directions. As a scholar, he was determined to defend Kant from being appropriated by German warmongers on the one hand, and systematically assaulted by most French Catholic scholars on the other. Thus his lecture, delivered in the Spring of 1915 to a predominantly Catholic audience, offered a principled, scholarly repudiation of contemporary attacks on Kant. But it was also a poignant farewell to a career devoted to German philosophy. Concluding his lecture, Delbos announced that he would henceforth turn his attention to the philosophers of France and rediscover his own intellectual origins. And so he did, until his death in 1916. Unwilling to denounce Kantian philosophy, he was, however, also unable to teach it with a clear conscience.

Unlike Delbos, who had no desire to use Kant to advance a political agenda, Basch and Alphonse Aulard, both leading figures in the League for the Rights of Man, defended Kant for political as well as academic reasons. Kant's moral and political philosophy provided the League with its first principles: his ethics emphasized the autonomy of the individual and the sanctity of individual rights; and his political philosophy anticipated an age of international peace rooted in collective security. To abandon Kant, therefore, would be to compromise the organization's essential ideals. In the aggressively nationalistic atmosphere of the war, however, the League could defend Kant only by separating him unconditionally from the Germanic tradition. Aulard and Basch effected this radical separation when they represented Kant as a cosmopolitan rather than a nationalist, a republican rather than a monarchist, a prophet of peace rather than an advocate of war. They challenged the signatories by asserting that Goethe, Beethoven, and Kant had each endorsed the French Revolution, and by insisting that Kant had developed a set of political principles that condemned in advance the "crimes" of contemporary Germany.[5]

When Aulard, who held the chair in the History of the French Revolution at the Sorbonne, addressed an audience gathered to hear the annual "Friends of the University" lecture series, he emphasized Kant's republican sympathies. As his moral and political philosophy made evident, Kant believed ardently in the freedom of citizens and of nations alike. He advocated constitutional "republicanism" (which for Kant meant, broadly speaking, the governance of all citizens through the rule of law), and insisted upon the rights and duties of all citizens and all states. Basch made the same point in two essays also published in 1915—the first a pamphlet for the League for the Rights of Man, the other a lengthy essay in the *Revue de métaphysique et de morale*—in which he insisted that Kantian philosophy was unequivocally incompatible with the destructive mentality of early-twentieth-century Germany. Kant's intention had been the "establishment of a rule of law as valid for nations as for individuals; the creation of a society of nations ruled by justice."[6] Thus Kant was not the father of pan-Germanism, which scoffed at treaty obligations and insisted that "necessity knows no law," but the defender of international law, justice, and cooperation.

Like Boutroux, Basch situated Kant within a cosmopolitan and classical tradition that had flourished in eighteenth-century Germany. He acknowledged that two intellectual tendencies—one rationalist, the other mystical—had coexisted in eighteenth-century Germany; and no German thinker, scholar, composer, or writer had been entirely immune to the appeal of mysticism. Not even Kant. But Basch insisted that it would be inappropriate to overemphasize the importance of mysticism, for in Kant, more than in any other German thinker, rationalism had prevailed over mysticism. Because Kant recognized that reason belonged not to one race but to *all* rational beings, Kantian rationalism was *universalist* and entailed a cosmopolitan point of view. Like Leibniz, Kant had exemplified a classical spirit of "humanity opposed to the egotistical and jealous individualism of nations" and inherently predisposed toward the achievement of "perpetual peace." For that reason alone, Kant shared nothing with the bellicose spirit of contemporary Germany.

Nor would he have endorsed the authoritarian spirit of Imperial Germany. Both Basch and Aulard emphasized Kant's essential republicanism. Aulard reminded his audience that Kant, following Rousseau, believed that one is obliged to obey only those laws to which one has freely consented. Freedom was the touchstone of Kantian ethics. Central to Kant's moral philosophy is the belief that man is capable of moral action only because he is endowed with freedom. Unlike the creature who is governed exclusively by the law of nature—by the commands of mechanistic cause and effect—and who cannot therefore choose how to act except on the grounds of base desires and practical interests, the rational being, who is endowed with the power to will his actions, is free to act in accordance with the moral law that his reason makes evident to him. Freedom, for Kant, is therefore the source of morality and the precondition of both duty and rights: as ends-in-themselves, rational beings have rights and the obligation to respect those rights in themselves and in others. Basch was careful to point out that Kantian negative freedom, which he and Kant defined as "independence from external constraint" (which is not to be confused with an independence from duty, or the *internal* constraint that reason and the categorical imperative impose on each rational being) did not entail unlimited licence to do anything one's natural appetites might incline one to do. Because reason is universal, and hence universally shared, the freedom which is the direct consequence of reason is also universal, and every rational being's freedom must, by definition, coexist with that of every other rational being. To ignore the freedom of others in a single-minded pursuit of one's own freedom would be to treat others merely as means and not also as ends-in-themselves. From this, Basch concluded that Kant's concept of freedom was "inseparable from that of equality."

Kant's rationalism led him to believe in the liberty and equality of individuals, and in the fraternity of all peoples. Essentially cosmopolitan, Kantian philosophy was inherently hostile to war. For French Kantians of the First World War, confronted by a nation that equated pacifism with defeatism, this principle represented something of a philosophical land-mine. Both Aulard and Basch were careful, therefore, to point out that Kant was by no means an unconditional pacifist. Citing *Perpetual Peace* (which Basch acclaimed as a "supreme charter of humanity"), they argued—with just cause—that Kant applied and extended his fundamental principles of morality to the domain of international relations.[7] Just as individuals are autonomous and equal under the universal law, so too are nations, which Kant considered to be "moral persons."[8] Thus the size and material power of a nation endowed it with no special rights, and eliminated none of its duties towards other nations. It was certainly the case that "no state had the right to intervene by violence in the con-

stitution and government of any other state." But if war broke out because a state violated this duty, and no international mechanism existed
to protect the rights or enforce the duties of all states, then it had to be
conducted in such a way as to guarantee the possibility of mutual respect
between antagonists once peace was secured.[9] Kant unequivocally "pro-
scribed all perfidious means which destroyed the confidence" of the enemy power in the responsibility and humanity of the belligerent. Aulard
concluded from this that Kant had condemned in advance the atrocities
and barbarous conduct of the German Army, as a consequence of which
the Germans forfeited their right to be considered international citizens.

As a philosopher Basch was more sensitive than Aulard to the nuances
of Kant's thought. He acknowledged, as did Aulard, that Kant both
countenanced the possibility of war and identified the conditions under
which war might be deemed legitimate; but he denied emphatically that
Kant ever *promoted* war (as he would have had to do if he had anything
in common with pan-Germanism). Like the French people, forced into
war by the wanton aggression of a lawless neighbor, Kant recognized
that war could be necessary; he denied that it could ever be desirable.
To make this point Basch had to tackle thorny evidence that suggested
a positive appreciation on Kant's part of war itself. Whatever allusions
Kant may have made about war as a noble experience or the consequences of war as sometimes laudable were fundamentally irrelevant.
Like an economist who might recognize that in an overpopulated nation
famine could relieve pressure on scarce food supplies, but who knew that
beneficial consequences could never make mass starvation desirable public policy, Kant believed that positive consequences did not in any way
justify the horror of war. Unlike the pan-Germanists who celebrated war
for its power to effect desired consequences, Kant rejected—categorically—the consequentialist ethic that informed such a view.

Basch was on solid ground when he pointed out that Kant would
refuse to consider a social phenomenon good simply because it maxi-
mized private or public utility. Such an argument would grant moral
legitimacy to an action based on its consequences and not on its intentions. But moral authority could never be derived from contingent consequences, for morality is determined not by the ends effected (which are
in many cases largely accidental) but by intentions (which are volitional
and thus the only thing over which moral agents can have direct control).
To contend that war might be good because it might sometimes bring
about beneficial consequences would be antithetical to Kant's entire
moral philosophy. In neither his moral nor his political philosophy did

he therefore have anything in common with the bellicose, authoritarian mentality of contemporary Germany.

Of all the republican apologia for Kant, Aulard's lecture (and the pamphlet that he subsequently published based on his lecture notes) was the most overtly political. According to Aulard, Kant was a disciple, and Kantian political philosophy a product, of the French Revolution. To make his case, Aulard identified the Revolution as an originative social act that redefined the moral principles upon which political authority rested. Until 1789 only one law had prevailed in international relations: that of the most powerful. Thus territory had been won or lost not according to a priori principles of justice or national self-determination, but by force of arms. The Revolution had changed all this by creating a new principle of legal authority: the nation forged in 1789 was one "united and free, in which the law was no longer the expression of the will of an individual, but the expression of the general will." And just as the general will of the nation (which was nothing but the product of "the federation of [many] small countries, the communes") was the expression of the collective revolutionary will of its many component parts, so also was an international general will the expression of nations. Aulard contended that the revolutionaries, when determining foreign policy, had "repudiate[d] the old law of conquest by force" and had resolved that henceforth France as a nation would not extend its frontiers by force of arms.[10] When the Convention extended "help and fraternity" to oppressed peoples and under these auspices authorized the liberation of the peoples of Belgium, Nice, and the Rhineland, it did so in compliance with the will of the people being liberated. Only with Napoleon did France return to the principle of conquest and territorial acquisition by military force. Thus the first principle of the Revolution was, in international affairs as in domestic policy, respect for the rights and freedoms of all people.

Aulard saw Kant's positive endorsement of the French Revolution to be most evident in two texts: the "Metaphysical First Principles of the Doctrine of Right" (the first part of *The Metaphysics of Morals*) and *Perpetual Peace*. There certainly is much in *The Metaphysics of Morals* that would have pleased a scholar sympathetic to the French Revolution. As Aulard knew well, Kantian political principles resembled in critical ways the ideas of Condorcet, Montesquieu, and the National Assembly. Like Condorcet, Kant spoke of the movement of states from the state of nature to that of civil society; like Montesquieu, he considered the separation of powers essential to constitutional governance; and like the

National Assembly, he believed that the state was authorized to confiscate church property. That Kant's political philosophy was consonant with the principles of the French Revolution, or at least with the principles and practices of the constitutional monarchy established in 1789 and abolished in 1792, was therefore indisputable.[11] But Aulard was not content to prove only that Kant had endorsed the principles of the French Revolution; he argued that Kantian political philosophy was a direct consequence of the French Revolution. Whereas Basch and Delbos situated Kant within a German tradition that was influenced by French antecedents and was well established by the mid-eighteenth century, Aulard spoke neither of Descartes nor of Leibniz. Instead, he spoke only of the French Revolution and appealed *only* to Kantian texts written after 1789. Thus he made no mention of *The Foundations of the Metaphysics of Morals,* which predated the Revolution by four years, and based his analysis exclusively on Kantian texts written during the Revolutionary era. This selective subtraction of a fundamental text that set forth the basic moral principles upon which Kant's political philosophy was grounded is extremely important. Had Aulard made the *Foundations* the canonical text upon which he built his interpretation of Kant's political philosophy, the French Revolution would have become either a direct product or an early instantiation of an existing Kantian philosophy. Such an interpretation would, however, have undermined his thesis that the French Revolution constituted an essential starting-point in the development of a new theory of international law. By dealing only with texts written in the 1790s, Aulard represented Kantian principles as products and not just coincident expressions of revolutionary ideals. The political implications of this argument, when delivered in 1915, were far-reaching.

Aulard believed, with Kant, that a lasting peace could be secured only if the appropriate political conditions prevailed. Kant considered permanent peace the state to which all rational beings aspire, but its attainment presupposed the existence *within* each state of a *republican* constitution predicated upon the freedom and equality of all citizens and the universal applicability of the law. When applied to the circumstances of war-torn Europe, it was clear that so long as Imperial Germany scorned republican principles and genuinely democratic government, peace would remain elusive. But Aulard did not want to impose an alien system of values on a defeated Germany. Such a strategy, he feared (rightly enough), would only breed resentment and increase the danger of future conflict. Germany, therefore, had to find the philosophical justification for republicanism within an indigenous philosophical tradition, not an imported one. For its own sake and the sake of its international neighbors, Germany had to return to Kant. When Aulard suggested that Kant represented the spirit of another Germany—when, in fact, he appealed to the thesis of two Germanies—he hoped to demonstrate that Germany could rid itself of the baleful influence of Prussia and yet remain true to itself.

If the concept of two Germanies allowed Germany to reform and yet remain true to itself, it also served to protect the patriotic credentials of French scholars loyal to Kant. Whether identified with the rationalism of Descartes or the politics of the Revolution, Kant belonged to an intellectual tradition honored in France but rejected in Germany. This was the interpretation Samuel Rocheblave put forth in an article published by the *Journal des débats* in 1916. Rocheblave, a *professeur* at the Lycée Janson de Sailly in Paris and at the Ecole des Beaux-Arts, insisted (as had Basch, Aulard, Delbos, and Boutroux before him) that the spirit of Kant absolutely repudiated the aggressive militarism of modern Germany, and his "entire philosophy [stood] opposed to . . . [that] of the Prussian state." For Kant, victory secured by material force alone did not establish virtue, and combat did not dissolve the categorical imperative. The "nobility of its universal principles" embedded in Kantianism insisted that no person and no state stood above the law. For Rocheblave, as for Aulard, Basch, and Boutroux, Kant was more a republican than a monarchist, more a defender of inalienable rights than an apologist for nationalist aggression, more French than German.[12]

"That there should be in France publicists and even philosophers who would affirm that Kant had sustained the German war" was for Basch beyond belief.[13] Yet as he knew very well, Catholic scholars and prelates on the one hand, and integral nationalist writers and polemicists on the other, had by the fall of 1915 been making that basic argument for the best part of a year. From the outset of the war, Catholics and neoroyalists combined rhetorical forces to attack Kant as essentially Prussian and Kantian principles as inherently antithetical to France. This was an argument so potentially subversive of republican institutions that French republicans, and especially the neo-Kantians of the League for the Rights of Man, could not ignore it. Nor did they. When Aulard identified republicanism as an indispensable precondition of peace, he implicitly condemned the ideology and arguments of antirepublicans in France. In their preference for the *ancien régime* (with its antipathy to egalitarianism and its international politics of territorial aggrandizement), they would *ipso facto* preclude the possibility of a lasting peace. A pseudonymous essay published in the *Grande Revue* in March 1915, entitled "La Guerre et philosophie," also castigated Catholics and neoroyalists for their attacks on Kant and impugned their loyalty: by agreeing with the signatories of the Manifesto of 93 that Kant was indeed responsible for *Kultur*, did they not show themselves to be suspiciously similar in intellectual spirit to the much-despised "ninety-three"?[14] Most interesting of all was Basch's representation of nationalism as essentially German and inherently aggressive. Not an original thesis perhaps, but in the ardently nationalistic atmosphere of 1915—when appeals to national loyalty were a mainstay of patriotic propaganda—a bold one nonetheless. Was the loyalty of every patriot in France thus compromised by inadvertent association with Germanic ideas? Not necessarily. Basch was no nationalist, for he despised the narrow, exclusionary inclinations of nationalists on both sides of the Rhine, but he was a patriot. He could and did support the French war effort, because he conceived of it as a struggle between the universal, democratic, and cosmopolitan principles of Kant and the French Revolution and the particularist, authoritarian, and nationalist principles of Germany and all other right-wing nationalists. With his defense of Kant and his attack on nationalism, Basch directed his criticism to those in France who would condemn Kant as the progenitor of *Kultur*.

The Catholic Assault on Neo-Kantianism

The French Catholic assault on Kant began with the publication in November 1914 of the manifesto of the Institut Catholique. In this text the Institut identified the three topics basic to all subsequent Catholic criticism of Kant. (1) By denying the possibility of knowing the noumenal world, Kant's epistemology placed God and divine law beyond human cognition. Man could know only himself. (2) This epistemological "subjectivism" gave rise to a subjectivist ethics that made *human* reason, essentially incapable of knowing divine will, the source of moral law. Man thus became a law unto himself. (3) In virtue of (1) and (2), Kantian subjectivism was effectively an extension of Lutheran theology, and thus essentially Protestant. In their repudiation of *Kultur*, the Catholic scholars decried German philosophy for "its fundamental subjectivism, its transcendental idealism, [and] its disdain for that which common sense took to be given." Kant, although not solely responsible for these philosophical errors, was guilty of every one. With his radical separation of phenomena and noumena, Kant dismissed ordinary perceptions as fundamentally inadequate for the disclosure of reality; his epistemology forever divorced the "world of reason" from the "world of ethics and religion," and the categorical imperative made the individual conscience the ultimate arbiter of morality. When human action was unrestrained by any transcendent authority, when man supplanted God, aggression and indulgence of even the basest of appetites inevitably followed. From Kant to Nietzsche was therefore but a small step. And German scholars, immersed in this intellectual tradition, could appeal to no higher law than that which man and the state, both autonomous and unrestrained by external moral law, had created. They endorsed the actions of their nation because they lacked any other benchmark for judgment.

Two lecture series, delivered in Paris between the fall of 1914 and the spring of 1915, elaborated upon the arguments put forth initially by the Institut Catholique. Jacques Maritain presented a public lecture series entitled "The Role of Germany in Modern Philosophy" at the Institut Catholique during the 1914–15 academic year. The title of the lecture series could just as easily have been inverted, for Maritain in fact discussed not so much the role of Germany in the development of modern philosophy as the role of philosophy in the creation of modern Germany. When the Catholic daily *La Croix* summarized the content of these lectures in a regular column, his ideas reached a substantially larger audience than that assembled each week at the Institut. In the spring of 1915, Fr. Paquier, the vicar at Holy Trinity Church in Paris, presented to an audience of more than two thousand a lecture series entitled, "German Protestantism: Luther, Kant, Nietzsche." Paquier, who held advanced degrees in both theology and philosophy, knew Maritain well enough to have him read his essays in advance of publication. Hence the similarity of their interpretations is not surprising.

Maritain opened his lecture series with a categorical rejection of the "two Germanies" thesis. There were not two separate and distinct cultural traditions in Germany, one lofty and creative, the other base and destructive. Rather, the modern Germany of 1914, which shelled cathedrals and committed unspeakable atrocities, was the natural and inevitable culmination of an indivisible German culture originating with Luther and including Kant, Goethe, and the other "great" Germans.[15] Collectively, they had created a culture which exalted the individual, denied the necessity of divine revelation, and dismissed metaphysical truth as unfounded. Maritain considered both German imperialism and modern atheistic materialism the natural consequences of Luther's "egocentrism."[16] For Luther, all things were understood and mediated through the individual human conscience. Ultimately, Luther's exaltation of the individual produced German "pantheism," which venerated the individual in place of a supernatural deity, and German imperialism, which upheld and reinforced this pantheism through brute force and the domination of matter. The world would be free of this pernicious spirit only when the Hohenzollern army and the *Kultur* that gave it authority were defeated. A cultural as well as military victory for France "would free the world, and Germany itself, of the influence of Fichte, Kant, and Luther."[17]

When Paquier presented his lecture series a few months later, he too identified German *Kultur* as an intellectual and moral continuum starting with Luther. Luther's principal error and the error from which all others followed was, in Paquier's judgment, his separation of salvation and moral action. By denying the efficacy of good works, and arguing that salvation occurred only through faith and as a consequence of divine generosity towards sinful man, Luther in effect concluded that "human activity had neither moral nor religious value." How one acted in the world, whether for good or for evil, mattered not at all. Paquier concluded that post-Reformation German political history reflected this indifference to moral law; how the state conducted itself and whether its actions conformed in any way to recognized principles of morality mattered not at all, because conduct, whether personal or public, was essentially irrelevant to man's prospects for salvation. Ultimately, this radical division between civil and moral life gave rise to a complete disregard for any law that would thwart one's natural inclinations. Absolute autonomy entailed the absence of any external rules and the denial of a moral order external to human existence. Hegel translated this moral autonomy into absolute moral relativism: "there no longer exists either good or evil, there exist only forces in a process of self-development."

If Luther set Germany on its path of moral and epistemological relativism, Kant confirmed the course. For Maritain and for Paquier, Kant was, after Luther, the critical linchpin in the evolution of pantheistic pan-Germanism. Paquier, who believed that Luther was Kant's most powerful intellectual influence, argued that Kant took Luther's theological principles and transformed them into a metaphysical system that stressed the absolute autonomy of the individual and the impossibility of transcendent knowledge. To be fair, this subjectivism, which Paquier identified as quintessentially Protestant, was not unique to Kant; it was evident in Cartesianism too, but that was only because Descartes had fallen under Protestant influences during his extended stays in Holland and Germany. Whatever his philosophical antecedents, Kant was, for Paquier, the "founder of subjectivist philosophy." With the publication of the *Critique of Pure Reason* in 1781, Kant created an epistemology that went one step beyond Luther, so that "not only does reason not have to adhere to a truth beyond itself; it is incapable of doing so." From this Paquier concluded that "philosophy became Protestant."[18] Henceforth, Lutheranism and Kantianism worked hand in hand "to destroy all objective truth," indeed, to destroy truth itself. When Kant asserted that it was impossible to *know* real essences—to know the thing-in-itself—and possible to know only that which presented itself to human perception, he made all knowledge relative or, to use the word Catholic scholars preferred, "subjectivist." Paquier disputed Kant's belief that the most human reason could provide was "a well-founded idea" of the noumenal world; that one could not "have the least knowledge of it" nor "ever attain to it by all the exertions of [one's] natural capacity of reason."[19] Because "the thinking subject, which is to say each one of us, closes himself in on himself and can no longer" transcend his self, after Kant it became impossible to "know the object of our knowledge." This expression of epistemological subjectivism heralded the "triumph" of a cosmological system that placed "the individual at the center and above all else, [and] which arrive[d] at the deification of the individual."[20]

Even though Kant denied the possibility of knowing things-in-themselves, according to Paquier, his subjectivist epistemology made no allowance for the possibility of error. When the self becomes the sole determinant of truth, there is nothing outside of the self to identify error; "everything that I think is therefore true." After Kant, German thinkers effected the transference of this epistemological relativism to the level of the state. If it is the case that "the subjectivist Protestant of Leipzig or Berlin does not have to submit to any objective, universal, and external truth," then only the "truth of each individual Protestant" exists. On the collective level—and how Kantian subjectivism allowed for this leap from the level of the individual to that of the social collective Paquier does not explain—the denial of universal, objective truth gave rise to the ascendancy of "German truth." From Kantian epistemology to German aggression was thus but a logical progression.

George Fonsegrive, another prominent Catholic thinker of the early twentieth century, suggested a slightly different connection between Kantian epistemology and German militarism. To avoid the shoals of skepticism entailed by Kant's denial of the possibility of transcendent knowledge, Germany after Kant took refuge in unreflective obedience. "In order to avoid skepticism . . . [*Kultur*] left aside all critical apparatus and by an act of free and voluntary authority, asserted the truth." Fonsegrive did not link Kantian critical philosophy to the automatic obedience of modern Germany; nonetheless, he believed that Kant's emphasis on critique contributed, ironically, to the ascendancy of a mentality fundamentally at odds with Kantian principles. German scholars after Kant, "not being able to think freely and by themselves, came to think by order."[21]

Maritain also condemned the consequences of Kant's "speculative philosophy." He considered Kant's epistemology and his representation of faith and reason as irreconcilable opposites, the "principal vices" Kant bequeathed to the world.[22] Because Kant separated the natural from the supernatural and contended that human reason could aspire only to knowledge of the natural world, Maritain held Kantian philosophy responsible for both "scientism" and "agnosticism." On the one hand, Kant bestowed on knowledge of the material world an exaggerated authority, hence "scientism." On the other, although Kant did not deny the existence of God, his philosophy made knowledge of God or God's will unlikely, hence "agnosticism."

Paquier and Maritain did disagree, albeit slightly, as to the character of Kantian ethics. Even though Paquier was determined to emphasize what he called the "negative" and "destructive" side of Kantian philosophy (he suggested that for balance his audience might wish to seek out Victor Delbos's "positive" interpretation of Kant), he initially exempted the categorical imperative from criticism. The categorical imperative was to him the one positive feature of Kant's philosophy. Insofar as it emphasized the power of man's free will to choose to do good, it was antipathetic to Lutheranism. Grounded in Kant's pietist past, the categorical imperative, and hence Kant's ethics, placed greater emphasis on good works than did Lutheran theology; in this—and only this—way did Kantian thought approximate Catholic moral theory. Nonetheless, in his final lecture (which was nominally concerned only with Nietzsche) Paquier presented an interpretation of Kantian ethics closer to that of Maritain than of Delbos.

Maritain considered Kant's ethics the logical and tragic consequence of his "subjectivist" epistemology. Having denied the possibility of transcendental knowledge, Kant "conferred on the human person a dignity which belonged properly to God." He thus made man the final arbiter of ethical decisions. According to Maritain's reading of the categorical imperative: "not only is man master of his own acts, but he is also a man of absolute liberty, a God who would be committing sacrilege against himself if he directed himself to an end other than himself or if he received his law from anyone other than himself."

Because the rule of the categorical imperative was to "obey only one-self," Kant's ethics "excluded all exterior authority."[23] "That which Luther had done to religion, Kant did to ethics: he made the 'I' the center of moral life." In the place of God, he installed the "law of duty" which conceived of the human being as moral legislator and end-in-himself. Maritain argued that Kant's concept of the self-regulating moral individual, unrestrained by any laws external to his will, ultimately justified the outrages and atrocities of 1914. The people of Germany, a law unto themselves, were authorized to "violate the so-called rules [of proper conduct] in the name of civilization and the vital interests of Germany."[24]

Catholics found the notion of man as an end-in-himself morally offensive because it seemed to render God unnecessary. In 1916, Paul Gaultier, who had received the distinguished Calmann-Lévy prize from the Académie Française in 1913, published *La Mentalité allemande et la guerre* in which he reiterated the Catholic case against Kant. Disputing those who held that the metaphysics of eighteenth-century Germany contributed nothing to the militarism of the nineteenth and twentieth centuries, Gaultier insisted that Kant was the keystone that brought together the metaphysical tradition of the eighteenth century and the aggressive *Kultur* of the modern age. By making man the absolute and humanity "divine," Kant had made German metaphysics and ethics from 1790 onwards fundamentally anthropocentric. Gaultier revealed to his wartime readers what he took to be the inevitable social consequences of Kant's ethical subjectivism: materialistic self-indulgence, sexual hedonism, and rampant secularization.[25] When man became the measure of all things, when human obligations became the foundation of morality, and the material assumed priority over the spiritual, the abandonment of religion was inevitable.

In his Introduction to the *Foundations of the Metaphysics of Morals*, Lewis White Beck points out that from the categorical imperative—"Act only according to that maxim by which you can at the same time will that it should become a universal law"—derive four separate formulae or ways of articulating that imperative.[26] It is significant that both Maritain and Gaultier paraphrased the "kingdom of ends" formulation, according to which "the moral agent [should] act as if he were a lawgiving member of a realm of ends, i.e. of persons, each of whom is an end in himself and an end for all others." Unlike republican scholars, who stressed the universality of Kantian ethics and thus emphasized the "universal law" formulation (given above), Catholic scholars all but ignored the universalizability principle. For them, the categorical imperative was an invitation to absolute moral license, according to which anything was permissible as long as it corresponded to an individual's inclination. It is essential to remember, however, that Kant insists upon the universal character of reason and the universal dominion of moral law. Because reason is universal, moral principles derived from reason are not strictly individual, even if it is individual rational beings who ascertain that moral action is required of them. The moral law, for Kant, must apply indiscriminately to all rational beings; if it does not, it lacks moral authority. The individual who asserts the moral law cannot rationally exempt himself from it, and there cannot be one law for Germany and another for the people it would subjugate. Thus when republicans perceived in the categorical imperative the essential precondition of universal moral order, they came closer to the true spirit of Kant's ethics.

Catholic criticism of Kant was tinged with political animus against the Republic. This was certainly true of an essay that the Bishop of Agen published in 1916. Bishop Vauroux called for the inauguration of a new intellectual order once peace was secured. He believed that this could and would occur, because the Germanic ideas upon which the existing intellectual culture of France rested had lost all authority. Indeed, he stated that "the firm desire of all good Frenchmen" was "to have no further contact with the [intellectual] systems from which this . . . barbarism had emerged." Henceforth, there should not remain in France even one scholar who would consent to serve as an instrument of "Teutonic infiltration." Vauroux anticipated that this much desired radical reorientation of intellectual culture could come only from Catholic leadership, because only neo-Thomism effectively countered Kantian subjectivism with its affirmation of the independent existence of God. For Kant, the idea of God was a necessary product of human reason; for Aquinas, God existed antecedently and independently of human will and representation.[27]

Vauroux's appeal to Thomism as a philosophical alternative for the postwar world was important, for it shows once again that much of the Catholic critique of Kant was rooted in fundamental philosophical disagreement. As we have already seen, there is much in Kantian philosophy that Catholics could neither accept nor assimilate. Both Maritain and Paquier were genuinely appalled by what they took to be Kant's thoroughgoing denial of traditional metaphysics and theology, and hence their disdain for Kantian "subjectivism" was authentic. And neither the notion of man as an end-in-himself nor the categorical imperative could be reconciled with the Aristotelian and Thomistic metaphysics informing modern Catholic thought. But philosophical disagreement alone does not explain the intensity with which French Catholics attacked Kant during the First World War. It was not just because they disagreed with him, and not just because they held his anthropocentrism responsible for the errors of the modern world—including the barbarism of the contemporary German state. Rather, French Catholic scholars attacked Kant because they sensed that there was political capital to be made within France and overseas if Kant were to be identified as responsible for the emergence of pan-Germanism. A repudiation of Kant could lend support to conservative educational reform in France, and could contribute to a rhetorical representation of Germany as both anti-Catholic and anti-Christian.

Vauroux's critique of Kant was certainly not disinterested: he denounced Kant in order to discredit the laic education the Third Republic had built on Kantian principles. Vauroux greatly regretted the influence of Kantian "subjectivism" upon French public education. Public school educators (like Liard, whose enthusiasm for Kant was well known) had, he feared, replaced the moral precepts of Catholic instruction with Kantian principles. Indeed, they had been so effusive in their admiration of Kant that they had exceeded even their master. Whereas Kant had acknowledged the necessity of the idea of God (he simply denied that one could know God through human reason), his epigones had made man entirely self-sufficient and the sole and ultimate source of morality. France could, however, be saved from the dangers of this ethical egoism by reintroducing Catholic moral principles to primary education and by refocusing higher education. It was time, Vauroux insisted, for another look at the Middle Ages and a return to the medieval synthesis of faith and reason, metaphysics and physics.[28] Like Etienne Lamy, who had already called upon the national intelligentsia to assert the "unity" of knowledge, Vauroux looked to the day when the medieval synthesis, ruptured by modern science, would once again dominate the intellectual culture of France. But this could occur only if religious education triumphed over the radical secularism of Third Republic.

However important it was to contemplate the intellectual character of the postwar period, in the darkest days of the war, when Vauroux wrote his essay, French Catholics confronted problems of greater urgency. At home, anticlericalism was on the rise and the French left publicly questioned the loyalty of French Catholics; abroad, Catholic antipathy to France—a reaction in large part to the anticlericalism of the Third Republic—undermined French efforts to win neutral powers over to the Entente cause. Confronted with such antipathy, noncombatant French Catholic scholars and prelates launched a counteroffensive on the home front and abroad. Prominent Catholic scholars disputed charges of Catholic disloyalty; visited neutral countries to deliver lectures in defense of France; and wrote essays to persuade international audiences that while Germany was fundamentally antipathetic to Catholic interests, France was more Catholic that it appeared.

French Catholics feared that their coreligionists in neutral countries believed that a German and Austrian victory would more adequately defend Catholic interests and hence showed little inclination to favor the Entente cause. As Imbart de la Tour contended in an open letter to *Journal des débats* written in February 1915, "Catholic hostility towards France, evident in more than one neutral country, [was] one of the [nation's] most serious problems."[29] It was certainly true that within months of the outbreak of war, significant sectors of Catholic opinion in Switzerland, Italy, Spain, and the United States had coordinated a systematic campaign against France. German-American Catholics lobbied actively against American support for England and France; and it was to counter these efforts that French scholars, Catholic and anticlerical, devoted much of their energy to proselytizing for the French cause in the United States. Catholics in other neutral powers, especially those in Spain, Italy (before 1915), and Portugal, were antipathetic to the Entente countries for a slightly different reason: they were "not so much for Germany as against France" and her allies. Persuaded that "atheist France," "Protestant England," and "schismatic Russia" were inherently hostile to Catholicism, they feared that an Entente victory would do nothing to protect Catholics or Catholic causes. The anticlerical record of the Third Republic did not dispel such concerns. Thus, although Spanish or Portuguese Catholics might have had no positive reason to support the Central Powers, or to lobby for intervention on their behalf, deep-seated antipathy prevented them from endorsing the Entente.

French Catholics were determined to discredit anticlerical attacks on their loyalty and on the policies of the Vatican as unfounded and illogical; in their desire to prove that a German victory would endanger the future of Catholicism—indeed, the future of Christianity itself—and to establish that only an Allied victory was consonant with Christian principles, they responded with assertions of Catholic piety and patriotism and evidence of German antipathy to Catholicism. The attack on Kant—in which Kant was identified as part of an intellectual continuum that started with Luther and ended with the Kaiser—was a significant part of this larger enterprise.

By linking Kant to Luther, French Catholics emphasized the essential culpability of Protestant thought: from Protestantism emerged the materialistic, relativistic, and aggressive spirit of contemporary Germany. The implication of this argument for French citizens was that only Catholicism could offer France adequate protection from such morally destructive ideas. A return to the faith would thus prove effective immunization against Germanic influence. Identification of "one Germany," from Luther through Kant to the Kaiser, also countered republican and international suspicions that the Catholic Church favored the cause of the Central Powers: because the German tradition was essentially Protestant it was, almost by definition, inimical to Catholicism. How, therefore, could Catholics around the world perceive in Germany the natural defender of the faith? Was it not obvious that only an Entente victory could protect the faith from the insidious effects of unrestrained Germanism? And for the same reasons, how could one accuse the Vatican of sympathy for a tradition so inimical to Catholicism?

To prove that Germany was hostile to Catholicism, the Catholic press in both England and France highlighted evidence of German aggression against Catholic monuments and atrocities against Catholic clerics in Belgium and France.[30] Lamy argued that if one judged Germany by its actions, rather than by its rhetoric, one would soon conclude that a country disposed to systematic cruelty against civilians and combatants alike could not be representative of true faith. Indeed, one could not help but observe in Germany "a long, persistent, calm and atrocious infidelity to religious law."[31] For Gaultier, this indifference to religious law originated with Kant. Contempt for religious artifacts and attacks on priests and nuns were, he lamented, the natural consequences of an irreligious cultural tradition that began with Kant and ended with the crass materialism and moral depravity of the Kaiser's Germany.[32]

Although Catholic critics frequently associated Kant with Luther, they found in Kant something even more pernicious than the spirit of Protestantism: the origins of modern Germany's antipathy to Christianity itself. The intellectual tradition that originated with Kant was not only un-Catholic but also un-Christian. Imbart de la Tour asked those Catholics in neutral countries who saw in contemporary German political culture the spirit of order, and in French democracy and individualism that of anarchy, to look beneath the surface of German ideology. They would discern that German order was built on a concept of "force, as an essential attribute of existence." This "Gospel of force was the negation of the Gospel of the Beatitudes."[33] "Respect for the weak, and regulation of the strong," essential Christian principles, had no place in the pan-Germanic system of values. Consequently, a German victory, inspired by the belief that might makes right, would be antithetical to Christianity. Lamy reinforced this argument when he reminded his readers in foreign countries that an ideology predicated upon the subordination and subjugation of lesser nations violated the Christian principle that all are equal in the eyes of God, and that "all human communities have the right to be respected by all others." Attempts to "infringe upon the freedom of peoples and of individuals" were, Lamy insisted, violations of Christian law. The ideology of pan-Germanism placed modern Germany outside and in direct contradiction of Christianity. France, whatever its flaws, fought to defend Christian principles and to guarantee the survival of Christianity itself.[34] It is in this context of the war as a conflict between antithetical religious traditions that the French Catholic critique of Kant must be read.

Maritain did this unequivocally when he held Kant responsible for modern atheism; Gaultier suggested as much when he represented the "rampant de-Christianization" of modern Germany as a consequence of Kantianism; and Paquier made a similar point with his critique of Kantian ethics. Paquier was particularly critical of Kant's apparent indifference to the *consequences* of human action and of what he took to be the excessive asceticism of Kant's concept of duty. He wondered why Kant considered it inappropriate to "have in view the well-being to be accrued" from moral action. Why did the *consequences* of human action seem to have such little moral weight for Kant? And why, indeed, could an individual not derive pleasure from acting in ways consonant with the will of God? It is certainly the case that for Kant the morality of any action rests not on its consequences but on the intention that informs it. Only actions inspired by and directed by a *good will* are moral, and even if they prove completely inefficacious, they remain moral. By contrast, actions inspired either by personal inclination or conscious calculation of benefits (whether in this life or the next) cannot be considered moral, although Kant acknowledged that they could be considered "praiseworthy." Kant did not, however, demand that moral agents take no account of the consequences of their actions. If a moral agent, inspired by a regard for the antecedently established universal moral law, examined the possible consequences of his action so as to determine better how to act upon the dictates of the moral law, then that agent would be acting morally; indeed, "an ardent desire to attain the goal do[es] not in the least detract from the morality of the men's action if they are indeed acting on the conviction that it is their duty to do these acts; their concern with the consequences may be an essential part of their conduct, necessary for the fulfillment of the obligation they have placed upon themselves."[35] For Catholics, however, whose actions are directed toward the end of salvation and who consider God both the ultimate end and the initial source of moral action, this argument only betrayed Kant's anthropocentrism: "since God was no longer either the end or the rule by which our activity is determined, man becomes an *end-in-himself*."[36]

When Paquier criticized Kant's apparent indifference to the consequences of moral action, he emphasized the way in which Kantian ethics differed from those of Aristotle and Aquinas. Clearly, Kantian ethics was anything but Catholic. But when Paquier criticized what he took to be the excessive asceticism of Kant's concept of duty, he insinuated that Kant was also fundamentally un-Christian. Was it really necessary, he wondered, to deny those who were acting from duty any sense of satisfaction?[37] This complaint, essential to the identification of Kant as un-Christian, was based on a misreading of Kant. He does not demand that individuals derive no satisfaction from doing their duty. When he states that "the good will seems to constitute the indispensable condition even of worthiness to be happy," he surely allows for the possibility that the individual who acts in "good will" can be happy, and thus that moral action can be a source of, and not incompatible with, human happiness.[38] Kant also concedes that there must exist "a power of reason to instill a feeling of pleasure or satisfaction in the fulfillment of duty"; all that he insists upon is that "it is wholly impossible to discern" how it is that reason, which contains "nothing sensuous," is able to produce this sensation of pleasure.[39]

Paquier's misrepresentation of Kant's concept of duty was, when read in the context of the Great War, particularly damning. Correspondence from the front suggested that soldiers suffered the horrors of the trenches because they were committed to doing their duty; moreover, they derived a profound moral satisfaction from doing so. Yet Kantian ethics, Paquier insisted, would deny troops at the front even the satisfaction of feeling contentment at doing their duty. To deprive them of this—when all else was denied them—was surely to demand more than was morally defensible. Like the German Army, which all French citizens now knew to be cruel, inhumane, and un-Christian, Kantian ethics, heartless and unrewarding as they were, were essentially un-Christian too. With such insinuations French Catholics reinforced their representation of the war as a conflict between two radically opposed religious traditions—one Christian, the other pagan—in which the protection of Christianity depended upon an Allied victory.

Neoroyalists and the Attack on Kant

The attack on Kant appeared not only in the Catholic press, but also in the essays and arguments of the antirepublican Action Française. Only days after *Le Temps* published the Manifesto of 93, Maurras published a lengthy editorial entitled "Individualism and Pan-Germanism" in which he too blamed Kant and Luther for the catastrophes of the modern age. Honoring the spirit of the *union sacrée,* he began by congratulating Boutroux for recognizing at last that German aggression had its roots in the ideas of Fichte, and that "German culture differ[ed] fundamentally from that which humanity understands as culture or civilization."[40] He took exception, however, to Boutroux's insistence that there were in fact two independent intellectual traditions in German culture: the Germany of the categorical imperative and the Germany of military aggression. Maurras insisted that these concepts were not opposite but inseparable: the one was the ground, the other the consequence. Employing a telling analogy (that made clear that his adherence to the *union sacrée* was in no way an acceptance of the republican tradition), Maurras suggested that just as the Terror was the natural product of the Declaration of the Rights of Man, so modern Germany was the logical consequence of Kantian philosophy.[41] For his final point, Maurras argued that Fichte's doctrine of national union was nothing but the ripening of Kant's "Jacobinism."

When Maurras spoke of Kant's "Jacobinism," he explicitly and purposefully united the German philosophical tradition and the French revolutionary tradition. By linking the ideas of the French Revolution to Kant and, through Kant, to Fichte and modern German nationalism, he exposed the treacherous consequences of revolutionary thought: the ideas of 1789 led inexorably to the advent of 1914. But Maurras did not wish to blame France itself or Frenchmen for German nationalism, militarism, and expansionism. (Elsewhere, he objected strenuously to Bergson's argument that pan-Germanism had its origins in the ideas of Gobineau.)[42] He was careful, therefore, to trace this individualist strain in German idealism and French republicanism back to Luther. With his break from established authority, repudiation of hierarchy, and commitment to individual autonomy, Luther had unleashed an unholy tradition responsible for the international calamities of both 1789 and 1914.[43] By tracing the intellectual lineage of German nationalism and French republicanism back to Luther, Maurras suggested that the ideas of Germany—not France—were ultimately responsible for modern German aggression, and, moreover, that the "so-called French Revolution" and the ideas associated with it had their origins in an alien, enemy culture. This was the reverse of Aulard's argument. By identifying Kant as a product of the French Revolution, he defied right-wing nationalists who represented the French Revolution, rooted in Germanic and Protestant principles, as alien and essentially German. He thus defended the Revolution and Kant from those within France who were hostile to both.

In characterizing the Revolution as a foreign aberration, Maurras implied that those who supported it and its principles were in fact defending an alien and enemy tradition. He could thus call into question the loyalty of those who defended the heritage of the French Revolution, without appearing to compromise his support for the *union sacrée*. Furthermore, he could suggest that opposition to the republican tradition was a patriotic necessity. If the Revolution were indeed the product of insidious German ideas—the same ideas that had led to the emergence of an aggressive, united German nation—it was the patriotic duty of loyal Frenchmen to combat it and its German accomplice. While congratulating ranking republicans for recognizing the acuity of Action Française criticism, Maurras challenged the legitimacy and authority of the Republic they supported.

With the publication of *Contre l'esprit allemand: de Kant à Krupp*, Léon Daudet developed in further detail the objections of the Action Française to the German intellectual tradition; and, significantly, he did so through the pages of the Catholic press. His essays appeared originally in *Le Correspondant* (which in the prewar years had expressed very little sympathy for the ideas of the Action Française) and were reprinted in 1915 by the Catholic publishing house, Bloud and Gay. Along with Maurras and Maritain, Daudet cast Kant and Luther as the progenitors of German *Kultur*. He denigrated the categorical imperative as an odious example of unrestrained individualism applied to ethics, which took its inspiration from the ideas of Luther and the Reformation, Rousseau and the Terror; and, in turn, it inspired the ideas of Hegel, Fichte, and Bismarck.

> All that had to be done, in effect, was to "nationalize" this essential principle of individualism, formulated by the Koenigsberg theoretician, to lead first to the crisis of 1813, then to that of 1870, and finally to that of 1914. This formula, transported from metaphysics to politics, has become that of German imperialism. It has created the legions, forged the cannon, and armed an entire people for conquest and the preparation for conquest.[44]

Daudet conceded that Kant alone had not engendered German imperialism. It was Fichte who had transformed the categorical imperative into a dictum of national self-determination and had thus converted intellectual principle into political practice. But the categorical imperative remained, in Daudet's estimation, "the mother" of all the outrages of modern history.[45]

When leading spokesmen of the Action Française attacked Kant in the early months of the war, their arguments and intentions were explicitly political. This was as true for Daudet as it was for Maurras. The purpose of *Contre l'esprit allemand: de Kant à Krupp* and its sequel, *Mesures de l'après-guerre,* was not merely to identify the insidious ideas that had stimulated Prussian aggression. Through his critique of Kant and (in *Mesures de l'après-guerre*) Wagner, Daudet also intended to attack the republican establishment of modern France. The two studies were supposed to demonstrate how "foreign intellectual influences, if strong and penetrating, could dismantle a nation in just the same way that failure to prepare for war could." Wagnerian opera, which had been particularly popular in France before the war, had undermined the integrity of French culture by infecting the minds of France with "Germanic poison." Wagner had thus served as the "vanguard" of the Kaiser's armies.[46] But Kant had "invaded" France even more effectively. French scholars, convinced of the superior merits of Kantian philosophy, had promoted a Kantian cult which had denigrated French culture and demeaned the French language. Daudet recalled how his own philosophy professor, when teaching the *Critique of Pure Reason,* had "insinuated that even if French had its charms . . . German was more properly the language of pure thought." In such hands, philosophy instruction became "more precisely, classes in Germanization." With these willing accomplices, Kant and his epigones had "invaded French philosophy, ethics, and education, in just the same way that the Kaiser's hordes [had]." Ultimately, the Kantian invasion of French higher education radically transformed French political culture. Daudet argued that the spirit of Kant's moral philosophy, which was the fundamental principle behind the practice of laic "neutrality," became the guiding spirit of the modern French state.[47]

Assigning equal weight to Kant and to the Kaiser, Daudet attributed direct responsibility for social and individual actions to intellectual principles. Given the insidious effect of German ideas, it was essential that France fight for an intellectual, as well as military, victory over Germany. Daudet was adamant on this point: he insisted that there would be no benefit to be gained from defeating the armies of Germany if the people of France "conserved the cult and practice of a philosophy which had presided at the formation of that army and a method which had unleashed it." To confirm its victory over Germany, France would have to purge French higher education of all Kantian influence, and institute in its place a return to the classical philosophy of Plato, Aristotle, and Aquinas. Daudet thus argued for the necessity of "educative *revanche*."[48] Given the intellectual origins of the Great War, intellectual reform was as necessary as military victory.

Daudet's essays constituted a justification of intellectual action during wartime. Insofar as destructive ideas had to be combated and productive ideas promoted, the efforts of the Action Française to encourage intellectual critique and effect intellectual reform were essential to the long-term success of the war effort. But Daudet's arguments did more than defend the intellectual deeds of his noncombatant colleagues. They called into question the loyalty of those who defended the Republic. Through his denunciation of German philosophy during the First World War, Daudet implicated, and attempted to discredit, the Republic which prior to 1914 had tolerated and indeed encouraged the proliferation of German ideas in French education. It was the secular Republic of Jules Ferry which had introduced, on a large scale, the foreign contagion of German philosophy and had thereby allowed for the intellectual invasion of France. In the process it had not only denigrated established French tradition, but had also endangered the future of France. How patriotic could such a regime be? If, as Daudet suggested, one of the happiest consequences of a victorious war would be liberation from the yoke of German ideas, surely France would also wish to be free of the regime which had harnessed the yoke initially.[49] Daudet thus began his attack on the loyalty of republican politicians and scholars in late 1914 when he insinuated that their voluntary intellectual association with the enemy was fundamentally unpatriotic. This campaign of public calumny—in which attacks on Kant would continue to figure prominently—culminated in the summer of 1917, when Daudet charged that the nation's Minister of the Interior, Louis Malvy, had entered into treacherous negotiations with the enemy.

For France—as for Russia—1917 was a year of crisis. In retrospect, of course, it is evident that the Russian crisis, which brought with it revolution, massive social upheaval, and withdrawal from the war, was of an entirely different order from that experienced in France. But at the time, for a nation exhausted by war, the French crisis of 1917 seemed serious indeed. Mutinous troops, striking munitions workers, acrimonious political debate, and the uncertain circumstances of France's principal Eastern ally combined in the spring and summer of 1917 to test to the limits the nation's ability to pursue the war until unconditional victory. And it was in this context of domestic and international crisis that the ongoing French debate over Kant acquired a new dimension. While republicans of all stripes, whether anxious for a negotiated peace or intent upon unconditional victory, insisted that they had found a neo-Kantian ally in Woodrow Wilson, neoroyalists, intent on discrediting some of the Republic's most powerful politicians, insinuated that those who expressed sympathy for the ideals of Kant were no better than traitors.

In the spring, the much-touted Nivelle Offensive that was intended to break the bloody deadlock on the Western Front failed miserably; and French troops, convinced that the military planners responsible for this tragically ineffective offensive operation considered front-line troops nothing but expendable *materiel,* mutinied. They would no longer tolerate the wanton disregard for human lives such ill-conceived and poorly executed military plans exemplified. To compound the problem, French workers, hard-pressed by spiraling prices and shortages of food and fuel, went on strike repeatedly. Jean-Jacques Becker has made a convincing case that the strike waves of 1917—one in spring, the second in late fall—were motivated not by revolutionary ideology nor by widespread defeatism but by economic anxiety.[50] But "defeatist" propaganda demanding an immediate peace settlement was evident enough in 1917. Much to the dismay of military advisers, French socialists met troop trains arriving in Paris and distributed pacifist pamphlets to soldiers arriving in the city for a few days' leave. Etienne Lamy suggested to his military superiors that when on leave, France's overburdened troops had to be protected from such insidious influence, and recommended that prostitutes (who had their own ways of undermining military might and morale) and socialists be banned from the city's railway stations.[51] Whether the nation would continue to hold out in all this adversity was the question Lamy had to analyze for his military superiors in late spring and early summer of 1917.

Mutinous troops and disintegrating morale at the front and behind the lines were not the only domestic problems confronting France in 1917. The political *union sacrée,* a marriage of convenience at best, strained under the combined tension of ever-increasing anticlericalism, on the one hand, and neoroyalist innuendo and invective, on the other. In February 1917, French socialists, convinced for some time that Catholic prelates had—with the active connivance of the government— avoided front-line duty, demanded a reform to the military service law. According to the terms of the existing law, Catholic priests and monks who had come of age before 1905 were required to comply with the nation's compulsory military service obligation through noncombatant service; those who were subject to the 1905 law had to serve in combat positions. By 1916, as many as 24,000 priests—including many who had been forced into exile when the Law of Associations had disbanded their religious orders and who had returned voluntarily in 1914 to enlist— had donned the uniform of the French Army.[52] Most, but not all, served in noncombat positions, as stretcher-bearers, chaplains, and medics. This by no means placed them out of danger, but it continued to feed anticlerical suspicions. Throughout 1915 and 1916, French socialists wondered aloud whether it was fair to give such protection (if protection it was) to Catholic priests, while loyal sons of France faced death in daily combat. Early in 1917, therefore, a socialist deputy presented a motion to the Chamber of Deputies that would require *all* religious personnel (Catholics, Protestants, and Jews) subject to military service to serve in combat positions.[53] Catholics resented the implication that priests were shirking their duty, and the Catholic-anticlerical divide deepened.

If domestic circumstances gave cause for grave concern, international developments were, in the main, equally alarming. Russia, in revolution from February 1917 onwards, seemed a most uncertain ally; and even before the Bolsheviks pulled Russia out of the war in late 1917, France had to consider the military consequences of a collapsed Eastern front. Was it any consolation to French observers that Germany had problems of its own? The Reichstag Peace Resolution, by which the German parliament called for a negotiated end to the war, suggested that Germany, too, was worn down by three years of war. But the resolution only compounded problems in France, for it gave added impetus to those on the left anxious for an immediate armistice. That the United States broke diplomatic relations with Germany in January 1917 and entered the war three months later on the side of the Entente was perhaps the only positive event to greet the war-weary French in 1917.

There is no evidence to suggest that Wilson's diplomatic principles derived directly from a reading of Kant, but sympathetic observers in France were eager to interpret them in this way. With his diplomatic note to the belligerent powers delivered in late 1916, and his address to the United States Senate presented in February 1917, Wilson appeared to give Kantian principles an unprecedented political immediacy. Kant's vision of international cooperation predicated upon the existence of free and independent states committed to collective security—arguments that had already won the approbation of Boutroux, Basch, and Aulard—might now become a reality. Although the United States maintained its neutrality through the early months of 1917, Wilson's address to the Senate articulated what he took to be the essential conditions for a lasting peace: an international organization to guarantee the peace, a reduction of armaments, and a nonpunitive, negotiated peace—a "peace without victory"—based on the equality of all participants.

Wilson's final condition angered many within the Entente, who believed that the President thereby ignored the moral right of those attacked by Germany to demand an unconditional victory. César Chabrun, writing in the *Revue des deux mondes* in February 1917, acknowledged that "peace without victory" was unpalatable to many within the Entente. But he defended Wilson's vision as a logical extension of Kantian principles, principles consonant with French republican ideals. For each of Wilson's arguments, Chabrun identified its Kantian antecedent. Thus Wilson's postwar international organization, respectful of the independence of sovereign states but committed by force of reason to the preservation of the peace, echoed Kant. And his call for a "peace without victory" did not intend to favor the Central Powers but to establish peace without rancor. Chabrun pointed out (as Rocheblave had done a year earlier) that because military victory would be determined by material force, victory alone would not establish moral worth; and thus military success could not by itself secure the peace. Peace had to be rooted "in the good will of independent peoples." If the unconditional victory of one side created only simmering animosity on the other, there would be no peace. Thus it was preferable to negotiate a peace between equals than to impose a peace upon the vanquished. Chabrun emphasized that Wilson, an unacknowledged neo-Kantian, was neither embracing a

"Germanic" ideology, nor favoring the German cause. He was, instead, endorsing principles of rationality and universality that Kant had inherited from the French *philosophes* of the eighteenth century.[54]

The republican nationalist weekly *L'Opinion* cited Chabrun's essay approvingly, for it seemed to confirm the thesis of its own contributor, André Fribourg, who had set forth two weeks earlier the ways in which Kantian principles differed from those of wartime Germany.[55] As many others had done before him, Fribourg found in *Perpetual Peace* ample proof of the author's antipathy to aggressive German nationalism. Kant had opposed large, standing armies; had warned against extensive borrowing for military expenditures; had reviled tactics of unrestrained and barbarous combat; and had denounced the territorial annexation of small nations by their more powerful neighbors. It was therefore quite clear from *Perpetual Peace* that Kant was no defender of pan-Germanism; but it was not clear—at least not to Fribourg—that Kant was a Wilsonian *avant la lettre*. Although Kant had insisted that there could be neither moral victors nor villains in a war and thus gave philosophical justification to Wilson's notion of a "peace without victory," the philosopher had not counseled peace at any cost. In the very first article of *Perpetual Peace* Kant had warned against peace treaties concluded in bad faith: "No treaty of peace shall be held valid in which there is tacitly reserved matter for a future war."[56] He feared that a premature peace, arrived at for the wrong reasons, would inevitably breed future conflict. Fribourg warned that the Reichstag Peace Resolution represented just such a trap: recognizing that for the moment the war had become "too dangerous" for Germany, the Reichstag had proposed peace, but it had hoped thereby only to buy time for the nation. Once it had caught its breath, Germany would resume the war, on its own terms and to its own advantage.[57] Thus Kant provided Fribourg and France with a philosophical rationale for ignoring overtures to peace and continuing the war. *L'Opinion* writers, although sympathetic to Kant, derived from *Perpetual Peace* a non-Wilsonian conclusion.

Although Catholics and neoroyalists agreed on a great deal during the war, when discussions turned to peace and international security, a notable difference of opinion emerged. In spite of their hostility to Kantian ideas, leading French Catholics spoke of preconditions for peace and prospects for international security in similar terms. This was evident as early as 1916, when Alfred Baudrillart, the Rector of the Institut Catholique, defended the French war effort—including the conscription of Catholic priests—to American Catholics. Although he would have preferred to exempt clerics from combat, he defended French clerical participation in the war as a necessity of democratic society—in a democratic and egalitarian society the moral authority of priests rested, at least in part, on their willingness to subject themselves to the same laws and the same dangers as their parishioners; and he defended the French war effort by appealing to the Thomistic criteria of a "just war." It was true that Christians should and always would prefer peace to war, but they also recognized the legitimacy of war fought in defense of victims of aggression. And they understood that a premature peace offered no lasting assurances: "in so far as resistance remains possible, if the peace that the enemy proposes does not conform to principles of justice, priests and laity alike have the right to reject it and prefer war to peace." Moreover, once engaged on a course of war, those committed to the principle of a just war must direct themselves to the establishment of a "just and perfect peace." Such a peace would "reconcile as well as possible the opposing wills [of the belligerents], would neither allow for the perpetuation of existing causes of conflict nor create new ones, and would not contain any germ of a new war."[58] Baudrillart never mentioned Kant, but the Thomistic doctrine of a just war and a lasting peace was in no way incompatible with Kantian principles.

It should not be surprising, therefore, that at least some French Catholics endorsed the idea of a League of Nations. Late in the war, Etienne Lamy participated in an international conference in Paris that brought together Catholics from the "Allied and Neutral Powers." In their closing declaration they denounced both pan-Germanism and Bolshevism, because neither the ongoing struggle of peoples nor that of classes would bring peace to the world. By contrast, they believed that Christian principles of fraternity and international cooperation offered the world a genuine prospect for peace. As Catholics, they "supported all measures that would substitute for the anarchy of violence the benefits of arbitration and order." They insisted that because "all nations were persons, all, even the weakest, had the same rights; and all, even the strongest, had the same duties."[59] And they called for the expansion of economic and political international cooperation: "While awaiting the formation of the League of Nations (if it should ever come about), it was to be hoped that international agreements would increase in number; they alone could curb aggression, expand production, stimulate exploration, and guarantee material progress." This was a far cry from the demand of the nationalist right for punitive postwar indemnities, and it pointed to a critical divergence in the ideology and rhetoric of some French Catholics and most French nationalists in the final years of the war.

If many republicans in 1917 continued to find philosophical sustenance in *Perpetual Peace* and if some Catholics considered collective security and international cooperation consonant with their faith, neoroyalists remained resolutely hostile to Kant, collective security, and international cooperation. Before the United States committed itself to military intervention on the side of the Entente, the Action Française had nothing but contempt for Wilson and his proposals for a postwar settlement. Maurras, for one, cast aspersions on Wilson's agenda by characterizing it as Kantian, Germanic, and socialistic. His critique appeared one day after the publication of Chabrun's essay in defense of Wilson's vision. Maurras, like Chabrun, heard in Wilson's plans for international peace echoes of Kant's essay on *Perpetual Peace*: "the philosopher of Koenigsberg gave the American president a thorough introduction to the ideas of international law."[60] This, however, gave Maurras little consolation, because he believed that history had proved Kant's ideas completely untenable, ineffective, and "inane." Since the publication of *Perpetual Peace* the incidence of war had not diminished at all; indeed, it had increased. Faulty logic—the numbing grossness of an argument based on the fallacy of *post hoc, ergo propter hoc*—did not seem to perturb Maurras; convinced that *Perpetual Peace* had failed to secure peace in the nineteenth century, he doubted that it would prove more successful in the twentieth.

It is clear from Maurras's articles that the Action Française attacked Wilson principally to discredit domestic enemies. Maurras admitted that "when we make our habitual objections to the pacifism of Mr. Wilson, it is really to Kant, to Rousseau, to Luther, to the spirit of the German Reformation and the so-called French Revolution that we are responding."[61] Because the "dangerous idealism" of the White House "found credit among the socialists in the Chamber [of Deputies] and at the editorial desk of *L'Humanité*"—indeed, it gave the left a new legitimacy—it had to be repudiated.[62] As heirs of the same tradition, Maurras implied, Wilson and the French left were agents of the enemy. When Wilson called for a "moral revolution," and Wilhelm II demanded a "moral act" to end the war, did not the American President and the German Kaiser speak in the same Kantian idiom?[63] And those in France who defended Wilson's peace proposals by appealing to Kant were nothing but dupes of the German empire: "If the socialist leaders are stupid enough to let themselves be manipulated by the German Emperor to work to save him from punishment and reparations, then let us instruct the country of their simplicity and show what new rivers of blood France will be immersed in if we are unfortunate enough to listen to them."[64] Wilson's ideas were to be excoriated not only because they were Kantian and hence alien in inspiration, but because they formed the foundation of the peace plans of French socialism. By identifying Wilson's ideology as that of the German enemy and the French left, Maurras condemned not only the liberal idealism of the American president, but also the ideas of the French Revolution, once again associated with the German enemy. It was only after the United States entered the war, and Wilson declared that it would fight to the bitter end, that Maurras, unwilling to insult, alienate, or antagonize France's new ally, abandoned his attack on Wilson.[65]

Maurras was not the only spokesman of the Action Française to denounce French democratic traditions as Kantian. In 1917, Henri Vaugeois, one of the founders of the Action Française, presented to the Institut d'Action Française a series of eight rambling lectures on Kant's ethics and the bankruptcy of French education. Much of what he had to say was by then well-worn anti-Kantianism. Like the Catholic critics of Kant, Vaugeois, a former philosophy professor, represented Kant as a radical individualist responsible for the mechanistic orientation of modern science and the ascendancy of atheism; a Protestant who, like the seventeenth-century French Jansenists, hoped to undermine established order and authority; and a puppet whose ethics led to the mindless obedience of Prussian militarism. And like Daudet, Vaugeois attacked Kant in order to disparage the Republic, which prior to 1914 had tolerated and indeed encouraged the proliferation of German ideas in French education.[66] From the time that Kantian ideals penetrated French education, the moral erosion of modern France had begun in earnest. Fortunately, Kantian principles had "failed" in France: "the stupid, Prussian mania for facts for facts' sake, and duty for duty's sake" had not taken hold, the concerted efforts of neo-Kantian reformers notwithstanding. And like Vauroux, Vaugeois concluded that if France were to save itself from these alien and injurious influences, it would have to reorient its intellectual culture by returning to Thomism.

Vaugeois, too, misrepresented the categorical imperative. He rendered it: "do this because I tell you to do it, and do it without questioning because my command to you is categorical rather than merely hypothetical," and held it responsible for most of the misfortunes of the modern world.[67] It gave moral authority to Prussian militarism because it

secured obedience not by "persuasion but by force." And its anthropocentrism informed German atrocities: it was "in the name of the individual conscience . . . knowing nothing but itself, that all the crimes [of the
war] had been committed." If one were to ask Wilhelm II why German
troops had bombarded Reims and burned Louvain, had defiled and
abused citizens of Belgium and France, he would reply that "it [was] out
of duty that I have killed, burned, murdered, pillaged, and raped."

But some elements of Vaugeois's attack were new, and were obvious
responses to the political circumstances of 1917. He talked of treason,
of anarchy in Russia, and of defeatism at home, and he implicated Kant
on each count. Although highly critical of French educational reformers,
Vaugeois insisted that he was not charging them with treasonous intent:

> If it has become necessary to combat the influence of German *Kultur*
> within our educational system *(Université)* . . .; if it has become nec-
> essary to criticize that which has been called "the official doctrine of
> the *Université*," it has never been necessary to suggest of any of those
> who have fallen—whether more or less strongly—under the influence
> of Germanism, a treasonous intention. . . . No! in most cases the ques-
> tion of sincerity, of intellectual probity does not need to be asked.[68]

Delivered at a time when the Action Française was in fact devoting itself
full-time to questioning the patriotism of prominent Republican politicians, Vaugeois's disclaimer was highly disingenuous. As we have seen,
a major objective of the Action Française campaign against Kant was to
place French neo-Kantians in the enemy camp by association. If, as Daudet alleged, Malvy, the French Minister of the Interior, was guilty of
treason for associating with individuals known to have contacts with the
enemy, were those who had brought Kantianism into the classrooms of
France any less guilty?

According to Vaugeois, Kant—already directly implicated in the rise
of Prussian militarism—was also responsible for the pacifism of the Second International, the revolutionary anarchism of Russia, and the "defeatism" of the French left. As always, the categorical imperative was to
blame. The unconditional authority of the autonomous will allows every
individual to decide how to act: "anarchism, whether manifest in private
or public morality, can be reduced to this: there is no law; there are no
rules; do what you wish, follow the inspiration of your heart since your
heart is human; and, friend of all humanity, do whatever you wish except
that which causes suffering, because you have no desire to suffer your-
self."[69] If such an attitude were to prevail, who would return to the

trenches in defense of France? France would collapse, and with it human civilization. Vaugeois was unequivocal on this point: only an unconditional French victory could guarantee peace, because France "was the leavening that generated in all other peoples a sense of the human and the divine." It was for this reason that individuals had to suppress their individual inclinations and sacrifice themselves for the survival of France.[70]

The debate over Kant exposed the political divisions of post-Dreyfus France that had been papered over by the *union sacrée*. Extensive and relentless, it brought to the fore fundamental, perhaps irreconcilable, differences that divided the French intellectual community: about the nature of human reason, the philosophical origins of freedom, the place of the individual in the political order, and the place of nationalism in the postwar world. Republicans saw in Kant's rationalism and respect for the moral autonomy of the individual the foundations of humanitarian republicanism and the fundamental ideals of the Third Republic, and they perceived in *Perpetual Peace* the foundations of postwar stability. Antirepublican intellectuals linked Kant to the Revolution and the Third Republic, denouncing all three. Consequently, when French intellectuals debated whether Kant could be held culpable for the Great War, they also debated the merits (or faults) of republicanism. Thus the debate over Kant, an apparently picayune matter, was in fact of great cultural and political importance, and the camps that emerged in the debate over Kant and *Kultur* revealed that the critical divisions between intellectuals evident during the Dreyfus Affair had by no means disappeared in the patriotic glow of the *union sacrée*.

CHAPTER FIVE

The Classicist Revival

In closing his presidential address to the Académie des Sciences Morales et Politiques in December 1914, Henri Bergson recounted a story of a little boy who had been asked what he would do if, when the war was over, everything around him had been destroyed. The boy, in no way disconcerted by the question, promptly answered, "I would go home." Bergson took this tale of the unflappable schoolboy as a morality tale for the French intellectual elite. In the chaos, confusion, and crisis of the war, those to whom Bergson addressed himself should "rentrons chez nous."[1] Implicit in this invitation to "return home" was the suggestion that the French cultural elite had strayed; impressed with and perhaps infatuated by the accomplishments of Germany, it had lost sight of France's essential cultural character. It was, Bergson suggested, now time for French scholars to return home from their spiritual pilgrimage across the Rhine and reclaim their own cultural heritage.

For many French scholars of the Great War to return home was to rediscover the rich literary, philosophical, and cultural traditions of ancient Greece and Rome and seventeenth-century France. In the aggressively modern atmosphere of prewar France many had scorned this composite classical tradition, with its celebration of order, moderation, discipline, and sacrifice, as archaic; and had criticized classical education, with its curricular emphasis on Latin and Greek, as elitist and impractical. During the war, however, when the nation affirmed the importance of order, the need for discipline, and the sanctity of sacrifice, the classical aesthetic, articulated in art, drama, and education, found a more receptive audience. Kenneth Silver has demonstrated how the war radically altered the dominant idiom of avant-garde French art. Erstwhile modernists abandoned their experimental strategies of the prewar years, turned their backs on Cubism (which the public and conservative commentators denigrated as Germanic), and recaptured the spirit of classical art.[2] A similar transformation occurred in the dramatic arts. When theaters reopened in early 1915, the French classical tradition of Racine and Corneille, almost ignored in peacetime, came to dominate the Parisian stage. Noncombatant audiences, with a rekindled appreciation for heroism, sacrifice, and tragic nobility, felt a new-found empathy for the great tragedians of the seventeenth century. The classical curriculum also acquired a renewed authority. In the early years of the war *lycée* students, prompted no doubt by parental urging, flocked to the classical option; enrollment in Section "A" (the Greek-Latin curriculum) significantly exceeded prewar totals. A Ministry of Public Instruction report noted that "the study of Latin was deliberately chosen as a way of participating in the new flourishing of French idealism and as a return to the sources of our national culture."[3]

Classicism found a receptive audience in wartime France for many reasons. With its examples of moral heroism and its acclamation of the redemptive power of sacrifice, it certainly offered invaluable moral solace to a nation in mourning. But the compatibility of classicism with this culture of bereavement does not of itself explain the broad appeal of classicism as a cultural idiom for wartime France. The French people sought—and found—spiritual consolation in the classical tradition, but they also found in it a cultural identity fundamentally distinct from that of the enemy. From a canvass of opinions of the moderate left, the center, or the extreme right, it is evident that nearly all French writers and scholars agreed that modern Germany was antipathetic to the classical tradition. Alfred Croiset insisted that an "abyss" separated German culture from the classical tradition; Paul Crouzet spoke of an "irreconcilable opposition between Germanism and Latin culture"; and Abbé Delfour, a Catholic prelate and ardent advocate of integral nationalism, insisted that when Germany had repudiated Catholicism—to him the only legitimate heir of the classical tradition—it had abandoned classicism itself.[4] Delfour's assertion was not remarkable, for the extreme right had long claimed the classical tradition as France's unique patrimony. Much more noteworthy, however, was the enthusiasm with which republican scholars—many of whom had consciously distanced themselves from the classical tradition before 1914—now embraced it.

During the war years classicism proved unexpectedly attractive to many republican intellectuals for several reasons. Identifying Republican France as the political heir of ancient Athens, they could justify with appeals to classical precedent the state's demands for individual sacrifice. According to the intellectual alignments forged by the Dreyfus Affair, Dreyfusard intellectuals, mistrusting classicism for its association with the antirepublican right, had rallied instead to the cause of modernism. Even those like Alfred Croiset, who were classicists by vocation, vigorously identified themselves after 1900 as modernists. In August 1914, however, these Dreyfusard scholars confronted a political dilemma: having affirmed the inviolability of individual rights, how could they now justify the Republic's demand that citizens forfeit their rights and sacrifice their lives so that the nation might survive? They found their answer in the example of ancient Athens. Croiset, the nation's foremost authority on Athenian democracy, argued that Greece had bequeathed to France "the idea of . . . liberty voluntarily submitted to the rule of law."[5] Respect for this principle, which the French revered and contemporary Germany scorned, allowed France to reconcile the demands of patriotism with the principles of democracy. French citizens voluntarily submitted to the rule of law, including the law compelling military service, because they knew that in doing so they were submitting to the will of a sovereign people.

Identifying themselves as guardians of classical values repudiated in modern Germany, republican scholars could also effectively distance themselves from any association with the enemy. For French scholars who had worked assiduously before the war to cultivate academic connections with Germany, this was of the first importance. If they could prove themselves as vigorous in their defense of classicism as German scholars were in their denunciation of it, then no one could reasonably suspect them of silent sympathy for the cultural values of the enemy. Thus it was essential that they establish their own affinity, and Germany's unequivocal antipathy, for the classical tradition. To this end, Emile Boutroux, only recently returned from his visit to Berlin, insisted in the fall of 1914 that at the very heart of the German cultural tradition was a fundamental "antagonism to Greco-Roman civilization." The German philosophical tradition after Kant and nineteenth-century German historiography had asserted unambiguously that "the first duty of [German] truth is to be opposed to that which Greek and Latin thought—classical thought—recognized to be true." All that the Greeks and Romans had taught subsequent civilizations to revere—morality, compassion, justice, virtue—the Germans denigrated as worthless. Germany was, therefore, not an heir of Greece and Rome but their belligerent adversary.[6] In a subsequent essay Boutroux pursued the argument further: the German people, unwavering in their enmity for all Latin peoples, had resolved "to construct a theory of a moral, religious, and intellectual culture opposed to the first principles of classical civilization, and to work systematically to bring about the triumph of that theory."[7] According to Imbart de la Tour, nothing revealed more clearly Germany's antipathy for "the first principles of classical civilization" than its xenophobic nationalism. Describing Germany's myth of cultural autonomy as antithetical to the cosmopolitanism of the classical tradition, he lamented that "the German race wanted to be indebted to no people but itself . . . [and thus] borrowed nothing from outside."[8] Because of this aspiration to cultural autarky, Germany consciously "isolated itself" from all foreign influences, renounced the internationalism of classicism, and cultivated in its stead a spirit of exclusionary, intolerant nationalism.

Finally, by insisting upon the cosmopolitanism of classical culture, republican scholars could seek allies for France among the other Latin nations of Europe and simultaneously defend their own well-established preference for the cause of intellectual cosmopolitanism. Although they no longer wished to maintain contact with scholars in Germany and Austria, they were eager to maintain, and in some instances establish, connections with scholars elsewhere. In this endeavor, their emphasis upon the cosmopolitanism of classicism proved of the first importance. France, they claimed, shared with the Latin nations of Europe and with the United States a common cultural heritage inherited from Greece and Rome: respect for the rule of law, the rights of individuals, and the universality of reason. The classical tradition thus bound them in common cultural communion, and made France's fight their own. Unlike the Germans who scorned the cosmopolitanism of classical culture, many French intellectuals acclaimed the classical, Mediterranean roots that committed them to intellectual cosmopolitanism. This proved of the utmost importance to the educational debates of the war years, for republican scholars who defined the classical tradition as inherently cosmopolitan could thereby urge the nation not to bow (as Germany had bowed) to nationalist pressures to abandon cosmopolitan education.

Although scholars of the left and right did not differ in their conviction that France was fighting to defend the classical tradition from German depredation, the classicist revival of the Great War did not erase the bitter disagreements that had divided the French intelligentsia before the war. Indeed, insofar as it became yet another occasion for conservatives and progressives to debate and disagree over the character of French education, the classicist revival ultimately sharpened, rather than softened, the fundamental divide between modernists and traditionalists within the

French intellectual community. Unlike conservatives who glimpsed cultural triumph in the classicist revival during the Great War and expected that France would soon return to the classical curriculum it had abandoned so recklessly in 1902, republican scholars recently converted to the classicist cause had no such expectation. Determined to preserve both the modern curriculum they had introduced a decade earlier and the spirit of intellectual cosmopolitanism associated with it, they affirmed the heterogeneous, internationalist, and essentially cosmopolitan spirit of classicism itself. Cultural conservatives, by contrast, insisted ever more emphatically that classicism could flourish in France only if French students immersed themselves in the texts, languages, and traditions of classical cultures. Their arguments proved persuasive. The classicist revival of the Great War successfully challenged the established, modernist orthodoxies of French education by affirming the importance of Latin in all secondary education, and thus prepared the ground for the Bérard reform of 1923.

Classicism and the Culture of Mourning

In January 1915, Etienne de Fontenay, a twenty-one year old junior officer in the French Army, noted with dismay that the Paris theaters had reopened. He found it astounding, disrespectful, and "a little sad, when you think about it dispassionately."[9] René Doumic, principal literary editor of the *Revue des deux mondes,* could not have known of de Fontenay's disquiet for the young soldier's letters were not published until after the war, but he would have respectfully demurred. Unlike de Fontenay he insisted that drama—at least, the morally uplifting drama of the classical tradition—had a part to play in a nation at war. Far from being a dangerous diversion from France's essential duty, it provided moral inspiration. Doumic believed that this was particularly true of the works of Corneille, which had at last acquired an appreciative audience. Whether ignored as irrelevant or dismissed as archaic, Corneille had found few enthusiasts in the modernist atmosphere of prewar France; but with their emphatic acclamation of duty, sacrifice, and patriotism, his plays had come into their own after August 1914. In the heroic, sacrificial atmosphere of the war, they seemed anything but archaic. Stressing the subordination of individual inclinations to national interests, prizing duty over romantic love, and acclaiming the virtues of martyrdom and individual sacrifice, Corneille had produced a dramatic form in which duty and honor took pride of place. This was drama tailor-made to the demands of wartime France. Thus in early 1915, Doumic argued that Parisian theatergoers applauded the masterpieces of seventeenth-century drama, and especially the works of Corneille, because they drew sustenance *(aliment)* from these stories of sacrifice and duty.[10]

As Doumic so astutely understood, classicism experienced a renaissance during the Great War in part because it offered the people of France a positive cultural paradigm through which they could come to terms with their suffering and not be overwhelmed by it. Somber and disciplined, respectful of the dead but never maudlin, this cultural form revels in remembrance and sustains sorrow. Surely it is what Vincent Scully means when he defines classicism so suggestively as "Memory and Sorrow."[11] Because the classical tradition presented the people of France with examples of self-sacrificing moral heroism; because it allowed them to transcend private bereavement by drawing inspiration from their dead; and because it gave the nation the ability to mourn and to remember without being incapacitated by grief, it was uniquely suited to an age in which memory inevitably served as a bittersweet salve for all-encompassing sorrow.

Both didactic and exemplary, the classical tradition also enjoyed a comeback in the schoolrooms of France. Inspired by a "passion for classical culture," parents urged their sons to opt for a classical education. Teachers and educational administrators often reinforced parental inclination and emphasized the moral value of a classical education. Like Doumic, they perceived in the classical corpus invaluable examples of moral courage needed to sustain a somber nation. Léon Cury, a teacher at the Lycée Janson de Sailly in Paris, argued that by teaching students the importance of patriotic sacrifice and by offering invaluable examples of moral courage, classical education had proved its worth under fire. With its emphasis on valor, it had become "a school for heroism" furnishing role models for French troops: Achilles was no longer only a subject of literary study but an inspiration to heroic action.[12] Cury's defense of classical instruction was particularly interesting because it inverted the utilitarian critique of classical education. Modernists had denigrated classical education as elitist, archaic, and insufficiently practical; concerned only with the disinterested pursuit of *culture générale,* it had failed to teach practical skills necessary to the modern world. Cury retorted that the war had revealed the true worth of classical education because it had fostered in its students the values essential to national survival. Thus a classical curriculum was useful less for the skills it taught than for the morals it inculcated. Raymond Thamin, a prominent French pedagogue who would be instrumental in the formulation of the Bérard reforms in 1923, made a similar point. Latin might be a "dead" language, but its literature offered a vibrant, vital moral example to the nation. These appeals to moral utility did not necessarily contradict those who championed the disinterested character of *la culture générale,* but they did suggest that the cultivation of practical skills was not the only measure of educational utility.

Not surprisingly, those who regretted that the classical curriculum had lost its pre-eminent position in the decade and a half before the war relished the classical revival. Significantly, however, it was not only die-hard classicists who now championed the classical curriculum. Albert Sarraut, the Minister of Public Instruction in 1915, urged students returning to their classrooms to study classical culture because it was in the classical tradition that the nation would find its defining principles.[13] This, too, was Lucien Poincaré's message to the students of Janson de Sailly when he delivered the prize-day address in 1915. Poincaré was a physicist and educational administrator who had served for several years before the war as Director of Secondary Education and had thus supervised the administration of the 1902 curriculum; in 1914 he became Director of Higher Education in the Ministry of Public Instruction. No enemy of modern education, he nonetheless defined French culture in 1915 as essentially classical. He argued that French troops were defending and were being sustained by "this immortal classical culture," and told the young students of Janson de Sailly that they could likewise draw sustenance from their classical curriculum. The classical tradition taught those at the front—and those too young to fight—the moral values essential to the preservation of the nation: discipline, devotion to ideals that transcend but do not ignore the individual, and stoicism. Poincaré urged his young audience to learn from the example of men at the front, and of those who remained behind, to fulfill their patriotic responsibilities. They should in fact imitate their own history teacher. Called from class to be told of the death of his son at the front, he had summoned the courage to return immediately to his classroom and continue his lesson. The classical tradition taught those who suffered, whether at the front or behind the lines, to be stoical in their grief and resolute in their responsibilities.[14]

The French were by no means the first people to recognize that classicism was a cultural construct eminently suited to a nation in mourning and overwhelmed by sacrifice. In his extraordinary analysis of the Gettysburg Address, Garry Wills writes that classical oratory provided Abraham Lincoln with the pre-eminent model of funereal rhetoric in celebration of sacrifice. As Lincoln knew, Greek funeral orations for soldiers dying young captured the pathos and impiety of war. Reversing the natural order, the old buried the young; physical incapacity outlived youthful energy; and teachers learned from their students. And rather than setting these polarities irreconcilably against one another, classical oratory with its reliance on parallel structure represented these antinomies as essential notes in a transcendent harmony: the many become one, death redeems those who die and those who live, and words become essential complements of heroic deeds.[15]

If the classical example served Lincoln at Gettysburg to sanctify what would otherwise have been the senseless slaughter of the Civil War, so too did classical rhetoric serve France in the Great War. There was no single French text that captured the essence of the war in compelling prose. But there was a great deal of public oratory, and given the pervasive presence of death and mourning, this oratory inevitably assumed the function of funerary speech. Prize-day speeches at prominent *lycées,* prefaces to anthologies of letters from the trenches, and public addresses all drew on classical rhetorical models and repeatedly rendered the experience of the war in terms of classical antinomies. According to this rhetorical tradition, the war was a redemptive act in which unity overcame division and individual sacrifice saved the nation; through their actions the young inverted the natural order and came to teach their elders; and the words of noncombatants became essential complements of combatants' deeds.

Nowhere were the themes, motifs, and rhetoric of classical oratory more persistently present than in Etienne Lamy's annual addresses to the Académie Française. It was customary for the Permanent Secretary of the Académie to report the results of its literary competitions at a public meeting scheduled for the end of each year. Throughout the war, the Académie continued this tradition, but with eligibility for nearly all literary prizes now restricted to front-line troops, most awards were bestowed posthumously. Thus Lamy's annual address became—like the Gettysburg Address—a form of funeral oration and commemorative address. Consciously invoking the rhythms of classical rhetoric, Lamy spoke in successive years of how the many had become one; how the dead had redeemed the living; and how words, by conferring immortality upon the dead, echoed their deeds.

Speaking to the Academy in December 1914, Lamy developed a dialectic of cultural decline and renewal. He argued that whatever its horrors, the war had saved France from the moral and social disorder of unrestrained self-indulgence that had marked the prewar era, by reaffirming the importance of duty. Confronted by a danger that threatened their nation's very survival, citizens had subordinated their own interests to those of the state, had recognized the imperative of duty over desire, and had relinquished their rights in a collective act of self-sacrifice. Lamy argued that the nation had thus returned to a tradition from which it had strayed two centuries earlier. He believed that until the eighteenth century the French people had taken comfort in the past, had nurtured faith in God and salvation, and had subordinated the interests of individuals to the well-being of society. This spirit of seventeenth century classicism—orderly and obedient, disciplined and dutiful—had succumbed, however, to the allure of individualism, which by the nineteenth century dominated French culture. Lamy regretted that by 1914 the celebration of individual desire had become the dominant cultural credo, and he rejoiced that the war had at last liberated the nation from its destructive inclinations. By reaffirming classical virtues, the French had reclaimed their classical heritage.[16]

If the tone of Lamy's 1914 address was almost celebratory, his initial (and perhaps only public) enthusiasm for the redemptive power of war gave way by December 1915 to unrelieved mourning. On this occasion the Académie Française awarded prizes to seventy-eight writers and scholars killed in the first year of war, and Lamy devoted his address to recounting the academic and literary merits of the men thus honored.[17] It would be another full year before he could derive some consolation for this unparalleled loss from classical precedent. In 1916, however, he reminded his audience that the many writers, students, and scholars who had taken up arms in defense of their nation had thereby revived a tradition long ignored in modern France but much honored in ancient Greece and Rome. Scholars-in-arms, they had eradicated a divide that for generations had separated "la France de la pensée" from "la France du courage." Certainly the often acrimonious history of civil-military relations during the Third Republic suggested that before 1914, those who had been "servants of peace" and those who had been "servants of war" had lived separate lives of mutual suspicion. Only when men of intellect imitated their classical forbears and fought side by side with career soldiers, was France able to transcend this artificial and debilitating division.[18]

Although the 1916 address was more subdued and more somber than that of 1914, on both occasions Lamy suggested that modern France derived its strength from classical antecedents. To prevail over adversity, it had to imitate classical examples, embrace the classical spirit of self-abnegation, and reaffirm its classical identity. To reinforce his classicist themes, Lamy used the classical rhetorical devices of parallelism and polarity. In 1916 he employed parallel structure to elaborate upon a theme he had first articulated in 1914: the war reconciled the one and the many, and indeed made the many one. "When one considers where all these soldiers came from, one is struck by their differences. When one considers what they have become, one is struck by their similarities." Before the war, religious, political, and regional differences had distinguished these citizens and had often set them against one another. All divisive distinctions had disappeared, however, in the collective enterprise of national defense. "Before arming these men, France had reconciled them," and from the "diverse multitude" a unified nation had arisen.[19]

Through their selfless actions, the soldiers of France not only reconciled but also redeemed its people: suffering thus secured salvation. This was true whether the suffering was endured by an individual or by an entire nation. Alluding to the correspondence of Maurice Masson (which would be published in the following year), Lamy spoke in 1916 of the redemption secured by each soldier's selfless sacrifice. Like many of his fellow scholars-in-arms, Masson had recognized "not only that courage finds its perfection in sacrifice, but that sacrifice contained within itself an efficacy" that could not be gainsayed: it permitted those who died to "repurchase" the destinies of those who lived.[20] In his 1917 address Lamy returned to this theme of redemptive suffering, and once again employed parallel structure to eloquent effect. "The people of France," he proclaimed, had borne their trials "without flagging, not through love of war, which has become ever more ugly, but through love of country, which has become ever more holy. . . . Awareness of all that they are saving holds them firm against all that they suffer."[21]

For the noncombatant intelligentsia of France, whose leaders were painfully aware that since 1914 their own freedom had been purchased with the deaths of their sons and students, the classical rhetoric of redemption resonated powerfully indeed. And so did the classical antinomy according to which students became teachers, and teachers became the taught. Lamy's rhetoric consciously evoked this inversion of the ordinary pedagogical hierarchy when in 1916 he described France as "a nation of orphans" that had "lost its incomparable guides." Cut down before their time, these youthful teachers continued through their deaths to offer direction to those who lived: "they left us with the most effective lesson of all: that of example."[22] Lamy was not the only noncombatant who spoke of the "lessons" of the war in terms of the youthful troops as teachers to a nation. In 1915 Raoul Narsy, editor of the *Journal des débats,* prepared for publication an anthology of letters written by front-line troops. Resolutely optimistic in tone, the anthology impressed upon those who read in it one of the "lessons of the war": that the nation had united in the collective enterprise of common defense. The volume functioned, in effect, as a primer of patriotism. Through their letters home, men at the front taught the old and the very young about heroism, self-sacrifice, and moral resolve.[23]

When Louis Liard delivered the prize-day address to the students of Lycée Condorcet, he also represented his former students as teachers to the nation. Identifying himself first and foremost as a teacher now learning from the examples and actions of his "beloved students," he took pride in their quiet courage and resolute determination. "We, their teachers *[ses maîtres],* we knew what strength coursed through their veins; and we had confidence in them." As events "from the Vosges to the North Sea" made evident, that confidence had not been misplaced: only another *Iliad* could adequately recount their heroic deeds. As was customary in a classical eulogy, however, Liard exhorted himself and his audience not to mourn: "the moment has not yet come to weep for those who have died." Rather, those who still lived should remain true to the cause for which so many others had died. Learning from the example of their sons and students, their brothers and fathers, those too old or too young to fight should also resolve to hold fast until victory was won.[24] That the survivors should learn from and become worthy of the fallen was a persistent message presented to the youth of France during and immediately after the war. But as Liard's and Lamy's remarks made evident, it was not only the very young who were to learn from the men in the trenches. The war was a schoolroom in which the collective courage of youth taught the elderly, as well as the adolescent, how to live. Thus students came to instruct their teachers, and all who lived learned from those who had died. In this way French oratory of the Great War captured the final element of classical oration, the *protreptikon,* by which the living are exhorted to prove themselves "worthy of the fallen."[25]

To be worthy of those who had died, noncombatant France had to become familiar with the truth about the war, for only then could those who did not fight appreciate and duly honor the quiet heroism of those who did. It became incumbent upon noncombatants, therefore, to complement the actions of those who fought with words of praise and public revelation. Bringing the truth of the war to light (which, as Jean Norton Cru subsequently argued, was a problematic enterprise even for eyewitnesses) became an important vocation for many noncombatant scholars. When Lavisse's anonymous correspondent begged him to make the truth of the war known so that everyone might come to share—if not equally then at least honorably—in the experience and the sacrifice, Lavisse took the charge to heart and urged civilians to read Maurice Genevoix's *Sous Verdun,* proclaiming the novel a "precious testimony to the war." With his trenchant yet subdued prose, Genevoix conveyed to his former professor the reality of warfare. To the "gentle" vision of the war presented in the press—with its omnipresent optimism, its simplistic explanations, and its reluctance to speak the truth—Genevoix offered a much needed antidote. Lavisse, having been thus instructed by a young man he had once taught, perceived no dishonor in Genevoix's honesty: "an event of the magnitude of this war deserves that we know about it in all its truth."[26]

The editors at Hachette agreed. Determined "to present to the public, in a form both vibrant and true *(fidèle),* all aspects of the Great War," Hachette published *Sous Verdun* in 1916 and in the following year worked with Victor Giraud and Paul Dupuy to prepare for publication the complete wartime correspondence of *normaliens* Maurice Masson and Marcel Etévé.[27] The project broke with established practice because, unlike earlier publishing ventures, the Hachette editions did not insist upon their authors' relentless good spirits: both Masson and Etévé wrote frankly and directly of combat, the inevitability of *cafard* (depression), vermin, and the intolerable conditions of the trenches.[28] The publication of their letters in 1917 was not, however, part of a defeatist conspiracy designed to undermine public support for the war. Far from it, for the letters testified to the unassuming heroism and patriotic resolve of those who endured the horrors of the war. These volumes sought to buttress national morale by moral example.

The prefatory essays of noncombatants like Giraud, Dupuy, and others performed a function essential to classical funeral oration: the written word rendered immortal those who died. Wills reminds us that the Greeks considered words an essential complement of action. It was only through words that deeds, otherwise soon forgotten, could enter the national memory and acquire heroic stature. And only words could confer the immortality of remembrance upon the dead. This was the message of Lamy's final wartime address to the Académie Française, when he spoke of how the war, having turned writers into soldiers, had by 1917 turned soldiers into writers. Ordinary men, confronted by the enormity and the horror of combat, had felt compelled to recount what they had experienced; and in bearing witness, they had guaranteed that the war would be forever remembered: "When they are no longer alive, they must be able [still] to speak of it."[29] Yet, as the classical tradition emphasized, only those who lived could confer immortality upon those who had died. The Académie Française did this by awarding posthumous honors to soldiers killed in the war. Other noncombatant scholars and writers worked to the same end when—in collaboration with widows and bereaved parents—they arranged for the publication of deceased soldiers' family correspondence.

Classicism and the Culture of French Republicanism

Whether moderate or progressive in their politics, republican scholars perceived in classicism the essence of republican principles. The values of ancient Greece and Rome were the values of the French Revolution and the Third Republic, and they were the values the French Army fought to defend in 1914. Addressing the scholars and students of the Sorbonne in the first November of the war, Alfred Croiset insisted that modern France prized "truth and justice, reason and liberty" because it was the direct heir of ancient Greece. Greece had "created the idea of human dignity" so essential to French republicanism and had forged a society in which social order was "founded on reason and harmony." Rome had subsequently received, and in its turn transmitted, this cultural legacy to France, where it had made itself manifest in the spirit of the French Revolution.[30] Victor Bérard, a regular contributor to the *Revue de Paris,* also identified a cultural continuum that started with Athens, continued in republican and Christian Rome, and culminated in the French Revolution. "To the liberty of ancient Greece and the equality of Rome, Europe—once converted to Christianity—added the aspiration to fraternity: between all men, sons of the same [divine] Father, Europe dreamed of a future of peace and charity."[31] For both Croiset and Bérard, the French Revolution of 1789 was therefore both the product and the natural expression of this tripartite tradition; and when the revolutionaries engraved "Liberty, Equality, Fraternity" on their public monuments, they acclaimed in one voice the principles of Greece, Rome, and Christianity.

For Boutroux, too, the political values of Republican France were modern expressions of the spirit and traditions of ancient Greece. Defining classicism as rationalist, humanitarian, and compassionate, Boutroux stated that it valued the human mind as an instrument of social progress, respected the weak, and cultivated a respect for right over force, justice over brute strength. The fundamental achievement of the Greeks had been, he believed, the subordination of matter to the superior moral power of mind. In the material world only "blind necessity" prevailed, but in the world of intellect prized by ancient Greece, the pursuit of truth and respect for beauty informed all considerations. "The God of Aristotle is truth and goodness, not force. His action consists in . . . spiritualizing the forces unleashed in the world of material necessity."[32] These were principles that Boutroux valued and for which France fought.

Along with scholars whose politics were further to the left on the spectrum of French republicanism, René Pichon identified the values that France defended as those of individualism and national self-determination, and he criticized the Germanic tradition for its indifference to all but the master races of history. Mommsen, Pichon's archetypal German, had had neither time nor compassion for the "little people" of the past; the qualities that he had admired in ancient Rome—the inclination to international hegemony, the repudiation of cosmopolitanism, the effacement of individual personality, and the subjugation of each individual to the collective will—were the very qualities that French republicans found repugnant. Mommsen was not afraid to assert that "the abdication of citizens' [rights] was nothing, if it allowed for the supremacy of the city." Pichon was no advocate of unrestrained individualism nor was he indifferent to the demands of the nation, even when they ran counter to individual inclination. But he faulted Mommsen for proposing an "absolute antinomy" between the interests of the individual and those of the nation, and between those of the nation and those of humanity. The German scholar failed to understand, as French republicans understood almost intuitively during the war, that it was possible to reconcile the interests of the individual and the interests of the nation. As a German, Mommsen favored the "mechanistic subjugation" of the individual to the state; as a French republican, Pichon preferred the self-discipline of individual will *(la discipline volontaire)*. Only the voluntary acceptance of external constraint was morally acceptable, compatible with the spirit of free men, and "fecund" in its effect.[33]

Republican scholars found in the classical tradition not only a moral justification for compulsory military service but also the promise of international alliances. In early 1915 the faculties of the University of Paris entered into correspondence with the Romanian faculty of the universities of Bucharest and Jassy. Claiming solidarity with their colleagues in France, the Romanian professoriate had some weeks earlier denounced Germany and Austria-Hungary for deliberately provoking the war. They had then gone on to declare that by defending French culture, the French intellectual community was in fact defending a "universal" culture.[34] Gratified by this evidence of international support, the scholars of the University of Paris urged their Romanian correspondents to join forces with France in defense of classical culture. They reminded them that France and Romania shared in Rome a common cultural ancestor, and so Germany's determination to supplant the principles of classicism with those of Germanism represented as great a threat to the cultural integrity of Romania as it did to France. It was only fitting, therefore, that Romanian scholars join forces with their French colleagues in the fight against Germany: "let us defend together our culture, our concept of law and justice, the clarity of our genius, the classical ideal of our art, our humanity."[35]

The Sorbonne scholars continued to lobby international colleagues with appeals to their common cultural heritage. On February 12, 1915, the Faculty of Letters coordinated an assembly in celebration of Latin culture which drew an audience of 3,000.[36] Distinguished guests from Greece, Portugal, Spain, and Romania listened while speakers representing Italy, Belgium, and France reminded them that the neutral powers thus represented in the assembly shared with the Allied powers of France and Belgium a classical heritage. All were direct descendants of Greece and Rome; all embraced the principles of universalism, reason, and humanitarianism grounded in the classical tradition; and all therefore stood to gain or to lose by the outcome of the war. In concluding the assembly, Ernest Lavisse summarized the principle arguments articulated by each speaker: "Since the time of Homer, Sophocles, Plato, Aristotle, and Phidias, our noble line of poets, artists and thinkers has come down through the centuries ... aspiring always to bring more enlightenment, more beauty, and more justice" to the world. This cultural tradition had given rise to a political tradition shared by all Latin cultures—but denigrated by Germany—of liberty:

> We are all free peoples who intend to govern themselves. We obey laws made for us and by us. ... We believe that all nations, by virtue of that which makes them nations, have the right to exist. ... We believe that relations between nations, like relations between individuals, must be governed by law; the Latin spirit is that of the legislator.

Thus the definition of classicism that emerged from the Sorbonne assembly was at once cultural and political. To be classical was to aspire to harmony and balance, whether in aesthetic judgments or international adjudication; it was to honor reason over brute force, clarity over mystical obfuscation, and the quality of expression over the quantity of production.[37]

Emphasizing the common cultural roots that bound France to Italy, Greece, Spain, and Romania, the Sorbonne scholars hoped to win allies for the French war effort. Louis Bertrand, writing in 1916, also emphasized the practical, diplomatic advantages to be gained by an alliance of those powers sharing the classical heritage. Even if Germany were to be defeated, he feared that pan-Germanism would not disappear. In all likelihood, it would flourish in the atmosphere of resentment that defeat would surely bring. Thus France could look to the future with confidence only if it secured for itself an alliance system sufficiently powerful to offset German ambition. Bertrand hoped that France could continue to count on Britain and Russia as allies in peacetime—as it now counted upon them as allies in war—but he saw no immediate prospect for the continuation of close diplomatic and economic relations among the major Entente powers once the war was won. The situation was, however, intrinsically different with Italy. As Latin nations, France and Italy were bound by cultural affinities that would outlast the war. Bertrand hoped that economic and political cooperation could be built upon this cultural foundation.

Bertrand insisted that France would not be the only beneficiary of such a postwar classicist alliance. Both powers stood to gain by mutual cooperation. Unlike France, Italy had a birthrate that exceeded its economic capacity; France, bled white by the war, would need to import manpower after the war if it were to revive economically. Before the war, France had employed German migrants. Would it not be more prudent to turn instead to Italy? Not only would such a reorientation protect France from the insidious effects of Germanic influence, but it would welcome into its midst a more naturally assimilable population. Similarities of language and cultural tradition would facilitate Italian absorption into France. And both countries would benefit by the economic consequences of closer international cooperation. Believing that a formal customs union was probably premature, Bertrand nonetheless advocated closer economic ties and increased trade between the two nations. Such an arrangement would balance the formidable economic power represented by the combined populations of the Central Powers.[38]

For many republican scholars, the great merit of classicism was that it allowed citizens and nations to reconcile the interests of the individual with those of the state, and the interests of the nation with those of humanity.[39] This was particularly important to scholars whose academic accomplishments testified to the power of cosmopolitan influences. After August 1914 Victor Delbos did not abandon his interest in Kant, but he did welcome the opportunity the war presented to reorient his philosophical focus. Having argued that German philosophy *after* Kant had abandoned the rationalism and universalism that had marked it during the seventeenth and eighteenth century, Delbos recommended that scholars refocus their attention on French philosophy. "Without enclosing ourselves narrowly in our tradition alone, let us come to know and appraise the reasons why we adhere to that which constitutes our most basic traditions."[40] It was this desire to rediscover the essential character of French philosophy that animated Delbos's subsequent lectures, delivered at the Sorbonne in 1915, on French philosophy. Eager to "defend that which is most intimate to the French spirit" by determining "in a kind of examination of conscience, what it has been and what it is worth," Delbos discovered that one of the most distinctive traits of French philosophy was its "tendency to search for clear ideas, and to link them one to another by clear connections." French philosophy, moreover, was intent on finding the mean; animated by a natural respect for "proportion and degree," it resisted the excesses of dialectics created by the juxtaposition of two essentially opposite propositions. French philosophy was, therefore, marked by a regard for clarity, moderation, rationality, and universality. In a word, it was classical.[41]

Imbued with the classical spirit, French philosophy eschewed any claims to innate superiority simply by virtue of being French. Indeed, the French philosophical tradition specifically rejected the notion that philosophy could be French, German, or in any way expressly national. According to Delbos, French philosophers never contended that their ideas "reflected the intellectual traits of a single nation." No French philosopher believed that his interpretations were valid for France alone; rather they were valid if and only if they were universally applicable and accessible to anyone endowed with reason. Devoted to the principle of universal truth, French philosophers "believed that their ideas could be upheld anywhere that human intelligence held sway." They strove, therefore, for the enlightenment of humanity, not for the enlightenment of any one people or one race.[42]

For Delbos, philosophy was intrinsically universal, and intellectual conversation necessarily international. Insofar as well-conceived ideas, whether generated in France or elsewhere, were of value to all rational beings, rational arguments originating outside of France could be justifiably integrated into French philosophy. It was a tradition that had "always welcomed many ideas that originated in other countries," in part because foreign ideas often "rendered the service of presenting . . . perspectives on things that French philosophy had not sufficiently considered."[43] But French willingness to welcome outside ideas was never excessive; French philosophy never abandoned itself entirely to foreign influences, and never embraced them uncritically and excessively. Balance, as in all French philosophical inquiry, prevailed. Although at first glance, therefore, Delbos's rediscovery of the French philosophical tradition appeared to be an abandonment of philosophical cosmopolitanism, this was not the case. In fact, he countermanded calls for the wholesale elimination of foreign influences. A Kantian antecedently committed to the universality of reason, he insisted that French philosophy should remain open to any argument posited on rational principles. Only the irrational had to be rejected. Thus he defended the cosmopolitanism of intellectual inquiry from those who favored a narrowly nationalist, exclusive absorption in that which was French.

To defend broad inquiry was also the objective of Victor Basch, who published in late 1915 a lengthy essay in the *Revue de métaphysique et de morale*. Like his colleagues who hoped to secure the support of Italian, Spanish, and Romanian scholars, Basch emphasized the international character of classical culture, but he did not speak of the cultural bonds that bound France to its would-be allies. Rather, he emphasized the common cultural denominator that linked France to its principal enemy: both countries had classical antecedents. He did not intend to suggest thereby that France should abandon its struggle against Imperial Germany. Germany had by the early nineteenth century forsaken its classical tradition in favor of an exclusionary and aggressive nationalism, and by 1915 represented a mortal threat to the classical principles it had once revered.[44] Nonetheless, like Aulard's belief in Kantianism as the moral grounds of postwar German reconstruction, Basch's emphasis on the German classical tradition allowed for the possibility of postwar reconciliation. Insofar as France and Germany still held philosophical and literary traditions in common, postwar intellectual rapprochement between the two powers remained a genuine possibility.

Prominent Dreyfusard and Vice-President of the Ligue des Droits de L'Homme, Basch—like Delbos—defined classicism as universal and cosmopolitan, and he suggested that the essence of German classicism was "*Humanity* opposed to the individuality of the ego and of nations." Originating with Leibniz (whose vision of an international community of scholars stood in stark contrast to the nationalist division of intellectual life in World War I), the German classical tradition in philosophy culminated with the Idealism of Kant, Hegel, and Fichte; in literature it reached its apotheosis with Lessing, Schiller, and Goethe.

For Basch, Lessing, who had declared in 1759 that "he had no idea of what 'love of one's country' might mean," was the ultimate cosmopolite. His great desire had been to "give birth to men worthy of the name, who rise above 'the prejudices of nationality and patriotism'." And when in 1772 he had written that he "had no desire to raise his pen for the honor of his 'dear' country," he had "affirmed that civilization consists in overturning the barriers that separate men and people from one another." This, Basch argued, had been the essential lesson of *Nathan the Wise*: in Lessing's great Enlightenment paean to religious toleration, Nathan successfully transcended his own national identity and came to recognize the humanity of all men.

In his praise of Lessing Basch sounded very much like Romain Rolland: the man of letters is the man without a country. But in his praise of Schiller, Basch implicitly rejected Rolland's injunction that scholars remain above the fray. Basch agreed with Rolland that a scholar's first loyalty was to *humanité* rather than to *la patrie,* to universal principles rather than to particularist passions; but upon rereading Schiller he concluded that there were times in the affairs of men when the active defense of first principles was appropriate and necessary. Like Lessing, Schiller had mistrusted patriotic sentiment and had refused to be limited by such a feeling: he charged that it was "a wicked and miserable ideal to write only for one nation, and this limitation is insupportable for a philosophical mind." *Don Carlos,* however, had suggested that there were occasions when it was appropriate to take up arms against an enemy. In this dramatic tale of the sixteenth-century Dutch revolt against Catholic Spain, Schiller's hero, the Marquis de Posa, had not hesitated "to contract alliances against his own country with those who fought for political and religious freedom." Thus what was laudable for Schiller (and for Basch) was not national loyalty but loyalty to first principles. The noble man was the one who fought for the protection of freedom, not the one who fought out of blind loyalty to his homeland. When applied to the circumstances of 1915, Schiller's thesis suggested that if it was evident that France fought to defend universal principles, then support for the French war effort was legitimate. While Basch was no advocate of blind patriotism, during the war he was neither a pacifist nor a defeatist. He believed firmly in the righteousness of the French cause, and he found in Schiller, and even more dramatically in Goethe, justification for this conviction.

Of all the great German writers of the eighteenth century, none was more profoundly classical than Goethe. Eschewing all nationalistic associations, he had celebrated the essential humanity of all men. Consequently, he had abhorred war, which reduced men to the level of beasts, and despised "those who unleashed it." He had railed against the Brunswick Manifesto (which had threatened the supporters of revolution in France with annihilation). Yet he had honored the "heroism of the revolutionary soldiers and had acclaimed the historical significance of the revolutionary victory at Valmy." Like Kant and Fichte (whom Basch praised as a "Jacobin" committed to the "universal liberation" of all people), Goethe had found in the Revolution a cause of universal significance, and hence a cause worth fighting for. Even though war in general was an abomination, Goethe held that war fought in defense of progressive principles was admissible, perhaps even admirable. Basch agreed.

Basch's essay thus proposed a solution to the problem Rolland had posed. Like Rolland, Basch believed that the function of intellectuals was to organize learned societies in each nation dedicated to improving relations *between* nations. But unlike Rolland, he did not think that noncombatant scholars could or should remain indifferent to the assault on civilization represented by German aggression. Thus in his essay he exposed the limitations of simple-minded patriotism—like Schiller, he could not understand the notion of "love of country"—but suggested that war in defense of first principles was entirely legitimate. By defining the French war effort as the defense of classical, republican, and universal principles, Basch allowed for the possibility of patriotic action within the parameters of cosmopolitan values.

Basch made it clear that it was not Germany per se that threatened the classical tradition, but nationalism. Indeed, much of his essay was an attack on nationalism and nationalists as the fundamental enemies of classicism. He identified Klopstock negatively as "the first great nationalist poet of Germany," precisely because he had disputed the cosmopolitan character of human culture built on reason; forcing reason to give way to sentiment, Klopstock had insisted upon the radical individuality of each nation. By the final decades of the eighteenth century, this particularist nationalist spirit "seemed to triumph definitively over rationalism," and *Sturm und Drang,* whatever its cosmopolitan roots, was "necessarily nationalistic and anti-cosmopolitan" in spirit. With his identification of nationalism as the antithesis of classicism, Basch not only revived the "two Germanies" thesis; he also called into question the moral value of nationalism itself and took issue with nationalists on both sides of the Rhine.

Classicism, Cosmopolitanism, and the Debate over German Language Instruction

Basch did not speak specifically of secondary-school curricula, yet his essay was laden with implications for one of the most divisive educational debates of the war years: should French students continue to learn German in school? As classicism was essentially cosmopolitan in spirit, a culture committed to classical values ought rightly to continue to offer a genuinely cosmopolitan curriculum. Furthermore, if—as Basch insisted—German literature and philosophy of the eighteenth century were expressly classical in spirit, then French educators, eager to immerse their students in the entire classical tradition, should give them the opportunity to study these German texts in their original language. Students would have to know how to read German. Nationalists, well-known for their denunciation of the "Germanization" of French education, considered any such suggestion outrageous: Léon Daudet, for one, hoped to rid the French curriculum of all German influences. And patriotic parents also urged the government to discontinue German language instruction. But many scholars and educational administrators, appealing equally to principle and pragmatic argument, continued to insist that French students be offered the opportunity to learn German. Only then could French republicans affirm their genuine commitment to the culture of cosmopolitanism the ancient Greeks had cultivated. It was a way to distinguish themselves from the narrow-minded nationalists of both France and Germany and prepare the "lost provinces" for full integration with France. Whether French patriots liked it or not, German remained the working language of Alsace, and if France hoped to welcome her Alsatian compatriots into the national community, her citizens—and especially her teachers—would have to have an active command of the language.[45] To give substance to this conviction, in June 1915 the Sorbonne renewed indefinitely the contract of Professor Rouge, who taught German literature and language.[46]

When Louis Liard and Alfred Coville, Director of Secondary Education, testified in 1915 before the parliamentary committee in charge of education, Coville's mind was made up: public antipathy to German-language instruction notwithstanding, "the time had not yet come to ignore absolutely everything that happens on the other side of the border."[47] He made an impassioned case for retaining German in the curriculum by reminding his audience of the academic advantages a rigorous study of German offered secondary students. Unlike Romance languages, whose structure, syntax, and vocabulary closely resembled those of French, German was linguistically distinct. Consequently, when French students studied German they developed cognitive skills of memory, synthesis, and analysis more thoroughly than when studying either Spanish or Italian. Confronted with the cases and declensions of German grammar, French students had to exercise their minds in a logical and rigorous way.[48] This, too, was the opinion of a *lycée* professor serving as a military interpreter: in an article published in 1916 he argued that the study of German, a language fundamentally different in structure, vocabulary, and syntax from French, offered students an intellectual challenge that studying Romance languages could not equal. Moreover, insofar as German syntax resembled that of Latin, it provided students with invaluable experience when preparing to study Latin. If the study of German did nothing else, it did hone the intellectual skills most highly regarded within the French secondary school system.[49]

Serious scholarship also required that French students be competent in German, for this alone would give them unmediated access to German scholarship. Setting aside the atrocities of modern Germany, it was evident to all men of learning that Germany had contributed substantially in the past to the advancement of knowledge. Its achievements had certainly eclipsed those of Europe's neutral powers. Coville defended the study of German by observing that knowledge of German would better serve France's students than a knowledge of Spanish, for in the history of "literary and scientific accomplishments, Spain's accomplishments did not equal those of Germany."[50] The military interpreter made a similar point. Patriotism notwithstanding, it would be a grave error to turn one's back on the genuine cultural accomplishments of Germany. To deny French students access to the great German classics would be "to condemn them to total ignorance of an essentially important moment in the evolution of human thought." And to deprive them of direct knowledge of Goethe would be to restrict their appreciation of the human condition, for "who could pretend to understand humanity who did not know

Goethe?" Finally, by showing students the greatness of Germany's past, the curriculum could demonstrate how tragically far modern Germany had fallen. For this enthusiastic teacher of the eighteenth-century canon, "the shame of modern Germany" was that it had "renounced its ancient ideal of humanity, denied the deities of Schiller, and put in their place the gods of barbarism, materialism, and force."[51]

Others who favored the continuation of German-language instruction argued that an exclusively national curriculum, so characteristic of the enemy, was unworthy of France. Victor Friedel, the assistant director of the Musée Pédagogique, feared that France would gravely compromise its most precious cultural principles if its educational system fell victim to narrow-minded nationalists determined to jettison all international influences, abandon instruction in foreign languages, and turn inward in a misguided absorption in that which was exclusively French. To discredit this agenda, Friedel identified it with that of contemporary Germany. He argued that since the turn of the century German nationalists, intent on making Germany culturally and intellectually self-sufficient, had insisted that modern Germany "turn its back on antiquity, to which it owed the purest masterpieces of German classical literature."[52] In spite of a vociferous campaign against classical, cosmopolitan education in that country, Friedel was convinced that the nationalists would not succeed in completely eliminating the classical curriculum. Iconoclastic German scholars—like the professor of English at the University of Gottingen who persevered in his defense of English culture in spite of "the grotesque Anglophobia of the German masses"—"continued to challenge the dominant nationalist spirit of contemporary Germany." He and other like-minded scholars "tried to turn their compatriots away from the thoughtless and sterile fight against the civilizations and cultures in the midst of which Germans had always lived and must continue to live, and from which it had drawn, and would continue to draw, precious benefits."[53]

Friedel took heart at this evidence, for it suggested that a scholarly spirit committed to a broad humanist education from a cosmopolitan point of view still survived in Germany. It raised some hope for the future, for Friedel anticipated that classicism could effect a postwar reconciliation. In a footnote at the end of his essay, he referred to a lecture delivered in June 1916 by the President of the Hungarian Academy of Sciences to the Viennese chapter of Austrian Friends of Classical Education. Speaking on the subject of "Humanism and the World War," the lecturer had insisted that it would be "the mission of the humanities, and especially Greek humanities, to bring together again, after the war was over, the civilized nations" of the world. Friedel concurred. He was convinced that "more than Christianity, ancient Greece offered the cultural grounds for international understanding because it was in Greece that all civilizations originated."[54]

Scholars eager to keep German studies in the French curriculum continued their campaign through the end of the war. Writing in late 1917, Lavisse rejected as ill-advised (and implicitly Prussian) any attempt to purge German studies from the French curriculum: surely it was better to know the enemy than to ignore and be ignorant of him. In Lavisse's opinion, one of Germany's great errors before the war had been the development of an excessively nationalistic curriculum. Beginning in the 1890s German pedagogues, with the active encouragement of the Emperor, had attempted to reform the curriculum by rejecting the cosmopolitanism of the classical tradition and emphasizing only indigenous cultural accomplishments. Assigning first priority to German language and literature, nationalists had insisted upon the importance of teaching only *German* classics; had dismissed foreign language instruction as unnecessary; and had tried "to proscribe . . . the usage of all words of foreign origin."[55]

Six months later, Germaine Goblot, writing in the *Revue pédagogique,* also deplored the xenophobic nationalism evident throughout the German curriculum. Taking aim at German nationalists, who in their determination to "form individuals who will be German to the bone" dismissed French literature as unimportant, unoriginal, and immoral, she subjected their anti-French sentiments to gentle ridicule. These cultural philistines denounced the study of French, denigrating it as "the instrument through which all evil ideas, originating in the West, penetrated the German people."[56] Like Friedel, Goblot was relieved that not all Germans endorsed this nationalist agenda. At the outset of the war, some teachers of French and English had abandoned their prewar scholarship in an outburst of patriotism, but others—unwilling to disavow their past or their principles—had insisted that French and English, the "source and inspiration of the great [German] classics," be retained. The most outspoken proponent of this dissenting view was Professor Robert Petsch, who urged his fellow Germans to remember the cosmopolitanism of the eighteenth century, to recapture the latitudinarian spirit of Lessing, and to acknowledge that even the enemy had contributed to the advancement of human culture. Petsch's vision of cultural inclusion closely resembled Goblot's own preference for a genuinely cosmopolitan education in France. Speaking tacitly to French nationalists, she and several other scholars suggested that France should not imitate the most odious characteristics of the enemy by pursuing a narrowly nationalistic educational program. To maintain its intellectual integrity, its principled commitment to the universality of reason, and its distinctiveness vis-à-vis Germany, France should avoid the temptation of nationalist education, remain true to its own traditions, and offer students a full, rich, and cosmopolitan curriculum that included German.[57] Turning the tables on their nationalist adversaries, they argued that insofar as the modern curriculum of 1902—notable for its preponderant attention to modern languages—gave expression to the essential cosmopolitanism of the classical tradition, it remained classical in spirit.

Classicism and Conservative Reaction

When Croiset conflated the classical tradition with that of the French Revolution or when Lavisse and others insinuated that the modern curriculum remained classicist in spirit, they endeavored—but ultimately failed—to reclaim the classical tradition from cultural conservatives. Enjoying the advantage of consistency and tapping a traditionalist and nationalist vein that the war had brought to the surface, conservative scholars and artists gained newfound authority from the classicist revival of the Great War. Demonstrating no tolerance for either the cosmopolitanism or the incongruous modernism of republican classicism, they offered the French people the familiar classicism of *Latinité:* rooted more in Rome than in ancient Greece, it eschewed the egalitarian universalism of republican classicism for the orderly, hierarchical universalism of Catholicism. Rejecting the political definition of classicism as "Liberty, Equality, and Fraternity," the French conservatives defined classicism according to an aesthetic trilogy of clarity, reason, and moderation.

Vincent d'Indy, whose compositions contributed to the revival of Gregorian chant and the rediscovery of traditional folk music, spoke for many others when he defined French culture as "nothing other than the ancient *Latin culture* that honored clarity, logic, and balance."[58] Epitomized by Virgil and Dante, these classical principles had found their most eloquent French expression in the literature of Molière and Racine, the philosophy of Descartes, the architectural splendor of Versailles, and Jesuit pedagogy directed to the formation of "honnêtes hommes." This composite list of classical accomplishments suggested, at least to cultural conservatives, that if France were truly to "return home," it had to recapture the spirit of the seventeenth century, contemplate the possibility of monarchical restoration, and initiate wide-ranging educational reform.

That Racine, Molière, and Descartes were all voices of the seventeenth century was by no means irrelevant. Unlike republican scholars who looked for inspiration to ancient Athens, cultural conservatives turned their attention towards the seventeenth century. Allusions to the *grand siècle* resonated in wartime France because the nation at war derived much-needed reassurance from the splendor, ideals, and triumphs of its past. Having conquered adversity and disorder in the seventeenth century, France could do so again in the twentieth. René Doumic reminded his readers that the year in which Corneille wrote *Le Cid* was also the year in which Corbie besieged Paris, "threw [the city] into panic," and prompted the national government to consider quitting the endangered capital.[59] The parallels with 1914 were striking indeed. No wonder wartime audiences flocked to the *Comédie Française* to applaud *Le Cid*: Corneille spoke as forcefully to the France of 1914 as to the seventeenth-century nation battered by the Frondes.

Vincent Scully suggests that part of the seventeenth century's wartime appeal lay in its masterworks of architectural classicism, Le Nôtre's gardens and Vauban's fortresses (of which perhaps the most famous was that of Verdun); both offered wartime France much needed reassurance. After 1914 seventeenth-century military fortifications served not just as a symbol of past military strength and ingenuity but as instruments of national defense and salvation. Although Le Nôtre's classical garden design offered modern France no such strategic advantage, it offered reassurance in a more subtle way. With its determined disciplining of nature, it was a "portrait of the order of the world" and a celebration of "the rationality of the human mind." Having imposed order on at least part of the fractious world of seventeenth-century France, Le Nôtre's gardens represented the power of "the human will . . . to control the environment."[60] Like French philosophy, which Delbos admired for its ability to render the human world orderly, Le Nôtre's landscape architecture brought the order of reason to unruly nature.[61] Powerfully compelling in its time, the classical pursuit of order was equally compelling in wartime France, when survival itself depended upon discipline and order. This pursuit of order and rationality, derived from seventeenth-century models, did not disappear with the Armistice. For example, Le Corbusier's plans for urban renewal, sketched out in the years immediately after the war, were consciously classical and Cartesian in spirit.[62]

The political implications of a classicist revival were not lost on those who acclaimed the accomplishments of the seventeenth century. French neoroyalists of the Great War perceived in seventeenth-century classical architecture, with its determination to impose order, rationality, and human control over a world fraught with chaos, the cultural analogue of absolutism: both sought to subdue anarchy and disorder. Identifying the reign of Louis XIV, not the age of the Revolution, as the apotheosis of classicism, they suggested that France could rediscover its classical culture only through a process of counterrevolution. This was the standing argument of the Action Française; and Abbé Delfour made this Maurrassian argument in *La Culture latine*. So did Maurice Denis, whose aesthetic sensibilities predisposed him to the Catholic and hierarchical order of the Old Regime, when he identified a classical continuum that originated with Aristotle and culminated with Maurras: "All masters of art and thought, from Aristotle to Maurras, from Phidias to Degas," devoted themselves to bringing out of the fog of uncertainty "pure truth and unadorned beauty." And Denis identified Versailles, the most enduring symbol of monarchical absolutism, as the "triumph of order" and the "masterpiece of classicism." To acclaim Versailles and Maurras as the authentic expressions of the classical tradition in France was to commingle the culture of classicism with the ultraconservative, distinctly counterrevolutionary politics of monarchism.[63]

Lamy, addressing the Académie Française in 1914, distanced himself from those who believed that a monarchical restoration was a necessary precondition of cultural renewal. It was possible, he argued, to recapture the spirit of the seventeenth century without reviving its political institutions.[64] Most admirers of the seventeenth century believed, however, that to be true to its classical identity the nation should return, if not to the political structure, then at least to the pedagogy of the seventeenth century. Charles Navarre, writing in the staunchly republican *Revue internationale de l'enseignement*, still found much to admire in the pedagogy of seventeenth-century priests. He defended both the Jesuits, with their pedagogical innovations that inspired young children with an enthusiasm for learning, and their arch-rivals, the Jansenists of Port Royal. The teachers of Port Royal had bequeathed to France an invaluable legacy, for they had demonstrated effectively that instruction in "classical culture, and especially in Latin culture, ought to be thought of not as an end in itself but as a means to an end." The study of Latin as taught at Port Royal was not directed to the formation of erudite Latinists, but to the formation of men of probity, "upright, honest, and serious."[65] And it was this respect for the formation of "honest men" that distinguished French education from the utilitarian instruction of both its allies and its enemies.

The most significant feature of conservative (as opposed to republican) classicism in the years of the First World War was its insistent defense of the classical curriculum and its determination to effect educational reform. Cultural conservatives like René Doumic believed that for France to "return home," it had to return to the educational tradition abandoned by would-be modernizers in 1902. A prominent literary critic well known to readers of the *Revue des deux mondes* (he would become editor of the journal in 1916), Doumic was also a familiar name to thousands of *lycée* students. By 1914 his *Histoire de la Littérature française,* a textbook for secondary school students, was in its thirty-first printing, and had sold more than 360,000 copies. In this regard at least, Doumic occupied a position comparable to that of Lavisse: as respected scholars and authors of popular introductory textbooks, both hoped to inspire in the nation's youth a regard and affection for their national cultural heritage. Unlike Lavisse, however, who had embraced the educational reforms of the Third Republic as essential to meeting the challenges of the modern world, Doumic lamented modernist innovations as alien and injurious to France.

Doumic's essay entitled "Retour à la culture française," which appeared in the *Revue des deux mondes* in November 1914, became the rallying point for educational conservatives who hoped to undo the reforms of 1902. Although Doumic welcomed Croiset's apparent conversion to the classicist cause, he did not absolve him of responsibility for the errors of educational innovation. It had been under the direction of Croiset and Lavisse among others that French education had lost sight of its essential objective and strayed from "the national path." They had acted not out of malice but from a false sense of security, for they had failed to realize that French civilization and its values stood in peril. The outbreak of war had exposed this belief as a cruel misperception. Doumic expressed confidence that the nation's educational authorities would now willingly engage in a frank examination of conscience, determine their past errors, and set them right.[66]

More than anything, Doumic hoped that erstwhile reformers would abandon the modern secondary school curriculum adopted in 1902. He feared that this innovation had critically undermined the classical tradition in France, and he insisted that France had to forsake this educational experiment if it hoped to preserve its classical heritage. For

Doumic, classical education was essentially instruction in *la culture gé-nérale:* "the knowledge that it embraces is that which ought to be common to all." For this reason the fundamental characteristic of a classical education was its emphasis on literary studies: "the object of all education is to prepare young men for life; and letters are the mirror of life." To this end students had to be well versed in classical languages, for Doumic contended that it was impossible to write good French if one knew no Latin, and impossible to write or to speak with a "certain degree of delicacy and purity" if one knew no Greek. Knowledge of Greek and Latin "put at one's disposal the patrimony of literary traditions that had attained perfection" and thus allowed the French to understand better their own literary achievement. A classical education did not ignore history and the natural sciences, but it did subordinate the study of both science and history to that of literature. Doumic argued that this ordering of intellectual disciplines was neither arbitrary nor unreal; rather, it reflected the fundamental reality that "before being a scientist, an engineer, a doctor or an architect, one must be a man."[67]

As a conservative republican Doumic believed that a classical humanist curriculum belonged to the entire French tradition, aristocratic and democratic, prerevolutionary and revolutionary; it was neither the exclusive patrimony of a cultural elite nor inherently incompatible with the principles of democratic society: "accessible to all, it was not the privilege of an elite although it did serve to create an elite." Nonetheless, classical education had fared poorly under the Third Republic. Unduly impressed by German accomplishments, the educational establishment of the Third Republic had introduced to France an alien spirit which, under the false guise of "science," had "perverted" and "contaminated" French education. Doumic reminded his readers that prominently placed scholars at the Sorbonne had directed this cultural offensive against indigenous educational principles. He considered it tragic that those in the vanguard of educational innovation had turned on the tradition that had created them. Lavisse, for one, had publicly denounced the classical curriculum of his youth, and had disparaged the classical curriculum as shallow instruction in "rhetoric."[68] Dismissing rhetoric as nothing but verbiage, Lavisse and his fellow reformers feared that classical education created talented sophists, but not capable citizens. Thus they had spearheaded a movement to purge all elements of classicism from the secondary and postsecondary curriculum. Doumic considered the results truly lamentable. Too many *lycée* students knew neither Latin nor Greek; and many didn't have much French either.

Arguing that the modernization of French education that occurred after 1870 was symptomatic of a "pedagogy of defeat," Doumic insisted that it was no longer appropriate to perpetuate the domination of the enemy in the school curriculum. Just as the French Army was repelling the German Army, so did the leaders of French education have to repel and eliminate all vestiges of German influence; nothing less than "the future of French intellect" depended upon it. From the Minister of Public Instruction down, all should now devote themselves to the restoration of the only educational system rooted in French cultural traditions. Believing these officials to have been mistaken in the past, Doumic nonetheless also believed them to be honorable and decent, willing to do that which was essential for the defense of France: "to be mistaken is human, but to persevere in one's error is unpardonable." Thus he called upon them to "give us back our traditional education" and "deliver us from the pedantic, mediocre and amorphous German curriculum."[69]

This had been Pierre Lasserre's argument before the war, and it is not surprising, therefore, that Lasserre reinforced Doumic's call for a "return home." In series of public lectures sponsored by the *Revue hebdomadaire*, he argued that the war had further strengthened his faith in the classical tradition. As he watched his younger comrades at the *Revue critique des idées et des livres* leave for the front and lamented his own inaction, Lasserre sought refuge in the classics and derived special inspiration from Virgil. Had not Virgil recognized that national revival would come from a rediscovery of that which was essential to a nation's identity? Lasserre believed that France, too, had to discover the validity of Virgil's insight: national regeneration would come if and only if France abandoned its prewar inclination to self-indulgence and decadence and embraced its true culture.[70] In a subsequent essay, he made it unambiguously clear that the nation could revive only if it restored classicism to its rightful place in French education. Like Doumic, Lasserre argued that the educational reforms implemented in 1902 had "dethroned" (though they had not totally destroyed) the classical tradition in France. Symptomatic of a national malaise and a tragically mistaken admiration for foreign, essentially alien, influences, the reforms of 1902 had critically weakened France. They had alienated the nation from its true cultural heritage and had permitted the ascendancy of pacifists and Germanophiles who saw in Germany a nation to be emulated rather than a power to be combated.[71]

It is significant that Lasserre published his essays and presented his public lectures under the auspices of the *Revue hebdomadaire*, for the

Revue had not been a standard-bearer of the classical cause in the years before 1914. It became one, however, during the war, and published several articles in addition to those of Lasserre that criticized the educational innovations of the prewar years as Germanic in inspiration. In 1915, for instance, Gaston Deschamps decried as antithetical to French culture the German influence in French education. Echoing Bergson, he condemned the German intellectual spirit as one of "barbarous discipline." "Nothing," he wrote, "was more inhuman than the programs of Germanic education, and nothing was more insipid than university education in the German style." The German spirit had neither taste nor respect for style, grace, or elegance; the inclination for perfection that characterized the efforts of elites in France, Greece, and ancient Rome enjoyed no currency in Germany. When this German spirit penetrated French education, the consequences were lamentable: "under the pretext of applying German method, war was waged on eloquence and poetry in France."[72]

A year later, an anonymous contributor to the *Revue hebdomadaire*, discussing "the necessary reparations" that the war demanded, insisted that France recognize that "order, clarity, and moderation *(mesure)*" were the essential traits of its own culture. The French spirit was "more accessible to ideas than to passion"; was committed to determining "what is real"; and respected "truth for itself." For all these reasons, it had no need to import German "objectivity"; the French tradition provided more than adequate foundations for discovering the truth. It was regrettable, therefore, that in the wake of the Franco-Prussian War, the nation had fallen under the baleful influence of Germany. Writers and politicians alike had been inclined "to welcome with the utmost unconcern ideas that were in no way favorable to maintaining intact a national culture." Referring his readers to Maurras for substantiation, the author enumerated the unfortunate innovations that had then followed: Latin had come under critical scrutiny, foreign literature had achieved a new authority, and German methods of instruction had been introduced to French education. What amounted to the evisceration of French education had only accelerated after 1900, when educational innovation, predicated on "an excessive confidence in German science," had turned France away from its native traditions. The classical curriculum, rejected as inadequate "for the needs of the modern world," had been supplanted by the study of science and the arid analysis of documents. Once highly regarded, the traditional intellectual qualities of originality and talent had lost credibility in an atmosphere that revered "application" and "patience."[73]

With its emphasis on the classicism of seventeenth-century France, the wartime discourse of French conservatives was consciously nationalist in tone. Unlike their adversaries on the left, they did not conceive of contemporary classical culture as essentially cosmopolitan; and they certainly did not agree that as a classical—and hence cosmopolitan—culture France had an obligation to offer and encourage instruction in modern languages. Recognizing that the French classical tradition, with its roots in ancient Greece and Rome, was not entirely indigenous, they insisted instead upon the importance of instruction in classical languages. Most significantly, they emphasized the importance of Latin to the classical curriculum. The "Latin question" thus became central to wartime educational debates.

Compulsory Latin, some scholars suggested, was an indispensable component of a truly "disinterested" education. This was true even of some pedagogues who endorsed the reforms of 1902. Charles Navarre argued that of the four options made possible by the 1902 reform, the three that required Latin were pedagogically superior to the one that did not. Only by maintaining compulsory Latin in the curriculum could France affirm the "disinterested" character of its secondary education. With little modern-day applicability, Latin offered students something more important than marketable skills: it provided a foundation in rigorous logical analysis and offered models of moral rectitude. The superiority of a Latin-based education was evident if one looked, for comparison's sake, to the one option within the secondary school curriculum that required no Latin. Navarre regretted that whatever other advantages might accrue to the "D" stream, it lacked the spirit of the other three options: it had not yet found the essential balance between idealistic, disinterested education and utilitarian instruction.[74]

Other defenders of Latin insisted upon its importance as a prerequisite for fluency in French. Among those who wished either to restore compulsory Latin to secondary education or to preserve its place in undergraduate instruction, several argued that because the French language had evolved directly from Latin, students needed to know it to develop full appreciation and fluent command of their own language. Thus in 1917, when the Sorbonne debated the merits of an undergraduate program in French studies *(licence française)* that would not require any Latin instruction, opponents of the innovation did not hesitate to voice their objections. Fortunat Strowski, a professor of French literature at the Sorbonne, put the matter simply: "to understand French literature, one must know how to read Latin." Professor Picavet, a medievalist, agreed. How could one study French thought of the Middle Ages, all of which had been written in Latin, without a command of the language? Speaking as a modernist, Professor Brunot (who would become Dean of the Faculty of Letters upon the retirement of Alfred Croiset) dismissed the study of Latin as the intellectual indulgence of "a small elite . . . no longer indispensable to the study of French." His colleague, Professor Puech, begged to disagree. "The classical heritage remain[ed]," in his opinion, "the foundation of our culture and it would be most imprudent to abandon it." He feared that such an innovation could occur only "to the detriment of our classical culture."[75]

The Sorbonne, after intense debate, voted to approve the *licence française* without any course requirements in Latin. To Abbé Delfour, the abandonment of compulsory Latin was proof of an anticlerical conspiracy to eliminate the cultural influence of the Catholic Church in France. Convinced that so long as Latin survived in French schools, the Catholic Church would survive in France, he feared that if the Republic eliminated Latin from the curriculum, the loss would, in effect, sound the death-knell of French Catholicism. Intensely antipathetic to the new Sorbonne, this integral nationalist charged that through their hostility to "Greco-Latin culture," republican leaders of higher education revealed their profound "hatred for the French, Catholic tradition." "Jewish and Protestant" reformers, "allied with such anticlerical Freemasons as Aulard and Seignobos," had expressed their aversion to Catholicism by declaring war on classical education. Believing that the study of Latin and Greek was essentially "reactionary" because it "favored the influence of the Church," they had resolved to "suppress" these essential elements of a classical education and "extirpate" from the French soul any remnants of Catholic influence. Looking to the future, he was no more sanguine: he feared that ministers of Public Instruction would remain, whether consciously or not, the executors of a vast "political, pedagogical, and religious plan the object of which would be the disappearance of classical studies" in French schools.[76]

Convinced that the Third Republic was intent upon the destruction of classical education and the Catholic Church in France, Abbé Delfour was probably dumbfounded when the Minister of Public Instruction in the summer of 1918 acclaimed the classical tradition as the very "root of our national education": "it is this that makes us forever French, and it is this which has prepared us for, and made us worthy of, victory."[77] These remarks suggest that—the outcome of the Sorbonne vote in 1917 notwithstanding—an unprecedented enthusiasm for classical education in France had emerged during the war years. The modernists feared that it had started in the early months of the war: in December 1914 a M. Edmond Pottier had written *Le Temps* to express his dismay that since the outbreak of hostilities educational traditionalists had gained the upper hand.[78] Nor did they lose ground as the war progressed. Félix Pécaut, writing in the summer of 1918, observed that the war had provoked a critical examination of all assumptions concerning public education, and had prompted teachers and educational experts to contemplate the necessity of "fundamental reforms in national education." Because the war had bestowed upon classicism and classical education a powerful new authority, "prominent men whose role within France was to defend classical education . . . believe[d] that events [had] worked to their advantage. Did not horror of German *Kultur* lead minds, disabused of their previous respect for Germany, back to the pure tradition of Greece, of Rome, and of France?" For Pécaut, the ultimate effect of this classicist revival had been a reassessment of the appropriateness of modernist educational reform, and especially the reforms of 1902.[79]

Called upon to consider abandoning the 1902 curriculum, educational administrators went on the defensive. When they addressed the parliamentary committee charged with overseeing education, spokesmen for the Ministry of Public Instruction rejected Doumic's argument that the protection of France's cultural patrimony depended upon the abolition of the 1902 curriculum. But they did acknowledge that curricular reform, having done much to improve instruction in the sciences and modern languages, had served the humanities less well; and they conceded that some kind of mid-course correction might be in order.[80] Liard admitted that there did indeed exist a *crise du français:* students of the last decade and a half had revealed an alarming inability to express themselves precisely and accurately in French. Their competence in classical languages was also questionable. Coville testified that even students who could translate from Latin into French were often hard-pressed to write comprehensible Latin. He anticipated that after the war France would have to undertake "a revision of its academic organization and its programs" to eliminate "the imperfections" evident in the current system.[81]

Whatever the imperfections of French secondary education, neither Liard nor Coville was willing to abandon the 1902 curriculum. Believing that compulsory Latin could be restored only at the expense of instruction in the sciences and modern languages, they articulated a cosmopolitan and modernist vision of French education consonant with the internationalist classicism of the Republic's academic reformers. Hence they urged the government to maintain the division, in place since 1902, between modern and classical instruction, because they believed that France should not sacrifice genuine advances in scientific and foreign language education on the altar of nationalist cultural conservatism. They shared with many scientists the fear that the classical revival of the Great War constituted a serious challenge to French science.

CHAPTER SIX

"Toujours la science"

Like their colleagues in the nation's faculties of letters, noncombatant scientists were susceptible to the imperative of patriotism and subjected to the pain of war. Those too old for active service regretted their inability to enlist and wished to make themselves useful as best they could. Aimé Cotton, a physicist at the Ecole Normale who would become one of France's most prominent scientists after the war, recalled "the mournful, deserted" character of the school's laboratories in August 1914 as students, research assistants, and laboratory staff responded to mobilization orders. Only forty-five years old himself, he found the enforced inaction of those early days "painful" indeed.[1] To lessen the pain of inactivity, he quickly absorbed himself in war-related scientific research. Scientists of an older generation, with sons away at the front, experienced an even more bitter anguish. Emile Picard, who spent many hours coordinating the various philanthropic efforts of the Institut de France, suffered the death of his only son in January 1915, and Camille Jordan, elected President of the Académie des Sciences in 1917, lost three sons in the war.[2] Thus French scientists shared with all noncombatants the embarrassment of initial inactivity and the agony of personal loss.

But scientists could make themselves useful in ways not available to philosophers, historians, and literary critics. They could—and did—apply their academic expertise to the military and medical challenges presented by modern warfare. Many resolved to do so immediately. In the spring of 1915, Gaston Bonnier, who succeeded Paul Appell as President of the Académie des Sciences, recalled how at the outbreak of war "all members of the Academy not mobilized in a public service" had placed themselves at the "disposal of the government to assist with the task of national defense, each one according to his [or her] expertise."[3] The French Society of Physicists and the scientists of the University of Paris, also under the direction of Paul Appell, were quick to follow suit. The government, perhaps not satisfied with voluntary efforts alone, made its own efforts to "mobilize" the nation's scientists, and circulated requests for counting and classifying nonmobilized scientists.[4] In the fall of 1915, the government, prompted by Paul Painlevé, moved to coordinate the disparate efforts of French scientists through the auspices of a newly created Division of Inventions, an undersecretariat within the Ministry of Public Instruction and Fine Arts. The division would complete the "mobilization of industry" already effected through the "mobilization of science." As Charles Nordmann wrote in the *Revue des deux mondes,* this was the first time that the French government had recognized the fundamental importance of science to modern society, and he considered the creation of the Division of Inventions "nothing less than a revolution" in French attitudes to science.[5]

The mobilization of science workers, distinct in this regard at least from that of nonscientists, did, however, resemble the mobilization of noncombatant men of letters in one critical way. Many of the nation's most prominent scientists devoted considerable time and effort not only to the practice and application of science for the war effort, but to the written defense of science as an intellectual enterprise. In part they acted out of outrage at the actions of scientists across the Rhine who endorsed the Manifesto of 93 and used their scientific expertise to develop chemical weapons. Thus they hoped to make a distinction between French science and French scientists and those of Germany. But French scientists also responded to domestic challenges. During the early months of the war science came under increased attack because it was too readily identified in French intellectual and popular circles as a "German" field of endeavor. Determined to combat this misperception, Louis Liard argued that "science stood outside" of *Kultur* and was untainted by any incidental association with it. But he feared that "the war had only accelerated" a pre-existing national suspicion of science.[6] To protect science from this internal attack, and preserve the educational advances in the sciences achieved in the years before 1914, it was necessary to prove it indigenous to France. Thus practical action, however important to the war effort, was not enough; it had to be complemented by discursive action in defense of science and in explanation of its nature and its origins.

Practical Action

From the very first months of the war, scientists applied their scholarly expertise to the service of the nation. They directed their intellectual energies to problems of munitions manufacture, the application of scientific knowledge to conditions of combat on land, at sea, and in the air, and to medical treatment of the wounded. Each year the Academy reiterated its determination to "mobilize" all scientists who might be "useful for the defense of the nation."[7] Albert Mathiez, the distinguished historian of the French Revolution, saw in the enterprise of French scientists the reenactment of a patriotic tradition established in 1794. In the critical Year II of the Revolution, French scientists, all devoted to the cause of democracy and the defeat of tyranny, had committed themselves to finding creative ways to manufacture saltpeter, to improve armaments production, and to expedite military communications. Their efforts, which included the invention and application of a rudimentary semaphoric system of telegraphy, had helped secure French victory.[8] Mathiez's essay was no simple exercise in disinterested historical scholarship; it was part of a much larger discussion, which tended to divide along political and sectarian lines, about the political character of science and its place in French culture. But the article also formulated one incontestable truth about the "mobilization of intellect," whether in 1794 or 1914: scientists could apply themselves directly to the technical problems of war. Mathiez, writing in late 1917 when many of the projects of French scientists remained hidden behind the veil of military secrecy, probably could not have known how apt his analogy was. Scientists who applied themselves to improving the technology of long-distance communication and finding French sources or synthetic substitutes for essential war materials, did indeed imitate the example of their revolutionary antecedents.[9]

Confidential documents compiled at the end of 1917 and now available in the archival records of the Ecole Normale allow us to observe one small, but highly prestigious, scientific community at work during the war years. In December 1917, Minister of Public Instruction M. Steeg asked Lavisse for a summary of scientific research undertaken at the school since the outbreak of hostilities.[10] With exemplary promptness, the directors of each of the major laboratories at the school prepared and submitted detailed reports outlining the contributions of ENS scientists to war-related research.

In the earliest months of the war (from August 1914 through April

1915), physicists enjoyed the upper hand, in part because they were able to continue military research initiated in the prewar years. Henri Abraham, the director of the physics laboratory, identified four areas of research to which more than thirty individuals (research scientists, associates, and laboratory assistants) had contributed since August 1914: (1) the use of sonics to pinpoint the location of enemy artillery emplacements; (2) the application of this process to submarine and subterranean combat; (3) the effect of air resistance on the projectory of shells; and (4) wireless telegraphy. Abraham had been personally involved since 1913 in the development of wireless telegraphy, and his research continued throughout the war years. In December 1914, his colleague, Professor Chilowsky, initiated research intended to extend the range of artillery batteries. Physicists at the beginning of the war had believed that this could be accomplished by one of only two means: increasing the initial velocity of the shell, or modifying the weight and/or shape of the shell. Chilowsky believed, however, that the desired result could be achieved by altering the density of air through which the projectile flew.[11]

In 1917 Abraham argued that each of these experiments had potentially important applications for artillery, submarine, and anti-aircraft combat. But the most noteworthy achievement of the ENS physicists belonged, without question, to Cotton and his colleague, Pierre Weiss (1865–1940), who worked on locating enemy artillery emplacements through sonics. Developed during the winter of 1914–15, the Cotton-Weiss system became the standard system used by the French Army. The necessary equipment was perfected at the ENS and adopted by the French Army in April 1915. It allowed French troops to locate the enemy's new artillery installations, to identify the position of guns in use, and "occasionally to adjust [French artillery] fire" accordingly.[12]

Until the spring of 1915, only the research undertaken by ENS physicists seemed of immediate and direct utility to the war effort. Thus in February 1915, when Lavisse submitted his budget requests for the forthcoming academic year, he asked for full funding for the physics laboratory because of the importance of the war-related research under way in Abraham's laboratory. By contrast, he requested only half-funding for the chemistry laboratory, where "the work was not, for the moment at least, of the same intensity as that undertaken in the physics laboratory."[13] Circumstances, unanticipated in February 1915, quickly changed all that. When the German Army used poison gas in April 1915 at the second battle of Ypres, chemical research immediately acquired an unprecedented importance. Indeed, the French Army was so anxious to counteract the effects of chemical warfare (and so determined to develop its own chemical weapons) that it authorized the jurisdictional transfer of chemists at the ENS from the Ministry of Public Instruction to the Ministry of War. Louis Simon, director of war-related research at the Ecole Normale, was charged with undertaking research into the production of chemical substances and compounds for the launching of "special projectiles." At the same time that French chemists investigated the possibilities of chemical warfare, they endeavored to identify the character and composition of chemicals deployed by the enemy.

Although it is clear that scientists offered their expertise to the nation with the best of intentions, good intentions did not always produce remarkable results. L. F. Haber has examined the development and deployment of chemical weapons in the First World War, and his judgment of French scientific initiative is harsh indeed. He contends that French research and development, whether for defensive or offensive purposes, was in most instances ill-conceived and severely inhibited by the obstinacy of the scientists involved. Disregarding considerable evidence establishing that hydrogen cyanide was "militarily useless," French research chemists continued to insist that it represented their best hope for an offensive chemical weapon. Researchers also resisted unwelcome evidence from the field when it came to designing and distributing effective gas-masks. When the British developed what would become the simplest and the most secure gas mask available, the French refused to follow the British lead. Instead, they persisted in developing, using, and selling to their eastern allies a much less efficient—albeit more comfortable—mask. In this instance, national pride, Haber suggests, proved a serious impediment to scientific progress.[14]

These shortcomings notwithstanding, the Army considered chemical research of sufficient importance that it agreed to the transfer of seven mobilized scholars, all former chemistry professors at lycées or universities, from the front to Simon's laboratory.[15] By contrast, Léon Bertrand worked alone for the first years of the war. Determined to devote himself to something that was "more urgent and of greater benefit to the nation" than the work he had undertaken before 1914, he reoriented the focus of his research and sought ways of applying the Cotton-Weiss system to underwater and underground sonic detection. With all of his regular research assistants at the front, Bertrand combined forces with Jacques Hadamard of the Institut de France and throughout 1916 they collaborated on experiments that seem to have entailed applications of the Cotton-Weiss system to naval combat. In late 1916 the Navy, convinced of the importance of this research, intervened to persuade the Army that the laboratory needed skilled research assistants. In December 1916 the Army authorized the transfer of one mobilized soldier from the front to Bertrand's laboratory; in 1917, faced with unrestricted German submarine warfare, the Ministry of War approved the appointment of a second research assistant. The research Bertrand supervised was of such sensitivity that even at the end of 1917 he could not inform the Ministry of Public Instruction of its precise nature. Presumably he and Hadamard were working to identify the underwater location of enemy submarines.[16]

However important applied research was to the French war effort, even the most eminent French scientists confronted critical problems of personnel shortages and inadequate funding. There was, indeed, an ongoing tension throughout the war between the immediate needs of the Army for manpower and the long-term advantages that the military might expect to accrue from advanced scientific research. At first, the Army seemed reluctant to approve the assignment of any able-bodied scientists to noncombat positions. Not only did Bertrand work alone for the first two years of the war, but even the directors of the physics and chemistry laboratories had to make special requests for staff. When Lavisse intervened in May 1915 on behalf of Simon's research, and requested the assignment of an unspecified number of mobilized *normaliens* to the chemistry laboratory, the Ministry of War seemed skeptical. Perhaps annoyed by Lavisse's constant intervention on behalf of his former students, the Army informed him that it would approve the transfers requested only when convinced that the work to be undertaken was of genuine importance to the war effort.[17] Lavisse's response must have been persuasive, because within the week the Army had approved the appointment of two *agrégés* in physics and graduates of the Ecole to Simon's laboratory.[18] Nonetheless, the Army continued to look warily on requests for the transfer of scientists out of the front lines. In December 1915, Lavisse forwarded to the Ministry of War a request from Henri Abraham for the transfer of two mobilized research assistants. Once again the Army insisted upon a "short note explaining the nature of the work currently being undertaken in the interest of national defense." And this time Lavisse recorded he was only half successful. One of the two *normaliens* requested by the laboratory was refused permission to return to Paris; perhaps to mollify Lavisse, the Army did, however, authorize his transfer from the infantry to the artillery.[19] As the need for front-line troops grew ever more emphatic, exemptions from combat for scientific research became more infrequent. In February 1917—no doubt in anticipation of the Nivelle Offensive—the Ministry of War requisitioned *all* able-bodied men under the age of thirty-five (those from the classes of 1902 and after) for front-line combat. If any men thus affected currently held a noncombat position, that position was henceforth to be filled by women or men over the designated age. Louis Simon, anxious to hold on to his two hard-won, skilled research assistants, made the case that as employees of the War Ministry's armaments and munitions subdivision, they were exempt from this new regulation.[20]

The overwhelming need of the infantry for manpower was only one of the obstacles confronting scientific research in wartime France. Another persistent problem was inadequate funding. In October 1914, Liard informed Lavisse and other directors of higher education that frugality was now the order of the day. Henceforth, all acquisitions budgets, whether for libraries or laboratories, were canceled.[21] Those responsible for budget requisitions seem, however, to have tried as best they could to protect the sciences from the full impact of financial austerity. When Paul Appell presented the 1915–16 budget to his colleagues within the Faculty of Sciences at the University of Paris, he had to announce a 25 percent reduction in income. Although government funding remained unchanged, declining enrollments had significantly reduced university income. The faculty approved Appell's proposal to reduce laboratory operating budgets, but expressed the hope that library acquisitions not be affected.[22]

At the ENS, a short walk from the Sorbonne, Lavisse confronted comparable problems. With even greater reductions in income, the school's anticipated budget for 1915–16 required that material expenses be cut almost in half (from 228,050 francs to 120,000 francs); the science budget, however, declined less drastically, from 61,850 francs to 50,900 francs. Lavisse explained this more modest reduction by appealing to the utility and essential nature of scientific research: "it is imperative that for the very sake of national defense, research in physics and chemistry be allowed to continue or be revived." Alluding to the valuable contributions the physicists had already made, he justified his decision to maintain that laboratory's operating expenses intact. The chemists had not yet proved their worth, but Lavisse believed it would be wise to maintain their operating and acquisitions budgets at levels that would allow for the possibility of defense-related research. Anxious to assure the Minister of Public Instruction that these budgets were neither extravagant nor unwarranted, Lavisse emphasized that the directors of each laboratory were determined to accommodate, to the greatest extent possible, the demands "circumstances placed upon them" for austerity.[23] By early 1917, with coal in short supply everywhere, these "circumstances" included the very real possibility of unheated laboratories. Lavisse noted that even though the school now housed a military hospital (funded by voluntary contributions from former students, the Académie des Sciences, and other distinguished donors) and laboratories devoted entirely to military research, the school was almost completely out of coal.[24]

Antipathy to Science

Perhaps even more debilitating for French science than either budgetary austerity or inadequate staffing was a general feeling of public antipathy to science—not all-encompassing but evident nonetheless. Scientists and those favorably disposed to the scientific enterprise were keenly aware of and disquieted by this sentiment. They feared that opponents of science had taken advantage of the war and of the Germans' use of science as a military instrument to launch "perfidious attacks" on the character and utility of science.[25] This certainly seemed to be the case in French Catholic circles, although Harry Paul has made a strong argument that French Catholic intellectuals of the Third Republic were not, properly speaking, hostile to science. Indeed, a few of the nation's most prominent scientists were also devout Catholics who believed strongly in the possibility of reconciling faith and reason.[26] Nevertheless, some of the nation's most prominent Catholic scholars, if not antipathetic to scientific inquiry itself, remained throughout the war hostile to the exclusively materialist world-view entailed by scientism and skeptical of the merits of technology.

When Jacques Maritain addressed the Institut Catholique in the fall of 1914, he reiterated his critique of modern science; furthermore, insofar as science was an essential component of the German intellectual tradition, it was morally suspect. His first lecture of the war (a summary of which appeared in the Catholic daily, La Croix, at the end of October 1914) was entitled "La Science allemande." Ostensibly a response to the Manifesto of 93, it was also a continuation of his prewar critique of modern science. As he had done four years earlier in "Reason and Modern Science," Maritain took care to define what he took to be the legitimate limits of scientific inquiry. He was not, he insisted, antipathetic to science tout court. In 1910 he had written that there were "properly defined limits within which [science] is competent." In 1914 he again emphasized that science was a valid form of intellectual inquiry; it was by nature universal, abstract, immaterial, and true for all times and all places.[27] Citing Maurras, he argued that it could not, therefore, be appropriated by any one nation or culture. Technically, "there [was] no such thing as German science, just as there [was] no such thing as modern science." Yet it was possible to give a meaning to the term "German science." Maritain contended that what Seignobos, Durkheim, and others understood by "German science" was "an intellectual product, made in Germany, intended to assure the hegemony of Germany over the development of thought." This intellectual enterprise was concerned only with materiality. "German science" presumed to arrive at total knowledge of the universe exclusively by analysis of its material character. To recall Maritain's prewar vocabulary, it was "pseudo-science."

Before 1914, Maritain had not identified pseudo-science as German; indeed, as a product of Cartesian rationalism, it was an attribute of modern *French* intellectual culture. In 1914, however, he argued that the pseudo-science that prevailed in the modern world was distinctly Germanic, with decidedly Germanic ambitions: the ultimate objective of "German science" was to establish the "sovereign domination of the German ego over nature." The inevitable consequence of this hubristic, antispiritual science was German militarism, which Maritain described as the "necessary fruit, the perfection, the culmination of [such] a civilization and [such] a culture." Predicated on principles of natural knowledge which recognized only the materiality of existence, modern Germany produced a "civilization without any principle of spirituality, without any God."[28]

In 1915 the Catholic literary critic Victor Giraud also identified the scientistic spirit that had pervaded French academic culture before the war as German, and insisted that its preponderant influence was injurious to France. Giraud's argument was not at this point with the physical sciences as such, but with what he took to be the systematic and misguided application of scientific method to the arts and humanities. Under the lamentable influence of "science," French historiography had cultivated an obsession for "documents" and "facts," at the expense of humanistic interpretation. Literary criticism had fared no better. Here, too, "the idol of 'Science' had exercised its fatal influence." Scholars by nature capable of genuine insight, elegance of style, and refined taste had abandoned all in a misguided pursuit of scientific objectivity. Their scholarship, ascetic in the extreme, lacked both "originality and, all too often, utility." Such was the regrettable consequence of voluntary subordination to Germany. Believing that French methods of analysis lacked rigor, scholars had "placed themselves in tow" behind Germany, a country both "arrogant and ponderous" that knew nothing of style, gave attention only to analysis *(l'esprit géometrique)*, and disdained insight *(l'esprit de finesse)*. Giraud hoped that if "the false idea of Science—*which comes to us from Germany*" were rightfully discredited, the writing of history and literature in France could be liberated from its pernicious influence. Historians and literary critics could then return to an authentically French literary tradition that eschewed arid, uninspired analysis, and rediscover elegance of expression. But only by abandoning its infatuation with the scientific method could France return to the classical tradition.[29]

When Giraud returned to his attack against scientism a year later, he was no longer content just to criticize the methodological error of literary scholars and historians enamored of scientism. He was determined to condemn as barbaric any culture grounded only upon the principles of scientific inquiry. Consciously alluding to Brunetière's essay of 1895, he defined his objective: he did not intend to claim that science itself was "bankrupt"; but he would insist very forcefully upon the bankruptcy of "scientism." Because the belief "that science—*and positivist science, at that*—is the only type of knowledge" had replaced theological faith, the modern world had come to believe that "without science, there is no salvation." In the absence of transcendental moral principles, all was justified in the name of science. And Germany, more than any other country, had been instrumental in this process of moral degradation. Not only had scientism originated in Germany, it had also been most enthusiastically embraced there: "Deifying science in order to deify itself, . . . Germany had pursued its materialist dream of universal domination." By 1916 "the results of this exploitation of science" were evident everywhere: one could not help but perceive in "the 'scientific' war and its horrors, pillage, rape, arson, bombardments, massacres, and torpedoing . . . the balance-sheet of a 'culture' founded solely upon science."[30]

Giraud held out a glimmer of hope: science itself was not inherently evil; indeed, it was essentially amoral, and could be used for good or evil. If science were developed within a metaphysical and epistemological framework that acknowledged its inherent limitations, it could still prove beneficial. But most Catholic critics insisted that the modern world could no longer afford to deify either science or the technology that accompanied it. Although technology was occasionally benign and sometimes beneficial, the war had revealed that it could also be powerfully destructive. Indeed, science had destroyed more lives in two years of war than it had saved in two centuries of peace.[31] And Abbé Delfour reminded his readers that "the marvelous mechanism of the modern age" should not be confused with civilization. It was perfectly possible, he claimed, to "imagine, without any trouble at all, a nation of savages using all the most up-to-date arms with a dexterity equal, or even superior, to that of the Europeans"; but such scientific acumen would not make these "savages" civilized. It was not by "using or perfecting" the technological marvels of the modern world—telephones, radios, airplanes, and submarines—that a people proved itself civilized.[32] A civilized nation was one that respected the arts and letters, not one that developed highly complex technology.

Toward the end of the war, Etienne Lamy developed in a more nuanced form the implications of Delfour's critique. He, too, conceded that the "positive sciences" had offered mankind "incontestable" material benefits, but he insisted that the fundamental epistemological premise of positive science—that human reason could arrive at an understanding of only the material world—had had "disastrous consequences." Indeed, the war and all the anguish it had unleashed were, he feared, the ultimate and tragic consequences of an epistemology concerned only with the immanent and the material. By compartmentalizing human intellect and limiting its domain, proponents of scientific inquiry had impoverished reason: "the most important question of all"—that of the connections that obtained between the visible and the invisible, the material and the spiritual—remained unasked and hence unanswered. Having proclaimed the sovereignty of science, the modern world had abandoned itself wholly to materialism. And "lacking any spiritual principle, force [had] affirmed its dominion . . . and [had] proclaimed its law." In Lamy's view, the naturalist epistemology of science had led directly to the outbreak and atrocities of war.[33]

Lamy did not insist, however, upon the wholesale elimination of scientific inquiry or upon the unmitigated evils of technology. Indeed, while serving in 1918 on an advisory panel investigating the development and deployment of air power, he spoke enthusiastically of the tactical advantages aerial reconnaissance could offer modern armies and expressed no serious reservations about the use of aerial bombardment as an offensive tactic. Lamy, like Pétain, was convinced that mastery of the air was essential to success in modern warfare. Looking beyond the famous dogfights of the First World War's flying aces, he suggested that "to destroy the enemy's airplanes is fine; but to destroy the enemy in large numbers [by aerial bombardment] and to discover [by aerial reconnaissance] his best hidden positions, that is much better."[34] Thus towards the end of the war Lamy's was a highly nuanced critique of modern science that tolerated—indeed, celebrated—the use of modern technology but decried the principles of philosophical materialism upon which modern scientific inquiry rested.

Lamy reconciled his modern enthusiasm for military aviation with his antimodernist repudiation of scientific materialism by insisting that the epistemological divide that had long separated modern science from metaphysics and theology could, and should, be bridged. This, he believed, was something that Catholic universities, under direct assault in the modern, materialist world, were uniquely qualified to do. It was surely significant that one of the first and most notable victims of the war should have been the Catholic University of Louvain, for in an age of relentless scientism Louvain represented an unrepentant challenge to the intellectual materialism of the modern era. The destruction of Louvain demonstrated Germany's utter indifference and contempt for the intellectual tradition fostered there. It also taught the people of Europe a harsh but necessary lesson: when knowledge was fragmented and science dissociated from faith—as it was in the scientistic culture of modern Germany—the monuments of European civilization fell victim to barbarity. To save civilization from such assault, men of intellect ought to abandon the destructive materialism of modern science and return to the Thomistic synthesis of faith and reason. But this could occur only through the active intervention of Catholic universities, which alone affirmed the essential "unity of mind" epitomized by medieval scholasticism but lost in modernity.[35]

The Catholic critique of modern science was clearly a continuation into the war years of the prewar repudiation of philosophical naturalism. It acquired a powerful cogency during the war, however, because by identifying scientism with Germany it tended to reinforce a more widely held belief that Kultur was "an authentic product of science."[36] As we have already seen in Chapter 3, many French commentators contended that Kultur was nothing but a superficially sophisticated cultural construct (to which historians, philosophers, and men of letters and of science had all contributed), the goal of which was to provide intellectual justification for the exercise of power. Critics of modern science contended that science had helped lay the foundations of Kultur and had implicitly endorsed the pernicious belief that "might makes right." Attentive only to the material world, the epistemological premises of modern science suggested, in effect, that matter was all that mattered. If this were so, then those who commanded its resources most efficiently and most effectively acquired a moral authority from their conquest of the material world. This criticism of modern science as unreflective materialism implied not only that science *could* give rise to *Kultur*, but that by its nature it necessarily would do so. Thus the association between science and *Kultur* became one of necessity rather than of contingency. And if science gave rise to *Kultur*, and *Kultur* justified the military efforts of the German Empire, then science ultimately grounded the atrocities of the German Army.

Both Henri Bergson and Camille Jullian, who by virtue of their appointments to the Collège de France enjoyed considerable intellectual prestige, questioned the utility—if not the morality—of science, suggesting that science offered little that was essential to the French war effort. Writing in November 1914 in an article intended for front-line troops, Bergson defined the war as a conflict of diametrically opposed philosophical principles. On the one hand, Germany represented "mechanism," or the systematic divinisation of material power; on the other, the Entente powers represented the moral authority of civilized people who recognized that material force had to be governed by moral law. Bergson, arguing passionately that moral authority would outlast material might, attempted to reassure the troops of the French Army that their cause would prevail. To this end, he distinguished between the "force that exhausts itself" and the force that does not. Material force, however formidable in appearance, was nonrenewable; built upon finite resources, its dominion would likewise prove finite. But the force that comes from moral conviction and principle sustains itself; immaterial, it is also inexhaustible. He urged the French troops to take heart, for "while the force which nourishes itself only on its own brutality" would wear itself out in time, the force that sustained the French Army would "renew itself" over and over again.[37]

Bergson's intentions were honorable: he hoped to sustain the morale of those who confronted the formidable power of the German Army. But by conceiving of the war as a conflict between matter and moral authority—in effect a conflict between *matériel* and morale sustained by moral conviction—he posited an interpretation that was perhaps deleterious to the nation's war effort. Bergson's pride in the moral authority of the French Army tended to reinforce the French conviction that they would win the war through the superiority of their troops' morale, and that material force was of only secondary importance. This notion indirectly belittled scientific accomplishment and scientific innovation: if victory depended more on the quality of one's troops than on the quality or quantity of their armaments, then it was more important to bolster morale than to improve *matériel*.

Bergson was not absolutely antipathetic to science, but he was extremely wary of the social and moral consequences of scientism. He acknowledged that science had brought unprecedented material progress to the world, but he believed that material progress had given rise in turn to "moral, social, and international problems." Most nations that had confronted the moral and social crises that material progress engendered had sought to resolve these problems through a transformation of political culture: offering more liberty, fraternity, and justice. This, however, had not happened in Germany, where material progress had not been accompanied by political progress. And in the absence of higher principles—whether of the rights of man, international justice, or human compassion—material power had given free rein to brute force.[38]

When Bergson ceded the presidency of the Académie des Sciences Morales et Politiques to Alexandre Ribot in January 1915, he used his final address to develop further the implications of his attack on mechanism. He asked his colleagues to think about the possible intellectual consequences of the war. Surely those who survived the war would question the value of progress obtained in the "mechanical arts" and secured through the application of positive science. He predicted that it would be "apparent to all that the material development of civilization, when it pretends to be self-sufficient, can lead to the most abominable barbarity." He anticipated that this realization would give rise to a new interest in questions of morality and mind, and that if the nineteenth century had been "the century of the physical sciences, the twentieth would become the century of the moral sciences."[39]

Camille Jullian, a historian of ancient France, also downplayed the importance of military technology. In a lecture delivered in early 1915, he argued that modern technology had not significantly affected the character of warfare. New weapons and instruments of war—and he spoke specifically of airplanes and submarines—had not "profoundly changed the moral or material conditions of war." If anything, scientific progress, which he considered only "a superficial phenomenon," had had a regressive effect on the character of warfare: Jullian hypothesized that an "excess of science" had led to a "return to the past." Because both sides were equal in industrial strength and scientific expertise, victory would not be found in material advantage. Rather, it would be secured through a revival of "ancestral tradition."[40] Thus he took comfort in the fact that the troops of France were, like their distant ancestors, digging themselves into the earth in order to defend, and be defended by, their native land.

Like Bergson, therefore, Jullian believed that the outcome of the war would not be fundamentally affected by the *matériel* available to the belligerents. The decisive factor would be the spirit that animated the opposing armies. "However well an instrument of war has been perfected, however cleverly conceived in the mind of the scientist who invented it, it is worth only what the arm, the eye, the body, and the heart of the soldier who uses it is worth."[41] This argument downplayed the importance of *matériel* and emphasized the importance of morale. By morale, Jullian did not mean just the state of mind created by material comfort or discomfort, but something more profound: morale was a product of moral conviction. The army that was most convinced of the justice of its mission and the rectitude of its cause would prevail. His argument not only assigned a fundamental significance to the conceptualizations of noncombatant intellectuals in their efforts to sustain the moral convictions of French combatants, but it also suggested that science would be of only incidental importance to the war. When Jullian first spoke to the matter in January 1915 his argument was perhaps plausible: this was before the use of poison gas, before the extensive use of airplanes and of submarines, and before the introduction of the tank. But he did not subsequently revise his assessment of technology's minimal importance to modern warfare.

With their emphasis on the primacy of morale, Bergson and Jullian tended to reinforce the beliefs of many military strategists who had developed in the decade before the war a strategy of the offensive *à outrance* that also emphasized the primacy of troop morale. Inspired in part (but not exclusively) by Napoleon's dictum that in warfare "morale is everything," strategists like Foch and Grandmaison had created a military plan that would simultaneously compensate for an underequipped artillery and exploit France's greatest advantage: the patriotic enthusiasm of its troops. When Foch delivered a series of lectures on the principles of war to the peacetime Ecole de Guerre, he, too, downplayed the importance of *matériel*. Endorsing Joseph de Maistre's judgment that "A battle lost is a battle one believes one has lost, for a battle is never lost materially," the future commander of the Allied Armies added: "And if battles are lost morally, they must also be won in the same way."[42] This, too, was Grandmaison's belief. The man whom Douglas Porch has called the "high priest of the offensive" affirmed a decade before Verdun the primacy of morale over *matériel*: "We are rightly told that psychological factors are paramount in combat. But this is not all: properly speaking, there are no other factors, for all others—weaponry, maneuverability—influence only indirectly by provoking moral reactions." In words that Camille Jullian would subsequently echo, he concluded: "The human heart is the starting point in all questions of war."[43] Perhaps Verdun proved him right. Relentless German firepower could not break French morale. But Captain Charles Delvert, who survived the battle and knew firsthand of his men's remarkable morale, wished that the General Staff would depend upon it a little less. Only Pétain seemed to realize that one "cannot combat *matériel* with men alone."[44]

Porch claims that the strategy of the offensive propounded before 1914 and practiced thereafter was not the proud challenge of an over-confident Army eager to exhibit the mettle of its professional officers. Rather, it "sprang from the army's very lack of confidence, its poor organization and material weakness."[45] Knowing that France could not match Germany man for man on the field of combat, and fearing that France could never equal—let alone exceed—Germany in armaments production, French strategists concluded that in the event of war, victory could be assured only if the *quality* of French manpower surpassed that of the enemy. Thus when training conscript troops already well-schooled in patriotism, instructors were urged to cultivate their love of country, inculcate in them a hatred of the enemy, and emphasize that an army convinced of the righteousness of its cause could not lose. And strategists were to develop a military plan that would best take advantage of the moral training of French troops. Persuaded that the patience demanded of a sustained defensive posture would inevitably erode troop morale, they developed a strategy predicated on a vigorous all-out offensive.

Advocates of the offensive *à outrance* were by no means ignorant of technical advances or scornful of artillery's power. They were, in the main, artillery officers well aware that an infantry offensive could succeed only if supported by appropriate and effective use of artillery. Reflecting upon the disastrous offensives of 1914 (in which the French suffered more than a million casualties), Joffre, Commander-in-Chief of the French Army, opined that the offensive strategy had failed because the generals responsible for it had not adequately coordinated the infantry's advance with the artillery's barrage.[46] But if generals understood in principle before 1914, and knew by experience thereafter, that modern warfare could not be waged without modern armaments, this recognition only reinforced their conviction that morale remained of the first importance. Writing a decade before the war Paul Simon, an instructor at Saint-Cyr, argued that the intensified firepower available to opposing armies made the morale of individual soldiers ever more important: "The more armaments are developed, the more dispersal becomes necessary and the more individual moral strength is needed."[47] Thus the development and deployment of new *matériel* only reinforced their faith in morale, a faith prompted in large part by the inadequacy of French armaments. Because parliamentary parsimony, the bane of French military life before 1914, had made the purchase and production of heavy armaments impossible, military planners had devised a strategy consistent with the equipment available to them; the plan of the offensive, with its heavy reliance on troop morale and mobile light artillery, was the result of the scarcity of heavy weapons. Porch concludes that " 'moral force' became the substitute for the arms which French soldiers did not possess."[48]

Convinced until May 1917 that the war would ultimately be won with men, not machines, the General Staff seemed skeptical that science could contribute much that was essential to the war effort. Thus every request for the transfer of personnel from the front lines to the nation's laboratories had to be defended with a demonstration of national and military utility. And transfers occurred one man at a time. Even when the Army was most anxious to exploit scientific expertise and improve the military technology available to it, its suspicion of civilians often thwarted the effective development of war-related innovations. Haber contends that even though the General Staff believed that chemical weapons held out promising possibilities for the prosecution of the war, there was very little open communication between the Army and the scientists responsible for war-related research. As a result, the scientists rarely understood what the Army needed them to produce or how their inventions would be used in the field.[49]

In Defense of French Science

It was in this climate of suspicion and skepticism that French scientists defended science as useful, honorable, and essentially French. The defense of science began, as was only fitting, in the Académie des Sciences. When the Academy assembled on November 4, 1914, to issue its response to the Manifesto of 93, it did not merely endorse the declaration of the Académie des Inscriptions et Belles-Lettres, as the other classes of the Institut had done. Rather, it repudiated the German text in terms specific to the scientific community. Having condemned the manifesto as an outrageous attempt "to tie the intellectual future of Europe to the future of German science" (which the Manifesto of 93 did *not* do),[50] the Académie des Sciences affirmed that science owed more to the contributions of French and British scholars than to all the efforts of German scientists: "it has been Latin and Anglo-Saxon civilizations that, over the past three-hundred years, have produced the majority of great minds in the mathematical, physical, and natural sciences, as well as the authors of the principal inventions of the nineteenth century."[51]

In the weeks and months that followed this statement, many scholars and scientists unaffiliated with the Academy joined forces with it in a concerted campaign in defense of science. Convinced that the successful prosecution of the war and the intellectual future of the nation depended upon the survival of science and the preservation of rigorous scientific education, they disputed Germany's putative leadership in science and acclaimed French (and, to a lesser degree, British) scientific achievement. They contended that German claims to scientific supremacy were unwarranted: German contributions to the sciences were, the record would show, usually of only secondary importance. By contrast, France had an illustrious but much neglected history of scientific accomplishment that proved beyond a shadow of a doubt that a disposition to scientific inquiry was indigenous to France.

Denying German Claims to Scientific Hegemony

French scientists intent on invalidating German claims to hegemony in science argued, on the one hand, that because science was universal by nature, it could not be the exclusive patrimony of any one nation; and, on the other, that German claims to leadership in the sciences were unwarranted. To make their first point, they frequently cited Pasteur's dictum that "science has no country." Concerned only with the pursuit of truth, science (like truth itself) was "independent of space and time." On this point, doctors Richet and Grasset were adamant. Charles Richet insisted that science was "neither French nor German, neither European nor Australian; [it belonged neither] to the twentieth century nor to the eighth."[52] Grasset concurred: it was ridiculous, in his opinion, to speak of "German science" or, for that matter, of "French science." There was only science.[53] Pierre Duhem, the nation's most distinguished physicist, disagreed on this point; as we will see, he believed that scientific inquiry could assume national characteristics. He did, however, agree that scientific achievement of the first order was free of national taint. Seminal achievements in the sciences were not, Duhem insisted, the products of national cultures but of individual genius. Rare by nature, genius—like truth—did not restrict itself to national boundaries; it could appear anywhere. Even, as Duhem openly acknowledged, in Germany.

Arguments affirming the universal character of science had an immediate utility, as Charles Nordmann (the science correspondent for the *Revue des deux mondes*) recognized. They could justify the use of German discoveries by French medical and military personnel. Universal by nature, science and its benefits belonged to all humanity. Hence Marie Curie could administer Roentgen's X-rays to French troops with impunity. Speaking with the unique authority of front-line experience, Nordmann insisted that it would be foolish to deny wounded troops access to the advantages X-Rays could offer; indeed, it would be tantamount to treason to shun discoveries that originated in Germany when such discoveries could offer France military or medical advantage.[54] Thus arguments affirming the universality of science did not deny Germany its genuine achievements in the sciences, but they did deny Germany's right to represent itself as the undisputed leader, innovator, and sole nurturer of modern science.

X-Rays were but one reminder of German achievements in the sciences; there were many others. Consequently, the French scientists' second task—to dispute German claims to sovereignty in the domain of science—was made most difficult by accumulated evidence of German technical superiority. As Nordmann reminded the readers of *Revue des deux mondes,* the Great War was (whether or not Bergson and Jullian admitted it) a war of science; and although technological innovation and industrial production sustained the military efforts of all major powers, Germany led the way. Outmanned on both fronts, Germany had not been outmaneuvered because its industrial production, built on the foundations of scientific innovation, gave it parity with its enemies. Writing in 1915, Nordmann observed that "the temporary advantages Germany enjoyed derived from its prewar ability to mobilize, better than its rivals, the resources of science."[55] In sharp contrast to Bergson and Jullian, Nordmann insisted that because France was engaged in a technological war, it too had to "mobilize the resources of science" if it hoped to secure victory. He recognized, however, that in the xenophobic atmosphere of war, national acceptance of science was going to be difficult. For many noncombatants, science was too closely associated with the enemy, and to embrace it would therefore be suspect. And so he countered this suspicion of science with an appeal to patriotism. Lest French readers fear that they were being urged to emulate the enemy, Nordmann emphasized that in mobilizing the forces of science, the French would in fact be reviving a tradition established during the Revolution. Science had saved France in 1794 and it could do so again in 1915. If Danton were alive in 1915, he would rally the nation with a new cry: "La science, la science, toujours la science!"[56]

Evidence from the front no doubt reinforced public perceptions of German superiority in science, but as Nordmann, Liard, and many others recognized, such beliefs predated the war by several decades. Indeed, critics could contend—with some justification—that republican pedagogues and academic reformers had done more than most French citizens to cultivate the belief in German superiority. For more than forty years, their imitation of German academic institutions and their words of praise had suggested that Germany did indeed lead the world in scientific accomplishment and output. The "Germanization" of French education evident in the triumph of "scientism" at the Sorbonne had done more than anything else to persuade French citizens that science originated in Germany. Liard denied that the reforms he had introduced after 1880 had "Germanized" French higher education; moreover, the scholars most immediately associated with them had, he insisted, always remained true to the cultural heritage of France.[57]

Although Liard refused to believe that his reforms had bestowed prestige on German science, other scholars identified with the republican academic establishment recognized that they had, however inadvertently, contributed to public perceptions of German scientific superiority. What Boutroux described as the "apparently indestructible prestige" of German science owed a great deal to scholarly opinion and enthusiasm.[58] Albert Dastre (who had held the chair in general physiology at the Sorbonne since 1887, and whose extensive academic credentials included election to the Académie des Sciences and appointments as Director of the Ecole des Hautes Etudes and President of the Société de Biologie) regretted that in the decades before 1914 English and French scholars of good intentions had willingly conceded superiority to Germany; they had done so, he believed, not because Germany merited such an advantage but because they admired German intellectual industriousness.[59] Alfred Croiset suggested ruefully that an "excess of courtesy," admirable under any other circumstance, had prompted the French to render homage (sometimes undue homage) to the accomplishments of their neighbors.[60] Emile Picard agreed. The French academic community, he feared, had unwittingly contributed to the international belief that Germany led the world in scientific accomplishment by "consecrating with their praise works of secondary importance."[61] It was now time to set the record straight.

Prompted to reassess the balance sheet of scientific accomplishments in the light of patriotic enthusiasm, many French scientists agreed with Nordmann's conclusion that Germany's putative hegemony in science was unwarranted.[62] As a careful examination would show, in most cases German contributions to scientific knowledge were of only secondary importance. This was certainly the conclusion Dastre, Picard, Duhem, and Richet (albeit with some reservations) arrived at when each of them reviewed the recent history of scientific achievement in Germany. Richet, anxious not to abandon objectivity entirely, judged Germany only "the equal" of France and Britain in scientific achievement. He recognized that in the years between 1850 and 1910 more scientific papers had appeared in German journals than in French ones: in his own field of physiology, German publications accounted for 48 percent of all papers published; French language publications accounted for 30 percent. It was important to remember, however, that the population of Germany exceeded that of France by exactly the same ratio, and that French output, when calculated per capita, equaled that of Germany. When the quality, rather than the quantity, of scientific knowledge was taken into consideration, Richet concluded that German scientists tended to spill "a lot of ink to very little effect."[63] Picard, professor of mathematics at the Sorbonne, concurred: Germany valued quantity over quality, and Germany's prodigious output, recognized by everyone, was no proof of merit. Insisting that "the majority of essential contributions, whether theoretical or practical, did not belong to German scientists and inventors," he concluded that "the true part Germany played in advancing scientific knowledge did not correspond to the role she purported to play."[64]

Picard's essay, entitled "L'Histoire des sciences et les prétentions de la science allemande," appeared originally in the *Revue des deux mondes* in the summer of 1915; frequently cited and subsequently reprinted, it constituted an important element in the French campaign against German science. Not only did Picard call into question the quality of German scientific accomplishments; like Bergson, he cast doubt upon the moral value of science founded exclusively on materialism. In this way he sought to distinguish the science that begat *Kultur* from the science developed in France, Britain, and Italy. In his two wartime addresses to the Académie des Sciences Morales et Politiques, Bergson had argued that "the material development of civilization, when it purports to be self-sufficient, can lead to the most abominable barbarism."[65] Thus in modern Germany, where the nation's intellectual elite provided philosophical justification for the triumph of force, material progress unrestrained by moral principle had led only to "scientific barbarism."[66] Writing only a few months after Bergson, Picard conceded (as had Bergson) that science could make life more comfortable, but he too argued that it could not make humanity more moral. Indeed, science was essentially amoral: its advances could be used to improve life and, equally easily, to bring about diabolical ends. Thus advances in science alone could not prove the "superiority" of one nation over any other. Even if Germany appeared to be more advanced in its command of science, it could not be concluded from such evidence that Germany was superior to either France or Great Britain.[67]

Most French scholars and scientists agreed with Picard that German scientists were lacking in inventiveness, and many accepted Bergson's characterization of *Kultur* as "scientific barbarism"; but they had to concede one clear advantage to Germany. Germany, without question, was more adept at applying scientific discoveries to practical purposes. What Nordmann called Germany's "temporary advantages" in the field—all too obvious to most French observers in 1915—derived in this view not from the superiority of its science but from the efficiency of its organization. This became a constant refrain for French scholars during the war years. If Germany *seemed* to surpass other nations, including France, in its scientific accomplishments, it was because Germany was better at applying others' inventions and at coordinating the efforts of science and industry. German "organization," not German intellect, accounted for the appearance of scientific accomplishment. This argument, which appeared in the essays of Picard and Duhem, as well as in the collection of essays entitled *Les Allemands et la science,* published in 1916, probably offered little comfort to French soldiers subjected to German barrages.[68] Whether German industrial output was the product of superior intellect or superior organization mattered very little to them. But the distinction between intellect and organization mattered a great deal to French scholars intent on protecting science from the criticism of domestic opponents. By suggesting that organization, rather than science itself, was Germany's unique advantage, they could contest the argument that science was essentially German and thus unwelcome and alien to French society.

It seemed clear to the Parisian scientists who contributed to the debate (but perhaps less clear to the provincial scientists who had worked for decades to improve connections between science and industry) that

France lacked the "organizational" acumen of Germany. Incubated in a culture that cherished individual achievement, science in France had, they feared, failed to coordinate its efforts or forge effective links with industry; as a consequence, many of its scientific achievements remained underutilized. Georges Lemoine of the Institut Catholique considered France's lack of "organization" a virtue: French scientists preferred the intellectual pleasures of pure research to the tawdry profits of applied science.[69] Most French observers, however, expressed grudging admiration for German "organization." The preface to *Les Allemands et la science* conceded that "Germany excels in application and organization: it is there that we ought to profit from her example and perfect our methods."[70] And Duhem believed that the French should cultivate the qualities of application and industry that seemed almost natural to Germans. The intellectual habits of discipline, attention to detail, and painstaking patience were, he surmised, "instinctive" for Germans; they derived from a national predisposition to order and obedience. But in countries where such qualities might be less natural, they ought to be acquired. Just as medieval monks, determined to achieve knowledge of fundamental truths, had imposed discipline upon themselves, modern French scholars could teach themselves to be as disciplined, orderly, efficient, and organized as their German counterparts. They could do so if they consciously adopted the spirit of medieval monasticism.[71]

When Duhem spoke of science as a monastic vocation, he spoke only for himself; but when he argued that distinct spirits of intellectual inquiry distinguished French and German science, he and his republican colleagues spoke in one voice. In November 1914, Alfred Croiset reminded his Sorbonne audience of Pascal's distinction between the "spirit of finesse" and the "spirit of geometry." "Finesse," according to Pascal, infused scientific inquiry with the creative play of imagination and intuition; it allowed scientists to transcend the constraints of logical deduction and see problems afresh. "Geometry" disciplined the imagination with the rigor of deductive logic. Croiset claimed that both inclinations were "indispensable to the perfection of intellectual life."[72] Emile Boutroux and Duhem agreed. But unlike Boutroux, who argued that French science and philosophy had achieved the necessary balance between intellectual imagination and intellectual discipline, Croiset and Duhem perceived imbalances on the two banks of the Rhine.[73] Croiset believed that France embraced both the careful rigor of geometry and the imaginative sweep of finesse, but he did concede that the "spirit of finesse," inherited from Greece and Rome and cultivated only in a community of *honnêtes gens,* was especially prized in France: "France considers the spirit of finesse an essential instrument in the search for truth." Germany, by contrast, scorned intuition entirely. Its intellectual culture lacked any sense of "justice, any spirit of finesse, . . . good sense, or humanity."[74]

While Duhem observed in German science an insufficiently developed spirit of finesse, he also sensed an underdeveloped spirit of geometry in French intellectual life. He argued that although men of genius of every nation successfully synthesized the imaginative, intuitive force of "finesse" and the rigorous deductive discipline of "geometry," scholars of lesser ability usually favored one inclination at the expense of the other. The spirit of finesse tended to dominate French scientific inquiry, and the spirit of geometry prevailed in Germany.[75] For Duhem, this was both the great strength and the hidden weakness of German science. Rule-bound, logical, and analytical, the spirit of geometry proceeded from axioms to logically valid conclusions. Duhem recognized this as a virtue: "It is by its power to deduce with the most extreme rigor, to follow without the least divergence, the most complicated, lengthy chains of reasoning that German science has marked its superiority . . . by this absolute submission to the rules of deductive logic, German mathematicians contributed usefully to the perfection of mathematical analysis."[76] But deduction alone did not produce scientific progress, because the rigorous application of rules of inference necessarily stifled the spirit of invention and intuition, both of which were indispensable to scientific creativity and advance.

Absolute reliance upon the rigorous method of geometry prevented logical error but occasionally led to intellectual absurdity. Duhem knew that rules of inference, when predicated on untenable or absurd axioms, could not lead to truth; they could arrive only at absurd, albeit valid, conclusions. And to his mind the great weakness of the German scientific tradition was that it lacked the intellectual flexibility needed to question the axioms from which it originated and to determine to what extent these axioms were consistent with a wider understanding of the world. Duhem was much too sophisticated a scientist to argue that common sense perceptions were infallible: one of the most important functions of scientific inquiry was to test common-sense assumptions, to refine them, and to modify them in ways consistent with scientific inquiry. But he believed that common-sense had a critical role to play in science, and a method that ignored it was inadequate and essentially flawed. It could lead to scientific nonsense, and relativity physics was a case in point.

Relativity physics proved for Duhem, France's leading theoretical physicist, the ultimate untenability of a scientific method inspired exclusively by the "spirit of geometry."[77] Einstein's theories formulated a "liaison" between space and time that "collided with the most formal affirmations of common sense." Duhem did not live to see his dismissal of relativity theory itself discredited in 1921, when Einstein received the Nobel prize; nor were his views wholly representative, for other French scientists of the war years were more receptive to the originality of relativity theory.[78] Nonetheless Duhem's critique of relativity does seem to have influenced subsequent French Catholic thought. In 1922, when the Collège de France welcomed Einstein to Paris, Jacques Maritain pointedly revived Duhem's critique. Contending that Einsteinian physics was grounded in "radical empiricism," Maritain—like Duhem—suggested that relativity theory betrayed a fundamental lack of Pascalian "finesse." Relying only upon empirical evidence rendered in mathematical formulae, Einstein made no allowances for "the interpretation of the data of the natural world according to the principles of the mind." Maritain also objected to what he took to be the transformation of relativity theory into a metaphysics of relativism, which "conceived of no other reality than that of sensible appearances." When dominated by such principles, modern science and modern philosophy were, he feared, in danger of disintegrating into intellectual anarchy.[79]

Rediscovering French Science

If German claims to scientific superiority were unwarranted, and their methods critically flawed, French achievements had all too often been underappreciated. Bedazzled by recent German accomplishments, the French people had forgotten how much modern science owed to French genius. This national amnesia had to be overcome for the sake of protecting the scientific enterprise and the educational reforms of 1902 that had promoted the serious study of science in France. Thus scholars who had developed and defended the Republic's system of modern education worked assiduously throughout the war to remind their compatriots of France's fundamental contributions to modern science. To this end, they revisited (and rewrote) the history of science, discovering in the process that modern science, although universal in character, was a spirit of inquiry that owed much to France's most honored intellectual traditions.

From the earliest days of the war, French scholars (often with the active encouragement of the French government) set out to prove that French scientific accomplishments, ignored by German scholars and often underrated by French citizens, were of singular significance. Thus when Lavisse and Croiset addressed students returning to the Sorbonne in 1914, Lavisse reminded them that the French intellectual tradition—from medieval scholasticism through Cartesian rationalism—had "opened all avenues to modern science."[80] And Croiset insisted that all scholarship undertaken during the war should remain true to this honorable tradition. To forsake science and the principles of scientific inquiry—application, attention to detail, and probity—would be to abandon something essential to the spirit of French civilization.[81]

In 1915 the French government sponsored an exhibit at the San Francisco World Fair which gave substance to Croiset's contention by documenting the vitality and variety of French science. Leading scholars contributed essays assessing French contributions in their respective disciplines and demonstrating that France had taken a back seat to none in the advancement of science. As if to prove his sympathy for science properly construed, Bergson pointed out in his contribution to the San Francisco exhibition that Descartes was the father of modern science. Although Cartesian mind-body dualism posed significant philosophical problems, it did not, in Bergson's opinion, engender unrestrained materialism (or the "mechanism" which he had only a few weeks earlier condemned in German science), because it ultimately subordinated matter to mind. And French philosophy after Descartes, most importantly the work of Maine de Biran (an almost forgotten eighteenth-century French metaphysician whose work enjoyed a renaissance in France during the war years) solved the problems posed by Cartesian dualism (and endemic in Kantian philosophy) by suggesting the possibility of complete knowledge of matter, on the one hand, and fundamental essences, on the other. Thus post-Cartesian French philosophy had encouraged the pursuit of knowledge of the natural world while at the same time fostering a scientific spirit essentially different from that which prevailed in contemporary Germany: France had cultivated, and contributed to, science without descending into brute materialism.

Innately sympathetic to the scientific enterprise, France had produced men of scientific genius. When Richet addressed an audience at the University of Christiania in Norway, he did not hesitate to remind them that from the seventeenth through the nineteenth centuries, each of the individuals whose work had fundamentally changed the character of modern science was French: Descartes in the seventeenth century, Lavoisier in the eighteenth, and Pasteur in the nineteenth.[82] This was also the message of Picard's "L'Histoire des sciences et les prétentions de la science allemande." His review of the history of science led him to conclude that in mathematics and physics (the two areas of his recognized expertise) first place rightly belonged to France and Britain. Indeed, France overshadowed its ally in essential contributions. Fermat had developed a calculus before either Leibniz or Newton; and Descartes, having preceded both in articulating the law of inertia, had been the first to set forth the fundamental laws of mechanics. If one "left Newton aside" (which the British, at least, were probably reluctant to do), the development of astrophysics ("celestial mechanics") was "almost uniquely" French. No less an authority than Lord Kelvin recognized that Sadi Carnot's contributions in the realm of thermodynamics were of the first importance; and Lavoisier clearly dominated the realm of chemistry.[83] Picard thus challenged German claims to scientific superiority by a review of the history of science that in each instance gave first prize to France. Richet's claims were somewhat more modest—he considered France's contributions to modern science equal to those of England, Italy, or Germany—but he too relished the thought that only France could claim both Lavoisier and Pasteur.[84]

This appeal to French genius was, however, potentially problematic. George Fonsegrive did not deny German accomplishments in the sciences, though he believed that even the most important German achievements were essentially derivative—"corollaries of earlier great discoveries, many of which were the work of French scientists." Was it not the case that Pasteur and Claude Bernard had led the world with their scientific discoveries, and this in spite of notorious shortcomings of French laboratories caused by inadequate equipment and persistent underfunding? "If one were to compare the contributions to knowledge that came out of the all-too-often ill-equipped laboratories of French universities with those emanating from the superb scientific workshops of Germany," one could not help but be impressed by the power of French science.[85] There is nothing in Fonsegrive's description to suggest that he was excusing the chronic underfunding of scientific research about which French scientists frequently complained. Yet his appeal to the power of genius contained the unfortunate implication that French science—creative, imaginative, and productive under the most inadequate material conditions—had not needed expensive up-to-date equipment to lead the world in scientific discovery. Perhaps unwittingly, Fonsegrive thus provided those responsible for funding scientific research with an excuse for persistently inadequate budgets. The strength of French science, like the strength of the French Army, resided in the power of the French mind, not in the plenitude of material resources.

Repeated references to the pre-eminence of nineteenth-century French science gave rise to yet another uncomfortable thought. Had France lost its competitive edge after 1870? Not at all, claimed the contributors to *Un Demi-siècle de civilisation française (1870–1915),* an anthology of essays proclaiming the vitality of French scientific and cultural accomplishments under the Third Republic. In the years after 1870 France had quietly persevered in the physical sciences, as in the arts, so that the nation "had made more progress, and more discoveries . . . than any other country during the same time period."[86] Whether in astronomy, chemistry, mathematics, physics or physiology, France had been at the forefront of human culture and had contributed to human progress in all its endeavors.[87] A similar survey, organized in the spring of 1915 by *Figaro,* also arrived at the conclusion that, from astrophysics to obstetrics, France led the world.

What accounted for France's remarkable, if only dimly recognized, achievements in modern science? Duhem provided a partial explanation with his characterization of French science as marked by a spirit of finesse. Like the spirit of geometry, the spirit of finesse was a two-edged sword: it was the source of the creative intuitions essential to true inquiry and discovery, but if left unchecked, it could be disastrous for science. When Duhem spoke of the dangers of "imprudent intuition," perhaps he had in mind the embarrassing scientific fiasco associated with the ultimately discredited "discovery" of "N-Rays" by French scientists at the University of Nancy in 1903.[88] He believed that in men of genius the inductive spirit of finesse and the deductive spirit of geometry naturally coexisted in harmonious balance; in men of lesser ability, this essential harmony would have to be cultivated. Recognizing that science dominated by the spirit of finesse could be fatally flawed, he urged his fellow—and future—scientists in France to moderate their intuitions with rigorous deduction; the spirit of finesse needed to be reined in by analytical rigor. Consequently, when looking to the future, Duhem did not wish to purge France of all "alien" influences; instead, postwar science would integrate the countervailing forces of geometry and finesse. He looked optimistically towards the day when "French and German science would flourish side by side, without looking to supplant the other; each one understand[ing] that it would find in the other its indispensable complement."[89] For Duhem, true scientific inquiry was marked by balance, moderation, equilibrium; of finding and following what might be called a classical mean. This made Duhem's theory of scientific inquiry consistent with principles of seventeenth-century French classicism and yet consonant with the cosmopolitanism of the republican university.

Science and French Education

Most French proponents of science agreed that science could flourish in an essentially classical culture. Liard, for one, believed that for centuries France had excelled in science *because* it had inherited the rationalism and intellectual universalism of ancient Greece and Rome.[90] But they also feared that a successful campaign in favor of classicism, when combined with a national reaction against science, could reverse the significant advances made since 1902 in the instruction of science and modern languages. Thus the acclamation of French scientific genius was more than an exercise in national self-esteem; it was an essential element in the education debates of the Great War. Those who defined science as an indigenous and honorable French intellectual enterprise hoped thereby to defend the reformed curriculum of 1902 as responsive to the needs of the nation and appropriate to its spiritual character.

In 1915, when Liard, Coville, and Lucien Poincaré addressed the parliamentary committee investigating the consequences of the 1902 program, they described the benefits of modern scientific education in France and urged the politicians not to dismantle the remarkably successful secondary school science curriculum. Liard and Coville were particularly insistent in their defense of the 1902 reforms as necessary, successful, and indispensable to a nation confronted with the challenges of survival in the modern world. It was of the greatest importance that France maintain a secondary school system "founded upon the classical tradition" and yet responsive to the needs of the modern world.[91] Thus they argued for maintaining the basic division between the modern and classical curricula.

A year later, Jacques Hadamard, by then not only Léon Bertrand's research associate but also the Director of the Division of Inventions, took time out from his already full schedule to address the parliamentary committee in writing. Almost three years earlier he had testified before the same committee in defense of the modern curriculum to dispel the belief, cultivated by such organizations as the Ligue pour la Culture Française, that "all men of science considered the classical curriculum in place before 1902 the ideal [form of education]." When in October 1916 he finally found time to return the corrected proofs of his earlier testimony, he considered the defense of scientific education even more imperative. "Not a week passes," he wrote, "that the pages of Le Temps do not affirm that all culture has been killed in France since the introduction of the reforms of 1902."[92]

Liard was equally disturbed by ever increasing evidence that France was turning its back on the modern curriculum. When he testified before the parliamentary committee in 1915 he spoke with especial enthusiasm of the advances made since 1902 in scientific education. Training in the scientific method had effected "a fundamental revolution" in scientific education, and the results were highly gratifying. Instruction in the positive sciences was, Liard concluded, "generally good; indeed, very good."[93] Convinced that the modern curriculum had been exceptionally successful, he nonetheless feared that by 1916 it was in grave danger. In an essay published in that year, Liard confessed his concern that French troops, having witnessed firsthand the formidable power of science in the service of the enemy, would subsequently shun science as uniquely German. Persuaded that no patriotic impulse could be more misguided, he asserted that not only was science a "natural vocation" for France, but the study of science was a "national duty." Only science could help the nation address adequately the many problems it would have to confront after the war. Thus he urged "those who love their country above all else" to apply themselves seriously to a scientific education; and he assured them that if they did so, they would not be ignominiously imitating the enemy. Rather, they would be continuing the traditions of Descartes and Pascal and thus preserving a priceless national legacy.[94]

History showed that modern science had its roots in an intellectual tradition originating in the seventeenth-century culture of the Old Regime; but more recently, science had been cultivated most productively in republican soil. Authoritarian monarchies did not advance science; rather, they stifled creativity under the weight of oppressive regimentation. This was true of Germany, where all the significant achievements of science had occurred before 1870. And it was also true of postrevolutionary France: if one analyzed the history of scientific development in France since 1789, it was clear that only republicans had recognized the importance of science to national security.

During the course of the war both Nordmann and Mathiez insisted that even though individual scientists—Lavoisier most notably—had perished at the guillotine, the Revolution had advanced the cause of science in France. Scientists had rallied to the revolutionary cause because they respected the ideology of equality and liberty it promoted; and they had repaid the Revolution with their genius. As the battle of Fleurus in June 1794 demonstrated, the Revolution profited directly from scientific innovation. At Fleurus, where the French used reconnaissance balloons for the first time in military history and thus inaugurated the age of aerial warfare, science helped win the day, turned the tide of the revolutionary war, and preserved the Republic. Nordmann noted, however, that in subsequent eras, when France had abandoned republicanism and had ignored science, it had been militarily unprepared and nationally vulnerable. Sedan had proved that.[95]

The implicit argument of *Un Demi-siècle de civilisation française (1870–1915)* was that only when republicanism returned to France did science regain its legitimacy. Professor Pinard, a leader in French obstetrics, contended that French superiority in obstetrical innovation derived from the national culture's fundamental respect for every individual. French doctors endeavored to improve childbirth conditions because they cherished "an absolute respect for all individuals, regardless of infirmity or origin."[96] Pinard believed that French dominance in obstetrics predated the Revolution by at least two centuries, but insofar as respect for the individual characterized French culture throughout, it followed that this national trait inexorably led to the Revolution and the triumph of republicanism. Perhaps this respect for the individual impeded "organization" (scholars in France were inclined and encouraged to pursue their inquiries free of government direction), but it was more an incentive than an obstacle to scientific inquiry itself. And as Nordmann and Mathiez argued, monarchism (and the quasi-monarchism of Napoleon III), with its cultural antipathy to science, endangered the nation, while republicanism, with its respect for science as well as for the individual, protected France. Such arguments suggested that national preservation, which was even more significant than national pride, was at stake. For France to survive, science had to flourish; and history demonstrated that it could do so only within a republican regime. From these various essays in defense of science, the educational program of 1902, and the political culture of science, a subtle syllogism emerged. The survival of France depended upon the nation's willingness to honor and promote a scientific culture; science would flourish only if the Republic and the modern curriculum it had created remained intact. Thus the curriculum of 1902 was essential to the very survival of the nation.

Throughout the war years, therefore, French scientists attempted to dismantle the prevailing stereotype that science was essentially German by identifying science as an international patrimony that owed an essential debt to French genius. Even though science was not uniquely French, it was nonetheless compatible with French cultural values and traditions. This argument had to be made because without it the character of the French curriculum, the nation's capacity to cultivate science, and the prevailing political culture of the nation would all be placed in jeopardy. If science were to be discredited as essentially German and an integral element of *Kultur,* it would be very difficult to sustain scientific education in France, to defend the educational reforms of the Third Republic, or to dismiss as unfounded neoroyalist charges that the Republic had imposed upon France an intellectual culture antithetical to the nation's essential traditions. If, however, it could be proven that science was, as Liard would have it, a "natural vocation" for France; if science could be shown to be as integral to the cultural tradition of France as classicism, then its place within the nation's curriculum and intellectual culture would be safeguarded. The outcome of the debate over science was thus of the utmost importance to French scientists, anxious as they were to convince a skeptical nation that their intellectual enterprise was compatible with the first principles of their nation's culture. It was equally important to educational reformers intent upon preserving the scientific character of secondary and advanced education in France, and to republicans eager to repudiate neoroyalists, whose vehement anti-Germanism gave them unprecedented prestige in wartime France.

Epilogue

The Great War wreaked havoc on France's intellectual community. In 1919, memorial services and commemorative plaques bore sorrowful witness to the deaths of hundreds of young scholars and students. Nor had the war been easy on those who had not fought. Overcome by age, physical infirmity and anguish, several of the nation's most famous scholars did not live to see the victory they had so confidently anticipated. Pierre Duhem and Victor Delbos died in 1916; 1917 claimed Louis Liard, Albert Dastre, and Emile Durkheim. Many others who had contributed to the mobilization of intellect survived the war but died shortly thereafter: Etienne Lamy in 1919; Emile Boutroux and François Picavet in 1921; Alfred Croiset in 1923. Peacetime prompted others to resign from their onerous posts. Having devoted himself tirelessly to the tasks of administration and personal commiseration through the war years, Ernest Lavisse retired as Director of the Ecole Normale in 1919. Croiset stepped down from his post as Dean of Letters in 1921. And Paul Appell—who had divided his apparently inexhaustible energy among the Secours National, the Académie des Sciences, and the University of Paris—resigned as Dean of Sciences in 1919. Giving up the restful retirement, he reluctantly accepted the position of Rector of the University of Paris a year later, upon the premature death of Lucien Poincaré.

Each of these men—and many of their colleagues—had resolved in 1914 to make themselves useful by contributing their energy, moral authority, and unique talents to the war effort. As the survivors looked back upon the war, could they conclude that the activities to which they had devoted themselves had proved of value and had in some way, however slight, contributed to victory? Certainly the philanthropic projects of noncombatant intellectuals had offered invaluable aid and an inspirational example to the nation. Because practical action of this sort had not, however, constituted their essential war work, they could not reassure themselves that they had made themselves useful thereby. From the earliest months of the war, they had devoted themselves most energetically to the cause of *intellectual* action, and it was here that their utility would have to be determined.

This chapter will argue first that the mobilization of intellect was important to France during the Great War because it reinforced the will of combatants and noncombatants alike to hold out until victory was secured. The essays of noncombatant intellectuals positively influenced national morale behind the lines and—perhaps more surprisingly—at the front, where the military high command worked to bring their ideas to front-line troops, and where junior officers proved in many instances receptive to the arguments and supportive of the efforts of the noncombatant intelligentsia.

But the impact, and hence the importance, of intellectual mobilization did not end with the Armistice. Indeed, the experience and debates of the war years so profoundly influenced French intellectuals after 1918 that they permanently marked the intellectual culture of the late Third Republic and of Vichy. On the one hand, the mobilization of intellect produced a bitter backlash among left-wing intellectuals, who were determined to hold the intellectual patriots of the Great War accountable for the slaughter of millions. Loath to imitate the men whom they so harshly denounced, they rejected not only the patriotism but also the engagement of the mobilized intellectuals. As Jean-François Sirinelli has argued, many writers and scholars of the left, led by Emile Chartier, Romain Rolland, and Henri Barbusse, denied the necessity, virtue, or utility of intellectual action and chose instead to take refuge in radical disengagement. In 1927, when the French government debated the Paul-Boncour law, which would have made intellectual mobilization mandatory in any future incident of general mobilization, left-wing intellectuals rejected it outright. After 1933 they heard in criticism of Nazi Germany echoes of wartime excoriation and failed as a result to take the Nazi threat seriously. Convinced that appeasement was preferable to war and capitulation preferable to combat, they perceived in Philippe Pétain a leader committed to not spilling French blood. Hence the intellectual left ultimately embraced the defeatism of Vichy.[1]

To recall the radical alienation of left-wing intellectuals is, however, to tell only half the story. The scholarly debates of the war transformed the intellectual culture of France in yet another way: they bestowed an unprecedented authority upon the cause of cultural conservatism. With integral pacifists still occupying the political left, and progressive reformers continuing to hold positions of cultural influence and authority at the Sorbonne and within the powerful Conseil Supérieur de l'Instruction Publique, the right did not gain uncontested ascendancy after 1918. But its influence within the intellectual community and within the nation at large did expand significantly, as evident in the emergence of "intellectual nationalism."[2] This new right-leaning orientation showed itself in the persistent anti-Germanism of French secondary and university students, in the cultivation of a self-satisfied intellectual insularity within French science, and—most vividly—in the debates surrounding the promulgation in 1923 of the Bérard reform of secondary education.

The Utility of Intellectual Mobilization

During the war Etienne Lamy had urged his colleagues to "make truth accessible to all" by teaching the nation "what it had to know." Albert Sarraut had insisted that "by illuminating national feeling with specific knowledge, [the intellectual community would] sustain and fortify the nation with an unshakeable confidence and a will for total victory." The utility of French intellectual action would be determined by assessing whether the many pamphlets and public lectures, essays, and inspirational addresses produced throughout the war years had "fortified the nation," sustained its morale, and encouraged the nation to persevere until victory was assured. Diverse sources suggest that the mobilization of intellect was indeed influential in this regard.

Whether ordinary civilians did or did not read the pamphlets and articles produced by prominent intellectuals, they were probably aware of their arguments and—in some documented cases at least—supportive of their efforts. Jean-Jacques Becker has pointed out that for the duration of the war public school teachers brought the arguments and ideas of the noncombatant intelligentsia to the nation at large. With the active encouragement of school administrators, teachers read the essays of national scholars and then made their arguments the basis of local public lectures and readings. Exercising their influence "to boost morale rather than to encourage opposition to the war," they worked diligently to cultivate and maintain the support of noncombatants for the war.[3] This became evident to Etienne Lamy in the summer of 1917, when he visited towns and villages close to the areas troubled by military indiscipline.

He was heartened to discover that "in spite of the length of the war, the firmness of public opinion remain[ed] unwavering: [civilians understood] the need to hold out still longer, so that all the sacrifices already made not be in vain."[4]

In the same year, Ernest Lavisse likewise received direct evidence that the mobilization of intellect was worthwhile. Although he seems to have preserved very little of his personal correspondence from the war years, he did keep two letters, both written in the summer of 1917, from private citizens acclaiming his contributions to the war effort. In June a shop-keeper residing close to the front-lines wrote Lavisse to acknowledge the receipt of one hundred copies of a recent pamphlet and to request ship-ment of another hundred. M. Gautrin took this opportunity to suggest that Lavisse write yet another pamphlet—and the sooner the better. An eyewitness to the breakdown of military morale that plagued the French infantry in 1917, Gautrin feared that the demoralizing forces responsible for the recent mutinies would gain the upper hand if not quickly offset by more positive influences. He recommended that Lavisse produce a pamphlet explicitly intended for the infantry's noncommissioned officers. These were the men best situated to combat the defeatism of their dis-affected troops, but they too needed to be inspired and their morale reinvigorated. Convinced that a carefully composed pamphlet could ef-fectively combat the "dangerous pessimism of the time and raise the morale of all," Gautrin urged Lavisse to remain committed to the cause: "do not let up in your efforts of propaganda at the very moment when it is most useful."[5]

A month later Lavisse published a brief article entitled "Why We Are Fighting" in the Paris daily Le Temps. The article summarized many of the arguments of previous essays: Germany, misled by a dangerously misguided philosophical tradition, had created an "atrocious philosophy of war" to justify territorial expansion and military aggression. France had been fighting since 1914 to prevent the triumph of Germany's heg-emonic ambition, to preserve its own political, economic, and intellectual freedom, to end the war, and to secure a lasting peace. With so much at stake, only unconditional victory was acceptable.[6] Moved by the power of Lavisse's argument, a Parisian reader wrote immediately to congrat-ulate him. The article had given him "great pleasure," and like M. Gau-trin, he urged Lavisse to produce still more: "I would like to see many more of your articles, and have them read by the general public and especially by our youth." M. Maupigny insisted that Lavisse's national stature bestowed upon him a unique responsibility: "renowned throughout the nation, you had to say that which was essential, and you had to say it often."[7]

Military commanders agreed. They encouraged scholars to address front-line troops and endorsed the circulation at the front of essays, pamphlets, textbooks, and classic works of literature and history. In early 1917 Lamy earned the approbation of staff officers when he spoke to troops stationed behind the lines. General Margot was convinced that by virtue of his "especial authority" as Permanent Secretary of the Académie Française, Lamy had done a great deal to inspire the troops and win their respect.[8] Only Lamy, however, seems to have ventured close to the front lines. Other scholars addressed the troops indirectly, through their essays and articles which circulated at the front thanks to the efforts of a philanthropic organization called Les Livres du Soldat. Founded in 1913, the association defined itself as a National Society for Intellectual Education determined to make the great books of French culture available to men fulfilling their military service obligations. When war came, the society resolved to work to maintain and strengthen the morale of the nation's troops. Convinced that France was fighting to defend "law, eternal justice, the liberty of all peoples" and French culture, the committee sent to the front textbooks of French literature and history (including Lavisse's much-read *Histoire de France*), of mathematics, physics, and chemistry; reminders of France's classical heritage in the works of Homer, Sophocles, Aeschylus, Virgil, and Cicero; and recent essays of patriotic propaganda, including titles by Boutroux, Aulard, Lavisse, Lamy, and Giraud. Among the journals sent up the line were the *Revue des deux mondes,* the *Revue hebdomadaire,* and the *Revue de Paris.*[9]

A manual of military morale written in late 1917 defined the role and acclaimed the importance of this scholarly literature. The author, Colonel G. Bernard, was an ardent advocate of the moral and cultural education of French troops: in 1916 he had delivered (and subsequently published) a lecture on "Civilization and *Kultur*" to convalescent soldiers at the military hospital of Autun.[10] In the wake of the 1917 mutinies, he revisited the issue of "the moral education of soldiers." Citing Napoleon's dictum that "in war, morale is everything," he wrote that junior officers could develop and sustain the morale of their men through personal example, effective leadership, and intelligent assessment of one's troops. But Bernard was convinced that junior officers could also strengthen the *poilus'* resolve by reminding them of what was at stake in the war. To be effective in this role, they first had to educate themselves as to why France was at war; how pan-Germanism and *Kultur* were responsible for German aggression; and why the defense of French culture and civilization was a task worthy of their sacrifices. Having familiarized themselves with the arguments set forth in the pamphlets and essays of the noncombatant intelligentsia, they would then be able and indeed obligated to convey their knowledge in simple, nonacademic prose to the men under their command.[11]

Front-line troops thus had ample access to the essays, articles, and ideas of noncombatant intellectuals. And much like public schoolteachers on the home front, junior officers in particular were expected to undertake the moral instruction of the men under their command. But did they do so? In some famous instances, they actively resisted the efforts of commanding officers and noncombatant intellectuals to educate—or, as their detractors would have said, to indoctrinate—the eight million men under arms. Emile Chartier, better known to his readers and students as Alain, considered these initiatives outrageous. A volunteer in the artillery until a shattered ankle forced him to return to civilian life in 1917, he had nothing but contempt for the mobilization of intellect, the "moral education" of combatants, and the "academic rhetoric" of his former teachers. In letters to his friends Elie and Florence Halévy, he insisted that "notions like the rivalries of nations, of [systems of] education, and of irreconcilable cultural beliefs" were utterly meaningless to men at the front. His troops were not at all moved by talk of pan-Germanism and the perfidy of Wilhelm II, and they had no tolerance for essayists who urged them to hate the enemy. In January 1917, he denounced those who formed public opinion in France as beset by prejudice, intellectual sloth, and fear of the truth; they were, he lamented, even worse than their counterparts across the Rhine.[12] Florimond Wagon, a socialist soldier killed in May 1916, agreed. A year before his death he had confided to a friend that he could not stomach the cultural arguments of noncombatant intellectuals: "Oh, that they would not talk any more about *Kultur* and culture, about atrocities and the savagery of one race and the perfection of the other. How that stuff makes me laugh." Preferring Rolland's defense of disinterested intellect to the patriotic propaganda of French intellectuals, he dismissed those "whose voices run on and on" as "either cowards or fools."[13]

But Chartier and Wagon did not speak on behalf of all scholars- and writers-in-arms. Many well-educated soldiers welcomed the reading material their friends, family, and commanding officers provided, and considered themselves under an obligation to educate their fellows as to why France was at war. Marcel Etévé, a classmate of André Durkheim at the

ENS, had no time for the drivel served daily in the nation's newspapers, but he was happy to receive copies of the *Mercure de France* from his commanding officer, and like Gautrin he read Lavisse's *Lettres à tous les Français* with approval.[14] Although he was not Catholic, Pierre Jourdan, a former law student sympathetic to the Action Française, read the Catholic periodical *Le Correspondant* with "great interest," and Etienne de Fontenay, whose studies at the Ecole Libre des Études Politiques were interrupted by the outbreak of war, welcomed the copies of the *Revue de Paris* that his father sent him.[15] Some of these men found intellectual solace in private reading; others hoped to inspire their men. Jean Rival, who had been a candidate for admission to the ENS before mobilization called him to the front, believed that the moral education of his men was one of his most important obligations. Farm and city boys, concerned only with their crops and the pleasures of civilian life, they had to be taught why France was at war. Rival hoped therefore to convince his troops "of the greatness of the task that confronted them."[16]

Many scholars-in-arms found themselves agreeing with the ideas of the nation's noncombatant intelligentsia. Robert André Michel, a distinguished graduate of the Ecole des Chartes and archivist at the Archives Nationales, was killed in October 1914. Thus he had no opportunity to observe the cultural debates of the war as they unfolded after 1914, but he did live long enough to perceive in the Manifesto of 93 proof of the bankruptcy of German intellect.[17] Both Jean Klingebiel, an ardent Protestant from Bordeaux, and Maurice Masson, an equally devout Catholic, shared Bergson's optimistic faith that the war would bring about the moral regeneration of France. Indeed, Masson was so moved by Bergson's 1914 address to the Académie des Sciences Morales et Politiques that he urged his wife to obtain a copy of the speech if she had not already read it.[18]

United in their regard for Bergson, Masson and Klingebiel differed when considering more broadly the merits and faults of intellectual mobilization. In early 1915 Masson learned to his horror that some of his academic colleagues in Switzerland had called upon French and German scholars to renew intellectual contacts broken by the war. When Gustave Lanson publicly repudiated this initiative, in an essay entitled "Un Projet de rapprochement intellectuel entre Allemagne et France," Masson was so gratified by his mentor's response that he requested an offprint of the article.[19] Like Lanson, Masson considered any overture to the enemy, whether intellectual or diplomatic, altogether inopportune and inappropriate. Klingebiel was not so sure. In December 1915 he confided to his brother that he did not disagree entirely with Romain Rolland. Lamenting the cultivation of hatred fostered by "too many of our intellectuals under the pretext of nationalism or patriotism," he would have preferred that men of intellect choose the interests of humanity over the narrow concerns of their nation. But unconsciously echoing Victor Basch, he believed that one could at once be true to France and to humanity. Given the opportunity he would have liked "to suggest to Rolland that from the point of view of humanity, France finds herself much better situated than her enemies; and it is for this reason that [the French] agree to fight with a good heart."[20]

Confident that France represented the cause of humanity, Klingebiel expressed the idealism of many of the nation's most highly educated troops, who believed—variously—that France fought to defend justice, to bring an end to war, and to preserve French civilization. Both Masson and Etévé were convinced that France had to secure Germany's unconditional surrender. While Masson insisted that France had "suffered too much in the name of justice to be able to accept a peace without justice," Etévé justified his *jusqu'auboutisme* on the grounds that France was fighting the war to end all wars.[21] This political rhetoric of the left had little appeal to Pierre Jourdan, but he too believed that France was fighting to defend more than the integrity of its frontier. Reflecting upon his inclination to spend his quiet moments in the trenches thinking about French literature, he reassured himself that "it is not inappropriate to speak of our literature, because that constitutes our intellectual and moral patrimony and it is that, too, which we are defending against the Barbarians." Etienne de Fontenay agreed. However "long and painful" the war was for everyone, the nation had to hold out, for the French fought "to save [their] intellectual and moral patrimony, [their] civilization." Recognizing somewhat apologetically that "these are grand words," he insisted nonetheless upon their aptness: "they describe the character and the necessity of the present war."[22]

Whether defining the French war effort as the defense of civilization or denouncing the enemy as barbarians, these troops adopted both the idiom and the cultural ideology of the noncombatant intelligentsia. Klingebiel was not the only front-line soldier to regret that contemporary Germany had strayed so far from the spirit and values of "the old Germany of Bach and Beethoven."[23] Robert d'Harcourt, whose memoirs of combat and captivity appeared after the war, also perceived the enemy through the lens of "two Germanies." Severely wounded in the spring of 1915, he had been removed to a German military hospital near Metz.

Having witnessed a German medic brutally harassing a mortally wounded French soldier, he subsequently reflected that "that day in Metz, in 1915, we were far removed from the Germany of Goethe and Weimar."[24]

Even troops embittered by their front-line experiences and contemptuous of civilians occasionally expressed themselves in the idiom of the noncombatant intelligentsia. This was true of Georges Bernanos, once an enthusiastic supporter of the Action Française, who had no patience for the patriotic propaganda and anti-German invective of his former colleagues, and of Charles Delvert, a graduate of the Ecole Normale, a historian, and a veteran of Verdun. Although Bernanos believed that those "who neither fought nor died" should have kept their counsel throughout the war, he did not disagree entirely with the intellectual arguments of the Action Française. For instance, he too conceived of Germany's industrial and technological expertise as the awful product of philosophical error; Krupp's cannon were, he opined, "Hegelian materiel."[25] Like Bernanos, Delvert disparaged the contribution of the daily press to the war effort, and he suggested that if noncombatants wanted to make themselves useful, they should abandon—if only for a while—their comfortable "well-outfitted Parisian offices" and venture up to the front line. But he shared the noncombatant intelligentsia's conviction that modern Germany was a nation of "brutes," indifferent to the wonders of nature and civilization alike. Reflecting upon the destruction of the French countryside, he likened the war to a conflict between Ariel and Caliban, in which Caliban sent "infernal machines" of destruction into the verdant, lush pastures of France and made of glorious nature "a horrible, blood-soaked desert."[26]

Finally, debates over classicism, literary aesthetics, and educational reform did not go unnoticed, unappreciated, or uncontested at the front. Not surprisingly, enthusiasts of the Action Française acclaimed the classicist revival. Although Jourdan, an ardent admirer of Lasserre's *Le Romantisme français,* admitted to a heterodox fondness for the Romantic poetry of the nineteenth century, he nevertheless held Racine, Molière, and Lafontaine in highest esteem: "these are our masters and our dearest friends."[27] The classicist cause won new enthusiasts, too. In July 1916, with the French Army embroiled at Verdun and on the Somme, the *Bulletin des Armées de la République* initiated an *enquête* into the effects of the war on French literary style. Several respondents suggested that the war had brought to the fore a new appreciation for the aesthetics of simplicity and clarity. One writer suggested that "the *poilu* has developed a taste for that which is brief, clear, and true. His motto will be that of Maupassant: the simple truth." The war had thus purged France of the "mannerisms and verbiage" of the prewar years.[28]

Even men unsympathetic to the classicist cause were attentive to the educational debate it generated. In February 1916, the parliamentary committee investigating the reforms of 1902 received a deposition from A. Decerf, an *agrégé* in mathematics who had held a teaching position at a *lycée* in Cherbourg before the war. In early 1916, while serving as an adjutant in the 25th Infantry Regiment, he reviewed what he knew of the reform debate, and his observations showed him to be remarkably well informed and critically engaged. From his vantage point at the front, he observed that advocates of educational reform could be divided into two camps—classicists and utilitarians—and he judged that since 1914 the classicists had progressively undermined the authority of educational modernists. Arguing that the "moral superiority" of France derived from its classical culture, they had worked to discredit anyone who had ever expressed an "exaggerated admiration" for German culture, and had demanded that France return to the "traditional education of the humanities." By contrast, the utilitarians had insisted that France could guarantee its victory only if it adopted "the methods, spirit of order, and intellectual organization" of its enemies. Advocating utilitarian education above all else, they demanded that France dedicate itself to the formation of cadres of engineers. Decerf, a defender of the 1902 curriculum, rejected both extremes, for he feared that if either school of thought emerged "completely triumphant," France would have to "sacrifice one part of [its] intellectual patrimony to the exclusive advantage of the other." Thus he urged the parliamentary committee to preserve instead the system established in 1902, which alone offered students a solid foundation in *culture générale* and an opportunity to develop their specific academic talents.[29]

Like Decerf, Daniel Mornet, who would establish himself after the war as one of the nation's most distinguished intellectual historians, observed the educational debates from the vantage point of the front. Publishing his reflections in the August 1918 issue of the *Revue pédagogique,* he disparaged neither the classical tradition nor the advantages offered by an essentially disinterested education, but he feared that an exclusively classical curriculum would effectively isolate French students and intellectual culture from positive external influences. Like Duhem, he believed that Anglo-Saxon pragmatism and German organization could successfully complement French qualities of mind. Unlike noncombatants and some military commanders, who had believed too eagerly that "enthusiasm and *élan*" would win the war, Mornet noted that troops had come to respect the less glamorous qualities of their allies and their enemy: American application and German discipline. The war had shown that "major accomplishments were not the result of superhuman *élan* but of the slow progression of modest efforts." Mornet believed that to recover from the war France would have to apply itself diligently to essential, albeit unglamorous, tasks; and it would have to develop in its youth a respect, heretofore lacking, for sustained effort. "One of the foremost duties of our education is to teach the sons of France that the future belongs to those who work courageously and methodically." Like Decerf, therefore, Mornet believed that France would be ill-advised to abandon the careful scholarly methods introduced before the war. Although disparaged by conservative critics as "Germanic," these methods were, he insisted, essential to the development of disciplined minds: "to teach the youth of France the value of hard work that is at once precise, modest, and perseverant, [was] not to place them in foreign hands."[30]

Educated front-line troops were, therefore, familiar with, and often sympathetic to, the writings of noncombatant scholars and writers. Whether they lamented the triumph of pan-Germanism, regretted the demise of "the other Germany," execrated the signatories of the Manifesto of 93, or believed that France fought to defend its intellectual and cultural patrimony from German depredation, their opinions were—on many occasions and many issues—essentially those of the noncombatant intelligentsia. According to Stéphane Audoin-Rouzeau's analysis of popular front-line opinion, this consensus of patriotic sentiment was not unique to the cultural elite. Whether highly educated or only marginally literate, French troops shared with their families at home an antipathy for the enemy, an affection for *la patrie,* and a conviction that theirs was the cause of justice.[31] This commonality of conviction, evident within the nation's cultural elite and the nation at large, effectively bound the military front to the home front and united the people of France in their determination to hold out until victory was secured. Recognizing that many other factors bolstered the determination of the nation to wage war *jusqu'au bout,* one cannot dismiss as unimportant or discount as ineffectual the efforts of noncombatant intellectuals. Civilians and soldiers alike read their articles, sought their opinions, valued their contributions, and endorsed their arguments.

This evidence confirms Jean-Jacques Becker's thesis that "the real explanation of French steadfastness . . . lay in the intellectual, spiritual, and political leadership of the people."[32] It also suggests that the French experience of the Great War was in some critical ways fundamentally different from that of its principal ally. Drawing their conclusions from English poetry and prose of the Great War, Paul Fussell and Samuel Hynes have argued that the experience of combat provoked within the British Expeditionary Force the profound alienation of highly educated front-line troops and prompted their intense disaffection for the Old Men of English academia. By 1916 young men of learning, literary imagination, and aesthetic sensibility fought only to maintain solidarity with their men, not to honor the Big Words bandied about by elderly academics, words like Glory, Country, and Civilization. There was, doubtless, some of this feeling in France too. Although Bernanos and Chartier had been bitter intellectual rivals before 1914, they spoke with one voice during the war when they damned the idealism of their elders. Bernanos confessed that he knew neither what he was defending nor what he was being asked to die for; all was "an astonishing stupidity." Convinced that "old glory ha[d] lied," he hoped that in the event of his death he would be remembered only as "a man who fought and died for his own personal satisfaction, and to enrage those who neither fought nor died."[33] And Chartier insisted that his men would fight to the death, but only because they were bound by "promises of friendship."[34] These sentiments notwithstanding, neither the alienation nor the disaffection of highly educated front-line troops was nearly as evident in France as it was in England. Members of the cultural elite who saw front-line action did not unanimously or even generally denounce the efforts, denigrate the integrity, or disparage the ideals of those who stayed behind. The mobilization of intellect did not alienate combatants from noncombatants; in the main, it united them.

The Consequences of Intellectual Mobilization
Intellectual Nationalism

To the extent that troops had appreciated the efforts of noncombatant intellectuals, it is not surprising that some veterans endorsed the principle of intellectual mobilization. This movement made itself evident in July 1919, when conservative veterans joined forces with equally conservative noncombatants to proclaim the virtue of "intellectual nationalism" in the Manifesto of the Parti de l'Intelligence. In a public rebuke to Rolland and Barbusse, whose own manifesto had criticized the mobilization of intellect as unworthy of men of learning, the Parti de l'Intelligence insisted that writers and scholars should remain "mobilized" in the postwar world of reconstruction and recovery. To secure the victory achieved by French troops, intellectuals had to dedicate themselves to the restoration of classicism and reason, essential elements of French culture endangered in recent years by Germanic influences.[35] The manifesto resolved to "revive the life of the mind and the prestige of French intellect in the world, by returning to the French tradition." So integralist was the tone of the text that many writers believed Maurras to be its principal author; in fact it was Henri Massis, whose service in the trenches had confirmed his cultural conservatism. An erstwhile republican affiliated before 1914 with the republican *L'Opinion,* Massis had until 1919 remained at arm's length from the neoroyalists. Once it became evident that the agenda of the Parti de l'Intelligence and the cultural agenda of the Action Française were indistinguishable, however, he did not hesitate to join forces with Maurras and Daudet.

Georges Aimel was another young conservative republican convinced by front-line experience of the merits of intellectual nationalism. In 1919 he published *Travaillons donc à bien penser,* a work widely praised by Catholic prelates and integral nationalists.[36] Although Aimel continued to believe that a democratic republic remained the form of government best suited to the character of France, he shared the contempt of the Action Française for German culture and intellectual cosmopolitanism. He praised Maurras for "liberating us from Kantian philosophy" and called for a fundamental reorientation of French culture along national lines. Speaking as a member of the "sacrificed generation" of 1914, he excoriated the cosmopolitanism of scholars committed to the cause of collective security and rejected all calls to renew intellectual cooperation between France and Germany. He feared that those who had done so much to "Germanize" French culture and education had not abandoned their faith in foreign ideas and had yet to learn the fundamental lesson of the war: that these were two radically incommensurable cultures. Aimel insisted that if postwar France were to avoid the errors of the prewar era, it had to free itself of its infatuation with German ideas and reconstruct its culture in a way consistent with French traditions. This much, surely, the survivors of the war owed to those who had died defending the integrity of French culture.[37]

After several sympathetic reviews of *Travaillons à bien penser* were published in the nonroyalist conservative press, the Action Française concluded that the tide of cultural opinion had at last turned in its favor.

Before the war, when the cultural elite had dedicated itself to the cause of intellectual cosmopolitanism, those who had dared to dissent had been in the minority. By the early 1920s, however, intellectual nationalists appeared in ever-increasing numbers.[38] In June 1921 Daudet reported proudly that *Hors du joug d'Allemand*—his wartime essay on the necessity of intellectual nationalism—had gone into several printings. For Daudet this signified that intellectual nationalism, characterized by its insistent call for the "de-Germanization of the Sorbonne and French culture in general," was gaining ground.[39]

It was to this constituency of intellectual nationalists that Jacques Bainville, Henri Massis, Jacques Maritain, and Charles Maurras addressed themselves in April 1920 with the first issue of the *Revue universelle*. Funded initially by a legacy Maritain and Maurras had received from a young soldier killed in the war, who wished that his fortune be used "to safeguard what remained of the intellectual and moral patrimony of our country," the *Revue universelle* dedicated itself singlemindedly to this task.[40] Edited by Bainville and Massis, with Maritain as philosophy editor and featuring frequent contributions from Maurras and Daudet, the new journal became a standard-bearer for intellectual nationalism. In the inaugural issue, Bainville aligned the *Revue universelle* with Massis's manifesto. Its purpose was to give individuals convinced of the necessity of intellectual renewal and committed to the principles articulated in the manifesto, "the means to bring their principles into play." Insisting that France could renew itself only if it embraced a set of intellectual principles fundamentally different from those that had held sway before 1914, Bainville believed that once France returned to its own intellectual traditions, it could then lead the world. The journal, although firmly rooted in French tradition, would thus become "universal," because through its commitment to "the principles of reason and enlightenment" it would bring together "men of intellect of all nations."[41]

However universal its professed aspirations, the *Revue universelle* in practice expressed little tolerance for German ideas. Maurras argued that true order would be restored to France only with the complete repudiation of the "Germanic spirit" that continued to pervade contemporary French culture.[42] This was also the principal message of Maritain's many essays published in the *Revue* between 1920 and 1926, when papal condemnation of the Action Française abruptly ended his association with that group and its affiliates. Maritain clearly found much that he could agree with in the cultural politics of intellectual nationalism. Like Bainville, he was convinced that France would benefit if the mobilization of intellect continued into the postwar era. It was necessary, he believed, to "mobilize all . . . interior forces" in order to preserve the common good of society and the vitality of intellect. And like Maurras and Daudet, he criticized the "intellectual anarchy" of the prewar Sorbonne, insisted that France had a special intellectual vocation to free European culture from the nefarious influence of German philosophy, and proclaimed that "the most universal and most truly human thought" was French. His antipathy to Kant, whom he denigrated as the Pontius Pilate of modern metaphysics, remained undiluted. Maritain was convinced that only a renewed scholasticism could cure the modern world of its post-Kantian malaise.[43] With his ardent advocacy of neo-Thomism, Maritain did more than merely carry into the postwar era the intellectual agenda of wartime Catholicism; he created a bridge of intellectual concord that (until 1926) brought French Catholics ever closer to the Action Française.

Intellectual nationalists worked vigorously because they realized that the war had neither fully repudiated the cause of intellectual cosmopolitanism nor dislodged its defenders from positions of intellectual and cultural authority. Although Daudet confidently proclaimed in 1919 that "the military genius of Foch had struck a serious blow against Kantianism" in France, he knew that "the heavy yoke of Germanism" had not yet been lifted.[44] A year later, he had to concede that Kantian philosophy (which with his characteristic hyperbole he now condemned as "the metaphysics of cemeteries") remained a force to be reckoned with. Although "a violent reaction . . . against this Germanization of intellect" had occurred within some circles in France, the purification of French thought and culture was, he conceded, not yet complete. "Others continue, in spite of the war, to represent Kant as the master of all philosophy."[45] Daudet's charge was not entirely correct. In the early 1920s the University of Paris offered its students very few courses in German philosophy.[46] Delbos's chair in the History of Philosophy remained unfilled, and Victor Basch, the department's remaining Kantian, concentrated his attention on the politically anodyne topic of "The Tragic and the Comic."[47] Nonetheless, Daudet's more general complaint—that some scholars at the Sorbonne remained sympathetic to German ideas and open to German intellectual influence—was true.

With his address to the Sorbonne delivered in 1919, Charles Andler proved their point. Eager to rebuild the foundations of Franco-German intellectual cooperation he had done so much to cement before the war, Andler outraged French nationalists by suggesting that France, intent upon reforming its system of higher education, should look once again to Germany for direction, since a spirit of democracy and egalitarianism now moved the German professoriate. Recognizing that no single group had been more discredited by Germany's defeat than her scholars, Andler took heart at their response to defeat and discredit: rather than deny their own culpability, they determined to rectify past wrongs by making higher education in Germany more democratic and more genuinely disinterested. Having been misled by the allure of practicality—an allure that had brought scholarship into alliance with industry and politics— German scholars now embraced the cause of knowledge for its own sake and hoped to cultivate "men of knowledge and understanding."[48]

Heartened by evidence that German scholars had adopted as their own the traditional values of French higher education, Andler was dismayed that the French were at the same time in danger of abandoning these ideals. Unlike the Germans, who did not hesitate to look abroad for examples of effective scholarship, the French were turning progressively inward. Andler feared that the French people's understandable antipathy to Germany and German studies was a great and regrettable error of judgment. It would profit France not at all if its people and its scholars, rejecting Germany entirely, purged German scholarship and culture from the collective consciousness. Acknowledging that blind imitation of Germany was unwarranted, he contended that ignorance of the former enemy was equally unwise.[49] He thus hoped that France would remain open to the possibility that she could continue to learn from German ideas, initiatives, and examples.

Andler's address proved controversial even within the confines of the Sorbonne. In a series of articles published from March through November 1919 in the *Journal des débats* (and subsequently reprinted in the *Revue internationale de l'enseignement* in 1920), Andler's colleague, François Picavet, denied that it was either necessary or appropriate for French scholars to look across the frontier for intellectual leadership. There were, Picavet insisted, "German methods" and "French methods," and France had no need to borrow from its discredited former enemy. Having published a critical edition and translation of Kant's *Critique of Practical Reason* in 1888 and in the process of completing a translation of the *Critique of Pure Reason* (which appeared in 1921), Picavet was by no means antipathetic to the German philosophical tradition. He was nonetheless incredulous that after four years of a war for which German scholars had provided the intellectual foundation and rationale, there remained in France "men who turn their gaze towards German universities" for guidance in educational reform. Convinced that recent Ger-

man scholarship had been completely indifferent to truth, Picavet counseled "circumspection and prudence when examining the methods and
the results that have come to us, and still come to us from German universities." He was not, however, categorically opposed to all international intellectual contact. If France's tradition proved inadequate in any
regard (and, like Duhem, he suspected that it might not be sufficiently
practical in its orientation), then French scholars and teachers should not
hesitate to borrow and learn from other traditions. As their forefathers
had always done, they should "take from other nations and other cultures . . . that which will allow us to attain the truth and advance the
cause of justice." Insofar as Britain and the United States shared this
respect for "truth and justice," France could profitably engage in intellectual contact with these former allies, but not with Germany.[50]

Picavet was not a narrow-minded nationalist convinced of the absolute superiority of French thought. He acknowledged that "in order to
conserve science, scholarship, ethics and civilization . . . it is without
doubt a good thing to draw upon all sources" consonant with the development of these values. But when he called upon the French to "return
[especially] to our own French intellectual masters who have since the
sixteenth century pursued truth and justice," he became (perhaps unwittingly) the acclaimed hero of intellectual nationalists, whose attacks
upon a Germanized Sorbonne intensified in 1920.[51] Unlike the *Revue
universelle,* which employed the refined tones of scholarly argument on
behalf of intellectual nationalism, the *Action française* denounced the
intellectual cosmopolitanism of the postwar Sorbonne with intentionally
objectionable language. During the 1920–21 academic year, the newspaper resumed with familiar vitriolic abandon its attack on the republican educational establishment, castigating its leading scholars for their
cosmopolitanism and continuing enthusiasm for Germanic ideas.

Maurice Pujo regretted that "the Sorbonne of today ha[d] not yet
liberated itself" of its dangerous infatuation with German culture.[52] Indeed, the University, infiltrated by "foreigners, spies, Jews, and Bolsheviks," seemed even more committed in 1920 to the nefarious allure of
cosmopolitanism than it had been before 1914.[53] Pujo was outraged that
Basch, Seignobos, Aulard—all representatives of the prewar Germanized
Sorbonne—continued to hold faculty positions. Was it not indisputable
that Seignobos had "falsified history to the detriment of the French people and to the advantage of the Germans and the Anglo-Saxons," and
that other scholars "continued to acclaim the superiority of German science, intellect, and virtue"?[54] But none was as execrable, in Pujo's opin-

ion, as Victor Basch. Castigated for his affiliation with the Ligue des Droits de l'Homme, despised as a Hungarian Jew, Basch was portrayed as the quintessential foreigner whose very presence at the Sorbonne was an insult to the idea of "French thought." Education would only benefit—in the eyes of French students and in the esteem of foreign students coming to Paris to learn firsthand about the essence of French culture—if it did "not admit foreign professors, who like Basch make a mockery of our Sorbonne."[55]

Determined to "purify" French culture and education, intellectual nationalists demanded that "strong restrictions" be imposed on the study of German. Daudet asserted that "we must no longer teach German to young children."[56] And Pujo insisted that "we stop according to the German language, German culture, and the products of German culture the disproportionate place given them by our educational system, and our culture more generally, before the war."[57] These integralist arguments found increasingly receptive audiences during and after the war. Whereas in the decade before the war French students had demonstrated what one observer called a "preponderant" interest in Germany and only a modest interest in the intellectual culture of the English-speaking world, this was reversed during the war. Students turned their backs on Germany, shunning instruction in German language, literature, and philosophy as unpatriotic.[58] The number of students within the jurisdiction of the Academy of Paris who continued to study German as their second language dropped noticeably during the war years; at one school the ratio of students opting for English instead of German was sixteen to one.[59] University students also shifted their attention away from Germany to England and the United States. By 1916, students at the University of Paris pursuing an advanced degree *(Diplôme d'études supérieures)* in English language and literature outnumbered students in German language and literature by eighteen to five. Adjusting its curriculum accordingly, the Sorbonne reduced the number of courses in German literature and culture and offered for the first time courses in American studies. Except in Alsace, where students were more at ease in German than in French, this rejection of German studies continued well into the 1920s. In 1922–23, only five candidates for the *diplôme d'études supérieures* in German took the examination; thirty-four took the examination in English.[60]

Students' persistent rejection of German studies, evident in secondary and higher education through at least the mid-1920s, offers compelling evidence that as a result of the war French academic life experienced a "nationalist turn" away from the cosmopolitanism many scholars con-

tinued to favor and towards the intellectual insularity advocated by proponents of intellectual nationalism. Sorbonne scholars could proclaim
the advantages to be gained from intellectual contact with German culture, but enrollment statistics in German language courses suggest that
students paid them little heed.

Intellectual Nationalism and French Science

Intellectual nationalism made its mark on French science, too. According
to Elisabeth Crawford's analysis of how the prominent scientists of the
war years—Nobel laureates and members of the national nominating
committees—assessed the qualifications of candidates from enemy countries, French scientists systematically refused after 1914 to recognize any
merit in the work of their German counterparts. The former intellectual
openmindedness, fostered by a belief that science was an international
enterprise, had simply disappeared with the outbreak of war, and "own-
country" nominations became the norm. This propensity to ignore the
genuine accomplishments of the enemy was evident on both sides of the
Rhine, but it was particularly pervasive in France, where it continued
well into the 1920s.

The spirit of internationalism of which European scientists had been
justifiably proud before 1914 disintegrated everywhere under the force
of national loyalty and international animosity. In France, it also fell
victim to the rhetoric of self-congratulation that characterized the scientific discourse of the war years. Having argued repeatedly that science
was not the privileged German domain everyone had believed it to be
before 1914, French scholars after 1918 continued their efforts to define
science as essentially French. Picavet took care to remind his readers in
1920 that French scientists from Pascal to Henri Poincaré had been in
the forefront of scientific research; and his list of world-renowned scientists included no Germans.[61] In the same year, the Faculty of Sciences
debated a proposal, brought to their attention by the Ministry of Public
Instruction, to create a series of public lectures accessible to nonspecial-
ists and detailing "recent discoveries in the sciences." Several professors
spoke in favor of such a plan, believing that lectures of this type would
be most valuable if delivered in the provinces![62] Parisian scholars preferred to direct their energies to educating foreign students. Coordinating
their efforts with the Friends of the University, members of the Faculty
of Sciences agreed to contribute to a public lecture series, the object of
which was to inform foreigners of the significant contributions France
had made to science.[63]

At the University of Paris a smug—and ultimately corrosive—sense of intellectual self-sufficiency increasingly marked the Faculty of Sciences, where the rhetoric of the war years, with its insistence that French science was more original and more rigorous than that practiced in Germany, continued to influence scientific thinking well into the interwar years. Paradoxically, integral nationalists, ordinarily vehement in their hostility to Germany, became amenable *in this case alone* to imitation of Germany. Scholars and writers on both sides of the issue articulated this unexpected inversion of attitudes most clearly in discussions about the merits of pure versus applied science. After the war Catholics and integral nationalists admitted to a newfound enthusiasm for science in general, and applied science in particular.[64] Impressed by Germany's industrial capacity and the military advantages the enemy had derived from it, they joined forces with advocates of technical education who called for the subordination of faculties of science to the needs of industry. At the same time, scholars affiliated with the most prestigious Parisian scientific institutions, fearful that the chronic underfunding of scientific facilities and the disinclination of students to pursue careers in scientific research and teaching would seriously jeopardize the future of scientific research in France, advocated the cause of pure research.

Led by Paul Appell, Parisian scientists expressed serious reservations about the virtues of technical education and the elevation of applied science.[65] As early as 1915 Appell had vigorously opposed a proposal to create faculties of applied science, believing that such institutions would be nothing but glorified technical schools. Employing the most disparaging comparison possible, he dismissed them as French equivalents of German *Realschulen*. He was convinced that *all* scientific research should be conducted within the established faculties of science, which cultivated the appropriately "scientific" environment for research and experimentation.[66] In 1918, Paul Painlevé (who as Minister of Public Instruction in 1915 had supervised the creation of the *Direction des inventions intéressant la défense nationale*) contended that German science was a "gigantic enterprise in which an entire people applied themselves relentlessly to creating the most formidable killing-machine ever produced." In contrast, French science remained committed to the "disinterested search for truth."[67]

Maurice Barrès, writing in the *Revue universelle* in 1920, spoke for the opposition. However hostile he was to Germany, he had to admit that Germany had derived considerable benefits, at the front lines and on the home front, from its well-known merger of science and industry.

Scientific innovation and application had sustained Germany's war effort. For Barrès this effective merger of science and industry constituted the "secret of [Germany's] economic power," and he believed that the French would do well to learn from this example. It was time for France to follow Germany's lead, support more generously its scientific infrastructure, and improve the ties between academic and applied science. He defended his apparently heretical recommendation by arguing that the marriage of science and industry that had served wartime Germany so well was, in fact, of French origin. "Descartes, Colbert, and Bonaparte had all advocated the development in France of a closer association between science and industry." Thus "the secret of German power [was] nothing other than the ancient secret of French grandeur."[68]

Regrettably, this "secret of French grandeur" had been lost in recent years. Barrès contended (although recent scholarship challenges the validity of his claim) that in the decades before the war France had neglected its scientific infrastructure and had done very little to develop a productive coalition of science and industry. The Germans, taking advantage of France's neglect and indifference, had developed chemical weapons and gained a strategic—albeit barbaric—advantage in the field. And as long as Germany's scientific and industrial infrastructure—its "criminal laboratories"—remained in place, it was incumbent upon the French to build more powerful and more efficacious facilities of its own. The population crisis made it impossible for France to match Germany man for man on the field of combat; hence the French had to recognize that their security depended upon their ability to surpass German quantity with superior quality.[69] Only when Germany became impressed by France's scientific might and expertise would it hesitate to move again against its neighbor.

Identifying science with national security, Barrès made evident an ironic inversion effected by the cultural debates of the war years. When considering the character of education in the humanities, integral nationalists demanded the complete elimination of all Germanic influences and the reintroduction of a purely French, classical curriculum. Yet in the case of scientific education, they were willing to countenance emulation of German practice. The discourse of the war years had assigned to Germany superiority in applied science and to France excellence in the domain of pure research. Even so, integral nationalists—in all other regards viscerally antipathetic to all things German—endorsed initiatives to improve technical education and the development of applied science.

Ultimately, however, the intellectual nationalism of postwar French science proved more a curse than a blessing. In spite of new and enthusiastic interest in the applied sciences, science foundered in interwar France. Penury, the bane of French academic life after 1919, was only partially to blame. Philippe Bernard and Henri Dubief have charged that after 1918 French science "became marginal and outdated" in large part because "pettiness and narrow nationalism" now prevailed.[70] Scientists, convinced of the intellectual superiority of French scholarship, isolated themselves from advances in other nations, failed to keep pace with new developments, and took comfort in past accomplishments. Professor Maurice Caullery of the University of Paris conceded as much in 1933 in a speech to an American audience on the importance of French contributions to science. As the war essayists had done, he insisted that "France has played one of the most important parts in the building up of modern science as a whole." But he acknowledged that French science had excelled in fundamental abstract discovery, rather than patient, concrete application: "French science is distinguished for the number and value of its great discoveries rather than for its general mass of scientific production." Having categorized organization and discipline as German attributes incompatible with the spirit of finesse that flourished in France, French science had taken refuge in the cult of national genius and had failed to accomplish much of great note: "in the name of common sense, and even the national genius and its peculiarities, the scientific establishment rejected all unorthodox discoveries, and even the most advanced teaching bodies spurned anything novel."[71] The failure of French science to flourish in the interwar years was, therefore, an ironic, unforeseen consequence of the efforts of the war years to bolster the international stature of French science by emphasizing the importance of national genius and demonstrating that France's great contributions to science lay not in the careful, systematic development of ideas and hypotheses, but in the imaginative spark of individual genius.

The Bérard Reform

Determined to overturn the 1902 curriculum and restore classicism to the center of secondary education, intellectual nationalists scored their most significant victory with the passage of the Bérard reform in 1923. Of all the intellectual debates to emerge from the ferment of the war, this one proved the most contentious, for it pitted the cosmopolitanism and modernism of the academic establishment against the now powerful intellectual nationalism of the right. The left castigated Bérard's proposal as elitist, undemocratic, hostile to science, and implicitly clerical; the right perceived in it the promise of cultural renewal. And if the passage of the Bérard reform bore witness to the new potency of cultural conservatism in postwar France, the passion of the debate showed how powerfully the cultural discord of the war years continued to shape interwar debate.

Following his appointment as Minister of Public Instruction in January 1921, Léon Bérard, a moderate, conservative, Catholic republican, resolved to act upon what he perceived as a "unanimous" conviction that secondary education had to be fundamentally reformed. Believing that the system established in 1902 had failed because it had insisted upon premature academic specialization, had institutionalized a rigid separation of the humanities and the sciences, and had provoked a crisis in national literacy, he sought to address each of these failings in turn. He was convinced that children of twelve or thirteen were in no position to decide intelligently whether they wished to pursue a career in the sciences or the humanities, and feared that the inflexibility of the existing system (which made it almost impossible for a student who started in one program to transfer to another) penalized students for ill-advised or inappropriate initial decisions. Bérard therefore proposed the creation of a unified curriculum for the first four years of secondary school, the essential requirement of which was that all students complete four years of coursework in Latin and two years of Greek. He defended this compulsory, classical curriculum by arguing that French students had to understand the literary and linguistic sources from which their language had evolved, and needed the rigor and discipline that only Latin and Greek—by virtue of "their clarity, logic, and analytical strength"—could offer. Bérard maintained that in the aftermath of war improved literacy, familiarity with the nation's cultural traditions, and intellectual rigor were essential to the nation's survival. The grievous losses France had sustained in the war made it "an imperious duty" to protect and preserve her unique intellectual traditions and to prepare the next generation to meet the challenges of the future.[72]

However much Bérard's rhetoric resembled that of René Doumic, his program differed from Doumic's in one essential detail. Reflecting the right's newfound regard for the sciences, it intended to establish "a rigorous balance" between the sciences and the humanities, rather than restore a classicist hegemony in secondary education. Writing in late 1914, Doumic had said nothing about the place or importance of science in the secondary curriculum; his concern had been exclusively with reasserting the primacy of the classics. By the end of the war, however, few conservatives still favored such a radical imbalance. One essayist, writing in the *Revue universitaire* in 1918, insisted that an integrated curriculum with equal instruction in the humanities and the sciences should become the foundation of secondary school reform. Adopting Bergson's powerful phrase, he argued that students instructed only in the sciences and modern languages would become nothing but "scientific barbarians." But he feared that France would be equally ill-served by those who learned only the classics. Lacking technological expertise, the nation would be vulnerable to attack—economic or military—by other, more technologically sophisticated "barbarian" states; thus to ignore the sciences would amount to the "ruin of the country in the economic struggle of the future." Bérard agreed. His proposal required that for the first six years of their secondary education all students devote equal time to the sciences and the humanities.[73]

Long before it became law, the Bérard reform won the endorsement of chambers of commerce, industrial syndicates, and teachers' societies. As they had done before the war, chambers of commerce from around the nation called for a return to a classical curriculum: to those who preferred the modern curriculum of 1902, the Chamber of Commerce in Lille responded that a classical education remained "the best instrument for disciplining the mind and the best preparation for life." Societies of engineers also adamantly opposed the modern curriculum: young engineers, they feared, lacked the judgment, breadth of understanding, and clarity of vision essential to success at their tasks, and many of them were "incapable of presenting their ideas in clearly-written, well-composed" prose. According to the Society of Hydraulic Engineers, foreign observers considered students subjected to the "premature specialization" of the 1902 curriculum ill-prepared for professional responsibility. Not surprisingly, the national society of teachers of classical languages endorsed the proposed reform, as did the alumni of the *lycée* in Bourges, who defended a return to the classical curriculum "because the classics constitute the French tradition."[74]

Initially, Bérard also secured the support of high-school teachers and principals. The Amicale des Proviseurs et Directrices de Lycée maintained that it was impossible to have a truly human culture not grounded in the classical tradition; and at its annual meeting in 1921 the Fédération Nationale des Professeurs de Lycée applauded the idea of a unified curriculum with a foundation in mandatory Latin.[75] Within two years, however, *lycée* professors repudiated their initial endorsement of Bérard's program: teachers of science argued that it was not necessary to know Latin to be a competent scientist; and teachers of foreign languages feared that administrators could find time for compulsory Latin and Greek in the daily schedule only by reducing the number of hours assigned to modern languages.

These groups found a powerful, albeit much divided, ally in the Conseil Supérieur de l'Instruction Publique. In 1921 when Bérard introduced the possibility of secondary school reform, this advisory body included Alfred Croiset, Paul Appell, Henri Bergson, Alfred Coville, Emile Hovelaque, Gustave Lanson, and Emile Picard. Defenders of the classical tradition, with convictions strengthened by the war, thus confronted advocates of modern education doing their best to scuttle Bérard's program.[76] Initially, the council considered two questions: (1) Should a unified curriculum be required of all students for the first four years of secondary education? (2) Should the mandatory study of Latin and Greek constitute part of this unified curriculum? A significant majority—including Appell, Bergson, Boutroux, and both Alfred and Maurice Croiset—favored a unified curriculum. Appell argued that a curriculum required of all students and comprising coursework in French, Latin, the sciences, history, geography, and one modern language would eliminate the problem of premature specialization and would allow students time to develop their individual interests. By a substantial but slightly slimmer margin, the council also voted to make classical languages a mandatory part of the unified curriculum. Several members argued that a classical curriculum should remain the foundation of *culture générale,* provided it could coexist with instruction in the sciences.

These votes did not, however, reveal the true sentiments of the Conseil, which undermined its endorsement of a unified curriculum by voting subsequently to retain the division established in 1902 between the moderns and the classics, and allowed only one substantive revision: to require students in the modern course to study Latin for a minimum of two years. But here, too, the council fell—as Lanson correctly observed—into self-contradiction. When asked to determine at what point in the secondary school cycle Latin should be required, the committee opposed, on successive votes, requiring the two years of Latin upon entrance to the *lycée* (6ème and 5ème), at the intermediate level (4ème and 3ème), or in the final two years (2ème and 1ère). Only nominally supportive of secondary school reform, the Conseil preferred, in effect, to retain the 1902 curriculum unchanged.[77]

Two years later when Bérard submitted his detailed program to the

Conseil, it remained obdurate. Only one proposal earned its unanimous endorsement: that the state grant deserving students scholarships to compensate for the costs of attending secondary school and wages forfeited by remaining in school. An astute politician, Bérard hoped that this innovation would appease his most organized opponents, the Compagnons de l'Université Nouvelle, by accommodating one of their most insistent demands—that secondary education be made more accessible to students of modest means—without undertaking the wholesale restructuring of French primary education they advocated. Eager to democratize French secondary education, the Compagnons believed that equal access to the elite *lycées* could be guaranteed only if France embraced a unified system of primary education *(école unique)* that would provide one curriculum for all elementary school students, whether they attended the prestigious, fee-paying preparatory schools preferred by the bourgeoisie or the free elementary schools patronized by children of the peasantry and working classes.[78] Sensitive to the appeal of the *école unique* but disinclined to take on a far-reaching reform of elementary education, Bérard promised to improve accessibility by increasing the financial support available for meritorious students. Ferdinand Brunot, who had succeeded Croiset as Dean of Letters at the Sorbonne, applauded the minister for this "truly democratic" initiative, but still refused to endorse Bérard's curricular recommendations.[79]

Bérard's program called for an examination at the end of the fourth year of secondary education to testify to students' competence in Latin and Greek; success in this examination would furnish students with a certificate for admission to the second stage of *lycée* education. This proposed *certificat d'études classiques* won the support of only five committee members. Some critics worried that students would be disqualified from further study solely on the basis of their knowledge of Latin and Greek. Still others objected to the political implications of such an initiative. Proponents of the *école unique* believed that secondary education should be accessible to students graduating from *écoles primaires* (at the age of twelve or thirteen) and also to older students graduating from the more advanced *écoles primaires supérieures* and the *écoles techniques*. They feared that the *certificat d'études classiques* requirement would make it impossible for students to transfer from the *écoles primaires supérieures* and *écoles techniques,* where no instruction in Latin or Greek was available, to the *lycées*.[80] Critics also complained that not only would secondary education as Bérard envisaged it remain inaccessible to the talented poor; it would become consciously clerical in spirit. Brunot suggested that if secondary schools required four years of training in Latin, France would return to the "Jesuitical" curriculum of the Old Regime.[81] Having rejected the proposed *certificat,* the modernists prevailed once again when the Conseil decided that students transferring from *écoles primaires supérieures* or *écoles techniques* into the modern course would not be required to study Latin. Contradicting its previous resolution that would have required some Latin of all secondary students, the committee reaffirmed the policy of 1902 that allowed students in the modern stream to qualify for admission to the *baccalauréat* and subsequently to higher education without any grounding in classical languages. This was a decision that Bergson, for one, regretted: fearful that the deliberations of the council only intensified the orientation of secondary education towards modern studies, he suspected that in voting against mandatory Latin and Greek and against the *certificat d'études classiques,* the committee had brought about the "end of study in Greek and Latin."[82]

In the short run, the modernists' opposition mattered little. On May 3, 1923, Bérard submitted his program to Alexandre Millerand for presidential authorization. The ministerial decree, which almost completely disregarded the dissenting opinions of the Conseil Supérieur, created a system of secondary education lasting seven years, established a unified curriculum for the first four, and required four years of Latin and two years of Greek within this initial cycle. Upon passing from the fourth year into the fifth, students would choose between a classical and a modern course of studies, but whatever their choice, they would continue to take the same number of hours in the sciences as in the humanities. Before registering to take the *baccalauréat,* students would have to furnish their examiners with a certificate of competence in classical languages.

If Bérard hoped that a presidential decree would shield him against his opponents' acrimony, he was mistaken. For the next six months, critics voiced their objections to the program in the press and on the floor of the Chamber of Deputies, where a protracted debate bore witness to the ongoing intellectual and ideological division of French culture. Speaking for the opposition, Edouard Herriot, Georges Leygues, and Gaston Deschamps upbraided the minister for ignoring the informed opinion of experts; criticized the new curriculum for failing to give adequate attention to science and modern languages; and charged that the reform—secretly clerical and unduly influenced by the Action Française—was antipathetic to the traditions of the Republic.

Deschamps, the chairman of the parliamentary committee on education, stated that with his arrogant dismissal of academic opinion, Bérard impugned the patriotism of France's most prominent scholars. If the Sorbonne judged the reform "retrograde" and "reactionary," it was not because the faculty were (as their opponents insinuated) inherently hostile to the classical tradition. Indeed, the war had demonstrated just the opposite, for the very scholars who opposed the Bérard reform in 1923 had demonstrated during the war years their profound regard for the classical tradition, and had devoted themselves to the defense of France's cultural heritage. Deschamps conceded that Germanic influences had once unduly swayed professors at the nation's universities—"there was a time when, from certain [academic] chairs, it was taught that the French Middle Ages were of Germanic origin"—but that day had passed. During the war, the nation's scholars had worked loyally "to maintain intact in our education, besieged on all sides by Germanic influences, the idealistic treasure of the French spirit." Having defined the French tradition as essentially classical, these same men had continued in the postwar era to teach that French culture, rooted in the heritage of ancient Rome, was in no way influenced or dominated by Germanic forces. Thus to accuse the leading *universitaires* of indifference to the classical tradition was a travesty, and to ignore the serious reservations they expressed towards the 1923 reform program was an insult. Deschamps demanded that Bérard accord the educational community "all the regard owing it," follow its counsel, and maintain intact the balance between classical and modern education that Victor Duruy had introduced.[83]

Georges Leygues had shepherded the 1902 reform through parliament, and believed that the great achievement of that reform had been the attention it paid to the sciences and modern languages. Disregarding Bérard's commitment to "rigorous balance" between the sciences and humanities, Leygues invoked the authority of contemporary scientists to argue that if implemented, this program would be fatal to the development of science in France: "Those who love science and who believe that present conditions do not permit that it be allowed to be replaced by a traditionalism and dilettantism are right to ask whether it is tolerable to allow the culture of science, especially if accompanied by a strong foundation in French and modern languages, to fall into such discredit as not to merit the status of a *bac*."[84] The scientific community did not dispute that France found its cultural origins in Greece and Rome, but scientists denied that the study of Latin was essential to the study of science. Leygues concluded, therefore, that the reform Bérard intended to introduce would "suppress" the spirit of modern education that revolutionary and republican France had long revered.[85]

It is also not surprising that the academics and their parliamentary advocates should have charged that the abolition of the modern curriculum would undermine modern language instruction. Bérard's proposal, in fact, gave almost as much time in the first four years to learning a modern foreign language as to learning French: only in the third year (4ème) would students receive one more hour of instruction in French than in their designated modern language.[86] Nonetheless, his critics charged that by limiting the study of foreign languages, another innovation introduced to French education with the Revolution of 1789, he was in effect repudiating the educational tradition of the Revolution, the Republic, and democracy.[87]

Arguing that Bérard's reforms represented a fundamental break from the educational traditions of the Revolution, Herriot, Leygues, and others questioned the minister's commitment to the principles of French republicanism. The deputy from Haute-Garonne condemned the reform as "a blow against democracy" and calculated that 17,000 working-class children would be barred from secondary schooling because they lacked the preparation in Latin that only private primary schools provided. Thus would "the sons of the bourgeoisie, whether intelligent or not" preserve their hegemonic hold over secondary education. To approve such an innovation would, he warned, make France "ripe for fascism."[88] With slightly less hyperbole, Herriot suggested that the Bérard reform would be "very dangerous for the future of institutions to which [the Republic] was dedicated." And Leygues contended that by returning to a compulsory classical curriculum, the minister advanced the cultural agenda of neoroyalists and conservative Catholics. He did not mince his words: with the implementation of the Bérard reform, the Action Française would finally have triumphed. At war with the Republic and its educational institutions since at least 1908, the neoroyalists, with Pierre Lasserre in the vanguard, had called for the demolition of modern education, the rejection of the 1902 reforms, and a return to classicism. Their prewar campaign had "led the way to the decree of May 3 [1923]."[89]

Opponents of the Bérard reform believed that requiring Latin of all students for the first four years in the *lycée* was an insidious attempt on the part of Catholics—both lay and clergy—to restore Latin to a central position in the curriculum. When Herriot took the floor, he contended that Jesuit-educated Bérard had succumbed to clerical influence. To substantiate his claim that this was a "campaign made . . . by the leaders of the Church," he reminded the Chamber that the Vatican had very recently emphasized the importance of teaching Latin in order to maintain a universal language for the Church. And had not the Catholic hierarchy in France endorsed Bérard's program, anticipating that a return to classical education would "strengthen religious feelings and convictions" of French citizens and protect French culture from the "ever more menacing spirit of decadence" that pervaded postwar society?[90] To the anticlerical Herriot, therefore, the true danger of Bérard's reform was that it would give undue influence to the Catholic Church.

In rebuttal, Bérard neither denied his faith nor denigrated his Catholic education, but spoke of compulsory Latin as essential to the preservation of French culture, not as essential to the preservation of the Catholic faith. There were valid cultural and pedagogical reasons for requiring Latin of all secondary school children, and mandating such a program had nothing to do with clerical influence. Revisiting familiar arguments, he emphasized the importance of preserving France's classical heritage: to protect it, children had to be schooled in its traditions, conversant with its literature, comfortable with its languages. Moreover, studying Latin was pedagogically valuable in that it helped students develop the academic skills at the very heart of a "disinterested" education.

Defending his reform as more democratic than the present system because it would increase funding for qualified poor students, Bérard and his supporters denied that his program was in any way incompatible with or antithetical to the spirit, values, or traditions of French republicanism. The minister acknowledged his friendship with Lasserre, but insisted that neither Lasserre specifically, nor the Action Française more generally, had influenced his deliberations.[91] Challenging those who would make support for the 1902 program the litmus test of modern day republicanism, he rejected as specious the complaint, frequently heard on the left, that the study of Latin and Greek was elitist, aristocratic, or undemocratic. Recalling arguments used frequently during the war years, he reminded his critics that French republicanism found its ideological and cultural roots in the Graeco-Roman tradition, and thus there was no *a priori* incompatibility between classical education and republicanism. Had not Jules Ferry, father of educational reform in the Third Republic, been an avid supporter of classical education?[92] And if defense of science were the standard by which education were deemed "republican," then this program, with its "rigorous balance" between the sciences and humanities, was inherently republican. Indeed, by that criterion alone it was more republican than the system introduced in 1902, for Bérard's proposal provided a more solid grounding in the sciences than that currently offered to students enrolled in the Latin/Greek or the Latin/modern languages courses.

Permeating this political discourse were the cultural arguments of the Great War. In his defense of a curriculum solidly grounded in the classical tradition, Bérard drew explicitly and implicitly upon the arguments animating the classicist revival: France was a classical culture that needed to preserve its heritage of Greece and Rome, and cultivate in its people a spirit of disinterested idealism distinct from the utilitarianism and aggressive materialism of its enemy. One of Bérard's defenders, responding to a critic who claimed that in this modern day it was more important to know how a tram worked than to know how to chat with Demosthenes, retorted that France could benefit little from such crass concern with the practical and the everyday.[93] "Now more than ever, all French citizens, and especially those who will lead the nation, must immerse themselves in a veritable bath of idealism."[94] And the regional newspaper serving Bordeaux applauded the reform as essential to maintaining "the intellectual supremacy of France."[95]

No one in the Chamber of Deputies used the discourse of the war years more explicitly than Alfred Oberkirch, a conservative deputy from Alsace, whose enthusiastic defense of the Bérard program commingled three fundamental arguments of the war years: that France and Germany were culturally distinct; that France, if it were true to its classical heritage, could offer the world a cultural model more worthy than that propagated by Germany; and that Germany could be redeemed if it returned to the cosmopolitan, humanistic, and rationalist traditions of the eighteenth century. Oberkirch claimed that his Alsatian background enabled him to know directly what his colleagues knew only indirectly, by reading the essays of prominent scholars: namely, that France and Germany were fundamentally culturally distinct. Unlike Germany, where the classical tradition had never fully taken hold, "France . . . had assimilated most completely and most thoroughly Graeco-Latin civilization." Nor could France now afford to turn its back on the classical tradition: it "had to reimmerse itself in this classical culture if it wished to give to its national genius the strength and vigor necessary to accomplish the difficult task that victory bestowed upon it." Finally, by reinvigorating the classical tradition, France could help Germany repudiate the anticlassical, antihumanist culture that had dominated it for the past century and rediscover the humanist traditions of "Goethe, Schiller, and Kant."[96] With this allusion to the "two Germanies," Oberkirch adopted the central

argument of republican cultural discourse during the war years and insinuated thereby that one could be a loyal republican, an ardent classicist,
and a supporter of Bérard's educational reform.

When put to a vote in July 1923, the Bérard reforms secured parliamentary approval by a vote of 330 to 255. Conservative republicans,
elected in the Bloc National election of 1919, rejected the argument of
the Left that to be loyal to the Republic one had to be loyal to the reforms
of 1902. The vote exposed a critical division within French republicanism
itself that the war had caused. After 1918 classicism ceased to be the
cultural hobbyhorse of neoroyalists alone; and academic modernism was
no longer the exclusive unifying rallying cry of republicanism. By 1923
there was a lack of consensus within republican ranks as to the character
of education most consistent with republican ideals.

The split within French republicanism did not disappear with the implementation of the Bérard reform. If anything, it intensified. On one
side of the divide, the Académie des Sciences Morales et Politiques acclaimed the new program. Several members considered the rigorous balance of the curriculum its greatest asset; one professor from the Faculty
of Law concluded that by giving equal attention to the humanities and
the sciences, it would strengthen the education of science students who
under the present system "knew a great deal but understood very little."[97]
The president of the Academy disputed the charge of prominent scientists
at the University of Paris, who feared that the program intended to undermine scientific culture in France, and took heart that the initiative
with its rigorous attention to classical languages would overcome the
crise du français.[98] Bergson, having urged his colleagues in 1914 to "return home," insisted nine years later that France had acted wisely in
strengthening the classical curriculum, and he applauded the decision to
give a more prominent place to the study of Latin and Greek. Recalling
his visit to the United States in 1917, he noted that the American people
had supported the French war effort because, convinced that France was
a country of great culture, they had feared that a French defeat would
have constituted "an irreparable ruin for civilization."[99]

The Compagnons de l'Université Nouvelle, as unbending in their opposition as the Academy was enthusiastic in its support, continued to
protest the Bérard reform as a danger to democracy and resolved to
repeal it as soon as an opportunity presented itself.[100] One of Herriot's
first legislative initiatives as leader of the Cartel des Gauches ministry
that took charge in the summer of 1924 was to revoke the reform he had

reviled a year earlier. Reinstating the modern curriculum of 1902, Herriot's minister of education replaced the unified curriculum of 1923 with a modern/classical division that eliminated compulsory Latin and increased instruction in French, science, and modern languages for students in the modern course. This program remained in place through the end of the Third Republic.

This story of bitterly contested cultural norms has a postscript: the finale occurred not in 1924, with the victory of the Cartel des Gauches, but in 1940, with the triumph of Vichy. Bérard the avowed republican eventually embraced Pétain's National Revolution, and became Ambassador to the Vatican. The Bérard reform re-emerged, too, to become an important inspiration for boys' secondary education under Vichy. Three significant amendments bear mention, however. Vichy abandoned Bérard's "rigorous balance" between the sciences and the humanities, and required Latin of most (but not all) boys.[101] In early 1924 Bérard had introduced his reformed curriculum to girls' secondary education, and in the process had won the enthusiastic support of those parents, students, and teachers who regretted that secondary education for girls in France had been until then structurally inferior to that available for boys.[102] Vichy rejected this notion of academic equality between the sexes, and imposed upon its adolescent women a consciously domestic curriculum.

Bergson, Bérard's great ally in 1923, did not share his enthusiasm for the National Revolution: appalled by the turn of events, he decided to observe the regulations of the Statut des Juifs and registered with the state as a Jew. A world-renowned scholar, Bergson could have been exempted from this dishonor, but he refused any such privileged treatment. He died in January 1941, citizen of a country that now banned Jewish scholars from teaching; had he lived he would also have worn the yellow star that distinguished his coreligionists from their fellows. Victor Basch, perhaps the most reviled of all Sorbonnards, fell even more cruelly victim to the institutionalized anti-Semitism that the intellectual nationalism of two decades earlier had done so much to foster: he was assassinated by the French *milice* in 1944.

These tragic continuities link the intellectual culture of France in the First War to the politics and cultural policies of France in the Second, and suggest that the cultural foundations of Vichy were laid between 1914 and 1918. The Great War helped create a cultural milieu in which classicism and technocracy came to coexist; in which intellectual nationalism gained ground against the established internationalism of the academic elite; and in which conservative republicans joined forces with neoroyalists to repudiate the cosmopolitan, rationalist, and modernist aspirations of the Third Republic.

Note on Primary Sources

Notes

Index

Note on Primary Sources

Between 1918 and 1923, Jean Vic, Librarian of the Bibliothèque Nationale, supervised the publication of a comprehensive three-volume bibliography entitled *La Littérature de la guerre* (Paris: Payot). Restricted to works published in French, this bibliography constitutes an invaluable guide to the intellectual culture of noncombatant France. Volume I, published in 1918 and listing pamphlets, books, and periodical articles published between 1914 and 1916, bears witness to the prolificacy of noncombatant intellectuals: the first section of listing alone, "La Philosophie de la guerre, ses origines profondes," runs to more than fifty pages. Subsequent volumes cite works published in the last two years of the war. The relevant published primary sources, cited at length in the notes of this book, are thus well catalogued in Vic's extraordinary bibliography.

At the same time, research in the National Archives in Paris convinced me that to review the published literature of the war years was not to tell the whole story of the mobilization of intellect. Whether as members of the University of Paris, the Conseil Supérieur de l'Instruction Publique, or the Institut de France, the scholars and writers who contributed to the mobilization of intellect also functioned within an institutional culture and debated their responses to the war in that environment. Thus the archival records of prominent cultural and educational institutions were indispensable to this project. Particularly revealing were the wartime and postwar records of the Faculty of Letters (*AJ^{16} 4752), the Faculty of Sciences (AJ^{16} 5123), and the University Council (*AJ^{16} 2589–2591, AJ^{16} 2640–2642) of the University of Paris; the records of the Ecole Normale Supérieure (AJ^{16} 2895, and from the 61 AJ series, nos. 85, 86, 115, 161–162, 195–197, and 206); and the F^{17} 17499 series from the Ministry of Public Instruction, documenting the history of the Bérard reform. The Archives Nationales also hold the papers of Etienne Lamy (333 AP 56, 58, 71, 72), which provide important documentation on the private initiatives of one very prominent individual and the institutional functioning of the Institut de France during the war years. Unlike the private papers of Henri Bergson, which revealed little of his wartime activities and reflections, the papers of Ernest Lavisse, also held at the Bibliothèque Nationale, proved both informative and intensely moving.

Notes

INTRODUCTION

1. As cited by René Doumic, "Frontispiece," *Revue hebdomadaire* 24, 11 (13 March 1915).
2. G. Blanchon, "La Mobilisation intellectuelle," *Journal des débats* 22 (3 September 1915): 370.
3. "Les Deux Cultures: Lettres à M. Scott Mowrer, de MM. Croiset, Aulard, Vincent d'Indy, Maurice Denis, Claudel, Trarieux et Verhaeren," *L'Opinion* 9 (19 August 1916): 153–154.
4. Pierre Imbart de la Tour, "Le Pangermanisme et la philosophie de l'histoire: Lettre à M. Henri Bergson," *Revue des deux mondes* (1 December 1915): 519.
5. Victor Giraud, "Le Miracle français," *Revue des deux mondes* (15 April 1915): 876–898.
6. Phyllis Stock, "New Quarrel of Ancients and Moderns: The French University and Its Opponents, 1899–1914," Ph.D. dissertation, Yale University, 1965.
7. Ernest Lavisse, "Un Sincère Témoignage sur la guerre," *Revue de Paris* (15 April 1916): 674.
8. Stéphane Audoin-Rouzeau, *14–18: Les Combattants des tranchées* (Paris: Armand Colin, 1986).
9. Antoine Prost, *In the Wake of War: 'Les Anciens combattants' and French Society, 1914–1939* (Providence, R.I.: Berg, 1992), 87–93.
10. Joseph Moody, *French Education Since Napoleon* (Syracuse, N.Y.: Syracuse University Press, 1978), 122.
11. William R. Keylor, *Academy and Community: The Foundation of the French Historical Profession* (Cambridge, Mass.: Harvard University Press, 1975), 3; George Weisz, *The Emergence of Modern Universities in France, 1863–1914* (Princeton, N.J.: Princeton University Press, 1983), 132–133, 368.

12. Madeleine Réberioux, "Histoire, historiens, et dreyfusisme," *Revue historique* 518 (April-June 1976): 407–432.

13. Keylor, *Academy and Community*, 3.

14. Christophe Charle, "Champ littéraire et champ de pouvoir: les écrivains et l'affaire Dreyfus," *Annales: Economies, Sociétés, Civilisations* 32 (March-April 1977): 245.

15. Keylor, *Academy and Community*, 209.

16. Claude Digeon, *La Crise allemande de la pensée française (1870–1914)* (Paris: Presses Universitaires de France, 1959), 334–336, 369.

17. Ibid., 160–162.

18. This was the explicit goal of the Ligue Franco-Allemande, founded in 1913 by the Dreyfusard scholars, Ferdinand Buisson and Gabriel Séailles; and it was an implicit objective of the Office National des Universités et Ecoles Françaises, established by government decree in 1910 and directed by Charles Petit-Dutaillis. Archives Nationales, C7732. "Office National des Universités et Ecoles Françaises: Statuts, Adoptés par l'Assemblée Générale du 29 juin 1910." Hereafter, all references to the Archives Nationales will be cited as AN.

19. AN AJ/70/29. Letter, dated 8 May 1914, from Rector of Friedrich-Wilhelms Universität, Berlin; letter, dated 16 May 1914 from the Berlin correspondent of *Le Temps*.

20. Mark Antliff, *Inventing Bergson: Cultural Politics and the Parisian Avant-Garde* (Princeton, N.J.: Princeton University Press, 1993), 17.

21. Kenneth Silver, *Esprit de Corps: The Art of the Parisian Avant-Garde and the First World War, 1914–1925* (Princeton, N.J.: Princeton University Press, 1989).

22. Weisz, *Modern Universities in France*, 178.

23. Guy Hartcup identifies the critical role that Paul Painlevé, scientist and Minister of Public Instruction in 1915, assumed in the formation and organization of the Direction des Inventions Intéressant la Défense Nationale, in *The War of Invention: Scientific Developments, 1914–1918* (London: Brassey's Defence Publishers, 1988), ch. 2: "Mobilising and Organising the Scientists."

24. Patrick Fridenson, "Introduction: A New View of France at War," *The French Home Front, 1914–1918*, ed. Patrick Fridenson (Providence, R.I.: Berg Publishers, 1992), 1.

25. Ibid., 9.

26. Serge Berstein discusses the shift to the right in French politics, effected during the war years, in "The Radical Socialist Party During the First World War," *The French Home Front 1914–1918*, 37–54.

27. Pascal Ory and Jean-François Sirinelli, *Les Intellectuels en France, de l'Affaire Dreyfus à nos jours* (Paris: Armand Colin, 1986), 66.

28. Becker's seminal study appeared in English translation in 1985 as *The Great War and the French People*, trans. Arnold Pomerans, intro. Jay Winter (Prov-

idence, R.I.: Berg Publishers, 1985). All subsequent references to this work are to this English translation.

29. Ibid., 326.

30. Ibid.

31. Jacques Fontana, *Les Catholiques français pendant la Grande Guerre* (Paris: Editions du Cerf, 199O); Jo Burr Margadant, *Madame le Professeur: Women Educators in the Third Republic* (Princeton, N.J.: Princeton University Press, 1990), ch. 9: "Sevriennes in a Nation at War."

32. Geneviève Colin, "Writers and the War," *Great War and the French People*, 161–179; Frank Field, *British and French Writers of the First World War: Comparative Studies in Cultural History* (Cambridge: Cambridge University Press, 1991), 5; Ory and Sirinelli, *Les Intellectuels en France*, 71.

33. Margadant, *Madame le Professeur*, 232–233.

34. Katherine Auspitz, *The Radical Bourgeoisie: The Ligue d'enseignement and the Origins of the Third Republic, 1866–1885* (Cambridge: Cambridge University Press, 1982), 8–9.

35. David Schalk, *War and the Ivory Tower: Algeria and Vietnam* (New York: Oxford University Press, 1991), 4; Tony Judt, *Past Imperfect: French Intellectuals, 1944–1956* (Berkeley, Calif.: University of California Press, 1992).

36. Jean-François Sirinelli, "Les Intellectuels français et la guerre," *Les Sociétés européennes et la guerre de 1914–1918,* ed. J.-J. Becker and S. Audoin-Rouzeau (Nanterre: Publications de l'Université de Nanterre, 1990), 152.

37. Ibid., 148–150; Fontana, *Catholiques français pendant la Grande Guerre*, 53.

38. Becker, *Great War and the French People*, 324.

39. Fridenson, "Introduction," *The French Home Front, 1914–1918*, 2.

40. Fontana, *Catholiques français pendant la Grande Guerre*.

41. Ory and Sirinelli, *Les Intellectuels en France*, 77; Sirinelli, "Les Intellectuels français et la guerre," 149.

42. Ory and Sirinelli, *Les Intellectuels en France*, 77–78.

43. Fritz K. Ringer, *The Decline of the German Mandarins: The German Academic Community, 1890–1933* (Cambridge, Mass.: Harvard University Press, 1969), 180, 12, 190–191.

44. Eberhard Demm, "Les Intellectuels allemands et la guerre," *Les Sociétés européennes et la guerre de 1914–1918*, 183–198.

45. Samuel Hynes, *A War Imagined: The First World War and English Culture* (New York: Atheneum, 1991), 10.

46. Paul Fussell, *The Great War and Modern Memory* (New York: Oxford University Press, 1975), ch. 5: "Oh What a Literary War."

47. Hynes, *A War Imagined*, 28.

48. Stuart Wallace, *War and the Image of Germany: British Academics, 1914–1918* (Edinburgh: John Donald Publishers, 1988), 4, 39.

49. Hegel found little favor among French philosophers until the 1930s, when

Jean Hyppolite, Alexandre Kojève, and Eric Weil launched a Hegelian revival in conscious opposition to the still prevalent neo-Kantianism of French academic philosophers. Michael S. Roth has examined the emergence of French neo-Hegelianism in the 1930s in *Knowing and History: Appropriations of Hegel in Twentieth-Century France* (Ithaca, N.Y.: Cornell University Press, 1988).

50. Wallace, *War and the Image of Germany*, 50.
51. Ibid., 172.
52. Hynes, *A War Imagined*, 74.
53. Marc Bloch, *The Historian's Craft*, intro. Joseph R. Strayer, trans. Peter Putnam (New York: Vintage Books, 1953), 107.
54. Stéphane Audoin-Rouzeau, "The National Sentiment of Soldiers during the Great War," *Nationhood and Nationalism in France: From Boulangism to the Great War, 1889–1918*, ed. Robert Tombs (London: Harper-Collins, 1991), 93.
55. On the frequency of letter-writing between the front and the home front, see Gérard Bacconnier, André Minet, Louis Soler, "Quarante millions de témoins," *Mémoire de la Grande Guerre: Témoins et témoignages* (Nancy: Presses Universitaires de Nancy, 1989): 141–169. On the relationship between combatants and civilians, see Audoin-Rouzeau, *Les Combattants des tranchées;* and the summary of his evidence in "Les Soldats français et la nation d'après les journaux de tranchées (1914–1918)," *Revue d'histoire moderne et contemporaine* (January–March 1987): 66–86.
56. Régis Debray, *Teachers, Writers, Celebrities: The Intellectuals of Modern France*, intro. Frances Mulhern, trans. David Macey (London: NLB and Verso, 1981).

One THE DISCORD OF THE ELDERS

1. George Mosse, "Concluding Remarks," *Journal of Contemporary History*, 2, 3 (July 1967): 217.
2. On the educational reform initiatives of the Third Republic see Evelyn M. Acomb, *The French Laic Laws (1879–1889): The First Anti-Clerical Campaign of the Third Republic* (New York: Columbia University Press, 1941); Françoise Mayeure, *Histoire générale de l'enseignement et de l'education en France,* vol. III: *De la Révolution à l'école républicaine* (Paris: Nouvelle Librairie de France, 1981); Joseph Moody, *French Education since Napoleon* (Syracuse, N.Y.: Syracuse University Press, 1978); and Antoine Prost, *L'Histoire de l'enseignement en France, 1800–1967* (Paris: A. Colin, 1968). The reform of higher education has been analyzed in William Keylor, *Academy and Community: The Foundation of the French Historical Profession* (Cambridge, Mass.: Harvard University Press, 1975); Fritz Ringer, *Fields of Knowledge: French Academic Culture in Comparative Perspective, 1890–*

1920 (Cambridge: Cambridge University Press, 1992); and George Weisz, *The Emergence of Modern Universities in France, 1863–1914* (Princeton, N.J.: Princeton University Press, 1983).

3. See Katherine Auspitz, *The Radical Bourgeoisie: The Ligue d'enseignement and the Origins of the Third Republic, 1866–1885* (Cambridge: Cambridge University Press, 1982); Weisz, *Modern Universities in France;* and Ringer, *Fields of Knowledge.*

4. Sandra Horvath-Peterson discusses Duruy's educational initiatives in *Victor Duruy and French Education: Liberal Reform in the Second Empire* (Baton Rouge, Louisiana: Louisiana State University Press, 1984). Ringer discusses the history of *enseignement spécial* in *Fields of Knowledge,* 114–117.

5. Pasteur insisted upon the inadequacies of nineteenth-century French science in *Pourquoi la France n'a pas trouvé d'hommes supérieurs au moment du péril.* Charles Nordmann cited Pasteur's arguments at some length in "Revue scientifique: Science et Guerre," *Revue des deux mondes* (1 December 1915): 701–702.

6. In his trilogy of the Third Republic, Allan Mitchell has argued that the German example figured prominently when French considered military, educational, and social welfare reform after 1870: *The German Influence in France after 1870: The Formation of the French Republic* (Chapel Hill, North Carolina: The University of North Carolina Press, 1979); *Victors and Vanquished: The German Influence on Army and Church in France after 1870* (Chapel Hill, North Carolina: University of North Carolina Press, 1984); and *The Divided Path: The German Influence on Social Reform in France after 1870* (Chapel Hill, North Carolina: University of North Carolina, 1991). Claude Digeon has examined in rich detail the impact of the "German question" on French intellectual development between 1870 and 1914 in *La Crise allemande de la pensée française (1870–1914)* (Paris: Presses Universitaires de France, 1959).

7. Weisz, *Modern Universities in France,* 66.

8. Moody, *French Education since Napoleon,* 112–113.

9. Weisz, *Modern Universities in France,* 285.

10. Mary Jo Nye, *Science in the Provinces: Scientific Communities and Provincial Leadership in France, 1860–1930* (Berkeley, Calif.: University of California Press, 1986), 21, 18.

11. Weisz, *Modern Universities in France,* 183.

12. Ibid., 194.

13. Harry Paul examines the significant accomplishments of Pierre Duhem in "The Crucifix and the Crucible: Catholic Scientists in the Third Republic," *Catholic Historical Review* 58 (1972): 195–219. In "The Issue of Decline in 19th Century French Science," *French Historical Studies* 7 (Spring 1972): 416–450, he questions how "backward" French science was at the turn of

the century. The quotation is from "Decline in 19th Century French Science," 448.

14. Weisz, *Modern Universities in France,* 76–79.

15. Keylor discusses the "scientization" of historical study in *Academy and Community,* chapter 4: "In Search of *La Méthode historique.*" Pierre Lasserre denounced the "scientism" of Gustave Lanson's literary scholarship in "Le Goût littéraire à la Sorbonne," *Action française: revue mensuelle* 27 (15 January 1911): 32–50; and in "L'Enseignement des Lettres à la Sorbonne," *Action française: revue mensuelle* 27 (15 April 1911): 251–283. William Logue discusses the spirit and limitations of Comtean-inspired philosophy in *Charles Renouvier: Philosopher of Liberty* (Baton Rouge, La.: Louisiana State University Press, 1993), 96–99.

16. Phyllis Stock-Morton traces the development throughout the nineteenth century of this secular ethic, in *Moral Education for a Secular Society: The Development of Morale Laïque in Nineteenth-Century France* (Albany, N.Y.: State University of New York Press, 1988).

17. Logue, *Renouvier: Philosopher of Liberty,* 74–76.

18. Linda Clark indicates that textbooks for young girls expressly appealed to Kant when they upheld the moral obligation to act in such a way that one's actions could become examples for others. Clark, *Schooling the Daughters of Marianne: Textbooks and the Socialization of Girls in Modern French Primary Schools* (Albany, N.Y.: State University of New York Press, 1984), 35. Phyllis Stock-Morton provides copies of the civics curricula taught in schools of the Third Republic, and their emphasis upon the importance of duty suggests a strong Kantian influence. Stock-Morton, *Education for a Secular Society,* 177–185.

19. Jo Burr Margadant, *Madame le Professeur,* 74–77.

20. Digeon, *La Crise allemande,* 336.

21. Léon Daudet, *Contre l'esprit allemand: de Kant à Krupp,* Pages actuelles, 1914–1915 (Paris: Bloud et Gay, 1915), 7, 11–12.

22. Lachelier defended his thesis, *Du Fondement de l'induction,* to the Faculty of Letters at the University of Paris in 1871, and the first edition of the work appeared in the same year. A second edition appeared in 1896; and until at least 1924 (when the eighth edition came out), the work became a standard text in French philosophy.

23. On the influence of Jules Lachelier upon generations of *normaliens,* see Robert Smith, *The Ecole Normale Supérieure and the Third Republic* (Albany, N.Y.: State University of New York Press, 1982); Celestin Bouglé, *The French Conception of 'Culture générale' and Its Influences upon Instruction* (New York: Bureau of Publications, Teachers College, Columbia University, 1938); and Bouglé, "Spiritualisme et Kantisme en France, Jules Lachelier," *Revue de Paris* (May 1, 1934): 198–215.

24. George Fonsegrive argued that the principal accomplishment of Boutroux's

dissertation was to "inaugurate the scholarly critique of 'science'." Fonsegrive, *L'Evolution des idées dans la France contemporaine: de Taine à Péguy* (Paris: Bloud et Gay, 1917), 126.

25. Allan Mitchell, "German History in France after 1870," *Journal of Contemporary History* 2, 3 (July 1967), 88–89.

26. Keylor, *Academy and Community,* 46.

27. Keylor stresses the important role Boutroux played in the intellectual formation of Henri Berr: *Academy and Community,* 132–135; Carole Fink, *Marc Bloch: A Life in History* (New York: Cambridge University Press, 1989), 33.

28. Christophe Charle, Madeleine Réberioux, and William Keylor discuss the relationship between academic reformism and Dreyfusism in: Charle, "Champ littéraire et champ de pouvoir: les écrivains et l'affaire Dreyfus," *Annales: Economies, Sociétés, Civilisations* 32 (March-April 1977): 240–264; and Réberioux, "Histoire, historiens, et dreyfusisme," *Revue historique* 518 (April-June 1976): 407–432; Keylor, *Academy and Community,* ch. 9 and 10.

29. Harry W. Paul, "The Debate over the Bankruptcy of Science in 1895," *French Historical Studies* 5 (Spring 1968), 299.

30. Harry W. Paul writes that the "essential theme" of his book is "the transformation of French Catholicism as a result of its trying to accommodate itself to science"; *The Edge of Contingency: French Catholic Reactions to Scientific Change from Darwin to Duhem* (Gainesville, Fl.: University Presses of Florida, 1979), 3, 179.

31. Raïssa Maritain recounts the story of the disillusioned scientists' suicide pact in *We Have Been Friends Together,* trans. Julie Kernan (New York: Longmans, Green, 1942), 73–76.

32. Paul, "The Crucifix and the Crucible," 219.

33. Paul, "The Bankruptcy of Science," 326.

34. Paul, "The Crucifix and the Crucible," 209.

35. Jacques Maritain, "La Science moderne et la raison," *Revue de philosophie* 16 (1910): 577, 601.

36. Ibid., 597–600.

37. Digeon, *La Crise allemande,* 476.

38. Ringer, *Fields of Knowledge,* 131.

39. Keylor traces the established tradition of elegant historical narrative to the *philosophes,* who "produced elegant histories whose popularity rested more on their indisputable stylistic excellence and polemical force than on their more dubious scholarly merits" (*Academy and Community,* 27–28). Championing the established narrative style, the Action Française, ironically, imitated and acclaimed the historiographical practices of those they held responsible for the decline of France.

40. Ibid., 57.

41. Maurice Pujo, *Les Camelots du roi* (Paris: Flammarion, 1933), 25.

42. Fritz Ringer shows that Croiset was a conservative traditionalist in the educational debates of the 1890s, skeptical of modern education and a supporter of the classical curriculum. Keylor makes it clear, however, that in the first decade of the twentieth century, however (probably in response to the Dreyfus Affair) he became much more clearly a member of the modernist camp. Ringer, *Fields of Knowledge,* 143–144, 150–151; Keylor, *Academy and Community,* 194.

43. Lasserre, "Lectures et discussions: L'antipatriotisme en Sorbonne (les définitions de M. Lalande)," *Action française: revue mensuelle* 25 (15 April 1910): 307.

44. Pierre Lasserre, "Le Goût littéraire à la Sorbonne," *Action française: revue mensuelle* 27 (15 January 1911), 33–35.

45. Phyllis Stock, "Students versus the University in Pre-World War Paris," *French Historical Studies* 7 (Spring 1971): 93–110.

46. "Aussi un enseignement national, qui ne serait pas résolument moderne par la substance et par l'esprit, ne serait-il pas simplement un anachronisme inoffensif, il deviendrait un péril national." As cited by Charles Navarre, "Le Latin dans l'enseignement secondaire," *Revue internationale de l'enseignement* 67 (1914): 199–215.

47. Henri Massis, *Evocations: souvenirs, 1905–1911* (Paris: Librairie Plon, 1931), 61–63.

48. Ibid., 72–73.

49. AN C7731. "Enquête de la Commission de l'Enseignement sur les Programmes de 1902: Réponses de la Ligue pour la Culture Française, présentés par M. Jean Richepin de l'Académie française, Président."

50. Bulletin de l'Association des Professeurs de Philosophie des Collèges, "La Classe de Philosophie et la Réforme de 1902: Rapport présenté devant la Commission parlementaire de l'Enseignement à la Chambre des Députés, par Louis Boisse" (Etampes: O. Lecesne, 1914).

51. AN C7731. "Rapport présenté, au nom de la Commission de l'Enseignement commercial, par M. Max Leclerc, et adopté par la Chambre de Commerce de Paris dans sa séance du 21 mai 1913."

52. Lallemand, "La Question du Latin et la culture scientifique."

53. Hubert Gillot, *La Querelle des anciens et des modernes en France: de la Défense et Illustration de la langue française aux Parallèles des anciens et des modernes* (Paris: Librairie Edouard Champion, 1914).

Two THE IMPIETY OF WAR

1. Marc Bloch, citing Herodotus, in *Strange Defeat: A Statement of Evidence Written in 1940,* intro. Sir Maurice Powicke, foreword Georges Altman, trans. Gerard Hopkins (New York: W. W. Norton, 1968), 130.

2. Pascal Ory and Jean-François Sirinelli, *Les Intellectuels en France, de l'Affaire Dreyfus à nos jours* (Paris: Armand Colin, 1986), 67.

3. AN AJ/61/206. "Charles Bayet," Association Amicale de Secours des Anciens Élèves de l'Ecole Normale Supérieure, *Annuaire, 1919* (Paris: Hachette, 1919): 36–37.

4. Raymond Thamin, "L'Université de France et la guerre," *Revue des deux mondes* 34 (15 July 1916): 307.

5. Pierre Duhem, "The Sciences of Reasoning," *German Science*, trans. John Lyon, intro. Stanley L. Jaki (La Salle, Ill.: Open Court, 1991), 6.

6. Emile Hovelaque, *Les Causes profondes de la guerre* (Paris: Alcan, 1914), iii.

7. Victor Giraud, *Pro patria: La Banqueroute du Scientisme, en marge de la Grande Guerre*, Pages actuelles, no. 109 (Paris: Bloud et Gay, 1917), 3–4.

8. Baudrillart, "Notre propagande," *Revue hebdomadaire* 25 (8 April 1916): 143.

9. Blondel, one of the leading philosophers in the prewar Catholic revival in France, published *L'Action* in 1893. George Fonsegrive described his theory of action in this way: "Our action exceeds ourselves . . . we are only a part of the whole, an important and often preponderant part, but a part nonetheless, and for this reason, dependent and not self-sufficient. We can act only on condition that we go beyond ourselves." *L'Evolution des idées dans la France contemporaine: de Taine à Péguy* (Paris: Bloud et Gay, 1917), 174–175. Fonsegrive noted that even though *L'Action* was out of print by 1914, loose copies still in circulation were so sought after that they went from hand to hand.

10. Maurice Blondel, *Carnets intimes*, vol. II (1894–1949) (Paris: Les Editions du Cerf, 1966), 218.

11. Pierre Assouline describes the efforts of Gaston Gallimard to avoid military service in *Gaston Gallimard: A Half Century of French Publishing*, trans. Harold J. Salemson (New York: Harcourt, Brace, Jovanovich, 1988), 55–63.

12. Jacques Maritain, *Notebooks*, trans. Joseph W. Evans (Albany, N.Y.: Magi Books, 1984), 82.

13. On September 15, 1914, Lavisse provided Louis Liard with the names of noncombatant *normaliens* available to serve as replacement teachers in *lycées* throughout France. AN AJ/61/85. A year later, seventeen *normaliens* were teaching either in France or, in one case, in the United States. AN AJ/61/86. Letter from Lavisse to Liard, 18 October 1915.

14. AN AJ/16/2895. Letter to Paul Dupuy, Ecole Normale Supérieure, from A. Robinet-de-Cléry, 21 May, 1915. AJ/61/85. Letter from Lavisse to Liard, 28 May, 1915, informing him of Robinet-de-Cléry's efforts on behalf of Alsatian students.

15. As cited in Jean Lacouture, *François Mauriac* (Paris: Seuil, 1980), 135.

16. Gonzague Truc, "La Vie intellectuelle pendant la guerre," *La Grande Revue* 88 (1915): 116.

17. AN 333/AP/72. Etienne Lamy's papers. Copy of a letter from Emile Picard to Mme Ernest Carnot, 15 August 1914.

18. Gaston Deschamps, "L'Institut de France et la guerre," *Revue des deux mondes* (15 February 1917): 902–905.

19. Ibid., 900.

20. BN, NAF 15995. Letter from Emile Boutroux to Raymond Poincaré, 22 April 1916, fiches 251–252. Boutroux's wife, Aline, was the sister of Henri Poincaré and first cousin to Raymond and Lucien Poincaré.

21. AN 333/AP/72. Copy of an undated letter from Emile Picard to M. de Vogué, President of the French Red Cross. Contents of the letter would suggest that Picard wrote it in August 1914.

22. AN 333/AP/72. Letter from Emile Picard to Etienne Lamy, 29 September 1914.

23. AN 333/AP/72. "Rapport sur le fonctionnement de l'Ouvroir fondé par l'Institut de France du 31 août 1914 au 15 mars 1915."

24. Payroll for the period from January 1, 1915, through March 15, 1915 totaled 5,413 francs: 3,709 for day-workers at the Institut; 1,704 for home-workers. If the Institut laid off home-workers first and continued to employ the full complement of seventy-five women at the *ouvroir* (and although the report is unclear on this point, this does seem to have been the established policy), then each day-worker received forty-nine francs for two-and-a-half months' work. Ibid.

25. Ibid., 3–4.

26. BN, NAF 25170. Papiers Ernest Lavisse, "Patronage National des Blessés, 45 rue d'Ulm, fevrier 1915."

27. Rosalynd Pflaum, *Grand Obsession: Madame Curie and Her World* (New York: Doubleday, 1989), ch. 12.

28. The prospectus from the Patronage National des Blessés concluded: "Le Patronage a conscience d'avoir fait oeuvre utile." BN NAF 21570. Papiers Ernest Lavisse, "Patronage National des Blessés."

29. AN *AJ/16/2589. Minutes of meeting of the Conseil de l'Université held on 26 October 1914.

30. In addition to Bloch's war diary, *Memoirs of War, 1914–1915*, trans. and intro. Carole Fink (New York: Cambridge University Press, 1989), Fink provides the details of Bloch's military service during the First World War, upon which this brief précis is based, in *Marc Bloch: A Life in History* (Cambridge: Cambridge University Press, 1989), 22–77. Lawrence K. Shook gives an extensive biographical sketch of Gilson's prewar and wartime activities in *Etienne Gilson*, Etienne Gilson Series 6 (Toronto: Pontifical Institute of Medieval Studies, 1984), 17–87.

31. AN *AJ/16/2589; *AJ/16/2590.

32. Almost half of the primary and high-school teachers in France were conscripted, and of those, three-quarters were wounded or dead by the fall of 1915. "Discours prononcé par M. Coville, Directeur de l'enseignement secondaire, à la distribution des prix du Lycée Charlemagne, 'Les Leçons de la guerre,' " *Revue internationale de l'enseignement* 69 (1915): 370.

33. Ory and Sirinelli, *Les Intellectuels en France,* 62.

34. Shook, *Etienne Gilson,* 80.

35. AN *AJ/16/4752. The written testimonials of Professors Croiset, Lanson, and Michart, principal readers of Masson's dissertation, take up fourteen pages in the Faculty registry.

36. Pierre-Maurice Masson, "A Monsieur Gustave Lanson, 19 octobre 1915," *Lettres de guerre, août 1914–avril 1916,* préface de Victor Giraud, notice biographique de Jacques Zeiller (Paris: Hachette, 1917), 145–146.

37. AN *AJ/16/4752. "Registres des actes et déclarations de la Faculté des Lettres de Paris, 1914–1918," 119.

38. AN AJ/61/206. Emile Durkheim, "Durkheim, André Armand," Association Amicale de Secours des Anciens Élèves de l'Ecole Normale Supérieure, *Annuaire* (1917): 201–205.

39. BN NAF, 16001. Letter from Victor Giraud to Raymond Poincaré, 10 May 1917.

40. AN AJ/61/197. Letter from Ernest Lavisse to Commandant Roussel, Major du Dépôt du 26ᵉ R. I., 22 October 1914.

41. AN AJ/61/206. "70ᵉ Réunion générale annuelle: Discours de M. Lavisse," Association Amicale de Secours des Anciens Élèves de l'Ecole Normale Supérieure, *Annuaire* (Paris: Hachette, 1917), 5.

42. Marie-Françoise Berrendonner, "Le Témoignage comme genre littéraire à partir de *Ceux de 14* de Maurice Genevoix," in *Memoire de la Grande Guerre: Témoins et témoignages* (Nancy: Presses Universitaires de Nancy, 1989), 44.

43. AN AJ/61/197. Letter from Lavisse to Minister of War, 6 November 1914. Lavisse informed the minister that "in constant touch with my students, I never ceased to recommend to them [the importance] of modesty, patience, and discipline" ("resté en relations constantes avec mes élèves, je n'ai cessé de leur recommander la modestie, la patience, et la discipline").

44. AN AN/61/206. Association Amicale de Secours des Anciens Elèves de l'Ecole Normale Supérieure, "Supplément: Les Normaliens mobilisés," *Annuaire, 1915* (Paris: Hachette, 1915).

45. AN AJ/61/197. Lavisse wrote to Commandant Roussel, 26ᵉ R.I., on 22 October 1914 on behalf of several students for whom he hoped to secure a transfer. He explained that "intimacy between professors and students was an essential element of the school's academic life," and he intended to act in accordance with that spirit throughout the war.

46. AN AJ/61/197. Letter from Lavisse to Minister of War, 6 November 1914.

47. AN AJ/61/197. *Journal officiel de la République française,* 3 September 1914.

48. AN AJ/61/197. Letter from Lavisse to M. le Lieutenant-Colonel, Directeur de l'Infanterie, Ministère de la Guerre, 7 October 1914, in which Lavisse cites a student's letter: "Il appartiendra alors à chacun de nous . . . de montrer qu'il sait être brave et de soutenir glorieusement la réputation de l'Ecole Normale."

The law providing the same procedure for the promotion of *normaliens* as for the promotion of *polytechniciens* went into effect in October 1916. AJ/61/197. *Journal officiel,* 17 October 1916.

49. AN AJ/61/197. Letter to Lavisse from Ministry of War, 8 December 1914.

50. AN AJ/61/197. Letter from Lavisse to Colonel Directeur de l'Infanterie, Ministry of War, 3 July 1915; response from ministry to Lavisse, 4 September 1915, informing Lavisse that military training undertaken as part of the curriculum at the Ecole Normale did *not* count towards years of military service when calculating pension benefits.

51. AN AJ/61/85. Letter from Lavisse to Louis Liard, 7 May 1915; AJ/61/86. Letter from Lavisse to Minister of Public Instruction, 5 July 1916.

52. AN AJ/61/197. Letter from Lavisse to Ministry of War, 30 October 1914.

53. AN AJ/61/197. Letter from Ministry of War, Section du Personnel du Service Etat-Major, 3 January 1915, to Lavisse.

54. AN AJ/61/197. Ecole Normale Supérieure, correspondence, 10 May 1915.

55. AN AJ/61/85. Draft of a letter composed by Lavisse, 1 March 1915.

56. Lieutenant Marcel Etévé, *Lettres d'un combattant (août 1914-juillet 1916),* préface de Paul Dupuy, "Mémoires et récits de Guerre" (Paris: Hachette, 1917), 134. The colleague of whom Etévé spoke, a former *normalien* by the name of Bouzol, died at Verdun. Etévé died at the Somme.

57. Robert Smith gives the number of *normaliens* mobilized in *The Ecole Normale Supérieure and the Third Republic* (Albany, N.Y.: The State University of New York Press, 1982), 98; "La Rentrée de l'Ecole Normale Supérieure," *Revue internationale de l'enseignement* 73 (1919): 85–86, gives the casualty rates for *promotions.*

58. J. M. Winter compiled statistics for Oxford (and Cambridge) graduates, "Britain's 'Lost Generation' of the First World War," *Population Studies* 31 (1977): 461.

59. BN NAF, 25170. Papers of Ernest Lavisse, fiche 523. "Lettre—extrait janvier 16."

60. BN NAF, 25170. Lavisse papers, ff. 520–552.

61. Ibid. "Lettre—extrait Janvier 16."

62. AN AJ/61/197. Draft of a letter dated 5 May 1917 from Lavisse presumably to the Ministry of War, on the military situation of students admitted to the ENS following the 1917 entrance examination.

63. AN AJ/61/197. Letter from Lavisse to Minister of War, 15 June 1917.

64. AN AJ/61/197. A one-page typed summary entitled "Les Normaliens tués et blessés," May 1917. From the *promotions* of 1910, 1911, 1912, and 1913: 250 combatants, all in the infantry; 113 [45%] dead, 111 [44%] wounded. *Promotion* of 1914: 44 combatants, of whom 28 were in the infantry, 16 in the artillery. There were 8 [28.5%] dead and 16 [57%] wounded from those in the infantry; one dead and one wounded among those in the artillery.

65. Brutus, "Guerre et philosophie," *La Grande Revue* (1915), 529.

66. Albert Sarraut, "Circulaire relative à la continuation de la vie scolaire dans l'enseignement public, Bordeaux, le 10 septembre 1914," "Circulaires du Ministre de l'Instruction Publique relatives à l'état de guerre," *Revue universitaire* 23, 2 (1914): 222.

67. Albert Sarraut, "Discours prononcé par M. Albert Sarraut, à l'occasion de l'ouverture des classes du Lycée de Bordeaux (2 October 1914)," *Revue universitaire* 23, 2 (1914): 192.

68. Université de Paris, "Discours de M. Alfred Croiset," *Ouverture des Conférences de la Faculté des lettres, le 5 novembre 1914* (Paris: Champion, 1914), 1.

69. Ibid., 1–2.

70. Etienne Lamy, *L'Institut et la Guerre. Pour la vérité, 1914–1915*, études publiées sous le patronage des Secrétaires perpetuels des Cinq Académies (Paris: Perrin, 1916), 14, 23, 35.

71. Albert Sarraut, "Pour la rentrée d'octobre 1915: Circulaire du Ministre de l'Instruction publique et des Beaux-arts à MM. les Recteurs des Académies," *Revue internationale de l'enseignement* 69 (1916): 329.

72. Ibid., 329.

73. Ibid., 326.

74. "*La Revue critique* et la guerre," *Revue critique des idées et des livres* 26 (July 1919): 323.

75. Pierre Lasserre, "Le Retour aux anciens," *Revue hebdomadaire* 24 (23 January 1915): 395.

76. Fernand Baldensperger, *L'Avant-guerre dans la littérature française, 1900–1914* (Paris: Payot, 1919), 34–39.

77. François LeGrix, "Un Temoin du temps de paix: M. Léon Daudet," *Revue hebdomadaire* 24 (27 February 1915): 418.

78. Alfred Vallette, "A nos lecteurs," *Mercure de France* 412 (1 April 1915): 657.

79. André Gide/Roger Martin du Gard, *Correspondance, 1913–1934*, intro. Jean Delay (Paris: Gallimard, 1968), 135–136. I have examined Gide's wartime activities and political allegiances in greater detail in "What Did André Gide See in the Action française?" *Historical Reflections/Réflexions historiques* 17 (Winter 1991): 1–22.

80. René Doumic, "La Réouverture des théâtres," *Revue des deux mondes* (15 January 1915): 446–450.

81. Giraud, *Pro patria,* 3–4.

82. Blondel, *Carnets intimes,* II: 218.

83. Letter of October 30, 1914 to Xavier Léon, as cited in Steven Lukes, *Emile Durkheim: His Life and Work* (New York: Harper and Row, 1972), 548.

84. Gustave Lanson, "Un Project de rapprochement intellectuel," *Revue de Paris* 22 (1 April 1915): 659–669.

85. AN AJ/61/85. Ministerial circular from Louis Liard, 6 October 1914.

86. AN *AJ/16/2589. Conseil de l'Université de Paris, Meeting of 1 October 1914, 329–330.

87. Leading members of the Conseil de l'Université at the University of Paris, including Lanson, Croiset, Liard, and Borel, opposed offering the annual competition while candidates for the advanced degree were at the front, believing that this would give an unfair advantage to those candidates who had not been mobilized. AN *AJ/16/2589. Conseil de l'Université, Meetings of 1 August 1914 and 1 October 1914.

    At least one *agrégation* candidate objected strenuously to the cancellation of the competition. It was not his fault that he could not serve at the front, and to deprive him of access to the *agrégation* was only to deprive the educational community of a qualified teacher. Although the student forwarded his objection to the President of the Senate Committee on Higher Education, political intervention was ineffective. The Ministry of Public Instruction decided in November 1914 to cancel the exam, but only for 1915. AN AJ/61/85.

88. On 1 February 1915, Louis Liard instructed all university administrators in Paris to develop appropriate procedures in the event of aerial bombardment of the capital. Posters appeared on the following day at the Ecole Normale Supérieure detailing what was to be done in such an eventuality. AN AJ/61/85.

89. Jean-François Sirinelli, *Génération intellectuelle: Khâgneux et Normaliens dans l'entre-deux-guerres* (Paris: Fayard, 1988), 27.

90. Enrollment statistics for the University of Paris are from "Discours de M. Alfred Croiset," *Ouverture des conférences,* 5; for the Ecole Libre des Sciences Politiques, from Ory and Sirinelli, *Les Intellectuels en France,* 62; and for the Ecole Normale, from AN AJ/61/85: the draft of letter, dated 1 March 1915, from Ernest Lavisse.

91. "Discours de M. Ernest Lavisse," "A L'Ecole normale supérieure," *Revue universitaire* 24 (1915): 24.

92. AN AJ/16/5123. Conseil de la Faculté des Sciences, Université de Paris. Minutes of meeting of 14 January 1915, 197.

93. Ibid. Minutes of meeting of 14 November 1914.

94. AN AJ/61/85. Letter from Louis Liard to Ernest Lavisse, 2 October 1914.

95. In the spring of 1915, Lavisse requested that Liard protect the library budget for the ENS. With the school's operating budget for material costs slashed from 228,050 francs to 120,000 francs, Lavisse feared the consequences for the library: "It is important that we not allow the value of our basic instruments of research to diminish. The experience of 1870–71 shows us that damage done by interrupting periodical subscriptions cannot always be repaired." Liard's reply, dated April 10, 1915, did not hold out any promise for increases to the library budget. AN AJ/61/85. The minutes of the meeting of the Faculty of Sciences, 14 January 1915, record the wish of the faculty council that budget cuts *not* affect the purchase of periodicals. AN AJ/16/5123. Conseil de la Faculté des Sciences, Université de Paris, 197.

96. In December 1914 the two faculties divided 2017 francs equally between the Secours National and the Secours Universitaire. In December 1915 the two organizations received 1048.55 francs each, 908.65 francs each in December 1916, but only 643.80 francs each in September 1918. Complete statistics of faculty donations, for the faculties of letters and sciences, are given in AN *AJ/16/4752. "Registres des actes et déclarations de la Faculté des Lettres de Paris, 13 janvier 1914–23 décembre 1918," 48, 53, 63–64, 77, 82, 84, 94, 97, 99, 104, 131, 167, 224.

97. AN *AJ/16/2589. Conseil de l'Université de Paris. Minutes of meeting, 26 April 1915, 403.

98. Liard, "La Guerre et les universités françaises," 70.

99. Ibid., 71. François Albert believed that female auditors lacked seriousness; Albert, "La Sorbonne de guerre," *L'Opinion* (29 May 1915), 346–347. The statistics on female enrollment during the war come from Liard; those concerning overall increases, from 1914 to 1922, appear in Ory and Sirinelli, *Les Intellectuels en France*, 63.

     German university enrollment evolved in a similar way. With 83% of German university students mobilized, places opened up to young women, and by 1916 almost one half of the students enrolled at German universities were women. Auguste Audollent, "L'Action intellectuelle de l'Allemagne et de la France pendant la guerre," *Revue internationale de l'enseignement* 71 (1917): 82.

100. Albert, "Sorbonne de guerre," 346.

101. Weisz, *Modern Universities in France*, 76–80. Ernest Renan lamented that public lectures inevitably lowered the lecturer "to the ranks of a public entertainer." Ibid., 79.

102. The *Revue de métaphysique et de morale* provided a list of all philosophy courses to be offered at French universities during the 1915–1916 academic year in a supplement to the November 1914 issue of the journal, which appeared in November 1915.

103. AN *AJ/16/2589. Conseil de l'Université de Paris, Meeting of 23 December 1914, 386.

104. Albert, "Sorbonne de guerre," 346–347. Albert noted that Seignobos was so determined not to be disturbed during his lectures that he locked the doors to the lecture hall as soon as he entered; thereafter, students could leave—if they dared—but the tardy could not enter.

105. AN *AJ/16/2589. Conseil de l'Université, Meeting of 25 October 1915, 439–440.

106. Charles Maurras, "Le Moral," *Action française,* 1 August 1914.

107. Louis Dimier, *L'Appel des intellectuels allemands: textes officiels et traduction avec préface et commentaire* (Paris: Nouvelle Librairie Nationale, 1914), 8; Léon Daudet, *Contre l'esprit allemand: de Kant à Krupp,* Pages actuelles, 1914–1915 (Paris: Bloud et Gay, 1915), 3.

108. In 1915 the Committee published 402,000 copies of each pamphlet; of the 88,000 printed in English, 20,000 were shipped to the United States for direct distribution, and the French Embassy in Washington received an additional 5,000 copies to distribute as the ambassador saw fit. Yves-Henri Nouailhat, *France et États-Unis, août 1914-avril 1917* (Paris: Publications de la Sorbonne, 1979), 167–168.

109. René Doumic, "Frontispiece," *Revue hebdomadaire* 24 (13 March 1915).

110. Mgr. Alfred Baudrillart, "Notre propagande," *Revue hebdomadaire* 25, 15 (8 April 1916): 144–169.

111. AN 333/AP/72. "Rapport de M. H[enry] Bloud, ancien éditeur, avocat à la Cour d'Appel de Paris, sur la propagande française à l'étranger par les méthodes usitées dans le commerce de l'édition."

112. AN 333/AP/72. Comité du Livre, "Note sur la collaboration possible des étrangers francophiles à l'oeuvre du Comité du Livre," stamped 2 September 1916.

113. Letter of André Gide to Edmund Gosse, 1916, as cited in *The André Gide Reader,* ed. David Littlejohn (New York: Knopf, 1971), 421.

114. Giraud, *Pro Patria,* 3–4.

Three THE *KULTUR* WAR

1. Brutus, "Guerre et philosophie," *La Grande Revue* 86 (1914), 529.

2. In 1915 Samuel Harden Church issued an English translation of the manifesto, complete with a list of signatories, in *The American Verdict on the War: A Reply to the Appeal to the Civilized World of 93 German Professors* (Baltimore: Norman, Remington, 1915), 26–32. Quotations from the manifesto that appear in this chapter are from this translation.

3. Republican writers, like the pseudonymous "Brutus" in *La Grande Revue* and Emile Hovelaque, Inspector of Schools, challenged the claims of the manifesto and denounced its signatories. Hovelaque was dismayed that Germany's "philosophers, professors, and infatuated pedants" were infected by a "fatal faith in the pre-eminence of *Kultur*"; Hovelaque, *Les Causes pro-*

fondes de la guerre (Paris: Alcan, 1914), v. "Brutus" welcomed French re-actions to the manifesto as proof of French intellectual vitality. George Fon-segrive, a regular contributor to Catholic periodicals and an enthusiastic historian of the pre-1914 Catholic revival, described his own study as a rejection of the culture German intellectuals defended as sacrosanct (Fon-segrive, *Kultur et Civilisation* [Paris: Bloud et Gay, 1916], 3). Paul Gaultier chastised Germany's most illustrious "scientists, artists, writers, theologians and professors" for approving the violation of treaties and the persecution of civilians. Paul Gaultier, *La Mentalité allemande et la guerre,* 3rd ed. (Paris: Félix Alcan, 1918), 2. The first edition appeared in 1916.

4. AN *AJ/16/2589. Conseil de l'Université de Paris, meeting of 18 December 1914.

5. "Déclaration de l'Académie des inscriptions et belles-lettres, en date du 23 octobre 1914," "L'Institut de France et la guerre," *Revue internationale de l'enseignement* 69 (1915): 6.

6. AN *AJ/16/2589. Conseil de l'Université. Meeting of 26 October 1914.

7. AN 333/AP/72. Letter from Paul Appell to Etienne Lamy, 19 October 1914.

8. AN *AJ/16/2589. Conseil de l'Université de Paris. Meeting of 26 October 1914.

9. Ibid.

10. Paul Crouzet, professor at the Collège Rollin in Paris and administrative assistant to Léon Bérard after the war, acclaimed Dimier's analysis of the manifesto as "the most detailed that has appeared to date." Crouzet, "La Guerre et la culture classique," *Revue universitaire* 24, 2 (1915): 654.

11. Louis Dimier, *L'Appel des intellectuels allemands: textes officiels et traduc-tion avec préface et commentaire* (Paris: Nouvelle Librairie Nationale, 1914), 10.

12. "La Nouvelle librairie nationale, rapport de Georges Valois," presented at the VIIe Congrès National d'Action française, *Action française* (19 March 1920).

13. J. Ernest-Charles, one of the signatories of the Manifesto of 100, denied that the Académie Française represented the collective voice of French literature and the arts. Ernest-Charles, "Les Ecrivains et la guerre," *La Grande Revue* (January 1915): 473.

14. "Un Appel des intellectuels français," *Journal des débats* 22 (12 March 1915): 397–398. The female signatories were: Mme Juliette Adam, Mme Virginie Demont-Breton, Mlle Marie Leneru, Mme Catulle Mendès, Mme de Noailles, and Mme Rachilde.

15. "Un Manifeste des universités françaises," *Journal des débats* 21 (13 No-vember 1914): 623–624.

16. Ernest Lavisse and Charles Andler, *The German Theory and Practice of War* (Paris: Alcan, 1915), 19–21. Lavisse and Andler cited Bédier's pamphlet, *Les Crimes allemands d'après les témoignages allemands,* in their essay.

17. John Horne and Alan Kramer, "German 'Atrocities' and Franco-German Opinion, 1914: The Evidence of German Soldiers' Diaries," *Journal of Modern History* 66 (March 1994): 1–33.

18. Charles Andler, *Pan-Germanism: Its Plan for German Expansion in the World,* trans. J. S. (Paris: Librairie Armand Colin, 1915).

19. Charles Andler, "Les Origines philosophiques du pangermanisme," *Revue de métaphysique et de morale* 23, 5 (1916): 659–695.

20. Ernest Lavisse, "Trois idées allemandes," *Revue de Paris,* 22 (15 May 1915), 225–227.

21. Victor Basch, "La Philosophie et la littérature classiques de l'Allemagne et les doctrines pangermanistes," *Revue de métaphysique et de morale* 22 (1914): 768–793. Basch conceded that pan-Germanists had appropriated Fichte's idea that the German language bestowed a unique character upon its people, but he denied categorically any pan-Germanist intent on Fichte's part: "On dira sans doute que ce magnifiement, cette glorification de la langue et du peuple allemands est la racine du pangermanisme. Il est possible, il est même certain que les pangermanistes se sont servis de ces pages. Mais il n'est pas moins certain, à mes yeux, que toute pensée pangermaniste était absente de l'esprit de Fichte lui-même," 783.

22. Emile Boutroux, "L'Allemagne et la guerre; lettre de M. Emile Boutroux," *Revue des deux mondes,* 23 (15 October 1914): 385–401.

23. Victor Delbos, *L'Esprit philosophique de l'Allemagne et la pensée française,* Pages actuelles, 1914–1915 (Paris: Bloud et Gay, 1915), 33–35.

24. E. Goblot, "L'Origine philosophique de la folie allemande: *Les Discours à la nation allemande* de Fichte," *Revue du mois* 19 (June 1915): 688.

25. Ibid., 692.

26. Edmond Barthélemy, "L'Idée allemande du développement: Hegel, Bismarck, Guillaume II," *Mercure de France* 111 (June 1915): 222, 225.

27. Pierre Imbart de la Tour, "Le Pangermanisme et la philosophie de l'histoire: Lettre à M. Henri Bergson," *Revue des deux mondes* 30 (1 December 1915): 482, 485, 488.

28. "Discours prononcé par M. Appell, Président de l'Institut, à la séance publique annuelle des Cinq Académies, du 26 octobre 1914, 'L'Institut de France et la guerre,' " *Revue internationale de l'enseignement* 69 (1915): 10–11.

29. Emile Boutroux identified the origin of the phrase "la barbarie savante" in "L'Allemagne et la guerre," 388.

30. Henri Bergson, "La Signification de la guerre," *La Signification de la guerre* (Paris: Bloud et Gay, 1915), 15.

31. Hovelaque, *Les Causes profondes de la guerre,* vi.

32. Université de Paris, "Discours de M. Alfred Croiset," in *Ouverture des conférences de la Faculté des Lettres, le 5 novembre 1914* (Paris: Edouard Champion, 1914), 2.

33. Paul Crouzet, "La Guerre et la culture classique (suite)," *Revue universitaire* 25 (1916): 116.

34. Lucien Maury, "Les Intellectuels allemands," *La Revue politique et littéraire: la Revue bleue* 52 (8 August-14 November 1914): 175.

35. Christian Pfister and Charles Bémont, "A Nos Lecteurs: L'Appel des Alle-mands aux nations civilisées," *Revue historique* 117 (September-December 1914): 1–2.

36. A. Dastre, "Du Rôle restreint de l'Allemagne dans le progrès des sciences," *Les Allemands et la science,* ed. Gabriel Petit and Maurice Leudet (1916; repr. New York: Arno Press, 1981), 80.

37. "Discours prononcé par M. Appell, 'L'Institut de France et la guerre,' " 10–12.

38. Charles Nordmann, "A Propos de la science allemande," *Revue des deux mondes* (15 January 1916), 464–465.

39. Imbart de la Tour, "Le Pangermanisme et la philosophie de l'histoire," 489.

40. Lavisse and Andler, *The German Theory and Practice of War,* 48.

41. Hovelaque, *Les Causes profondes de la guerre,* 43.

42. Goblot, "L'Origine philosophique de la folie allemande," 706–708.

43. Fridel-Cortelet, "Der Professor ist die deutsche Nationalkrankheit," *La Grande Revue* 88 (October 1915), 547, 551.

44. Ibid., 547.

45. Ibid., 552.

46. Gonzague Truc, "La Vie intellectuelle pendant la guerre," *La Grande Revue* (July 1915), 116.

47. Dr. Grasset, "Lettre à Professeur G. Petit," *Les Allemands et la science,* 202.

48. De Miomandre, "A Propos du Manifeste des cent," 172–173.

49. Romain Rolland, "Above the Battle," in *Above the Battle,* trans. C. K. Og-den (Chicago: Open Court Publishing, 1916), 37–55. Rolland's essay ap-peared originally in the *Journal de Genève* (15 September 1914).

50. Henri Massis, "Romain Rolland parle," *L'Opinion* (24 April 1915): 258.

51. Julien Benda, "Lettre ouverte à M. Romain Rolland," *L'Opinion* (19 Feb-ruary 1916): 169.

52. "Discours de M. Alfred Croiset," in *Ouverture des conférences,* 5.

53. The complete text of the manifesto of the Institut Catholique appeared in "Chronique politique" column of *Le Correspondant* (21 November 1914): 618–622. The reference to scholarly methodology appears on p. 619.

54. The texts of each declaration appear in "L'Institut de France et la guerre," 6–9. Paul Flat criticized the Académie des Sciences for failing to act more promptly, in "L'Institut de France et la guerre," *Revue politique et littéraire: la Revue bleue* 53 (January 1915): 12.

55. Paul Flat, "Le Devoir des Intellectuels," *Revue politique et littéraire: la Revue bleue* 53 (1915): 47–48.

56. Flat, "L'Institut de France et la guerre," 13.

57. Maury, "Les Intellectuels allemands," 174–176.

58. Etienne Lamy, "Les Intellectuels d'Allemagne et l'Institut de France," *Le Correspondant* (10 March 1915): 737–755.

59. Charles Richet, "Science française et science allemande," *Les Allemands et la science,* 346. The essays that appeared in this collection were responses to an enquiry published in April 1915 in *Le Figaro.*

60. Georges Lemoine, "Les Sciences chimiques," in *Un Demi-siècle de la Civilisation française,* ed. Baillaud, Boutroux, Chailley, et al. (Paris: Librairie Hachette, 1916), 220; Pierre Duhem, "Quelques réflexions sur la science allemande," *Revue des deux mondes* 25 (1 February 1915): 665, 675.

61. Emile Picard criticized German scientists for refusing to recognize the genuine accomplishments of French scientists: Picard, "L'Histoire des Sciences et les prétentions de la science allemande," *Revue des deux mondes* (1 July 1915): 68; Charles Nordmann repeated the charge in "A Propos de la science allemande," *Revue des deux mondes* (1916): 463.

62. In his review of *La Science française,* a collection of essays written by France's leading scholars on the accomplishments of French scholars in more than two dozen disciplines, André Beaunier cited Langlois. "Revue littéraire: *La Science française,*" *Revue des deux mondes* 30 (1915): 687.

63. "Discours de M. Alfred Croiset," in *Ouverture des Conférences,* 5.

64. Basch, "La Philosophie et la littérature classiques de l'Allemagne," 711.

65. Hovelaque, *Les Causes profondes de la guerre,* iii, 47.

66. Lavisse and Andler, *The German Theory and Practice of War,* 17.

67. René Pichon, "Mommsen et la mentalité allemande," *Revue des deux mondes* (15 October 1915): 762–763, 765, 770–771.

68. "Discours prononcé par M. Appell, 'L'Institut de France et la guerre,'" 11.

69. "Discours de M. Alfred Croiset," in *Ouverture des Conférences,* 3–4.

70. Gaston Deschamps, "Le Retour à la culture française," *Revue hebdomadaire* 24, 14 (3 April 1915): 5–29.

Four THE CONTROVERSY OVER KANT

1. Emile Boutroux, "L'Allemagne et la guerre, lettre de M. Emile Boutroux," *Revue des deux mondes* (15 October 1914): 399–400.

2. A complete copy of the manifesto of the French Universities appeared in *Journal des débats,* 21 (13 November 1914): 623–624. A commentary on the manifesto, written by A. Albert-Petit, appeared in the same issue under the title, "La Réponse des Universités françaises," 609–610.

3. Victor Delbos, *L'Esprit philosophique de l'Allemagne et la pensée française,* Pages actuelles, 1914–1915 (Paris: Bloud et Gay, 1915), 32.

4. Ibid., 12–14, 32, 35–36.

5. Alphonse Aulard, *La Paix future d'après la Révolution française et Kant,*

Conférence faite à la Sorbonne pour les Amis de l'Université de Paris, le 7 mars 1915, 2ème édition (Paris: Librairie Armand Colin, 1915), 20.

6. Victor Basch, *La Guerre de 1914 et le droit* (Paris: Ligue des Droits de l'Homme et du Citoyen, 1915), 111. Basch had established the first provincial chapter of the Dreyfusard society in Rennes, was vice-president of the League in 1915, and assumed its presidency in 1926.

7. Victor Basch, "La Philosophie et la littérature classiques de l'Allemagne et les doctrines pangermanistes," *Revue de métaphysique et de morale* 22 (1914): 760.

8. Immanuel Kant, *Metaphysics of Morals*, trans. and intro. Mary Gregor (Cambridge: Cambridge University Press, 1991), 343.

9. Basch, "La Philosophie et la littérature classiques," 761.

10. Aulard, *La Paix future*, 11.

11. Aulard acknowledged that in his political beliefs Kant was neither a Jacobin nor a Girondin: "his ideal seemed to be that of a constitutional monarchy like that which the members of the Constituent Assembly had created"; *La Paix future*, 18. Aulard failed to mention that Kant condemned the execution of the king as "a crime that remains forever and cannot be expiated." Kant, *Metaphysics of Morals*, 132.

12. S. Rocheblave, "Kant contre l'Allemagne," *Journal des débats*, 23 (18 February 1916): 254.

13. Basch, "La Philosophie et la littérature classiques," 762.

14. Brutus, "La Guerre et philosophie," *La Grande Revue* (1914): 535–536.

15. Jacques Maritain, "Le Rôle de l'Allemagne dans la philosophie moderne," *La Croix*, 17 December 1914.

16. Maritain, "Le Rôle de l'Allemagne dans la philosophie moderne: le luthéranisme," *La Croix*, 7 January 1915. Maritain uses "egocentrism" and "pantheism" interchangeably to describe the concept of autonomous individualism according to which human beings regulate their existence independently of divine authority.

17. Maritain, "La Science allemande," *La Croix*, 25/26 October 1914.

18. Abbé J. Paquier, *Le Protestantisme allemand: Luther, Kant, Nietzsche* (Paris: Bloud et Gay, 1915), 73.

19. Immanuel Kant, *Foundations of the Metaphysics of Morals: Foundations of the Metaphysics of Morals and "What is Enlightenment?"*, trans. and intro. Lewis White Beck (Indianapolis: Bobbs-Merrill Educational Publishing, 1959), 81.

20. Paquier, *Le Protestantisme allemand*, 58, 60.

21. George Fonsegrive, *Kultur et Civilisation* (Paris: Bloud et Gay, 1916), 30, 31.

22. Maritain, "Le Rôle de l'Allemagne dans la philosophie moderne: la philosophie speculative de Kant," *La Croix*, 27 May 1915.

23. Ibid.

24. Maritain, "Le Rôle de l'Allemagne dans la philosophie moderne: la philosophie morale de Kant," *La Croix,* 31 May 1915.

25. Paul Gaultier, *La Mentalité allemande et la guerre* (Paris: F. Alcan, 1916), 51, 12–14.

26. Lewis White Beck, "Introduction," in Kant, *Foundations of the Metaphysics of Morals,* xiii.

27. S. G. Mgr. du Vauroux, *Du Subjectivisme allemand à la philosophie catholique,* Pages actuelles, 1914–1916 (Paris: Bloud et Gay, 1916).

28. Ibid., 15, 58–60.

29. Pierre Imbart de la Tour, *L'Opinion Catholique et la Guerre,* suivi d'une lettre de Don Miguel de Unamuno, Recteur de l'Université de Salamanque, Pages actuelles, 1914–1915 (Paris: Bloud et Gay, 1915), 10.

30. The Catholic Committee for International Propaganda issued a pamphlet in 1915 to provide proof of German atrocities against Belgian and French clerics. Identifying twenty-two French priests killed by German troops, the pamphlet argued that Germany showed no favor towards the Catholic Church. Abbé Eugène Griselle, *Le Martyre du Clergé français,* Pages actuelles no. 51 (Paris: Bloud et Gay, 1915).

31. AN 333/AP/72. Etienne Lamy, typewritten manuscript, "La Guerre allemande et le catholicisme" (n.d.).

32. Gaultier, *La Mentalité allemande,* 67–68.

33. Imbart de la Tour, *L'Opinion catholique et la guerre,* 16–17, 18.

34. AN 333/AP/72. Lamy, "Guerre allemande et catholicisme," 3–4.

35. Lewis White Beck makes this point in his introduction to *Foundations of the Metaphysics of Morals,* ix.

36. Paquier, *Le Protestantisme allemand,* 110.

37. Ibid., 108.

38. Kant, *Foundations of the Metaphysics of Morals,* 8.

39. Ibid., 80.

40. Maurras, "L'Individualisme et pangermanisme," *Action française,* 17 October 1914.

41. Ibid.

42. Maurras, "Pour nous empêcher de penser," *Action française,* 13 December 1914, as cited in Charles Maurras, *Les Conditions de la victoire* (Paris: Nouvelle Librairie Nationale, 1917), 2:44.

43. Maurras, "L'Individualisme et pangermanisme," 120.

44. Léon Daudet, *Contre l'esprit allemand: de Kant à Krupp,* Pages actuelles 1914–1915 (Paris: Bloud et Gay, 1915), 18.

45. Ibid., 17.

46. Léon Daudet, *Contre l'esprit allemand: Mesures de l'après-guerre,* Pages actuelles 1914–1915 (Paris: Bloud et Gay, 1915), 3, 13, 10.

47. Daudet, *De Kant à Krupp,* 12, 13, 31.

48. Daudet, *Mesures de l'après-guerre,* 46–47, 49.

49. Ibid., 59.

50. Jean-Jacques Becker, *The Great War and the French People*, trans. Arnold Pomerans (Providence, R.I.: Berg, 1985): ch. 14: "The Strikes of the Spring of 1917."

51. AN 333/AP/71. Report prepared by Etienne Lamy on the Chateau-Thierry mutinies, dated 4 August 1917.

52. Jacques Fontana, *Les Catholiques français pendant la Grande Guerre* (Paris: Editions du Cerf, 1990), 136.

53. Ibid., 159.

54. César Chabrun, "Kant et M. Wilson," *Revue des deux mondes* (15 February 1917): 857, 861.

55. "Kant et M. Wilson," *L'Opinion* (24 February 1917): 190.

56. Immanuel Kant, "Perpetual Peace," *Kant's Political Writings*, ed. with introduction and notes by Hans Reiss (Cambridge: Cambridge University Press, 1970), 85.

57. André Fribourg, "Kant contre l'Allemagne," *L'Opinion* (3 February 1917): 117.

58. Alfred Baudrillart, "Un Prêtre catholique peut-il vouloir la continuation de la guerre?" *La France, les Catholiques et la guerre: Réponse à quelques objections,* Pages actuelles (Paris: Bloud et Gay, 1917), 9, 11. Published in France in 1917, these essays were written in 1916 at the request of the National Editorial Service for distribution in the United States.

59. AN 333/AP/72. Declaration of Catholics of Allied and Neutral Powers, undated.

60. Maurras, "Kant et M. Wilson," *Action française,* 16, February 1917, as cited in Maurras, *Les Conditions de la victoire* (Paris: Nouvelle Librairie Nationale, 1920), vol. 8: 22.

61. Ibid.

62. Maurras, "L'Idéalisme dangereux," *Action française,* 28, January 1917.

63. Maurras, "Ni Vainqueurs, ni vaincus," *Action française,* 24 January 1917.

64. Ibid.

65. After April 1917, Maurras represented Wilson as a model of executive authority. Maurras, "La Tradition américaine," *Action française,* 6 July 1918, as cited in *Les Conditions de la victoire,* vol. 8: 73.

66. This argument is most explicit in Vaugeois, *La Morale de Kant dans l'université de France* (Paris: Nouvelle Librairie Nationale, 1917). The third lecture in Vaugeois's series was entitled: "Convenance de la morale de Kant avec les besoins pédagogiques de l'état français décatholicisé."

67. Ibid., 18.

68. Ibid., 15–16.

69. Ibid., 266.

70. Ibid., 286.

Five THE CLASSICIST REVIVAL

1. Henri Bergson, "La Signification de la guerre," *La Signification de la guerre* (Paris: Bloud et Gay, 1915), 23.
2. Kenneth Silver, *Esprit de Corps: The Art of the Parisian Avant-Garde and the First World War, 1914–1925* (Princeton, N.J.: Princeton University Press, 1989).
3. Paul Crouzet, "L'Enseignement secondaire dans l'Académie de Paris depuis la guerre," *Revue universitaire* 29, 2 (1920): 187.
4. "Discours de M. Alfred Croiset," in *Ouverture des conférences de la Faculté des Lettres, le 5 novembre 1914* (Paris: Edouard Champion, 1914), 3; Paul Crouzet, "La Guerre et la culture classique (suite)," *Revue universitaire* 25, 1 (1916): 118; Abbé Delfour, *La Culture latine* (Paris: Nouvelle Librairie Nationale, 1916), 8.
5. "Discours de M. Alfred Croiset," in *Ouverture des conférences*, 3.
6. Emile Boutroux, "L'Allemagne et la guerre; lettre de M. Emile Boutroux," *Revue des deux mondes* 23 (15 October 1914): 390–394.
7. Emile Boutroux, "L'Allemagne et la guerre, deuxième lettre," *Revue des deux mondes* (15 May 1916): 249.
8. Pierre Imbart de la Tour, "Le Pangermanisme et la philosophie de l'histoire: Lettre à M. Henri Bergson," *Revue des deux mondes* 30 (1 December 1915): 485.
9. Letter from Etienne de Fontenay to his mother, dated 24 January 1915. Charles et Etienne de Fontenay, *Deux frères morts pour la France: Charles et Etienne de Fontenay, Lettres du Front, 1914–1916,* préface de M. Paul Deschanel (Paris: Plon-Nourrit, 1920), 175.
10. René Doumic, "La Réouverture des théatres," *Revue des deux mondes* (15 January 1915): 446.
11. Vincent Scully, *Architecture: The Natural and the Manmade* (New York: St. Martin's Press, 1991), 297.
12. Léon Cury, "La Guerre et les humanités," *Revue universitaire* 24 (1915): 14.
13. Albert Sarraut, "Pour la rentrée d'octobre 1915: Circulaire du Ministre de l'Instruction publique et des Beaux-Arts à MM. les Recteurs des Académies," *Revue internationale de l'enseignement* 69 (1915): 324.
14. "Discours prononcé par M. Lucien Poincaré, Directeur de l'Enseignement supérieur, conseiller d'état, à la distribution des prix du lycée Janson de Sailly, 'Les Leçons de la guerre,' " *Revue internationale de l'enseignement* 69 (1915): 289–290.
15. Garry Wills, *Lincoln at Gettysburg: The Words That Remade America* (New York: Simon and Schuster, 1992), ch. 2.
16. Institut de France, Académie Française, "Séance publique annuelle du jeudi 17 décembre 1914: Rapport de M. Etienne Lamy, sur le concours de l'anneé 1914" (Paris: Firmin-Didot, 1914), 25–26.

17. Institut de France, Académie Française, "Rapport de M. Etienne Lamy sur les concours de l'Année 1915," *Séance publique annuelle* (Paris: Firmin-Didot, 1915), 5–20.

18. Institut de France, Académie Française, "Rapport de M. Etienne Lamy sur les concours de l'Année 1916," *Séance publique annuelle* (Paris: Firmin-Didot, 1916), 3–5.

19. Ibid.

20. Ibid., 30.

21. Institut de France, Académie Française. "Rapport de M. Etienne Lamy sur les concours de l'Année 1917" (Paris: Firmin-Didot, 1917): 4–5.

22. "Rapport de M. Etienne Lamy sur les concours de l'Année 1916."

23. Raoul Narsy, *La France au-dessus de tout: Lettres de combattants,* Pages actuelles (Paris: Bloud et Gay, 1915), 1.

24. "Discours prononcé par M. Louis Liard, Vice-recteur de l'Académie de Paris, à la distribution des prix du lycée Condorcet, 'Les Leçons de la guerre,'" 283–284.

25. Wills, *Lincoln at Gettysburg,* 60. Lamy also spoke directly of a nation—and not just a younger generation—educated by a generation of youthful heroes. Calling the French an "orphaned people," he took solace in the fact that the dead had offered the living "the most effective lesson of all, that of personal example." "Rapport de M. Etienne Lamy sur les concours de l'Année 1916."

26. Ernest Lavisse, "Un sincère témoignage sur la guerre," *Revue de Paris* (15 April 1916), 673–674.

27. Lieutenant Marcel Etévé, *Lettres d'un combattant (août 1914-juillet 1916),* preface Paul Dupuy, "Mémoires et récits de guerre" (Paris: Hachette, 1917), frontispiece.

28. Maurice Masson, *Lettres de guerre (août 1914-avril 1916),* preface Victor Giraud (Paris: Hachette, 1917) and Etévé, *Lettres d'un combattant.* Reviewing French war literature a decade after the war, Jean Norton Cru considered these two volumes more truthful in their description of the war than either of France's two classic war novels: Henri Barbusse's *Le Feu* and Roland Dorgelès's *Croix de bois.* Jean Norton Cru, *War Books: A Study in Historical Criticism,* ed. and trans. Stanley J. Pincetl, Jr., and Ernest Marchand (San Diego, Calif.: San Diego State University Press, 1976), 156, 160.

29. "Rapport de M. Etienne Lamy, secrétaire perpétuel, sur les Concours de l'année 1917: Académies et Corps savants: Académie française: Séance publique annuelle du 20 décembre," *Journal des débats* 24 (December 1917): 1143.

30. "Discours de M. Alfred Croiset," *Ouverture des conférences,* 3.

31. Victor Bérard, *L'Eternelle Allemagne* (Paris: Armand Colin, 1916), 43.

32. Boutroux, "L'Allemagne et la guerre, deuxième lettre," 254.

33. René Pichon, "Mommsen et la mentalité allemande," *Revue des deux mondes* (15 October 1915): 781.

34. "Les Universités françaises et la guerre," *Revue internationale de l'enseignement,* 69 (1915): 22–28.

35. Ibid., 27.

36. "Pour la Civilisation latine: l'union des groupements latins au grand amphithéâtre de la Sorbonne," *Revue hebdomadaire* (20 February 1915): 268.

37. "Déclaration de M. Ernest Lavisse," "L'union latine à la Sorbonne," *Revue universitaire* 24, 1 (1915), 93.

38. Louis Bertrand, "Vers l'unité latine," *Revue des deux mondes* 35 (15 September 1916): 314–338.

39. Pichon, "Mommsen et la mentalité allemande," 780–781.

40. Delbos, *L'Esprit philosophique de l'Allemagne et la pensée française,* Pages actuelles, 1914–1915 (Paris: Bloud et Gay, 1915), 42.

41. Delbos, *La Philosophie française* (Paris: Plon, 1919), ch. 1.

42. Ibid., 2.

43. Ibid., 14.

44. Victor Basch, "La Philosophie et la littérature classiques de l'Allemagne et les doctrines pangermanistes," *Revue de métaphysique et de morale* 22 (1914): 711–793.

45. In 1915 a member of the Committee of Public Instruction observed that German remained the working language of Alsace. Two years later, when a committee of scholars including Paul Appell, Christian Pfister, and Charles Andler issued a series of recommendations for the integration of the University of Strasbourg into the French academic system, they, too, recognized that classes at the University would have to be conducted in German for at least the first three or four years until students were sufficiently adept in French to attend classes conducted in French. AN C7731. Christian Pfister, "Rapport sur l'Université de Strasbourg" (Paris: Ministère de la Guerre, Service d'Alsace-Lorraine, 1917), 74.

46. AN *AJ/16/4752. "Registres des actes et déclarations de la Faculté des Lettres de Paris, 13 janvier 1914–23 décembre 1918," 65.

47. AN C7731. "Chambre des Deputés. Commission de l'Enseignement et des beaux-arts: Enquête sur la réforme de l'enseignement secondaire de 1902: Déposition de M. Coville, Directeur de l'Enseignement secondaire, 23 septembre 1915," 41.

48. Ibid., 42.

49. J. P, "L'Enseignement des langues vivantes et la culture classique," *Revue universitaire* 25 (1916): 23–30.

50. AN C7731. "Déposition de M. Coville, Directeur de l'Enseignement secondaire," 42.

51. J. P., "L'Enseignement des langues vivantes," 23–30.

52. V. Friedel, "L'Allemagne contre la culture classique," *La Grande Revue* 91 (1916): 697.

53. Ibid., 710.

54. Ibid., 712.

55. Ernest Lavisse, "Lettre à une normalienne," *Revue de Paris* 24 (15 December 1917): 780.

56. Germaine Goblot, "La Guerre et l'enseignement des langues vivantes en Allemagne," *Revue pédagogique* 62 (June 1918): 415.

57. Ibid., 411–431.

58. "Les Deux Cultures: Lettres à M. Scott Mowrer, de MM. Croiset, Aulard, Vincent d'Indy, . . ." *L'Opinion* 9, 34 (19 August 1916): 155.

59. Doumic, "La Réouverture des théâtres," 446.

60. Scully, *Architecture: The Natural and the Manmade,* 277.

61. Delbos argued that French philosophy "aspired to an ever more comprehensive order, in which all things of this world are explained in terms of the place they occupy." *Philosophie française,* 6.

62. Scully, *Architecture: The Natural and the Manmade,* 299–300.

63. "Deux cultures," 156–157.

64. Etienne Lamy, *Du XVIIIᵉ Siècle à l'Année sublime,* Pages actuelles, 1914–1915 (Paris: Bloud et Gay, 1915), 28.

65. Charles Navarre, "Le Latin dans l'enseignement secondaire," *Revue internationale de l'enseignement,* 67 (1914): 211.

66. René Doumic, "Le Retour à la culture classique," *Revue des deux mondes* 24 (15 November 1914): 317–328.

67. Ibid., 320.

68. Fritz Ringer, *Fields of Knowledge: French Academic Culture in Comparative Perspective, 1890–1920* (Cambridge: Cambridge University Press, 1992), 177.

69. Doumic, "Retour à la culture française," 328.

70. Pierre Lasserre, "Le Retour aux anciens," *Revue hebdomadaire* (23 January 1915): 396.

71. Lasserre, "Les Etudes classiques et la vie nationale," *Revue hebdomadaire* 24, 49 (4 December 1915): 37–38.

72. Gaston Deschamps, "Le Retour à la culture française," *Revue hebdomadaire* 24, 14 (3 April 1915): 5–29.

73. Anonymous, "Les Réparations nécessaires:—VII La Culture Française," *La Revue hebdomadaire* 25, 31 (29 July 1916): 561–577.

74. Navarre, "Le Latin dans l'enseignement secondaire," 199–215.

75. AN *AJ/16/4752. "Registres des actes et déclarations de la Faculté des Lettres de Paris," 142.

76. Abbé Delfour, *La Culture latine* (Paris: Nouvelle Librairie Nationale, 1916), 20, 27.

77. "La Culture grecque et latine: Un discours de M. Lafferre, ministre de l'Instruction publique," *Journal des débats* 25 (19 July 1918): 97.

78. As cited in Cury, "La Guerre et les humanités," 11.

79. Félix Pécaut, "La Guerre et les pédagogues," *Revue pédagogique* 72, 5 (May 1918), 316.
80. AN C7731. "Déposition de M. Coville, Directeur de l'Enseignement secondaire," 4. Liard made a similar point in his written deposition to the Committee: "Déposition de M. Liard," 8.
81. AN C7731. "Déposition de M. Coville," 22–23, 48.

Six "TOUJOURS LA SCIENCE"

1. AN AJ/61/86. "Rapport du Laboratoire de Physique de l'Ecole Normale Supérieure. Rapport sur des recherches faites part MM. Weiss, Cotton, et leurs collaborateurs, par M. A. Cotton," 1917.
2. Institut de France, Académie Française, "Rapport de M. Etienne Lamy sur les concours de l'année 1915," 6. Lamy told of the sacrifice of Charles Picard. To protect a soldier who was married and had young children, Picard had volunteered for a wire-cutting detail on the night of January 8, 1915, and died on that mission.
3. Gaston Bonnier, "L'Académie des Sciences et la guerre," *Revue hebdomadaire* 24 (20 March 1915): 235.
4. At the faculty meeting of 25 November 1915, Paul Appell informed his colleagues that the Ministry of Public Instruction had requested names of all nonmobilized laboratory staff who might be used for military-related research. AN *AJ/16/5123. Conseil de la Faculté des Sciences, Université de Paris.
5. Charles Nordmann, "Revue scientifique: Science et guerre," *Revue des deux mondes* 30 (1 December 1915): 698.
6. Louis Liard, "La Guerre et les universités françaises," *Revue de Paris,* 23 (1 May 1916): 52–55.
7. Edmond Perrier replaced Bonnier in 1915 as president of the Académie des Sciences; at the annual public meeting of the society, held in December 1915, he spoke of how the Academy had become "sous la main du ministre de la Guerre, un puissant instrument, capable de mobiliser tout ce qui, dans la science et dans les industries chimiques ou physiques, était susceptible, de près ou de loin, d'être utile à la défense nationale." As cited in Gaston Deschamps, "L'Institut de France et la guerre," *Revue des deux mondes* (15 February 1917): 899.
8. Albert Mathiez, "La Mobilisation des savants en l'An II," *Revue de Paris* 24 (1 December 1917): 551–559.
9. Scientists at the ENS applied themselves to the development of wireless telegraphy and to the production of silica bricks. Silica was an essential component in the manufacture of blast-furnaces for the production of high-grade steel, but until 1914 France had relied almost exclusively upon silica imported from Germany. During the war Léon Bertrand, director of the

Geology Laboratory at the ENS, successfully identified the means and methods for its domestic production. AN AJ/61/86. Letter and report, dated 22 December 1917, prepared by Léon Bertrand for submission to the Ministry of Public Instruction.

10. AN AJ/61/86. Letter dated 20 December 1917 from the Minister of Public Instruction to Lavisse.

11. AN AJ/61/86. Covering letter and confidential report, dated 28 December 1917, prepared by Henri Abraham on behalf of the Physics Laboratory at the ENS on research conducted since the beginning of the war.

12. AN AJ/61/86. "Rapport du Laboratoire de Physique de l'Ecole Normale Supérieure. Rapport sur des recherches faites par MM. Weiss, Cotton, et leurs collaborateurs, par M. A. Cotton," 1917.

13. AN AJ/61/85. Letter dated 9 February 1915 from Lavisse to Liard, Director of Higher Education.

14. L. F. Haber, *The Poisonous Cloud: Chemical Warfare in the First World War* (Oxford: Clarendon Press, 1986), 117–118, 74–76.

15. AN AJ/61/86. Letter dated 26 December 1917 from L. J. Simon to the Minister of Public Instruction.

16. AN AJ/61/86. Letter dated 22 December 1917 from the director of the Geology Laboratory at the ENS to the Minister of Public Instruction.

17. AN AJ/61/197. Letter dated 11 May 1915, to Lavisse from the Ministry of War, Direction générale des services de l'Administration de la Guerre.

18. AN AJ/61/85. Letter dated 17 May 1915, from Lavisse to Liard.

19. AN AJ/61/197. Letter dated 1 December 1915 to Lavisse from the Ministry of War, Under-Secretariat of State for Artillery and Munitions; and letter dated 7 January 1916, to Lavisse from the Ministry of War, Department of the Infantry.

20. AN AJ/61/197. Letter dated 21 February 1917 from Louis Simon to Ernest Lavisse.

21. AN AJ/61/85. Letter dated 2 October 1914 from Liard to Lavisse.

22. AN AJ/16/5123. Conseil de la Faculté des Sciences, University of Paris. Minutes from the Faculty meeting of 14 January 1915.

23. AN AJ/61/85. Letter dated 8 February 1915 from Lavisse to Liard.

24. AN AJ/61/86. Letter dated 8 February 1917 from Lavisse to the Ministry of Supplies.

25. Nordmann, "A Propos de la science allemande," *Revue des deux mondes* (15 January 1916): 458.

26. Harry Paul, *The Edge of Contingency: French Catholic Reaction to Scientific Change from Darwin to Duhem* (Gainesville, Fl.: University Presses of Florida, 1979), 3.

27. Jacques Maritain, "La Science allemande," *La Croix* 25/26 October 1914.

28. Ibid.

29. Victor Giraud, "La Littérature de demain et la guerre européenne," *Revue des deux mondes* (15 May 1915): 387, 385.

30. Victor Giraud, "La Banqueroute du scientisme," *Pro patria: La Banqueroute du Scientisme; En marge de la Grande Guerre*, Pages actuelles, 1914–1917 (Paris: Bloud et Gay, 1917), 5–9.

31. Ibid., 8.

32. Abbé Delfour, *La Culture latine* (Paris: Nouvelle Librairie Nationale, 1916), 38.

33. AN 333/AP/72. Etienne Lamy, "L'Avenir de nos universités catholiques," typed, undated manuscript.

34. Guy Pedroncini discusses Pétain's conviction that mastery of the air was essential to victory: *Pétain: Général en Chef, 1917–1918* (Paris: Presses Universitaires de France, 1974), 41. Lamy expressed his opinions on the strategic uses of airpower in an interview given in October 1918: Félicien Pascal, "Nos Conversations: chez M. Etienne Lamy," *Les Annales* (13 October 1918): 322.

35. AN 333/AP/72. Lamy, "L'Avenir de nos universités catholiques."

36. Liard, "La Guerre et les universités françaises," 54.

37. Henri Bergson, "La Force qui s'use et celle qui ne s'use pas" (Extrait du *Bulletin des Armées de la République*, 4 November 1914), *La Signification de la Guerre* (Paris: Bloud et Gay, 1915), 39, 42.

38. Bergson, *La Signification de la guerre*, 19.

39. Bergson, "Allocution prononcé à l'Académie des sciences morales et politiques, le 16 janvier 1915, à l'occasion de l'installation de M. Alexandre Ribot au fauteuil de la présidence," *La Signification de la guerre*, 34–35.

40. Camille Jullian, "Les Eléments du passé dans la guerre actuelle," *La Guerre pour la patrie: Leçons du Collège de France, 1914–1919* (Paris: Bloud et Gay, 1919), 17, 23.

41. Ibid., 17. "Si perfectionnée que soit une arme de guerre, si merveilleusement conçue qu'elle ait été par l'intelligence du savant, elle ne vaut que ce que valent les bras, l'oeil, le corps et le coeur du soldat qui l'emploie."

42. General Ferdinand Foch, *The Principles of War*, trans. J. de Morinni (New York: H. K. Fly, 1918), 314.

43. Grandmaison, *Dressage de l'infantrie en vue de l'offensive* (Paris, 1906), 2–3; as cited by Douglas Porch, *The March to the Marne: The French Army, 1871–1914* (Cambridge: Cambridge University Press, 1981), 215.

44. Capitaine Charles Delvert, *Carnets d'un fantassin: Massiges, 1916, Verdun*, ed. Gérard Canini (Paris: Editions du Mémorial, Collection témoignages et mémoires, 1981), 56. Daniel Mornet also feared that civilians and strategists, far from the front lines, had "believed too readily that *élan* and enthusiasm were all a nation needed to win a war." Mornet, "La Guerre et l'enseignement après la guerre," 85.

45. Porch, *March to the Marne*, 214.

46. Joffre wrote: "Above all, there was hardly ever cooperation between artillery and infantry. As soon as these facts became known, I told the armies to be more prudent in their attacks and above all to pay more attention to inter-arm coordination. It was precisely this perfecting of the offensive doctrine that I had proposed in the training camps that was now imposed in the rude conditions of battle." Joffre, *Mémoires* (Paris, 1932), 303–304; as cited by Porch, *March to the Marne*, 223–224.

47. Paul Simon, *L'Instruction des officiers, l'éducation des troupes et la puissance nationale* (Paris, 1905), 176, 184–185, as cited in Porch, *March to the Marne*, 226.

48. Ibid., 231.

49. Haber, *The Poisonous Cloud*, 126.

50. The Manifesto of 93 did not expressly "tie the intellectual future of Europe to the future of German science." Although scientists predominated among the signatories, who identified themselves as "representatives of German science and art," the manifesto did not speak explicitly of the place of science in German *Kultur*. It insisted only upon the need to defend *Kultur* from the assaults of Entente powers intent upon its destruction. But to a nation convinced that "*Kultur* was a product of science," the association between science and *Kultur* was so intimate that to conflate *Kultur* with science was an ever-present danger, even for the most educated.

51. "Déclaration de l'Académie des sciences, en date du 3 novembre 1914," as published in "L'Institut de France et la guerre," *Revue internationale de l'enseignement* 69 (1915): 9.

52. Charles Richet, "Science française et science allemande: les Allemands et la science," *Les Allemands et la science,* ed. Gabriel Petit and Maurice Leudet (1916; rpt. New York: Arno Press, 1981), 346.

53. Dr. Grasset, "Lettre au Professeur Gabriel Petit," *Les Allemands et la science,* 200.

54. Nordmann, "A propos de la science allemande," 464.

55. Nordmann, "Science et guerre," 700.

56. Ibid., 703.

57. Liard, "La Guerre et les universités françaises," 62–63.

58. Boutroux, "La Science allemande," *Les Allemands et la science,* 48.

59. Dastre, "Du role restreint de l'Allemagne dans le progrès des sciences," *Les Allemands et la science,* 82.

60. "Dans la conception même de la vérité, un côté chevaleresque et desintéressé . . . nous conduit à pousser parfois la justice à l'égard de nos ennemis un peu au delà de ce qui leur est strictement dû. Si nous trouvons . . . quelque trait qui nous paraisse digne d'éloge, nous avons plaisir à le mettre en lumière, et l'on a pu nous blâmer en certaines circonstances d'un excès de courtoisie." Université de Paris, "Discours de M. Alfred Croiset," *Ouverture des confér-*

ences de la Faculté des Lettres, le 5 novembre 1914 (Paris: Edouard Champion, 1914), 4.

61. Emile Picard, "L'Histoire des sciences et les prétentions de la science allemande," *Revue des deux mondes* (1 July 1915): 68.

62. Nordmann, "Science et guerre," 701; "A Propos de la science allemande," 460.

63. Richet, "La Science française, la science allemande," *Les Allemands et la science,* 349–350, 358.

64. Picard, "Les Prétentions de la science allemande," 64, 75, 56.

65. Bergson, "Allocution prononcé à l'Académie des sciences morales et politiques, le 16 janvier 1915," *La Signification de la guerre,* 34.

66. Bergson, *La Signification de la guerre,* 19.

67. Picard, "Les Prétentions de la science allemande," 55.

68. The contributions to *Les Allemands et la science* appeared originally in response to an *enquête* published in *Le Figaro* in April 1915. The inquiry, framed as an explicit rejection of the Manifesto of 93, asked French experts to judge the quality of German accomplishments in their fields of study.

69. Georges Lemoine, "Les Sciences chimiques," *Un Demi-siècle de la civilisation française,* ed. Boutroux, Baillaud, and Chailley (Paris: Hachette, 1916), 220.

70. "Préface," *Les Allemands et la science,* vii.

71. Duhem, "La Science allemande et vertus allemandes," *Les Allemands et la science,* 149.

72. "Discours de M. Alfred Croiset," in *Ouverture des conférences,* 4.

73. Boutroux argued that French scholarship had achieved the essential balance of intuition and deduction. Boutroux, "La Philosophie," *Un demi-siècle de la civilisation française,* 44.

74. "Discours de M. Alfred Croiset," in *Ouverture des conférences,* 4–5.

75. Pierre Duhem, "Quelques réflexions sur la science allemande," *Revue des deux mondes,* 25 (1 February 1915): 660–661.

76. Ibid., 662–663.

77. Ibid., 680–681.

78. Harry Paul observes that some French scientists spoke favorably of relativity physics even during the war years. E. M. Lémeray published a scholarly treatise, entitled *Le Principe de relativité* in 1916, based on a course he had taught the previous year at the University of Marseille; unlike Duhem, Lémeray considered relativity theory a "discovery of singular power." Paul, *The Sorcerer's Apprentice: The French Scientist's Image of German Science, 1840–1919* (Gainesville, Fl.: University of Florida Press, 1972), 72–73, fn. 48.

79. Maritain, "De la métaphysique des physiciens (à propos d'Einstein)," *Revue universelle* 10 (15 August 1922): 434, 439.

80. "Discours de M. Ernest Lavisse," in *Ouverture des conférences,* 12.

81. "Discours de M. Alfred Croiset," in *Ouverture des conférences,* 8.
82. Richet, "La Science française, la science allemande," *Les Allemands et la science,* 354.
83. Picard, "Les Prétentions de la science allemande," 57–61.
84. Richet, "La Science française, la science allemande," *Les Allemands et la science,* 361.
85. George Fonsegrive, *Kultur et Civilisation* (Paris: Bloud et Gay, 1916), 16–17.
86. Raphaël-Georges Lévy, "Préface," *Un Demi-siècle de Civilisation française,* v–vi.
87. Many of the scholars who responded to Leudet and Petit's *enquête* of 1915 also contributed to *Un Demi-siècle de civilisation française:* Lemoine spoke for chemistry, Picard for mathematics, Richet for medicine, and Perrier for the natural sciences.
88. Mary Jo Nye argues that institutional pressures to produce and prove the international competitiveness of French science contributed to the "N-Ray" fiasco: *Science in the Provinces: Scientific Communities and Provincial Leadership in France, 1860–1930* (Berkeley, Calif.: University of California Press, 1986), 53–77.
89. Duhem, "Réflexions sur la science allemande," 685.
90. Liard, "La Guerre et les universités françaises," 56.
91. AN C7731. "Chambre des Deputés, Commission de l'Enseignement et des Beaux-Arts: Enquête sur la Réforme de l'Enseignement secondaire de 1902: Déposition de M. Coville, Directeur de l'Enseignement secondaire, 23 septembre 1915," 4.
92. AN C7731. "Déposition de M. Hadamard, Membre de l'Institut, Professeur au Collège de France." Hand-written letter dated 7 October 1916, accompanying corrected proofs of his deposition to the Committee of Public Instruction, 1914.
93. Ibid., 16, 21.
94. Liard, "La Guerre et les universités françaises," 56, 58, 63.
95. Nordmann, "Science et guerre," 702–703.
96. Prof. Pinard, "Puériculture: Obstétricie française, obstétricie allemande," *Les Allemands et la science,* 323.

EPILOGUE

1. Jean-François Sirinelli, "Les Intellectuels français et la guerre," *Les Sociétés européennes et la guerre de 1914–1918,* ed. J.-J. Becker and S. Audoin-Rouzeau (Nanterre: Publications de l'Université de Nanterre, 1990), 156–157.
2. The earliest reference to "nationalisme intellectuel" seems to have occurred in Pierre Lasserre, *Le Germanisme et l'esprit humain* (Paris: Librairie An-

cienne Edouard Champion, 1915). Subsequently it became a rallying cry of the nationalist right. In the summer of 1919 Camille Mauclair, a conservative republican and signatory of the Manifesto of the Parti de l'Intelligence, insisted that France not squander the advantage it had secured on the battlefield: "France must conserve its 'nationalisme intellectuel' and remain the leader and director of that set of moral principles that has saved the world." As cited in "Revue de la presse: Parti de l'Intelligence," *Action française* 6 August 1919.

3. Jean-Jacques Becker, *The Great War and the French People,* trans. Arnold Pomerans (Providence, R.I.: Berg, 1985), 155–156.

4. AN 333/AP/71. Report on the state of civilian and combatant morale in the region of Senlis, 30 June 1917.

5. BN NAF 25170. Letter dated 27 June 1917 to Ernest Lavisse, President of the Committee of *Lettres à tous les français,* (Librairie Armand Colin), from A. Gautrin, Givry-en-Argonne (Marne).

6. Ernest Lavisse, "Pourquoi nous nous battons," *Le Temps* 26 July 1917.

7. BN NAF 25170. Letter dated 26 July 1917 from M. E. Maupigny to M. Ernest Lavisse.

8. AN 333/AP/71. Letter dated 14 January 1917 from General Margot, Director of the Infantry, to Major Etienne Lamy.

9. AN 333/AP/72. "Le Ravitaillement moral des héros."

10. Lt. Colonel G. Bernard, *Civilisation et Kultur* (Paris: Berger-Levrault, 1916).

11. Colonel G. Bernard (Infanterie), *Guide d'education morale du soldat* (Paris: L. Fournier, 1918), 8–12.

12. Alain [Emile Chartier], *Correspondance avec Élie et Florence Halévy,* préface et notes par Jeanne Michel-Alexandre (Paris: Gallimard, 1958), 171, 174, 249.

13. Florimond Wagon, "Lettres du front, extraits," *Anthologie des écrivains morts à la guerre, 1914–1918,* vol. 3, préface Roland Dorgelès (Amiens: E. Malfère, 1925), 707–709.

14. Lieutenant Marcel Etévé, *Lettres d'un combattant,* preface Paul Dupuy (Paris: Hachette, 1917), 105, 172.

15. Pierre Jourdan, "Lettres de guerre," *Anthologie des écrivains morts à la guerre, 1914–1918,* vol. 2, préface de José Germain (Amiens: E. Malfère, 1924), 403; Charles et Etienne de Fontenay, *Deux frères morts pour la France,* preface Paul Deschanel (Paris: Plon-Nourrit, 1920), 175, 202.

16. Jean Rival, "Du Front," *Anthologie des écrivains morts à la guerre,* vol. 4, préface Claude Farrère (Amiens: E. Malfère, 1926), 675.

17. In posthumously published remarks of November 1914, Michel's comrade Claude Cochin wrote that the abject reasoning of the "manifesto of the *Intellectuals*" had intensified their shared antipathy for "Germanic methods of scholarship." *Anthologie des écrivains morts à la guerre,* 4: 557.

18. Jean Klingebiel, *Jean Klingebiel (5 Mai 1892–16 avril 1917): I Les Cahiers; II Les Nouveaux Cahiers; III Les Lettres; IV Les Notes* (Paris: Fédération Française des Associations Chrétiennes d'Étudiants, s.d), 3: 42; Maurice Masson, *Lettres de guerre*, preface Victor Giraud (Paris: Hachette, 1917), 208, 26.

19. Masson, *Lettres de guerre*, 26, 85.

20. Klingebiel, *Les Lettres*, 57.

21. Masson, *Lettres de guerre*, 103; Etévé, *Lettres d'un combattant*, 102.

22. Pierre Jourdan, "Lettres de guerre," *Anthologie des écrivains morts à la guerre*, 2: 407. De Fontenay, *Deux frères morts pour la France*, 241.

23. Robert d'Harcourt, *Souvenirs de captivité et d'évasion* (Paris: Nouvelle Librairie Nationale, 1922), 51, 34. Klingebiel, *Les Lettres*, 3: 41.

24. D'Harcourt, *Souvenirs de captivité et d'évasion*, 51.

25. Georges Bernanos, *Correspondance*, recueillie par Albert Béguin, choisie et présenté par Jean Murray, O.P. (Paris: Plon, 1971), 1: 145.

26. Charles Delvert, *Carnets d'un fantassin: Massiges, 1916, Verdun*, ed. Gérard Canini (Paris: Editions du Mémorial, 1981), 52, 116, 190–191.

27. Jourdan, "Lettres de guerre," *Anthologie des écrivains morts à la guerre*, 2: 407.

28. "Art et littérature du front: Notre enquête littéraire," *Bulletin des Armées de la République* (Réservé à la zone de l'Armée), 2, 204 (26 July 1916), 10.

29. AN C7732. "L'Organisation des études secondaires et la spécialisation des élèves au lycée." Etudes et voeux, présentés à la Commission Parlementaire de l'enseignement, par A. Decerf, agrégé de l'Université, professeur de mathématiques au lycée de Cherbourg, adjutant au 25e R.I. 7 February 1916.

30. D. Mornet, "La Guerre et l'enseignement après la guerre," *Revue pédagogique* 73 (August 1918): 79–89.

31. Stéphane Audoin-Rouzeau, "Les Soldats français et la nation de 1914 à 1918, d'après les journaux de tranchées," *Revue d'histoire moderne et contemporaine* (January-March 1987): 66–86.

32. Becker, *The Great War and the French People*, 155, 326.

33. Bernanos, *Correspondance*, 1: 102.

34. Alain, *Correspondance*, 174.

35. Henri Massis, *Maurras et notre temps: entretiens et souvenirs* (Paris: Plon, 1961), 104.

36. In October 1919, the *Action française* drew to the attention of its readers the forthcoming publication of *Travaillons à bien penser*, which the review *Renaissance* had already issued in serial form. "Revue de la presse: la vie intellectuelle, *Travaillons donc à bien penser*," *Action française*, 29 October 1919. Abbé de la Valette-Montbrun, writing in the *Revue du clergé français*, borrowed Aimel's title when he insisted that France, instructed by the

great lessons of the age, now had a duty to "bien penser." "Revue de la presse," *Action française,* 30 January 1921.

37. Georges Aimel, *Travaillons donc à bien penser* (Paris: Edition Bossard, 1919), 56, 7–11, 32.

38. In January 1920, the *Action française* commented on a review by Pierre Champion of Aimel's *Travaillons donc à bien penser,* in which Champion explicitly compared Aimel's work to *L'Avenir de l'intelligence.* The newspaper went on to observe that before the war "those who had engaged in healthy thought [ceux qui pensaient sainement] had been only a minority" but that had changed as a result of the war. "Revue de presse," *Action française,* 16 January 1920.

39. Léon Daudet, "La Dégermanisation intellectuelle," *Action française,* 20 June 1921.

40. Jacques Maritain, *Notebooks,* trans. Joseph W. Evans (Albany, New York: Magi Books, 1984), 129.

41. Jacques Bainville, "Notre programme," *Revue universelle* 1 (1 April 1920): 1–3.

42. Charles Maurras, "L'Avenir de l'ordre," *Revue universelle* 1 (1 April 1920): 22.

43. Jacques Maritain, "La Liberté de l'intelligence," *Revue universelle* 1 (1 April 1920): 104–106; "Ernest Psichari," *Revue universelle* 8 (1 March 1922): 615; *Theonas: Conversations of a Sage,* trans. F. J. Sheed (New York: Sheed and Ward, 1933), 169; Maritain and Albert Kasel, "L'État actuel de la philosophie allemande," *Revue universelle* 4 (15 March 1921): 720; Maritain, "La Philosophie americaine et les continuateurs de William James," *Revue universelle* 7 (1 October 1921): 51; "Premier cahier de Théonas," *Revue universelle* 9 (15 April 1922): 242; and "La Pensée moderne et la philosophie thomiste," *Revue universelle* 13 (15 May 1923).

44. Léon Daudet, "Les Fruits intellectuels de la victoire," *Action française,* 19 August 1919.

45. Léon Daudet, "L'Étude, en France, de l'allemand," *Action française,* 24 October 1920.

46. In 1919 the University of Paris offered *no* courses in German philosophy, and offerings in subsequent years were scant at best. AN AJ/61/161. Posters listing philosophy courses for 1919–1920 through 1925–1926.

47. AN *AJ/16/4752. "Registres des actes et déclarations de la Faculté des Lettres de Paris, 1914–1918," 159–161. Academic positions left vacant by the retirement or death of a scholar were not filled during the war years. Looking to regain its prewar strength, the Faculty of Letters urged the government to fill these positions as soon as circumstances allowed. But the faculty had to decide on a case by case basis the fate of each academic chair. Having deliberated on the issue of what to do with Delbos's chair in the History of Philosophy, the Faculty of Letters voted in February 1918 to let

it lapse, and to create a Chair in Italian Literature and Language in its place. This decision was confirmed by ministerial decree on 19 May 1918.

AN AJ/61/161. Poster: Université de Paris, Faculté des Lettres, 1921–1922. Philosophie: Cours généraux, Licence et agrégation.

48. Charles Andler, " 'La Rénovation présente des Universités allemandes et des Universités françaises,' A la Faculté des lettres de l'Université de Paris," *Revue internationale de l'enseignement* 39 (1919): 433–435.

49. Ibid., 438.

50. François Picavet, "Méthodes allemandes et méthodes françaises," *Revue internationale de l'enseignement* 40 (1920): 305, 317, 323.

51. Ibid., 317.

52. Maurice Pujo, "Nationalisme intellectuel," *Action française,* 30 October 1920.

53. The phrase "la République . . . a installé carrément à la Sorbonne des étrangers, des espions, des Juifs bolshevistes" appeared originally in an article by Urbain Gohier in *La Vieille France;* the *Action française* brought it to the attention of integralist readers in "La Revue de la presse," *Action française,* 2 May 1921.

54. In a letter to the *Action française,* Marius André (identified as a "friend" of integral nationalism and a member of the French consular corps) leveled these charges against Seignobos's scholarship in "Les Erreurs de fait de M. Seignobos," *Action française,* 25 March 1921. Urbain Gohier criticized André Lichtenberger for his excessive regard for German scholarship, as reported in "La Revue de la presse," *Action française,* 2 May 1921.

55. Maurice Pujo, "A la Sorbonne," *Action française,* 20 March 1921.

56. Daudet, "L'Étude, en France, de l'allemand."

57. Maurice Pujo, "Nationalisme intellectuel."

58. J. P., "L'Enseignement des langues vivantes et la culture classique," *Revue universitaire* 25 (1916): 23.

59. Paul Crouzet, "L'Enseignement secondaire à Paris depuis la guerre," 188.

60. The preference among students of modern languages for English over German, perhaps the predictable outcome of the war, was not evident, however, at the level of the *agrégation,* where the number of degrees awarded in German was almost equal to the number of degrees granted in English. Nor was it evident at the ENS, where students specializing in modern languages were in a distinct minority. In the *promotion* of 1920–21, only 3 of the 30 students who gained admission to *Lettres* specialized in modern languages: two (of whom one was Alsatian) studied German; one studied English. For the *promotion* of 1922, modern language enrollment increased slightly, to 7 of a class of 32: four specialized in German, two in English, and one in Italian. But by 1925 there were no candidates in either German or English; the two students who identified themselves as modern language specialists both opted to study Russian. AN AJ/61/162. Annual reports

submitted by the Director of the Ecole Normale Supérieure to the Minister of Public Instruction, 1920–21, 1922–23, 1923–24, 1925–26.

61. Picavet, "Méthodes allemandes, méthodes françaises," 320.

62. AN *AJ/16/5123. Conseil de la Faculté des Sciences, meeting of 2 December 1920, 328. Professor Borel (director of the School of Pharmacy) argued that public lectures for citizens interested in science were already offered in Paris at the Conservatoire des Arts et Métiers, but they did not exist outside of the capital.

63. Ibid., meeting of 17 March 1921.

64. In July 1919, *La Croix* praised Duhem for bringing to light the medieval origins of modern science. His research had demonstrated that scholastics of the twelfth and thirteenth centuries had laid the foundations for all subsequent scientific research in France. Having thus recovered the scholastic origins of modern science, Duhem gave his discipline a legitimacy for Catholics it had previously lacked. B. Latour, "Les Origines de la science moderne," *La Croix,* 9 July 1919.

65. Daniel Mornet shared the scientists' disdain for utilitarian education and purely practical careers. Insisting that "our education not become entirely oriented towards utilitarian ends," he maintained that "it is not necessary— indeed it is dangerous—to propose incessantly that our children and our youth think only of practical problems and future profits." Mornet, "La Guerre et l'enseignement après la guerre," *Revue pédagogique* (August 1918): 82.

66. AN *AJ/16/5123. Conseil de la Faculté des Sciences, 207–208.

67. As cited by Harry Paul, *The Sorcerer's Apprentice: The French Scientist's Image of German Science, 1840–1919* (Gainesville, Fl.: University of Florida Press, 1972), 27.

68. Maurice Barrès, "La Réorganisation intellectuelle de la France, I," *Revue universelle* 2 (15 August 1920): 387, 404.

69. Ibid., 403.

70. Philippe Bernard and Henri Dubief, *The Decline of the Third Republic, 1914–1938,* trans. Anthony Forster (Cambridge: Cambridge University Press, 1985), 164–165.

71. Maurice Caullery, *French Science and Its Principal Discoveries since the Seventeenth Century* (New York: Arno Press, 1975), 210–212.

72. AN F[17] 17499. "Rapport au Président de la République" from the Minister of Public Instruction, 3 May 1923, as printed in the *Journal officiel,* Chambre des Députés, 4 May 1923.

73. Significantly, the program Bérard envisaged was the program most *lycée* students already preferred. Three of the four curricular options ("A," "B," and "C") established in 1902 required coursework in Latin. In 1914, 67.2% of secondary school students had chosen one of these three options; by 1917, this proportion had increased to 73%, and the most heavily en-

rolled was the section that required students to take both Latin and science. Evidently, secondary school students sought out the curriculum that gave them a solid grounding in the sciences (in order to prepare for a career in industry) and a sufficient grounding in classical culture (in order to understand the foundations of French culture). Crouzet, "L'Enseignement secondaire à Paris depuis la guerre," 187.

74. AN F¹⁷ 17499. Letter from the Lille Chamber of Commerce to the president of the Association des Professeurs de Langues Vivantes, 8 October 1921. The chambers of commerce of Paris, Lyon, Bordeaux, Foix, Tours, Perpignon, Alais, Le Havre, Troyes, Bethune, Agen, and Limoges also supported the Bérard reform, as did the Association Nationale d'Expansion Économique, the Syndicat Médical de Paris, the Association des Anciens Élèves du Lycée de Bourges, the Union des Industries Métallurgiques et Minières de la Construction Mécanique, Electrique, Metallique, and the Chambre Syndicale des Forces Hydrauliques. Letter dated 15 December 1921 from the Union des Industries Métallurgiques et Minières de la Construction Mécanique, Electrique, Metallique, to the Minister of Public Instruction; and letter dated 12 November 1921 from the Chambre Syndicale des Forces Hydrauliques to the Minister of Public Instruction.

75. Léon Bérard, *Pour la réforme classique de l'enseignement secondaire* (Paris: Librairie Armand Colin, 1923), 8–9.

76. The Bérard reform proved just as controversial abroad. The Committee for the Maintenance of Classical Education, headquartered in Amsterdam, praised Bérard for reassuring the world that culture and civilization remained intact in France. In the wake of the French occupation of the Ruhr (which led foreign observers to fear that France had succumbed to the allure of militarism and barbarism), it was reassuring to learn that France remained committed to humane values and civilization. Eugène Lautier, "Pour le salut des humanités," *L'Homme libre* (1 June 1923). Although some American observers deemed the reform one of the most influential developments in modern education, others, especially those inspired by Dewey's belief in pragmatic education, called the program regressive. I. L. Kandel spoke in favor of the reform in, *The Reform of Secondary Education in France* (New York: Teachers' College, Columbia University, 1924); Frederick William Roman denounced it in *The New Education in Europe: An Account of Recent Fundamental Changes in the Educational Philosophy of Great Britain, France, and Germany*, 2nd ed. (New York: E. P. Dutton, 1930), 199–203.

77. AN F¹⁷ 17499. Although the minutes of the Conseil's meetings for 1921 are not included within this archival file, the members of the Conseil reviewed the debates of 1921 and the Conseil's ultimate decision to maintain the modern curriculum intact in the January 1923 meetings.

78. John Talbott's classic study of interwar educational policy, *The Politics of*

Educational Reform (Princeton, N.J.: Princeton University Press, 1969), focuses on the *école unique* as the principal—but admittedly not the only— reform proposal to emerge from the Great War. The Compagnons de l'Université Nouvelle believed that the future of France depended upon the democratization of French education, and in 1918 published their manifesto, calling for a *"université nouvelle"* dedicated to educational accessibility for all. By creating one and the same primary school system for all students, the *école unique* would abolish the practice of two parallel and unequal systems of early education.

79. AN F^{17} 17499. Minutes of the morning meeting of the Conseil Supérieur de l'Instruction publique, 16 January 1923.

When Bérard defended his program to the Chamber of Deputies, he called the new Dean of Letters at the University of Paris "head of the modernist school of strict observance," and insisted the Dean was antecedently hostile to classical education. Bérard reminded the Chamber that at the turn of the century Brunot had called upon the Ribot commission to abandon what he took to be an archaic system of education: "One must acknowledge that what is dead is dead, and Graeco-Roman education, as it once existed, is finished." *Journal officiel,* Chambre des Députés, 2nd session, 22 June 1923, 2723.

80. AN F^{17} 17499. Conseil Supérieur de l'Instruction Publique, minutes of afternoon meeting, 17 January 1923.

81. AN F^{17} 17499. Conseil Supérieur de l'Instruction Publique, minutes of the morning meeting, 17 January 1923.

82. AN F^{17} 17499. Conseil Supérieur de l'Instruction Publique, minutes of morning meeting, 21 January 1923.

83. *Journal officiel,* Chambre des Députés, 1st session, 11 July 1923, 3366–3371.

84. Ibid., 3374.

85. *Journal officiel,* Chambre des Députés, 2nd session, 11 July 1923, 3382.

86. *"Arrête* concerning the time-schedules and programmes of Secondary Education in the classes in the *lycées* and *collèges* for boys, December 3, 1923," appendix to I. L. Kandel, *The Reform of Secondary Education in France* (New York: Teachers' College, Columbia University, 1924), 81–82.

87. Herriot read into the parliamentary record the opinion of the Comité de l'Association des Professeurs de Langues Vivantes that the reform would "discredit and gravely compromise the instruction, now more important than ever, of modern languages." *Journal officiel,* Chambre des Députés, 1st session, 5 July 1923, 3120. At a meeting in August 1923, the Conseil Général of the *département* Loir-et-Cher reiterated arguments brought to the floor of the Chamber of Deputies: the Bérard reform would "overturn" secondary schooling, weaken instruction in science and modern languages, and constitute a "blow against democracy." AN F^{17} 17499. "Conseils gé-

néraux, 1922, 1923." But in a letter to Jean Molinie, the deputy from Aveyron, Bérard rebutted this charge, claiming that it was "specious" to criticize the new curriculum for neglecting modern languages. F¹⁷ 17499. Letter of June 1923 from Léon Bérard to Jean Molinie, député de l'Aveyron.

88. H. Ducos, "Le Décret Bérard est un coup de force contre le Parlement," *Le Quotidien,* 11 May 1923.

89. *Journal officiel,* Chambre des Députés, 1st session, 11 July 1923, 3371.

90. Ibid., 5 July 1923, 3121.

91. Ibid., 11 July 1923, 3371.

92. Ibid., 2nd session, 22 June 1923, 2716–2717.

93. Ibid., 11 July 1923, 3402.

94. Ibid., 3403.

95. "La Réforme de l'enseignement sécondaire," *La Petite Gironde,* 10 May 1923.

96. *Journal officiel,* Chambre des Députés, 2nd session, 11 July 1923, 3385–3386.

97. AN F¹⁷ 17499. "Communication de M. Berthélemy à l'Académie des Sciences Morales, le 25 novembre [1923]," 3.

98. AN F¹⁷ 17499. Transcript of the Académie des Sciences Morales.

99. AN F¹⁷ 17499. News clipping, "L'Institut étudie la réorganisation de l'Enseignement secondaire" [no header, no date], November 1923.

100. In December 1923 the Compagnons coordinated a meeting of protest attended by Paul Painlévé, Alphonse Aulard, and Charles Seignobos, and with Herriot presiding. "La Réforme de l'enseignement," *Le Petit journal,* 12 December 1923.

101. Robert Paxton, *Vichy France: Old Guard and New Order, 1940–1944* (New York: Norton, 1975), 159–160.

102. AN F¹⁷ 17499. "Rapport au Président de la République" from the Minister of Public Instruction, n.d. [1923].

Index